SOUTH AFRICA

A DIFFERENT KIND OF WAR

FROM SOWETO TO PRETORIA

JULIE FREDERIKSE

DESIGNED BY PETER BONNICI

BEACON PRESS   BOSTON

Acknowledgements

Beacon Press
25 Beacon Street
Boston, Massachusetts 02108

Beacon Press Books are published under
the auspices of the Unitarian Universalist
Association of Congregations in
North America.

© Julie Frederikse 1986
Published by arrangement with
James Currey Ltd.
First published as a Beacon
paperback in 1987
All rights reserved
Printed in the United States of America

94 93 92 91 90 89 88 87   87654321

LC: 86-047875

Unless otherwise indicated, all interviews and statements from political meetings were recorded in South Africa between 1979 and 1984. It should be noted that for most of those I interviewed — Africans, Afrikaners and many people of mixed race — English is a second language, and this is often reflected in their speech. Even with whites and Asians who grew up speaking English, readers will notice peculiarly South African idiomatic expressions.

For the laborious task of transcribing the more than 300 tapes I recorded over the years, I am grateful to Pat Brickhill, Charles Mutangebende, Terry Barnes, Helen Chigorimbo, Lillian Nguruve, Andrea Findlay, Joan Jack, Ayesha Minty, Eric Itzkin and Helene Berold. While I am indebted to the World Council of Churches, the Commission of Interchurch Aid of the Netherlands Reformed Church, the Steve Katz Foundation and the Ford Foundation for funding the transcription of this veritable tape archive.

I wish to thank Richard Wicksteed, who spent hours clipping newspapers and organising my ever-expanding files; Margaret Ling, who tracked down photographs and graphics in London; Eileen Maybin and Iden Wetherell, who proofread the final manuscript; and Andy Meldrum, without whose help I could not have continued my journalistic work while writing this book. Hubertus Welck often offered me the use of his office facilities — a great boon to one who writes at home.

I am grateful to all the photographers whose pictures make the words of this book come alive, especially Paul Weinberg, Wendy Schweggman, Jimi Matthews, Biddy Partridge and Gideon Mendel, who responded to specific requests for photos, and to the German Protestant Association for World Mission for covering the cost of the photographers fees. Because of the complex lay-out process involved in producing a book of this format, a subsidy from the Canadian University Services Organisation was indispensable to the goal of marketing the book at an accessible price.

Finally, I wish to express my appreciation to Hugh Lewin, who read through endless drafts of this manuscript, responding with a most effective blend of constructive criticism and moral support. Of the many more people I would like to thank for offering advice, recommending reading, assisting with research, commenting on drafts of my manuscript, and generally lending encouragement, most preferred not to be named for political reasons. And then there is Stelios Comninos, who was always there — whether to help re-work a paragraph or woo our kids from my study: I thank him most of all.   J.F.

CONTENTS

POPULATION IN SOUTH AFRICA

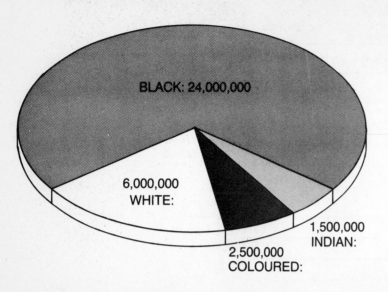

BLACK: 24,000,000

6,000,000
WHITE:

1,500,000
INDIAN:

2,500,000
COLOURED:

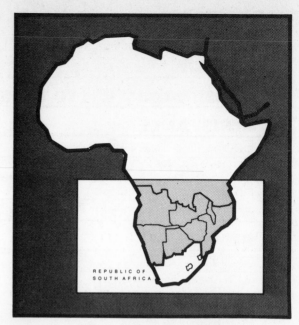

REPUBLIC OF
SOUTH AFRICA

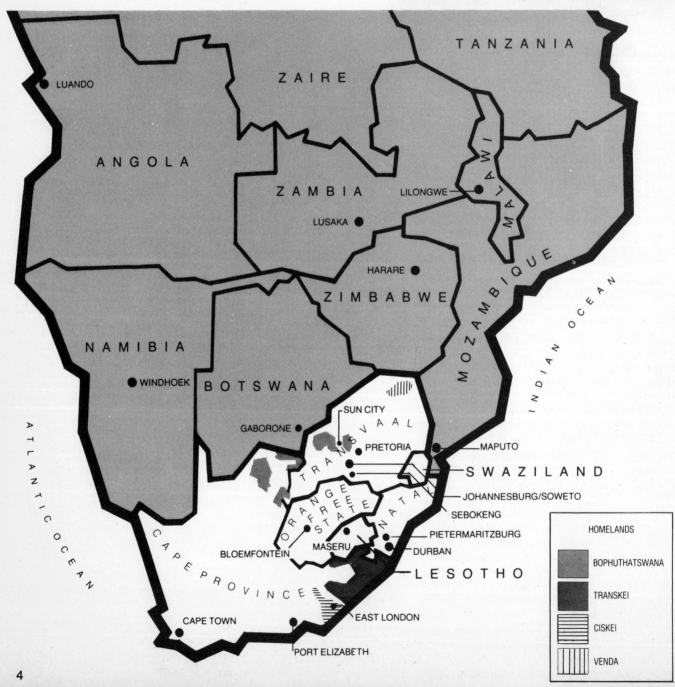

TANZANIA

ZAIRE

LUANDO

ANGOLA

ZAMBIA

LILONGWE

MALAWI

LUSAKA

HARARE

ZIMBABWE

MOZAMBIQUE

INDIAN OCEAN

NAMIBIA

WINDHOEK

BOTSWANA

ATLANTIC OCEAN

GABORONE

SUN CITY

TRANSVAAL

PRETORIA

MAPUTO

SWAZILAND

ORANGE FREE STATE

JOHANNESBURG/SOWETO

NATAL

SEBOKENG

PIETERMARITZBURG

BLOEMFONTEIN

MASERU

DURBAN

CAPE PROVINCE

LESOTHO

CAPE TOWN

EAST LONDON

PORT ELIZABETH

HOMELANDS

BOPHUTHATSWANA

TRANSKEI

CISKEI

VENDA

Prologue

As a journalist based in southern Africa, first in Johannesburg and now in Harare, I have witnessed first-hand the unfolding of the most decisive decade to date in the long history of struggle against white minority rule. *A Different Kind of War* documents how the deep anger unleashed by the Soweto student uprisings of 1976 has been organized and mobilized into the inexorable nation-wide resistance of today.

The format of this book represents neither a journalistic chronicle of events nor an academic analysis. It lets the ordinary people of South Africa, as well as their leaders, speak for themselves, through interviews and the proliferating media of their organizations. It portrays the government as it presents itself, mainly through its pronouncements over the state-controlled broadcasting system. The visual counterpart to this oral history approach is the book's design, which shows—rather than tells—the dynamics of contemporary South Africa, by allowing readers to see the ephemera spawned by the conflict: newspapers, posters, pamphlets, and songs, juxtaposed against the compelling images recorded by documentary photographers.

Events in South Africa are moving at such a pace that predictions are not only impossible but inappropriate. *A Different Kind of War* delineates the patterns of resistance—some historical, others still evolving—that have propelled the country into a state of civil war.

Many of the trends first identified in these pages have since been made clearer still by the stark picture of a country under siege beamed world-wide by the international media. For example, those initially skeptical of the book's characterization of the array of anti-apartheid forces in the country as "non-racial"—as opposed to the conventional wisdom of South Africa's "race war" —will by now have noted the abundance of images that defy the description of black versus white: black policemen shoot protesting black youths, who in turn attack black collaborators, while white opposition figures are jailed by the white minority government for their involvement in the fight for majority rule. By the same token, Pretoria's continued truculence in the face of international demands for change, and its unabashed militarization while proclaiming itself a force for regional stability, clearly strengthen the book's indictment of the government's "reform" and "détente" strategies. Anyone confused by the government's claim to have abolished its dehumanizing pass laws must soon realize that all but a privileged minority of blacks remain the "aliens" described in this book.

Sadly enough, some of the potential disasters foreshadowed here have since come to pass. An official of the inaptly named ministry of "Cooperation and Development" is quoted in the book as vowing that the famous squatter community of Crossroads, seen as "a symbol of provocation," would be "destroyed at all costs"; today Crossroads is no more, the "provocative" squatters having been routed by state-supported vigilantes.

Similarly, the rent and school boycotts mounted by the black communities and the strikes and stay-aways led by the burgeoning black trade unions are no longer isolated incidents, but have spread throughout the country, forcing the government to impose two recent "states of emergency" in a desperate bid to quell the relentless resistance. What is more, the collection of material that I undertook to produce this book, including interviews with activists and recordings of rallies, would be severely restricted under the censorship laws that now restrain not only the media but all free expression of ideas.

While it is the South African people themselves who will fight and win this war, the international community has begun to counter the widespread cynicism felt by many among the oppressed majority in South Africa about the role of the West in helping to change their country. "People regard the West as a friend of their enemy," explained a Soweto student I interviewed, "and you know a friend of your enemy cannot be your friend." Yet a wide range of Americans, from students to senior citizens, backed up by veteran anti-apartheid campaigners, are finally forcing our government to decide who are our enemies and who are our friends, and to forge a southern Africa policy accordingly.

Ultimately, then, my goal is neither to catalog the past nor prophesy the future, but instead to let the words and pictures on the following pages enable readers to make sense of the emerging situation, in terms of how the people of South Africa perceive and express their own experience. With the publication of this book in the United States, I hope a process will begin whereby those concerned about South Africa can continue to study the situation and respond to it, better equipped with a context in which to analyze current trends, and perhaps even anticipate future developments.

Julie Frederikse has covered southern Africa since 1979 for America's National Public Radio. Her first book is *None But Ourselves: Masses vs. Media in the Making of Zimbabwe.* She lives in Harare, Zimbabwe with her husband and two children.

**Julie Frederikse
Harare, Zimbabwe
January 1987**

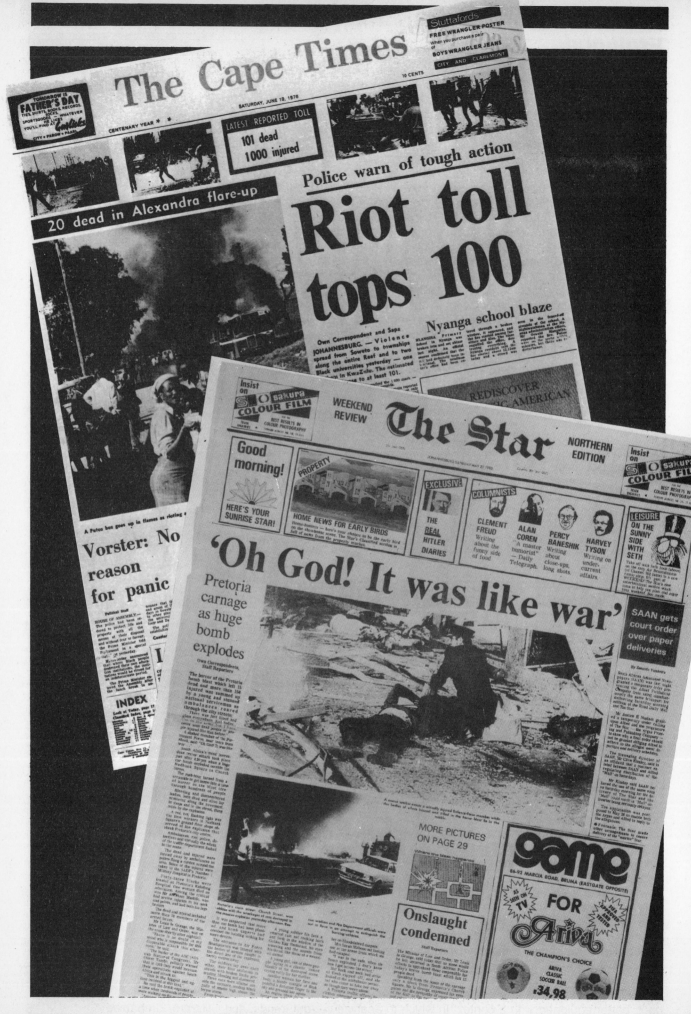

1. An Introduction to the System

Two of the most striking images to come out of South Africa in the last decade are those of the schoolchildren of Soweto marching toward armed police in June 1976 and the devastated streets of Pretoria after the May 1983 bomb blast. The uprisings dramatized a political awakening – the conscientization of a new generation of young black South Africans, facing a predictably brutal response from the state. The Pretoria bombing symbolized the inevitable outgrowth of that consciousness, as hundreds of young blacks who had fled the country in 1976 began returning to South Africa as trained guerillas. In the words of one black priest interviewed, the attack on the Pretoria military offices by the African National Congress resistance movement meant that 'the war has started'.

In reality, South Africa has been a country at war with itself since the seventeenth century, when white settlers landed at the Cape and began robbing the indigenous people of their land. Three hundred years of African resistance brought South Africa into the twentieth century with its black population still in the vast majority, unlike North America or Australia, where the indigenous people were all but exterminated. South Africa's white minority has built a thriving capitalist economy through the enforced labour of more than three-quarters of the population.

That is not the history that is taught in South African government schools today. On the contrary, South African schoolchildren learn that theirs is a political system with all the trappings of any other western-style democracy – parliaments, opposition parties, an independent judiciary – and that blacks who demand majority rule already have it – in those distant, impoverished, but black-ruled rural dumping grounds called 'homelands'. White education, for which the government spends seven times as much as it does for African education, follows the tenets of an Afrikaner,[1] Calvinist-inspired syllabus. Perhaps the best way to understand the whites who rule South Africa is to speak to schoolchildren and listen to the lessons they have learned from 'Christian National Education'.

Inhabitants of the Surroundings.

A. Europeans – Whites
1. Dwellings: They live in houses, flats, hotels and boarding houses.
2. Activities: They may go to schools, churches and synagogues.
3. Relaxation: Swimming, tennis, golf, soccer, cricket.
4. Professions: bowls, doctors, lawyers, accountants, engineers, architects and many more.
5. Transport: cars, buses, taxis and bicycles take people to and from city.

1981-02-11   The Indians.

1. They are the 'fourth' largest group.
2. They are darker in colour than the coloureds.
3. Different tribes like the Hindus. Different dialects and speech.
4. They are originally from India.
5. They come to work in the sugar fields in Natal.
6. They are mostly traders and they work in factories and ships and also as waiters in hotels.
7. Some of them are very well educated.
8. They have a township in Laudium and they have beautiful homes and facilities.

1981-01-27   Different Population groups in the area.
Non-whites in our neighbourhood.
The Bantu.

1. They all have their own language culture, land and tradition.
2. You can tell some of the tribes by their adornments – and clothings.
3. Outside Pretoria live the Ndebele tribe. The women wear thick head necklaces around their necks and legs. Their huts are decorated with beautiful designs.
4. Two of the native townships near Pretoria are atteridgville and mamelodie.
5. They work as gardeners, cleaners, and waiters.
6. There are radio programmes and books, newspapers and magazines in Bantu languages.

1981-01-20   The Coloureds

1. They are the nearest in colour, culture speech etc. to the European / race.
2. They are the 3rd largest group in Pretoria. (Bantu. European. Coloured.)
3. They are well educated and are in good positions.
4. The coloured township is at Eersterust near Pretoria.
5. They work in shops, doctor, tradesman, and cafes.

Interview with English-speaking Johannesburg high school students.

Marie: The settlers came and they built up this country.

Roseanne: There were blacks here, but if the whites hadn't come we wouldn't have been civilized, we wouldn't have what we have today.

Michelle: No, but when the whites came to South Africa originally, the blacks weren't at the very tip of Africa, they were moving down. The trouble only started when the blacks and whites started meeting. So there wasn't any conquering – they just sort of met halfway.

And what are you taught about South Africa as it is now?

Debbie: We learn about the way other countries overseas are always saying that we treat the blacks badly.

Marie: I hate the way other countries are always saying that we're racialist. Because even in America or Britain, I don't think the blacks are treated the same as whites. They have these faction fights all the time. Look at Ireland – they're about ten times worse than we are. But the rest of the world is always condemning us. It's just that we've got our laws written down. In other countries they don't have laws like us, but they act exactly the way we do. Even worse. Much worse.

Roseanne: But you know, most of my life I've been around blacks. I had a nanny since I was nine months old, and, like, I had nothing against them.

Marie: Look, I think it actually works both ways: we need the blacks and the blacks need us I mean, with a black government this country would be chaos, because we are more educated than blacks and we are more civilized than they are, so we can rule the country better. But then again, without the blacks, we wouldn't have the manpower we need. You're not going to find a white who's going to work like these blacks do – as a maid or sweeping the streets, in the mines, things like that. So it actually works both ways.

Debbie: Also you know, the thing with the blacks is that there are so many tribes and there'd always be fighting, so I think that's why it's good to have a white government, to keep order so there's not chaos.

Are there special classes where you learn about politics?

Marie: In 'Youth Preparedness'[2] we learn about terrorists and all that, and Russia …

Michelle: We learn about how bad terrorism is, and which countries it's infiltrated and how it's affecting society, how it's bringing downfall to certain countries.

Marie: And that we shouldn't let it happen here.

Michelle: This country would go like Rhodesia if it was handed over to the blacks.

Marie: But it won't be! This country will never be handed over to the blacks. We'll fight for it.

What do you mean when you talk about 'terrorism'?

Roseanne: Terrorism is a group of people trying to fight for a country and they want it so badly that they're going to go out in any way to get it.

Marie: It's like communism, you know. Russia's trying to take over South Africa for the strategic position, and the gold and all that and the blacks don't know any better because they're not properly educated, and if a communist is going to come to them and say, do this and that and the other and we'll give you a black government – well, they just won't know any better, the blacks won't, and they'll believe the communists.

The daily dose of Christian National Education and the weekly dose of Youth Preparedness is reinforced in many whites-only schools by intensive, week-long 'veld schools' (field schools) held in rural camps. According to the Transvaal (provincial) Education Department, the veld school programme should focus on 'love of that which is one's own, raising and lowering the flag, communism, a love of our own fauna and flora, and community singing'.[3]

Debbie: In veld school, we did communism, we did the South African flag, we did terrorism, and one whole lecture was about how sex, communism and drugs all goes into the music we listen to.

Did you agree with everything you were told in the lectures?

Roseanne: I think it was too old-fashioned. I mean listening to music doesn't automatically make you take drugs or have sex every night or become a communist.

Marie: But I do believe what they said about Rhodesia. You see, even though the Rhodesian Army was one of the best bush-fighting armies in the world, they were beaten by the terrorists who aren't really well trained. They said it was actually through terrorism, and that now, here in South Africa it's not the army that's got the hard task, it's us that stay at home, because we have to guard our homes, and our families and young children. And that's what the terrorists are going to attack – not the army, which is strong. They're going to attack the weakest point: us!

It seems that you were taught a lot about what the communists want to do when you were at veld school. Did you ever learn what communism *is*?

Marie: It's a government by which you don't have any religion, you don't have any say in how the country's run, you don't have any rights. I mean everybody is equal, there's no poverty or anything, but you can't strive for anything in a communist country. No matter how hard you work, you don't get, you don't move up, you just stay at the same level.

Veld School Lecture on 'Insurgency'.[4]
Today South Africa is experiencing a total onslaught. Weapons naturally play a part, but 80 per cent consists of the silent war. They are trying to get *you*. You are the youth of our country. They are not interested in the older generation – you are the leaders of tomorrow. The communist says, 'Give me a child between 0 and 6 and I will win the war.' They are not in a hurry – they want the whole world and they won't stop anywhere. The insurgents will try to create chaos, as we saw in the Soweto riots. They were part of a communist onslaught. They used the youth, hoping we would panic, but our Prime Minister was too clever, and luckily, handled the riots. The so-called freedom fighters on our borders are not fighting for freedom, but for communism. This can be seen in urban terrorism. In Soweto there are hundreds of terrorists. You must be aware of them. Speak to your servant – she will tell you. If you notice something strange about her, don't be afraid to tell the police. We must make use of our superior knowledge to outwit the communists. How do we get this knowledge? Listen to the radio. Read all the papers. We must be spiritually prepared. We must be like David against the Philistine Goliath, and South Africa will triumph against the Red Onslaught.

What if someone were to argue that the situation you've just described as communist is not unlike the situation of most blacks in South Africa?

Michelle: I don't agree with that, because blacks might not have the vote, but they have a lot of things that we have. I mean they have houses ...

'Questions and Propositions for Group Discussion', compiled by the Johannesburg College of Education after a visit to the Schoemansdal Veld School in 1981: [5]

1. Distorted reports of South Africa appear frequently abroad. How must we criticize this and what must we do about it?

2. Can the West, and especially America, stop Russia's expansionism? Give examples.

3. What steps will you take to prepare the homelands against communism?

4. How should strikers be dealt with?

5. How would you gain the support of a non-white for your government?

6. Must we rebuild the schools that have been burned down by the blacks? Who is going to pay for the rebuilding of the schools?

7. Darwin brought us his evolution theory and maintains that man descends from the baboon. My dear young friends, his ancestors may have been baboons, but most certainly not mine. Science rejects this theory because no animal developed from one kind to another. Discuss.

8. When the Voortrekkers[6] started out from the Cape, there was no European civilization in Johannesburg – or do you think the Bantu[7] could have built Johannesburg? No, it was built by Europeans. Discuss.

9. Must I feel guilty because I am white?

Marie: We build them schools and they just burn them down!

Roseanne: I know some people say that – why should we pay to teach the blacks proper subjects when they're just going to grow up to be a nanny or garden boy – but I know that's the wrong attitude.

Marie: But that's exactly why they shouldn't burn their schools! If they got some education, maybe they could do more. It's just that it takes time. It can't be done just like that, you have to …

Michelle: Go slowly, you just have to go slowly and listen, all our taxes go to their houses. Okay, Soweto's nothing fantastic, but at least they've got a roof over their heads. They want all the facilities that we've got, but you can't all of a sudden just give them everything. They're not prepared to take it in stages.

Debbie: You know it's already got to the stage where the blacks are starting to do our jobs, that's how much of a chance we're giving them.

One last question: can you tell me, from what you've learned in veld school, what's the opposite of communism?

Debbie: Christianity!
Roseanne: No it's freedom …
Michelle: Democracy?
Marie: Capitalism!

 Nicky is a schoolgirl the same age as Marie, Michelle, Roseanne and Debbie. Nicky is also a product of Christian National Education. Yet she found her veld school experience disillusioning.

Nicky: They don't tell you what it's going to be about, they don't tell you why you're going. It's just supposed to be a kind of awareness of nature weekend. It sounds wonderful, and you think, wow, this is going to be fun – and then you get a shock when you get there.

What happened when you first arrived at the veld school?

Nicky: I think it was the longest day of my life. They made us run an obstacle course. We learned how to camouflage ourselves and how to do certain crawls through the bush. They told us it was all for exercise and self-discipline and fun, but it was really more like a survival thing – how to survive, I don't know – a war, I guess?

Why do you think it had to do with war?

Nicky: Because they gave us a lot of lectures about war and there was a movie about the South African Defence Force. We had lots of lectures on politics. They said that any kind of opposition to the government is just opting for communism. They told us things like, 'Do you like the kind of things you have in your house, your luxuries? Then how would you feel if half your stuff was given to some black man? And how would you feel if the government controlled everything? Just think how free you are now. Think of your garden.' That was the kind of thing they were telling us. And they were always telling us to be glad about South Africa's big defence force, and that we must encourage our big brothers to kind of rush to the army and not dodge the army and that we must buy defence force bonds and stuff.

Did you ever say anything to the veld school teachers about how you felt?

Nicky: When I tried to, I really got into trouble. Like they had one of their lectures on politics, and this guy was telling us about how you should choose to buy South African products over other products, over anything imported, because people overseas boycott South African products. And they never said that maybe the reason for these boycotts was because of South Africa's policies. Oh, no, it was as if the rest of the world was just being nasty.

I was very nervous about saying anything because all the teachers were really authoritarian and they'll tell you to kind of know your place and that sort of thing. I mean, they can do what they like with you for the time that you're there. Veld school is perfectly legal and they can be quite harsh. But finally it got so ridiculous that I said something – just to try to point out that, well, South Africa likes to trade with other countries anyway. And the guy got really angry. He just turned round and glared at me and said, 'Nicky, you're a communist!' So I said to him, 'Surely I'm allowed to think freely in this country!' and he just kind of looked at me and didn't say anything else. I wanted to say to him, 'How can you just sort of throw that big word at a little girl who's just trying to make some sense out of this rubbish that you're talking?' But of course, I didn't dare to.

So what did you tell your friends about veld school when you got back home?

Nicky: Well, I actually had to write a speech, telling my school what the veld school camp had been like. I told my teachers that I wasn't prepared to say that it had been fun and that all the girls should go next year, because it is supposedly optional, even though they really pressurize you to go. But in the end, I was manipulated and convinced to write something decent in their terms, to write that it would be a worthwhile experience, the kind of things we did, and how much fun it was, how much we all wished for home and our hot baths – not mentioning that a lot of people in this country don't have a home and a hot bath.

My speech was read before I said it, and anything vaguely suspicious was crossed out and I was told to write it again. They would say, 'You didn't really think that, did you?' So in the end, nobody in my school really knew what I thought. I guess they will just have to go to find out for themselves. Anyway, that's how things always work in the school system in this country: you're not supposed to ask too many questions and you're never supposed to challenge the line they're putting out.

South Africa's rulers were brought up on Christian National Education. The whites who support the system of apartheid – literally 'separateness' of blacks and whites – are merely putting into practice the lessons of their schooldays. It was white farmers who provided the backbone of the 1948 National Party election victory that entrenched apartheid in its present form. Apartheid ensured these whites a continuous supply of cheap black labour, and a comfortable way of rationalizing the inequitable division of land: 87 per cent for whites and 13 per cent for the overcrowded black 'homelands'.

Leon Maré, farmer in Hectorspruit, eastern Transvaal: There's no reason that blacks can't farm in the homelands – it's just that they aren't developed to that stage yet. They've got to be led to that stage, and somebody's got to do that for them. That is what out government is trying to do, to train them to be independent, to look after themselves, to farm independently.

Annette Maré, Leon's wife: I'm glad you came here to see things for yourself, because people don't understand how we get along with the blacks. They think we don't treat them well on the farms, and that's far from the truth. You see, we grew up with these people, we played with them when we were kids. We know what they think like, how they live and all that. But you see, they aren't educated like we are, so that's why they are operating on a lower basis.

So you see the solution to South Africa's problems in 'separate development'?

Leon Maré: Yes, only we can't do it completely because we've got a big percentage of blacks in the cities that's westernized already. We're interdependent, you know. We need them for labour, and they need us for their extra money that they can send back to the homelands, to their women and their kids.

How many people from the homeland do you employ on your farm?

Leon Maré: I bring in about fifty or sixty by lorry every day, and the rest stay here, on the compound.

Annette Maré: The mines and SASOL (para-statal oil-from-coal plant) is recruiting labour here and they're taking all the strong men out of the area, so it's only women left behind who come work for us. And they are quite willing to work, the women. They don't mind work where they've got to bend. A man can't do that kind of work, say, picking tomatoes, or at least a woman is much better at it than a man, because they've been doing it for their whole lives, since they were kids. Although they all do need our guidance. You know how you teach a small child? You must always hammer it into them, repeat everything three, four times, you know.

How long have you been here on this farm?

Leon Maré: We only bought this farm two years ago. We'd been dreaming of owning our own farm for years, and then we got a big loan from the government. You see, they want to try and get the population more thick in this area because it's a border area. We've got threats outside and all that and the more people that stay here on the border, the better it is. It's a weapon against terrorism.[8]

Doesn't that make you nervous?

Annette Maré: Oh no. You know, my husband is going sometimes for a week to the (military) commando[9] and I'm staying all by myself on the farm. I'm not scared at all. Not at all. Actually, we're on such good footing with our labourers that if anybody unknown will arrive they would come and tell us.

Leon Maré: We've got a good relationship with all the black people in the area. We've got no problems here.

Do you think the blacks are satisfied with the division of the land in South Africa, with working on your big farm and then going back to their small plots in the homeland?

Leon Maré: If it's such a bad situation, it isn't logical to me why people should laugh and make jokes during their work time. They'll be singing on the lorry when they go back home. To me they seem friendly, quite content – I won't say happy, but I think, content.

Annette Maré: I think they *are* happy. We've got a beautiful lot working for us. We're so happy together. And when they die, we give them a proper funeral, you know. We stop all the work on the farm and pay respect.

The Afrikaans-speaking farmers and workers who helped install the National Party in 1948 were united in their resentment of the 'Anglo-Jewish capitalist conspiracy'[10] which controlled the country's economy. By 1976, Afrikaners had achieved income parity with English-speakers, joining them in enjoying one of the highest living standards in the world, and the National Party had become the party of Afrikaner capital. Afrikaner and English businessmen have now joined forces to defend their economic gains. The symbolic start of the rapprochement came in November 1979, when Prime Minister P.W. Botha summoned the country's top business leaders to a conference at Johannesburg's Carlton Hotel, followed up by the 'Good Hope' summit in Cape Town two years later.

Racial segregation and intensive state control laid the foundations for South African capitalism over the past century. Beginning in the late 1970s, such crude constraints were dismissed as anachronistic, and the cure for the country's ills – from the skills shortage to labour unrest – was seen in unfettered 'free enterprise'. Business and government promoted the theory that a bigger 'economic cake' was all that was needed to bring greater economic gains for all, but the reality for South Africa's black workers was that their slice of the cake was as small as ever.[11] The equation for change in South Africa today is simple: the power of the state versus resistance to the state. And if anyone doubts which side the money is on, they need only listen to the candid views of South Africa's wealthiest individual.

HOW THE RICH GET RICHER.

'The only answer for SA is capitalism'

Harry Oppenheimer, retired chairman of South Africa's Anglo-American Corporation, which controls the world's richest gold and diamond mines , with assets of $15 billion:[12] No doubt I started out with more advantages than I deserved. But don't you think life would be a terrible bore if one only got what one deserved? Have you ever noticed how in countries where millionaires flourish ordinary people themselves tend to live better?

SA whites strike it rich

Lay off the taxes, and leave it to free enterprise

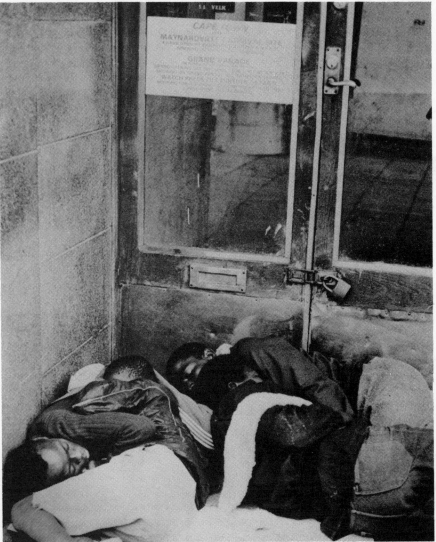

SABC (South African Broadcasting Corporation), 12 November 1981: The scope of the challenge has never been greater. Demographers point out that the black population will double in size in the next quarter of the century. The implications are obvious; rapidly rising black unemployment, while economic growth is retarded by the shortage of skills, rural stagnation and massive migration to the metropolitan areas. Left unchecked, it will result in one-and-a-quarter-million black people moving to these areas during the next eight years. Those are the unavoidable realities.

It is a daunting task in its magnitude and complexity. As such, it is also a challenge to the ingenuity and determination of business and political leaders in co-operating for a stable and just dispensation for all South Africa's peoples. Leading South African industrialist Dr Anton Rupert sounded an optimistic note about the 'Good Hope' conference.

Anton Rupert: I think the advantage of today's gathering was that it brought together government with the majority Afrikaans-speaking people, and the business sector, which is a majority of English-speakers. Finally, it showed that there is a common patriotism, a great feeling of common patriotism, which spells wealth in the future.

13

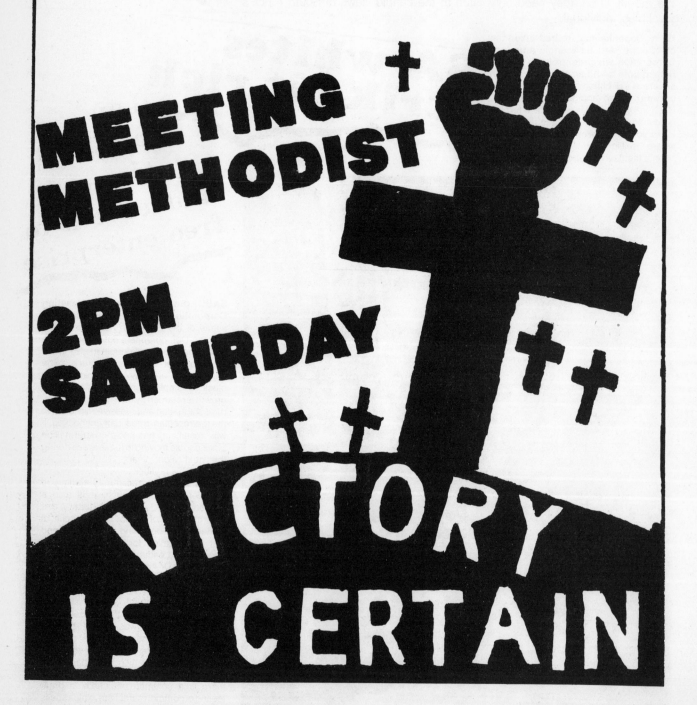

REMEMBER JUNE 16

MEETING METHODIST

2PM SATURDAY

VICTORY IS CERTAIN

2. Resistance

It was the inferior black education system that kindled the uprisings that erupted in Soweto on 16 June 1976. Since then, black education has been so discredited that it now serves only to further crystallize opposition to the government. The classroom plays a far less influential role in shaping black perceptions than the informal schooling blacks get from their peers, their parents and political organizations. Siphiwe, Ben, Jabulani and Peter are students in Soweto, veterans of the 1976 uprisings.

 Siphiwe: The thing that made me politically minded was the influence I got from 1976, because so many of our brothers and sisters were shot dead for their rights. In fact, June 16th was the day I started to have interest in political activity in this country.

Ben: My awareness was limited because of my education, all the things that we were told at school, you know, about how life is. One of the things they wanted us to believe is that nobody can change the system as it is, in fact, that it is God's wish that we live this type of life. So that was limiting my awareness, because whenever I would see people having problems and sufferings, I would say this is God's will, you know. But because of the challenge that was presented to the system by the students, I began to realize that, no, these things are man-made and it is possible to change things.

Jabulani: It was the 1976 experience that made us start to ask questions, you know, about the poverty of our people, the living conditions of our people. We started questioning why whites live in that type of life and we live in these conditions, and we began to realize also that our whole education system is a very big lie. Because it's a system that tells you that certain people must be rich and others must be poor, and if people are poor, it must be their own fault – that it's because of the system, you see. These are the values that our education system teaches us, and in '76 we started questioning those values.

Peter: The '76 experience was, for us, a kind of physiotherapy. You know how a physiotherapist trains patients to be independent and to do everything for himself and that he shouldn't rely on the next person. So I say the June '76 uprising was just like a physiotherapist who trained the blacks to use their own initiative and not to depend on other people. It motivated us, especially the youth, to become more powerful.

Are you taught politics at school? Are you taught who are the black political leaders of South Africa?

Siphiwe: They only tell us about those homeland leaders, those puppets, and those we don't want to know about. For instance, we never learned why Nelson Mandela is in prison for life, or why the African National Congress turned to violence, or about Oliver Tambo and the other leaders who are out of the country.[1] We just learn about these things from talking to other knowledgeable people who can inform us about the situation we are living in, and what can be done about it.

Do you remember how you felt when you first heard about the jailed and exiled political leaders?

Siphiwe: My reaction was that I wanted to know the reason for their imprisonment. So when I was told that these people were trying to lead our people to victory, I was very depressed.

Jabulani: I remember I was very much depressed to hear this, but then I knew that I would have to alter the present situation for the coming generation, irrespective of detention (without trial) or any other thing that the government may impose.

Siphiwe: I can say that I heard about those true leaders from my parents, because we had some political books at home which I used to read. But they also told me not to go and talk with each and every person I came across in

A. Each One, Teach One

'No More Lullabies' (excerpt),
Mafika Gwala,
Ravan Press, 1982:

It is seedtime in Soweto
What went round has come around
This time the plants will grow
and bear fruit to raise up more seed
There'll be a refreshing persistence
of the wits
Because this time
There'll be no more lullabies.

CONGRESS OF SOUTH AFRICAN STUDENTS
COSAS
EACH ONE TEACH ONE

the street because some of them are not to be trusted – they could be spies for the government.

Jabulani: That's the main problem: people are scared, you see. That is why so many people, they just keep quiet about politics. People are scared to talk openly, unless they trust a person, for fear that he will just run to the police. But personally, I am not worried, I believe that no amount of such fear, and no amount of propaganda, will stop the mental revolution in this country. And no matter how they try to hinder us from getting the right kind of influences to counteract our inferior education, change will come.

Siphiwe: We know that through education – our kind of education – we can make it. But we must work hard now to get everybody conscientized.

Following the hundreds of shootings and detentions of 1976–7, the students regrouped to study the lessons they had learned from their violent confrontations with the police and army. In October 1977, the government banned nearly all the black political groups founded since the late 1960s, but by 1979, new mass-based organizations were emerging. The first new student grouping founded after the Soweto uprisings was the Congress of South African Students, whose effectiveness can be measured by the response of the security police: its first president was convicted of subversion and jailed for eight years, and the entire executive committee spent its first year in office in jail.[2] Against these odds, COSAS persevered with the task embodied in its motto, 'Each one, teach one', to become the leading national organization in the country's black secondary schools.

The government, too, reassessed its response to student grievances. The notorious 'Bantu Education' Department – named in 1953, when blacks were seen solely as 'hewers of wood and drawers of water' – was re-named the Department of Education and Training (although the government refused even the recommendation of its own commission for a single educational ministry for all races.[3] Government and industry had suddenly awoken to the desperate need for more skilled and semi-skilled black labour, and improved black education and training seemed the only means of incorporating a core of blacks to alleviate this crisis.[4] At the same time, the generation politicized in 1976 began articulating its disenchantment with the free enterprise system that black skills were supposed to help salvage.

You can give him charity. Or you can give him knowledge.

Without us, Miriam Kabako would be an illiterate, hungry, cold little girl.

Tshediso Matona, National Organizer for the Congress of South African Students: There has been a great shift in education, from academic to technical, and the idea is to get young blacks to be part and parcel of the free enterprise system . Most of these big capitalists say it in clear terms, that as long as black people do not have a stake in the free enterprise system, they will never support it and therefore they'll fight against it, you see. You find that these capitalists have bursary funds which sponsor young blacks to study. The idea is to co-opt them into the capitalist system – so-called free enterprise. They actually offer scholarships for students to go to America, because they know that after having the experience of life in America – you know, that luxury life, having a television and homes and all the facilities they don't enjoy in South Africa – they will come back having a capitalist mentality. So the government is on a campaign to draw young people to free enterprise, and to keep them away from what they see as communism.

There seems to be such a fear of communism among whites in this country; how do blacks feel about communism?

Tshediso Matona: The government wants to give blacks the impression that communism is a system where nobody will be allowed to own anything and everything will be owned by the state. But this is exactly what is already happening today among blacks, because even the houses we live in are not ours.

What do you have against capitalism?

Tshediso Matona: We see capitalism as that system where the wealth of the country – the means of production, the things that are necessary to make people live – they're owned by few. You'll find people begging for jobs, whereas they're still going to be exploited. And that's the system which creates a majority of the people to be poor. Whereas if you're rich, for instance, take the example of Oppenheimer: he owns a lot of mines, a lot of firms, and he enjoys all the wealth alone. He gets millions and millions of rands profit, while our people are suffering. We hardly have houses, we have people without water, we have starvation, we have such diseases as cholera and polio, which are of course economic diseases. So that's what we have against capitalism.

What would you see as an alternative to capitalism?

Tshediso Matona: That system that I want to see is a system where the wealth of the country is going to be shared amongst all the people, and there'll be work for everybody, and students will be educated to serve their people, to make sure that the wealth of the country is distributed amongst all and everybody has his needs catered for. I don't know whether it's communalism, communism or socialism, but that's what I'd like to see.

In early 1980, the embers that had been smouldering since 1976 burst into flame again. This time it was the Coloured students in the Western Cape who led the protest against their 'gutter education', and this time the protest evolved through a deeper understanding of the role students play in the greater South African political context. The students pressed their demands for 'equal education in an equal society' through a boycott that spread beyond the Cape Coloured schools to involve over 150,000 school and university students throughout the country.

The students' success in linking educational demands to national political grievances was evidenced when an estimated 70 per cent of the workers in the Western Cape observed a two-day stay-away in June 1980, to commemorate the 1976 uprisings. In contrast, the government had learned no lessons from 1976: it dispatched camouflage-clad armed riot police to the Coloured townships, with orders from the Police Commissioner to 'shoot to kill'. A public outcry forced the

'From the Schools to the People' pamphlet distributed by the 'Committee of 81' (student leaders) in May 1980: The wider and deeper the present boycott action has developed, the more we have become aware of one of the main lessons of 1976. This lesson was simply that we should not allow any serious action by black students to become isolated in the schools. Every student action, in order to be successful, has to be linked up with the struggle of the rest of the oppressed people. The condition of the ghetto schools and the gutter education are the outcome of the whole system of racist oppression and capitalist exploitation. This much all of us know well. Who makes this system work? Our parents are workers. It is the workers of this country who produce its wealth. If the workers could be put in a position where they could say for a few weeks: 'We will not work to maintain apartheid and capitalist exploitation', the present loudmouthed *kragdadige* (Afrikaans for rule by force) government would be shaken to its very foundation.

Our parents, the workers, are therefore strong. They have power. We, the students, cannot shake the government in the same way. We can only warn them; we can serve notice on them that the youth will not tolerate the old order. They know as we know, that the future belongs to us. But we have got to get our parents on our side. We have got to link up our struggle with the struggle of the black workers. Our parents have got to understand that we will not be 'educated' and 'trained' to become slaves in an apartheid-capitalist society. We must convince our parents that the only way is to reject, to challenge and to replace this system. It is therefore of very great importance for the success of our present action that we go out to the organizations of the people: to the Parent-Teacher Associations, to the residents, civic, tenants' associations, to the churches and to other organizations of the community. We must explain to them our struggle for national liberation. From the schools to the people! This must be our slogan.

order to be withdrawn and the Minister of Police apologized for the 'unfortunate choice of words' – nevertheless, at least sixty people were killed by police during the following week.

The victims included 17-month-old Belinda Moore, who was struck in the head while sleeping in her cot by a police bullet that passed through the corrugated iron wall of her family's temporary council shack, 14-year-old Shirley September, who was shot when her mother sent her on an errand to buy candles, and 10-year-old Arthur Prinsloo, who ran outside his home to see what was happening when he heard screaming and shots. These details emerged only days later, however, because the police banned all journalists from 'trouble spots', on the pretext that it was the press that was responsible for instigating the unrest. On 17 June 1980, at a press conference at Soweto's Protea Police Station, Police Public Relations Officer Colonel Leon Mellet faced a hostile crowd of foreign and local reporters, demanding to know the reason for the media ban.[6]

Colonel Mellet: Of course, we cannot say the press is to blame for all the trouble. But if you could just understand what is happening at the moment: there is a riotous situation within the country, and the people behind this are seeking all the publicity they can get out of the situation. I want to note this point very clearly: the moment you lift those cameras, those people will start throwing stones. There have also been incidents where television crews have been seen by not only the police, but also by other pressmen, where they are standing behind cameras, inciting the people with black power salutes. Particularly for the cameramen to photograph them.

The unmistakeable impression that is created is that you want to prevent unfavourable coverage. Can you comment on that?

Colonel Mellet: I deny that. It is not only because of unfavourable coverage; it is distorted coverage. The most important reason for banning these media crews is because it has come to our notice that some of the newsmen have openly incited people to stone-throwing and riotous behaviour.

You have laws prohibiting incitement to riot. Do you propose to arrest and charge the people who you say did that?

Colonel Mellet: I don't want to talk about laws; I'm just explaining to you what is happening at the moment.

'Boycott as a Tactic of Struggle', Committee of 81 pamphlet, June 1980: Once the average student has reached the level of conscious militancy, when they see how short-term demands and long-term goals are linked and act on it, then the ground is ripe for unified and effective action. We must see how our short-term demands are linked up with the political and economic system of this country. We must see how the fail-pass rate in schools is linked up with the labour supply for the capitalist system, how low-quality school buildings are linked to the unequal allocation of funds to education for children of the oppressed and children of the oppressor, how inadequate library facilities are linked with the need to confine and limit the thoughts of the oppressed, how distorted history textbooks are linked with the need to obscure and propagandize against the proud history of resistance of the indigenous people against economic slavery, how, in fact, the whole educational system against which we are rebelling stems from the fact that we are denied basic political rights, and thus political power.

The boycott is not an end in itself. It is not a holiday: neither will it transform South African society overnight. It is a planned political act, which is designed to achieve specific short-term victories within a given space of time, and also to raise the general political consciousness of broad layers of students. The boycott can achieve short-term victories. These are important because they give students confidence in themselves, teach them through practical experience the basic lessons of organization and create the climate wherein political consciousness can flourish.
Power to the people! Amandla Ngawethu! Alle Mag Aan Die Mense![5]

What about the little children who've been shot dead?

Colonel Mellet: Yes, well, it is quite obvious that the instigators are using children as a pawn for a confrontation with the police and the demonstrators. And when the police are in such a position where they have to safeguard their own lives and property, it has become necessary for the police to use birdshot. And in this regard, there have been injuries.

Who are these instigators?

Colonel Mellet: They are people who would start off a riotous situation. They are exploiting certain grievances, no doubt. Intimidation is the main cause of the problem. The intimidators are behind in the back rows and they are urging these youngsters to start throwing stones and to start looting buildings. They are using them as shields. It is quite obvious, and then they want publicity. Many, many threats are taking place and it develops in a process where the mobs are urged to take part in violence, and are urged to take part in mass stay-aways from work. And the ones that do not stay away and do not take part, they are then threatened with violence themselves. So you have a situation where most of the people who do stay away from work are staying away because they fear violence, not because they want to stay away from work. The whole thing is an effort to try and break down law and order and discipline, and they are using the children for that particular purpose. They are trying to intimidate the various races in this country to a situation of confrontation, hoping that the races would fight each other. And then the enemy would move in and want to take the spoils. That is what they are trying to do.

SABC, 18 June 1980: The Minister of Police, Mr le Grange, has given assurances that relentless action would be taken against the violent elements and hooligans responsible for the disturbances. Mr le Grange said neither he nor the police had any sympathy with criminal elements who behave in the way they have done. The authorities were prepared to talk to responsible people about grievances, but those who had got out of hand deserved what they would get. Mr le Grange said he was grateful, though, to the large number of black, Coloured and Indian people who were acting responsibly and not taking advantage of what the hooligans were doing. The police would support these people. And that's the end of the news. Our next bulletin will be at seven o'clock.

News commentary tonight is on the criminal element in the brown unrest.[7] Despite the publicity given to the radicals, and the tendency of the news media to sensationalize and exaggerate isolated incidents of unrest, it was moderate opinion which carried the day on June 16th and subsequently. Too often, black South African leaders with moderate views, such as the leaders of the independent black homelands, are discredited by foreign news media as being unrepresentative of majority black opinion. The reason for this is that they preach negotiation as a means of resolving South African problems, as opposed to confrontation.

As never before, June 16th, 1980 has indelibly underlined that the mass of black people in South Africa subscribe to the views of the moderates and are not interested in the demands of the politically motivated agitators and intimidators. During this sensitive period, the black people of South Africa demonstrated in a concrete fashion that South Africa today is further away from revolution than it ever was and that the changes which the government has brought about, and the other ones which are being contemplated, are having a positive impact.

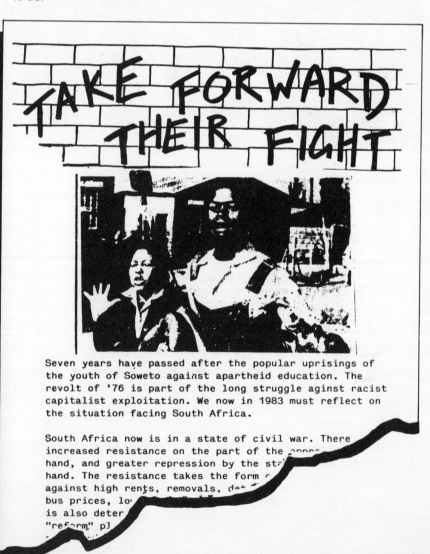

Seven years have passed after the popular uprisings of the youth of Soweto against apartheid education. The revolt of '76 is part of the long struggle aginst racist capitalist exploitation. We now in 1983 must reflect on the situation facing South Africa.

South Africa now is in a state of civil war. There increased resistance on the part of the oppre hand, and greater repression by the sta hand. The resistance takes the form against high rents, removals, det bus prices, lo is also deter "reform" pl

20

The government communicated its intolerance of the unrest, not just with teargas and bullets, but also via the state-controlled South African Broadcasting Corporation, the only radio and television service that most South Africans receive daily in their homes. The message hammered home on the SABC after the police and army quelled this latest uprising: anti-government protest is instigated by a small clique of 'radicals', whose criminal conduct is deplored by the 'moderate' majority, which is patiently awaiting the government's long-promised reform.

By the time the schools reopened, a month after the June violence, the students had abandoned all hopes of negotiating a settlement with the authorities, and were in no mood to suspend the boycott. The government responded by 'indefinitely' closing eighty schools around the country for the rest of the year; then in 1981, it declared black education compulsory for the first time. This anti-boycott ploy – forcing students to partake of 'gutter education' – was guaranteed to further alienate students who had seen their classmates protest and die, in 1976 and again in 1980, in pursuit of free, non-racial education for all.

'What Did You Learn in School Today?' adapted from a protest song by American songwriter Pete Seeger by South African Jessica Sherman:

What did you learn in school today,
Dear little child of mine?
We learnt that West is always best,
And white is usually right,
That rich and poor will always be,
And that's what makes us free.

What did you learn in school today,
Dear little child of mine?
That education brings opportunities,
In this advancing age,
But we'll end up working in the factories,
For a measly weekly wage.

What did you learn in school today,
Dear little child of mine?
We learnt that teargas burns the eyes,
We learnt how police dogs bite,
We learnt that batons break our bones,
And we're learning how to fight!

What did you hear on the news today?
Dear little child of mine?
That agitators stir us up,
And lead us all astray,
But we can think and we can see,
And we want change today!

Resistance
B. We Speak For Ourselves

'Work for all', song by South African band, Juluka:

Keep the home fires burning,
While Papa's earning the pittance he calls his pay,
You've got to get up so early in the morning,
To keep your job, let alone find one these days,
Hear them sing in the streets now,
Hear the sound of marching feet now,
Sifun'umsebenzi – work for all!
We need to work to be,
Sifun'umsebenzi – work for all!
There's a jobless army in the street,
Sifun'umsebenzi – work for all!
In a wage, a hidden war,
Sifun'umsebenzi – work for all!
There's a jobless army at my door.

Labour's 'June 16th' came before 1976, with an unprecedented wave of strikes by some 100,000 black industrial workers in Durban in 1973. The black trade union movement, which had been crushed in the early 1960s, was on the rise again. The government had concluded that repression alone could not control the unions and it appointed a commission to investigate ways of stabilizing the volatile labour force. As a result of its findings, the government passed legislation in 1979 allowing Africans to join unions for the first time, and permitting black and multi-racial unions to register and obtain official recognition. These changes still inhibited political activity among unions, stiffened penalties for illegal strikes, and further tightened government controls, so many of the new black unions refused to register, yet they succeeded – much to the government's dismay – in forcing management to negotiate with them. Membership in these independent non-racial trade unions grew by 200 per cent between 1980 and 1983, and national unions began to be formed in key sectors. For the first time in three decades, a union was formed in the industry that brought in 70 per cent of the country's foreign exchange earnings – mining.[8] The unions' increased strength and bargaining power led to more strikes. An estimated 1000 black workers a day went on strike in 1982 – the most widespread labour unrest since the 1973 Durban strikes — and each of the following years saw even more strike action than during that record high year. The government found the new climate among workers inevitable in theory, but threatening in practice.

The oldest and largest member of the new independent trade union movement was the Federation of South African Trade Unions, with unions representing 130,000 workers by 1984, mainly in the motor, metal and textile industries. FOSATU's impressive membership was a testament to the painstaking and time-consuming process of shopfloor organization, factory by factory and industry by industry. The marathon labour dispute between one of FOSATU's largest affiliates, the Metal and Allied Workers Union, and South Africa's major steel furniture manufacturer, the B & S company in Brits, Transvaal, illustrates the kind of odds facing black unions in the fight for recognition and against retrenchment of workers.

SABC, 10 August 1982: The Director-General of Manpower, Dr Piet van der Merwe, says the main causes of strikes are inexperience and unrealistic expectations. There are, however, also people who exploit trade unions for ideological or personal gain, and who are not particularly concerned about improving the lot of the workers. Speaking in a radio programme, Dr van der Merwe said the degree of labour unrest in South Africa would have been higher if the reforms of the past three years had not been introduced. He said the labour scene here was still relatively calm, if compared with other countries.

Metal and Allied Workers Union organizers David Modimoeng and Fred Modau, shop stewards Ellen Khoza and Joseph Boikanyo, and B & S factory workers Harrison Masedi, Robert Ramorula and Johannes Matjima traced the development of the dispute, beginning in May 1982, when MAWU first started organizing the factory's nine hundred workers.

Ellen Khoza: I had been with B & S for eleven years, and all this time there had been no union, so many of the workers, they were scared at first to hear that the union was coming. They were afraid maybe this would lose their jobs. But then we did hear about the union from some other people from Johannesburg, and they told us the union is very good for the workers, that it can demand a lot for us, so finally we did trust to join it.

What problems at the factory were you hoping that the union would help to solve?

Ellen Khoza: In the factory there was very, very bad conditions. We didn't have safety clothes or gloves or masks and all that. And when somebody is sick, when he is from the doctor, they don't pay him. And when the woman is from the maternity they don't pay her. They just fire him, fire her.

What was the reaction to you, as organizers, when you first started talking about the union to the workers?

David Modimoeng: They were afraid at first, of being fired. They didn't understand what the union is and they want someone maybe to give them an example.

SABC, 7 September 1982: A Johannesburg company has dismissed its entire work force in a labour dispute at the company's two factories near Brits. The financial director of B & S Steelbrite Furniture Company, Mr Keith Haskell, says almost 1000 workers were paid off and discharged after a dispute over the dismissal of a member of the workers' liaison committee earlier this week. Mr Haskell said that both factories had been closed, but that both factories would begin recruiting a new work force on Friday. All those dismissed will be reconsidered for re-employment, but the company was not prepared to reinstate the worker discharged earlier in the week.

Fred Modau: But that was a problem, because we were the first people to establish the union in Brits, and then at the only other factory where we did organize for MAWU, the management provoked a strike and fired all the workers. So, people were really scared that this would happen at B & S.

Can you remember what those first union meetings were like?

Ellen Khoza: They told us the whole story about how MAWU can help us, but they did say that we mustn't think that we are going to see a somebody who's coming to help us. They said, no, we must be prepared and be strong for ourselves, that we must know that when we speak about the union, there's nobody – the union, it's us.

Robert Ramorula: I heard from some friends in Johannesburg that this MAWU, it is a good thing, that I must join with these people and push with them. They told me that I mustn't worry that they can fire me at any time, that someone's coming to fire me because I went to the toilet for five minutes. They said I must be free at work. Now I think that it is a good thing because previously, they would just fire anybody, without any problems.

Fred Modau: So by September (1982), we were having already 85 per cent of the workers at the factory joining MAWU.

And what did management think when they saw people getting excited about the union?

Fred Modau: The boss, he was playing tricky, sort of delaying and delaying before he would recognize us.

Ellen Khoza: I can say from the first, when the management heard that we're joining the union, he did try to victimize all the union members, especially all

the shop stewards. He told us this factory doesn't belong to the union, he's the boss, and his son owns monies and shares, not us. But still, we were sticking together. Then he dismissed the chairman of our shop stewards.

David Modimoeng: Now when the shop stewards went to management to know the reason why they dismissed him, they dismissed all the workers. All nine hundred workers! They just switched off all the machines and ordered the workers outside. They said, 'We will employ workers again – selectively.' They told them to come the next Monday and collect their money and they will be rehired.

Fred Modau: Now, we feel something like that is no good. If they select, they will select people who they know are not union members.

So what did you do?

Ellen Khoza: We called all the union members and we said, 'People, are we coming to fetch our money and be rehired, or what?' and the people said, 'We're not coming to take that money.'

What was the incentive for people just to leave that money?

Harrison Masedi: We knew, in fact, that to take that small pay packet would mean that they could just say, 'You – union members – you're fired.'

Joseph Boikanyo: And I knew, I'm not going to get work any more in the district of Brits, because those people of B & S they do this: they tell the administration they mustn't give us more jobs here.

Fred Modau: The (government) Administration Board, the Labour Bureau, they can kind of blacklist you. For every worker they have a file, so when you go to get another job, they say, 'No, you are a striker, you can't get a job any more in the area of Brits.'

Song sung by Brits workers:

Stay with us, united,
Because where we are going is near,
Cowards are wavering,
They say where we are going is too dangerous,
But we know, the day we win,
The only people who'll cry,
It's only management and the informers.

A TRADE UNION IS ...

A PERMANENT DEMOCRATIC ORGANISATION ...OF WORKERS...

TO BETTER THE CONDITIONS OF THEIR LIVES.

IMPROVE THE CONDITIONS OF THEIR WORK

...TO PROTECT...

...THROUGH COLLECTIVE BARGAINING...

Joseph Boikanyo: So then we could see, the better thing we must do is to stick together and we must try to push our case through to the end.

From that day on, and every day for the next year, the workers met together in the Brits township church hall. Some eventually went back to the factory, and others sought jobs elsewhere, but nearly three hundred workers decided, with the support of MAWU, to take the company to the Industrial Court for its unfair labour practices.

What were you fighting for?

Ellen Khoza: We were fighting for the right to work, and to have the union to be recognized inside the factory.

Fred Modau: In fact, it was not a strike. The workers were dismissed; we must make that clear. We started at first to try to negotiate with management, we tried by all means, but all that that boss could do was to get two of our guys arrested for 'intimidation'.[9]

David Modimoeng: The harassment was large, because even in the factory, management used to call the security police. You'd find them right in the office while our shop stewards were trying to negotiate. Even here at the church hall, they were arresting our people for not carrying passes, and the security police would take people for interrogation.

How did you manage to survive the whole year?

Ellen Khoza: We were suffering like nobody's business. We had to sell our belongings, if we couldn't manage to borrow enough money from our relatives and friends. We couldn't pay rent, we couldn't pay school fees. We just had to all help each other.

Robert Ramorula: Sometimes, what kept us going was to sing songs. For twelve months we were thinking about the day that we will go back to work, and we were singing about our victory that we knew was coming.

In September 1983, the workers' perseverance paid off: just before the case was to come before the court, the company arranged an out-of-court settlement with the union, and agreed to take back the dismissed workers.[10]

What did this whole experience teach you?

Joseph Boikanyo: It taught me so many things, but I think the most important is that through unity, we will survive.

Harrison Masedi: Another thing it did teach me is that we are so many different kinds of nations, so, before the strike, if I am Tswana and the other one is Xhosa, if I saw him here in the street, suffering, I don't care. But now, if I saw him there, I would just know that black is black, he's my friend, so I must help him. So that strike is teaching me a lot.

Why do you think that unity is so important?

Joseph Boikanyo: Because if we people are always united, there's nothing can break us. Before, if someone will be chased out of the factory, we don't care about it. But today we know we must be together and make our union to negotiate to save that person.

Ellen Khoza: Yes, really, unity is strength. When I'm alone, I can't do nothing. They will just dismiss me immediately and I have no say. But when we are united, really, it's sound. Even the employers, they see, these peoples are united, so they can't oppress us like before.

The happy ending was shortlived. The company was sold and the new management spent the next six months working to undermine the union's support, then suddenly announced the closure of one of the two plants in March 1984. As a result, 240 workers found themselves worse off than they had been during the campaign of the previous year: jobless, and – since management had stalled on the agreed-on union recognition – with no recourse against the short notice and pitiful severance pay. Still, the workers' unity survived this setback, some setting up income-generating projects through an unemployed workers' committee, and others working voluntarily as union organizers.[11] The Brits workers also showed that there is a lot more to trade unionism than wage disputes. Workers are demanding union recognition, better working conditions, the right to factory-level negotiations with management, and a voice in dismissals.

South Africa had seen an era of overtly political trade unionism, culminating with the campaigns of the South African Congress of Trade Unions in the 1950s, but when the African National Congress was banned in 1960, SACTU was forced underground. Since then, the unions permitted by the government to organize dared not stray far from shop floor issues. By the late 1970s, a number of independent (unregistered) non-racial unions had arrived on the scene, and the line separating workplace issues and community matters was again becoming fainter. In 1979, a strike called by the African Food and Canning Workers Union (a former SACTU affiliate revived in the Cape) at the Fattis and Monis factory led to a boycott of the company's food products. This first national consumer boycott since the 1950s helped to re-establish the links between trade unions and the wider community.[12]

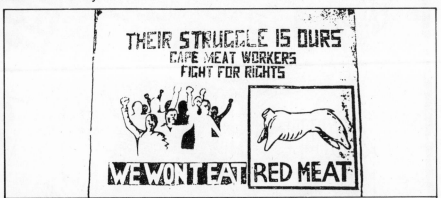

In 1980, a strike by meat workers in the Western Cape-based General Workers Union led to a call for a boycott of red meat products. The union compared its strike for the right to elect a non-racial factory committee democratically with the demand of the majority of South Africans for the right to choose non-racial political representatives. The meat boycott coincided with the 1980 school and bus boycotts, and, as a result, the unions and the budding community and student organizations began co-ordinating strategies. When the South African Allied Workers Union struck in support of dismissed workers at the Wilson-Rowntree sweet factory in 1981, the workers called for a national boycott of the company's products until Rowntrees agreed to negotiate, and the community responded with posters, pamphlets and fund-raising concerts.

For the vulnerable independent unions – whose workers were largely unskilled, often migrants and ever threatened by unemployment – community support seemed an indispensable bulwark against the power of both management and government. For the communities, the calls for support from the unions presented a challenge: to translate the sporadic, high profile campaigns of strike support and boycotts into long-term, mass-based structures for change in both the workplace and the community.

As the young community organizations or 'civics' started putting down roots, they applied a few lessons from the trade union movement. These civics launched membership recruitment drives, then charged small membership fees which could be used to rent offices and even employ full-time organizers. Just as the unions sought to groom shop stewards from among rank-and-file workers, the civics aimed to develop leaders from among local residents. There was certainly no lack of issues to organize around, from rent, bus fare and rate increases, to the demolition of squatter camps.

The civics also discovered the value of long-term projects in mobilizing community support, such as health and education centres, crèches and pre-schools, advice offices, culture clubs, and, perhaps most importantly, news media. Newspapers, newsletters and pamphlets have become a valuable means of consolidating organization, educating the community, and ensuring two-way communication.

Grassroots community newspaper, April 1983: All over South Africa people are hearing the words of the bosses, and the government TV, the radio, the newspapers and films control what we know and think. We need to answer back. We need to speak for ourselves, to find ways of reaching people and passing on our own message. *Grassroots* is one way of doing this. *Grassroots* brings us news about our organizations and what is happening in other areas. But there are other ways of reaching people. Slogans on walls, buttons, T-shirts, stickers, plays, posters, pamphlets, meetings – all these are ways of passing on the message.

We don't have money or machines, or specially trained experts. But we are creative. This means that even if we don't have printing presses, we can learn to explore whatever means are available to us. We can learn to use anything that will leave a mark to help us reach people. While making posters, banners and newsletters, people are coming together to share ideas and learn skills, so media helps our organizations in two ways: firstly it informs and educates people about our organizations. Secondly, in producing media, people learn to work together. We must learn the skills of communicating, and we must teach others. If the bosses and government shout loudly, we must pass on the message to others. The state uses media to control the people. We must use it to liberate ourselves.

WORKERS & TENANTS IN YOUR FACTORIES & TOWNSHIPS
UNITE TO DEFEND YOUR LIVING STANDARDS

Wilfred Rhodes, 1983 Chairman of the Cape Areas Housing Action Committee, an umbrella group representing more than twenty civics: To build strong, democratic organizations means more than a show of hands at meetings. It calls for greater involvement by all affected people. The task is not for those with confidence to make decisions on their own. Rather, their job is to reach out and involve others in day-to-day work. It is this collective involvement in decision-making and action which will be the real measure of how successfully we are organizing. The goal of organizations must not only be to fight high rents and bus fares. We must see these problems as being only the smoke. Our work must be to put out the fire which causes the smoke. We must wipe out from this society all the causes of our hardship.

Women's freedom song from the 1950s, sung in English, Zulu and Afrikaans:

You have tampered with the women,
You have struck a rock,
You have dislodged a boulder,
You will be crushed.

Unzima lomthwalo ufuna manima,
Unzima lomthwalo ufuna madoda,
Asikhathali noba siyabotshwa,
Sizimisele inkhululeko.

Die gewig is swaar,
Die moeders is nodig,
Ons gee nie om as ons gevang is nie,
Ons is bereid vir onse vryheid.

The weight is heavy,
We need our mothers,
We won't give up, even if we're jailed,
We are ready for our freedom.

The leaders of the civic movement tend to be men, and the most energetic members are usually the youth, but when it comes to the actual spade-work of community organizing, it is often the women who make the greatest effort. Because South Africa's labour and influx control laws prevent women from joining their husbands who have migrated to the cities to work, it is the rural women who often shoulder the responsibility for their families' upkeep. It is these women who have led the campaigns for urban rights, travelling illegally to the urban areas and squatting in makeshift shacks on the outskirts of cities when they could find no 'legal' accommodation.

Increasingly, political activists have come to see their organizations as historically rooted – and women, especially, have stressed the continuity of their struggle from the 1950s to the 1980s. South African Women's Day has been commemorated annually in the communities: the events of 9 August 1956 recalled, when 20,000 women of all races marched on Pretoria's Union Buildings in a massive display of solidarity against the extension of passes to women.

The communities, workers, students and women have a powerful ally in their efforts to organize resistance: the church. On a purely practical level, the churches make their halls available for meetings, help collect food and funds for striking workers, and support the families of jailed activists. More and more churches are refusing to accept the thesis that religion and politics should not mix.

It is the three white Dutch Reformed Churches that have done the most to discredit religion in the eyes of blacks, with their biblical justification of apartheid. After 1976, blacks felt that any church which did not actively support their struggle was against them. Thus the challenge to the churches – to oppose the

WE WOMEN WILL STAND SHOULDER TO SHOULDER WITH OUR MENFOLK IN A COMMON STRUGGLE AGAINST POVERTY, RACE AND CLASS DISCRIMINATION

government with action in addition to prayer – gave theologians a chance to try and win back some respect from the Soweto generation. Fifty top clergymen and women marched through the streets of Johannesburg in 1980, in protest against the detention of a fellow minister, and were arrested for violating the Riotous Assemblies Act. In 1981, the Presbyterians called on their ministers to ignore the Mixed Marriages Act and marry couples across the colour bar. The Catholic bishops publicly branded the South African Defence Force an 'army of occupation' in Namibia in 1982; and later that year, 123 dissident Dutch Reformed ministers signed a document condemning apartheid. In 1983, a Durban ecumenical group released a declaration supporting workers' rights, and the World Alliance of Reformed Churches declared apartheid a heresy.

A sure sign that all these actions had indeed boosted the churches' credibility came in the government's response. The South African Council of Churches, representing twenty-two of the country's main churches, and its outspoken General Secretary, Bishop Desmond Tutu, became the targets of vitriolic government attacks.

► Shortly after that tirade, the government appointed a commission of inquiry, whose lawyers tapped into the well-financed international right-wing lobby against the World Council of Churches and its alleged support of 'terrorism' through humanitarian grants to the liberation movements.[13] After months of public hearings that condemned the churches on charges ranging from financial mismanagement to subversion, the Minister of Police warned the SACC that he would 'not allow any wicked acts to be committed under the cloak of religion', but

Father Lebamang Sibidi, preaching to the Soweto Civic Association, 23 November 1981: Now what does theology have to say to a landless people, to a disinherited people, to a people dispossessed of their most precious heritage, a people whose land has been stolen from them? I am going to admit right from the outset that for many people today, Christianity holds no appeal in terms of the practicalities of life. There is just too much emphasis in Christianity on personal, private preparation for the life beyond, and much less emphasis on the deep hurts, the struggles, the agony of a people deprived of their land. Such Christianity and theology hold no appeal for the majority of our people, especially for the young ones who identify so vitally with the Soweto of 1976, June the 16th.

SABC, 10 September 1981: The Minister ◄ of Police, Mr le Grange, has appealed to members of the South African Council of Churches, to reconsider their links with the council and its General Secretary, Bishop Tutu, in view of his encouragement of or support for revolutionary elements. Speaking in the debate on his budget votes in the Senate chamber in Parliament, he said the government found it increasingly difficulty to tolerate the situation. Our political correspondent, Johan Pretorius, reports that in the debate, Bishop Tutu and other clerics were also accused of helping to promote disorder and violence.

Johan Pretorius: The Minister said the SACC and its General Secretary, Bishop Tutu, wanted to undermine the preparedness of the South African Police and the Defence Force. They were accusing the government of following policies which could lead to a confrontation between church and state, and yet the SACC had been propagating the same policy as the ANC since 1961.

Bishop Tutu and the SACC supported and initiated programmes of education which were making things extremely difficult for the government, and in all this Mr le Grange said the SACC did not rely on its own finance, but rather on funds from abroad to launch policies similar to that of the ANC. Among the sources of the funds were the World Council of Churches, the International University Exchange Fund, as well as money from Scandinavian countries. Mr le Grange said Bishop Tutu supported civil disobedience, preached disinvestment, distorted the facts of the government's endeavours to better black education, and had abused the squatter problem.

stopped short of implementing a threatened ban on international funding.[14] The SACC remains, after all, the most respected international religious symbol of opposition to apartheid, and the government obviously concluded that the witch hunt was not worth the attendant, very negative publicity – especially after Bishop Tutu became an international celebrity when he was awarded the 1984 Nobel Peace Prize.

Letter to Reverend Frank Chikane from the Apostolic Faith Mission of Africa: Christian greetings. I have been instructed by the West Rand District Committee to write you this letter. The Committee has suspended you from the 6th August, 1981, for the following reason: that you are still active in politics, but on the 31st January, 1980 you promised the Committee to stay away from politics. The Committee found that you are still appearing in the newspapers. Yours in His Service, V.F. Pieterse, Chairman.

There was no such protection for Reverend Frank Chikane, as he fought a similar battle in the tiny black township of Kagiso, on the West Rand. Between 1978 and 1982 Chikane was detained four times without charge or trial, and spent 450 days in jail. He was three times refused a passport to attend theological seminars abroad. His church, the white-run Apostolic Faith Mission, seemingly endorsed the police action against the pastor by suspending Reverend Chikane from his religious duties, citing his involvement in politics.

Reverend Frank Chikane: They claim that their position is such that they do not participate in the political issues of the country, that they are neutral as a church. And they said I was an embarrassment to the church because of all the press reports about what I was saying. You see, I argued that the church must be involved in the South African problem, that we must guide the people, that we cannot just leave them to face the bloodbath that is coming. Because in the history of struggles, a ruling class has never voluntarily given in. It is only when you produce power equal to theirs that they start thinking and talking.

Therefore, the situation is such that the government challenges people to take up arms. So, from the point of view of the oppressed, they are saying, 'We have tried everything else and the only thing left to do is to match the power that the oppressor has got.' It is the violence of the state that keeps the state in power, so people feel that to match that power you must also use the same method.

So my Christian appeal was that if South Africa is not going to change, you are going to have a situation where people reach the stage of 'don't care'. And once they've reached that stage, guns won't stop them. Remember, June 16th presented itself and people – children! – simply walked into guns. Once people are so frustrated by oppression, they can do anything.

What was the response of your church when you told them all this?

Reverend Frank Chikane: Their response was very negative. They said, well, they've got the separate development policy of the government, which they think will work. And I told them, 'It will not work. You're going to have revolution on top of those Bantustans (homelands).' The other problem they

had with me was this business of me getting detained. They asked, why was I detained? They had this idea that where there's smoke, there's fire. And I said, 'Well, I get detained because I differ with the state, I'm critical of them.' They wanted me to make sure I wouldn't be detained again, as a kind of negotiation to keep me in the church. But I had to tell them, 'It's beyond my control, I don't decide that I should be detained tomorrow. These guys simply come during the night without an appointment, so I can't control it, and therefore I can't give that type of assurance.'

And that was what broke down our talks. They felt, well, they cannot have such a person in their church, and they suspended me. The funny thing was, we never even touched on the Bible to try to prove that I was sinful or a heretic to be worth suspending. And that's when I realized that talking with those people was futile. Actually, my feeling is now that in South Africa today, those kind of Christians have become more dangerous – or at least they are more prone to cause people to resort to unfortunate methods – than non-Christians. That's a hard statement, but that's the feeling today in the black community.

What did you do after your suspension?

Reverend Frank Chikane: Well, it didn't really matter, because the police came for me soon after, so I was detained for most of the year that I was supposed to be suspended.[15] And, during my detention, the type of things the police said to me! As a Christian, it taught me that any young person who is exposed to this system would come out being an atheist, completely. If Christians can say those things that they were saying about Christianity – that the Bible has nothing to do with blacks, the Bible only talks about whites – well, then you can understand why so many blacks feel so negative about Christianity. I remember the police tried to threaten me: 'Ons will niks van jou Bybel hoor nie (We don't want to hear anything from your Bible). Nothing about your Bible, we just want you to answer our questions.' But I had to tell them that everything I did – even if it was against the government – I did because of my commitment as a Christian. So I could not explain anything I had done without calling on the Scriptures to reveal my position.

Freedom Charter

A call for peace and justice

Twenty five years ago this week, 3 000 people from various organisations in the country gathered in Kliptown to draw up the Freedom Charter.

The gathering in Kliptown, known as the Congress of the People, unanimously adopted the document as the policy and manifesto of the organisations.

The meeting was convened by the African National Congress (ANC), the South African Indian Congress, the South African Coloured People's Organisation and the mainly white Congress of Democrats. The Freedom Charter came after the Defiance Campaign of 1952 to record the demands for change that had been made over a period stretching back to the turn of the century.

The ideals set out in the charter still live in the hearts of millions of South Africans.

● With the help of the United Nations Special Committee Against Apartheid, the ANC this week observed the 25th anniversary of the Freedom Charter, with a performance by South African musician Hugh Masakela and the screening of a film tracing the history of the Charter.

We, the people of South Africa, declare for all our country and the world to know:

● That South Africa belongs to all who live in it, black and white, and that no government can justly claim authority unless it is based on the will of all the people;

● that our people have been robbed of their birthright to land, liberty and peace by a form of government founded on injustice and inequality;

● that our country will never be prosperous or free until all our people live in brotherhood, enjoying equal rights and opportunities;

● that only a democratic state, based on the will of all the people, can secure to all their birthright without distinction of colour, race, sex or belief.

And therefore, we the people of South Africa, black and white together — equals, countrymen and brothers — adopt this Freedom Charter. And we pledge ourselves to strive together, sparing neither strength nor courage, until the democratic changes set out here have been won.

The people shall govern!

Every man and woman shall have the right to vote for and to stand as a candidate for all bodies which make laws;

All people shall be entitled to take part in the administration of the country;

The rights of the people shall be the same, regardless of race, colour or sex;

All bodies of minority rule, advisory boards, councils and authorities shall be replaced by democratic organs of self-government.

All national groups shall have equal rights!

There shall be equal status in the bodies of state, in the courts and in the schools for all national groups and races;

All people shall have equal right to use their own languages, and to develop their own folk culture and customs;

All national groups shall be protected by law against insults to their race and national pride;

The preaching and practice of national, race or colour discrimination and contempt shall be a punishable crime;

All apartheid laws and practices shall be set aside.

The people shall share in the country's wealth!

The national wealth of our country, the heritage of all South Africans, shall be restored to the people;

The mineral wealth beneath the soil, the banks and monopoly industry shall be transferred to the ownership of the people as a whole;

All other industry and trade shall be controlled to assist the well being of the people;

All people shall have equal rights to trade where they choose, to manufacture and to enter all trades, crafts and professions.

Chief Albert Luthuli, who chaired the Congress of the People.

The land shall be shared among those who work it!

Restrictions of land ownership on a racial basis shall be ended, and all the land redivided amongst those who work it, to banish famine and land hunger;

The state shall help the peasants with implements, seed, tractors and dams to save the soil and assist the tillers;

Freedom of movement shall be guaranteed to all who work on the land;

All shall have the right to occupy land wherever they choose;

People shall not be robbed of their cattle, and forced labour and farm prisons shall be abolished.

All shall be equal before the law!

No one shall be imprisoned, deported or restricted without a fair trial;

No one shall be condemned by the order of any government official;

The courts shall be representative of all the people;

Imprisonment shall be only for serious crimes against the people, and shall aim at re-education, not vengeance;

The police force and army shall be open to all on an equal basis and shall be the helpers and protectors of the people;

All laws which discriminate on grounds of race, colour or belief shall be repealed.

All shall enjoy equal human rights!

The law shall guarantee to all their rights to speak, to organise, to meet together, to punish, to preach, to worship and to educate their children.

The privacy of the house from police raids shall be protected by law;

All shall be free to travel without restriction from countryside to town, from province to province and from South Africa abroad;

Pass Laws, permits, and all other laws restricting these freedoms, shall be abolished.

There shall be work and security!

All who work shall be free to form unions, to elect their officers and to make wage agreements with their employers;

The State shall recognise the right and duty of all to work, and to draw full unemployment benefits;

Men and women of all races shall receive equal pay for equal work;

There shall be a 40-hour working week, a national minimum wage, paid annual leave, and sick leave for all workers, and maternity leave on full pay for all working mothers;

Miners, domestic workers, farm workers, and civil servants shall have the same rights as all others who work;

Child labour, compound labour, the tot system and contract labour shall be abolished.

The doors of learning and culture shall be opened!

The government shall discover, develop and encourage national talent for the enhancement of our cultural life;

All the cultural treasures of mankind shall be open to all, by free exchange of books, ideas and contact with other lands;

The aim of education shall be to teach the youth to love their people and their culture, to honour human brotherhood, liberty and peace;

Education shall be free, compulsory, universal and equal for all children;

Higher education and technical training shall be opened to all by means of state allowances and scholarships awarded on the basis of merit;

Adult illiteracy shall be ended by a mass state education plan;

Teachers shall have all the rights of other citizens;

The colour bar in cultural life, in sport and in education shall be abolished.

There shall be houses, security and comfort!

All people shall have the rights to live where they choose, to be decently housed, and to bring up their families in comfort and security;

Unused housing space shall be made available to the people;

Rent and prices shall be lowered, food plentiful and no one shall go hungry;

A preventive health scheme shall be run by the state;

Free medical care and hospitalisation shall be provided for all, with special care for mothers and young children;

Slums shall be demolished, and new suburbs built where all have transport, roads, lighting, playing fields, creches and social centres;

The aged, the orphans, the disabled and the sick shall be cared for by the state;

Rest, leisure and recreation shall be the right of all;

Fenced locations and ghettoes shall be abolished, and laws which break up families shall be repealed;

South Africa shall be a fully independent state, which respects the rights and sovereignty of nations.

There shall be peace and friendship!

South Africa shall strive to maintain world peace and the settlement of all international disputes by negotiation — not war;

Peace and friendship amongst all our people shall be secured by upholding the equal rights, opportunities and status of all;

The people of the protectorates — Basutoland, Bechuanaland and Swaziland — shall be free to decide for themselves their own future;

The rights of all the peoples of Africa to independence and self-government shall be recognised, and shall be the basis of close co-operation;

Let all who love their people and their country now say, as we say here:

"These freedoms we will fight for, side by side, throughout our lives, until we have won our liberty."

Resistance
C. People's Republic-Yes!

With the building up of trade unions, student and community organizations came a renewed attempt to define and articulate an ideology of resistance. What emerged in the 1980s was a body of beliefs that had matured through the 1976 experience, but was rooted in a broader historical context. Workers, students and the communities had gained self-confidence in the 1970s, largely through the Black Consciousness organizations inspired by Steve Biko, and banned after his death at the hands of the security police in 1977. In the years that followed, Black Consciousness began to be seen more as a developmental stage than a strategy for liberation. This view led to a resurgence of interest in Africa's oldest liberation movement, the African National Congress, founded in 1912. The ANC was banned in 1960, and in 1961 launched an armed struggle for majority rule. Its leaders were all jailed or out of the country, and its members forced underground, so to the Soweto generation, the movement was surrounded in awe and mystery.

26th June 1980 marked the 25th anniversary of the ANC-sponsored Congress of the People, when 3000 delegates from all over South Africa drew up a document calling for democratic rights for all and redistribution of land and wealth. In a bold move, the black newspaper, *Sunday Post,* published the Freedom Charter in its entirety, and over the next year, political leaders, community organizations, trade unions, student groups and churches began affirming their allegiance to its 'minimum demands' for change.[16] This rediscovery of the Freedom Charter gave birth to a new alliance of 'progressive

BIKO AND SOLIDARITY

**BLACK PEOPLE'S CONVENTION
TRIBUTE TO THE LATE
HONORARY PRESIDENT
BANTU STEPHEN BIKO**

One Azania: One Nation

democrats' – Africans, Coloureds, Indians and some whites – who saw class as well as race as the determining factors in the South African conflict.

The Congress of South African Students, the Azanian (university) Students Organization, and independent trade unions such as the South African Allied Workers Union and the General and Allied Workers Union led the shift away from Black Consciousness to the progressive democrat or 'Charterist' stance, sparking bitter attacks from the sole Black Consciousness grouping to survive the 1977 bannings, the Azanian People's Organization.[17] The government watched nervously from the sidelines, its wariness over revived support for the ANC curiously translated into a seeming tolerance for Black Consciousness – an attitude that only made people sceptical of Black Consciousness and its potential to confront the state. Even more disturbing was the far higher incidence of detentions, prosecutions and jailings of leaders of non-racial organizations, as compared with the treatment of Black Consciousness adherents.[18] The president of the General Allied Workers Union, Sampson Ndou, said he had seen

Harald Pakendorf, editor of the Afrikaans newspaper, *Die Vaderland*, **the Transvaal mouthpiece of the National Party:** I've no quarrel with Black Consciousness as such; there is nothing wrong with it. It's part of a nationalist feeling and it's understandable and we shouldn't react negatively. We should react positively to it. It would be foolish not to recognize that there are grievances and that those grievances can be addressed best through a nationalist organization, and if it's a nationalist organization that can base itself on colour, it makes it so much easier.

a shift in the government's approach toward the independent trade unions over the course of several detentions, from the 1960s through the 1980s.

 General and Allied Workers Union President Sampson Ndou: You can tell that the security police have changed: Black Consciousness is no longer their problem. From what I have experienced during detentions, their problem today is the ANC. You know, I have been detained several times and lately, the security police have stopped talking about BC (Black Consciousness). They no longer bother us about BC. To them, they think that all non-racial organizations within the country are a front for the ANC.

What do you think was the purpose of detaining you?

Sampson Ndou: Well, I was questioned about the ANC, and it seemed they thought I have links with the ANC and its military wing, Umkhonto we Sizwe. The security police just don't see any line of demarcation between the ANC outside and the union movement within the country, particularly the independent trade unions and other non-racial organizations. You see, to the security police, when they look at me, or any other progressive person, to them, they are seeing guerillas. The true situation is that people are simply more radical now. Those who were at school in 1976, who were first supporting the BC line, they are now workers, some of them are even in the labour movement. And these young people today, they are much more active than we used to be in the past. Oppression has sharpened their political views.

The experience of Tshediso Matona, a national organizer for the Congress of South African Students, and a young woman named Thandi, who is active in community organizations, typifies this 'sharpening of political views', away from Black Consciousness to the progressive democrat camp.

Tshediso Matona: When I first started involving myself in politics, I was BC because I had a very strong feeling against whites. I thought whites were those who were oppressing us because they call us 'kaffirs' (niggers) and they ill-treat us and they don't pay us living wages, so I had this anti-white feeling. But as time went on, I realized that it is the strategy of the government to divide the people in terms of their living standards: Africans were the most oppressed and the Indians and the so-called Coloureds were better off. I realized that, no, whites are not our oppressors, but they're rather being used by the system. And that within the white group you can find certain individuals who are committed to the struggle, like, for instance, Bram Fischer, Joe Slovo, Denis Goldberg[19] and others.

So this explains the difference between COSAS today and the past student organizations. They were predominantly Black Consciousness, they believed in 'Black is beautiful, black is proud', you know. But we realize the loopholes in these slogans. You cannot tell me Matanzima and Thebehali[20] are beautiful – they are oppressors of the black people. And you find that many of the traitors and collaborators hide behind this Black Consciousness philosophy while they continue to collaborate in the oppression of their own people.

Thandi: I was still at boarding school at the time when BC had quite a lot of support. Like, we knew about Steve Biko – I mean, he was a kind of hero. And when he was killed, it had such an impact. I see the philosophy of Black Consciousness was important, in the sense that people had been seeing whites as the best stage to develop to. Like the skin should be light to be beautiful, and the hair should be straight. And that was the whole reason for Black Consciousness: for us to be able to take pride in ourselves. But it's not an end in itself. BC can't be an end in itself.

Why not?

Thandi: Because it ends up pushing people into racism – just another kind of racism. It can outgrow its time, so that people find themselves in racism, without understanding it, without seeing it as racism.

Tshediso Matona: People have realized that BC doesn't provide solutions for the problems of South Africa; they come with impractical concepts like driving the white people into the sea. So, people begin to lose confidence in these types of things, because they do not even give people a semblance of an idea as to how this is going to come about.

In any case, I shouldn't say that we don't support BC, because our understanding of BC is not that it should be anti-white. Our understanding is that black people must unite and fight for their liberation. So our understanding of Black Consciousness is the advocation of black unity. That was expressed as early as 1912, when the African National Congress was formed, when Pixley Seme[21] said there should no longer be any talk of Zulu or Xhosa, for we are all one people. He said all these racial aberrations and ethnic divisions are the causes of all our oppression, as such. So, we understand Black Consciousness to advocate the unity of black people, rather than the rejection of whites.

Thandi: But one problem I worry about is that I think the system is going to come down harder and harder on the non-racial line.

Tshediso Matona: I think that the system is realizing that the great threat is non-racialism. Because this means that even those people who they rely upon for defence and security – the whites – are going to be drawn to the cause of liberation. You see, the system is realizing that South Africa is in a very deep crisis and the majority of whites are gripped by a lot of insecurity about their future. And because non-racialism advocates that whites have a role to play, the system is scared that the whites are going to turn their backs against the government and join forces with us in fighting against the system. And what also worries them is that the principles of non-racialism are more economically inclined, because we believe it is the taking of economic power which will solve our problems, not only political power. So this is also why the repression of the non-racial organizations is so high.

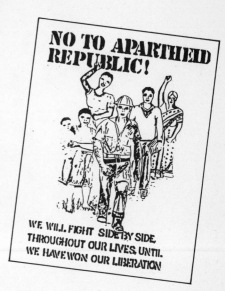

In response to the widespread disenchantment with Black Consciousness, Azanian Peoples' Organization stalwarts made a concerted effort to update the philosophy and recruit new members. One of the most articulate exponents of the Black Consciousness of the 1980s is Saths Cooper, a founder member of the banned Black Peoples' Convention, along with the late Steve Biko. Cooper and several of his contemporaries served six years in jail for their Black Consciousness beliefs – convicted under the Terrorism Act on a charge stemming from a 1975 Durban rally in support of Mozambican independence. After his release, Cooper was elected Vice-President of AZAPO, and set to work revitalizing the traditional Black Consciousness line, redefining the enemy, not as whites, but as the forces of 'racial capitalism'.

 Saths Cooper: We basically analyze the problem as one constituted by racism and capitalism; there is an amalgam, the one bolsters the other. The solution to that problem can never come from within the ranks of that problem.

Do you accept the Freedom Charter as a minimum demand for changing South Africa?

Saths Cooper: The problem with the Charter is that it has remained static from 1955 till today. It is a document which arose out of post-war conditions, out of conditions that are almost three decades old. They need to be constantly revised in the reality of dynamic processes. At best the Charter is a bourgeois democratic programme. It doesn't contain the seeds of socialist transformation for this country.

Can you elaborate on what seems to be a fundamental difference between your point of view and that of non-racial groupings: the role of whites?

Saths Cooper: Look, we don't say whites are irrelevant. Whites can play a very meaningful role in the struggle, but we don't think they're going to do the revolution in this country a whole lot of good if they continue in positions of leadership, but not at grassroots level. This is the challenge facing the white left in this country – even the liberals: to attempt attitudinal changes amongst the people they live with, their wives, their brothers, their sisters, their parents and their little communities, the suburbs that they come from. That is a much more difficult task than standing up on a platform and lifting your fist and shouting 'Amandla!'

What is your view of the ANC?

Saths Cooper: Look, the ANC was banned in 1960. What presence did they maintain in this country until Black Consciousness came up? Nothing. No presence whatsoever. They had abrogated responsibility in this country for leadership, they left the people in a state of hopelessness and despair, until BC arose. Then BC arose in the late 60s and early 70s and took the people to a cataclysmic type of awakening that you saw happening in 1976. Now, this wasn't attributable at all to the ANC or any previous positions, but purely to BC orientation. This is a fact: these organizations which were haemorrhaging got new blood transfusions from the exodus of post-76. The ANC's frontline slaughter sheep are products of Black Consciousness. They are the products of Soweto, of BC, who have been reorientated into a vicious anti-BC line.

That sounds a bit like the government's line, that the children of 1976 have got into the grips of 'communists' and are being used as cannon fodder.

Saths Cooper: I'm just saying that the ANC had no membership. Their membership came from us. Another unfortunate thing is the attachment of the Communist Party to the ANC in a form of symbiotic relationship, which has tended to bring in Moscow. But then, who says Moscow's socialist?

Are you anti-communist or anti-Soviet?

Saths Cooper: I think largely that I am anti-anything that's going to be an imposition, an affliction. Basically, we're opposed to Big Brother imposition, particularly from the super-powers. But our problem is not as much with communists; we have problems with detached armies which have no roots with the people. We have no links with any country, we have no support from anybody, except what we actually get from our membership in this country. We've been accused of being sponsored by various international agencies like the CIA, and I'm sure the CIA is laughing all the way to the bank because they've got us for free. But that's just an effort to discredit our movement, mostly by those who feel that Black Consciousness is becoming a threat to what they regard as the long-established organizations.

Cooper's criticism of the Freedom Charter for its lack of explicit socialism is suspect to Charterists who feel they are forced to play down their radical views, so as to avoid being detained by the police as 'terrorists' and 'communists'. Cooper's criticism of white involvement and communist influence in the black struggle for majority rule is reminiscent of the 1959 breakaway of a group of Africanists from the ANC to form the Pan-Africanist Congress. While internal squabbles and the virtual inactivity of its military wing since the 1960s have debilitated the PAC as a political force,[22] the memories of that period of disunity are still strong. Veterans of that era, like Dr Nthato Motlana, leader of the Soweto Civic Association, saw the same dangerous potential for divisiveness in the debate between Black Consciousness supporters and the progressive democrats.

Dr Nthato Motlana, speaking at a June 16th commemoration, Regina Mundi Church, Soweto, 1981: Those of us who are united in our utter dedication to freedom, to freeing ourselves, must stop fighting among ourselves. Let us not give joy and comfort to our enemy. Our commitment, sons and daughters of the soil, is to liberation, and at this moment in our history, the one unifying factor is Nelson Mandela. I know that even if we may have differences on ideology, the one unifying symbol about which there is no doubt at all in our minds, is Nelson Mandela. Let us resolve that from this day onwards, ladies and gentlemen, sons and daughters of Africa, that our struggle for freedom is bigger than our little differences. In the famous words of (the ANC's) Radio Freedom,[23] let us say, 'Victory is certain!'
Crowd: Victory is certain!
Dr Nthato Motlana: Amandla!
Crowd: Ngawethu!

The name of imprisoned ANC leader Nelson Mandela does seem to transcend ideology. Even Black Consciousness adherents supported a petition for his release: the Azanian People's Organization publicity secretary, George Wauchope, stated publicly in 1981 that his group saw Mandela as a symbol of all those in prison and exile, and that 'We were never anti-him at any stage.'[24] From the 1950s through the 1980s, hardly a freedom song was sung that did not mention his name.

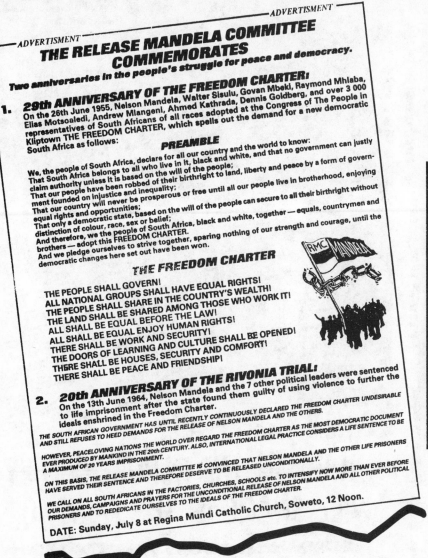
Freedom songs sung at protest meetings:

Mandela says fight for freedom,
Freedom is in your hands,
Mandela says freedom now,
Now we say away with slavery,
In our land of Africa.
Rohlihlahla[25] Mandela,
Freedom is in your hands,
Show us the way to freedom,
In our land of Africa.

Vula Botha siyanqonqoza,
Khulul' uMandela asikhokele,
Open Botha, we are knocking,
Release Mandela, so he can lead us.

In all my trouble and suffering,
Mandela is with me,
Even amidst hippos,[26]
Mandela is still with me.

In 1981, when this incipient unity was still tenuous, the strength of the non-racial organizations was put to a test. The government called for all South Africans to join in celebrations to mark the twentieth anniversary of the break with the British Crown and the founding of the Republic of South Africa.

The anti-Republic Day campaign brought hundreds of thousands of people to protest meetings all over the country, but, even more importantly, the successful boycott vindicated the efforts of the non-racial movement to mobilize a campaign on a national political level. A simultaneous anti-Republic Day campaign was waged on another front: the ANC launched a spectacular series of attacks against strategic targets in Soweto, Durban, the Orange Free State, East London and Ciskei. Guerillas blew up rail links and a Defence Force recruiting office, attacked a police station, and cut power lines. While many of the ANC's attacks over the past two decades had often been dismissed as isolated and amateurish, these attacks were seen – by both the government and its opponents – as a well-co-ordinated demonstration of support for a popular campaign of mass resistance.

State President Marais Viljoen, speaking on the SABC, 1 May 1981, to open month-long Republic Day Celebrations: This festival is an attempt to bring together all the citizens of our country, and also all the strangers within our gates. We should be inspired to undivided loyalty to our fatherland, and be willing and prepared, as good citizens, to serve and to offer up whatever South Africa may ask of us. What occasion in the life of a nation could be better suited to fostering a sense of unity than the commemoration of the coming into being of a constitutional order in which its freedom and independence are fully guaranteed?

Sammy Adelman, President of the Students' Representative Council of the University of the Witwatersrand, chairing an anti-Republic Day meeting at Johannesburg's Selbourne Hall, 27 May 1981: People from all sections of the community, throughout South Africa – the unions, the students, the churches, political organisations – are boycotting the twentieth anniversary celebrations of the Apartheid Republic! We are gathered here today, as people are gathering all over the country, to voice our opposition to the festival, to voice our opposition to the fact that over three million rand is being spent, while black people in this country are still subject to gutter education. There is a housing shortage; over one-and-a-half-thousand people are detained daily for contravening the pass laws; there are 22 million people unemployed in this country. The opposition is country-wide. It goes across racial lines, across the political spectrum. What do we have to celebrate?

Crowd: Nothing!

Azanian Students' Organisation leader Reveal Nkondo: For 350 years, the majority of the people of South Africa have been suffering from the ravages of colonialism, of imperialism, and from capitalist exploitation. And now they want us to celebrate! Those who will be celebrating the twentieth anniversary of the Republic will be celebrating the massacre at Sharpeville,[27] they will be celebrating the death of the children in 1976. On the eve of the so-called celebrations, we have roadblocks all over. We ask ourselves why – because freedom is knocking at our doors. Amandla!

Crowd: Ngawethu!

Reveal Nkondo: Mayibuye!

Crowd: i Afrika![28]

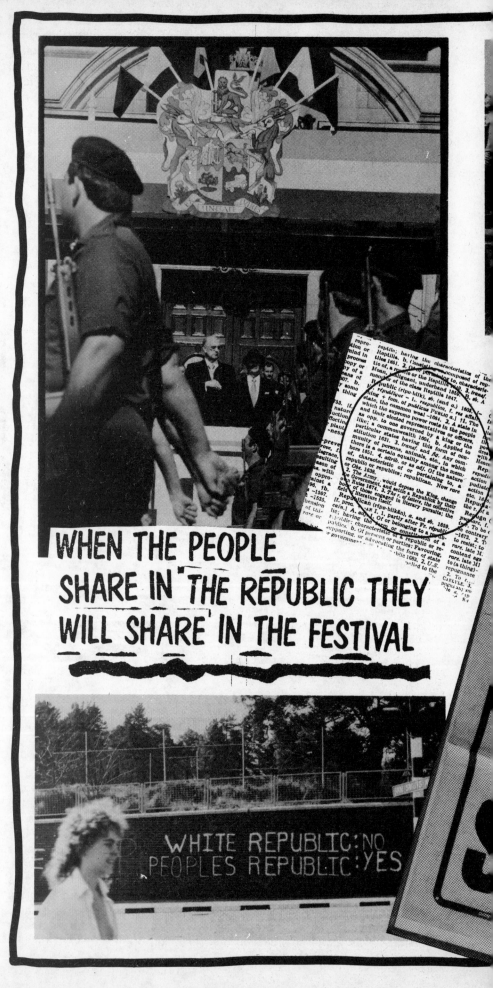

WHEN THE PEOPLE SHARE IN THE REPUBLIC THEY WILL SHARE IN THE FESTIVAL

WHITE REPUBLIC: NO
PEOPLES REPUBLIC: YES

Challenge

Whose Republic Day?

TOWARDS A FREE AND DEMOCRATIC SOUTH AFRICA

REJECT REPUBLIC DAY CELEBRATIONS

RAND Daily Mail

REPUBLIC FESTIVAL: TROUBLE SPREADS

Resistance
D. Action Speaks Louder Than Words

Unidentified Soweto poet at a June 16th commemoration at Regina Mundi Church, 1981:

Azania is tired of detentions,
Azania is tired of bullets from the enemy,
Azania is tired of holding gatherings,
Year after year without any success,
Azania is tired of working for you, white man in the cities,
Azania is tired to go deep down to dig gold for you,
Azania wants to dig gold for its own children,
Azania is tired, Azania is tired,
Azania is tired of crying.

Sons and daughters of Africa, this is where my poem ends, and I want to put it straight to you that I'm also tired of coming into this big church and standing here rendering poems. From now on, I think there is a better solution: instead of standing here and talking, I should be doing something deep in the bushes of Africa!
Crowd: (Wild applause.)

By the late 1970s, the children of Soweto – those who fled the country after the 1976 uprisings – had started to come home. The trail of these thousands of newly trained guerilla fighters, from their military bases 'deep in the bushes of Africa' to their strategic targets in the heart of the white regime, is little known to most South Africans. News reports of the guerillas' successes are censored: a cable sent from the US Embassy in Pretoria told Washington that 'the overwhelming majority of security trials and incidents are not being reported in the South African Press'.[29] Accounts of the trials of guerillas who are arrested tend to focus on incidents and individuals. Nevertheless, the themes of this intensifying conflict are clearly emerging.

Resistance

Charge sheet detailing the case of the State vs. Mosima Gabriel Sexwale and eleven others tried in Pretoria Supreme Court in 1978: The State intends to lead evidence which proves a conspiracy: the establishment of a national underground organization, pyramidal in shape and built of cellular units. Evidence will be led on how the twelve accused established or attempted to establish such cells throughout the Transvaal. Evidence of the establishment of bases, from which the accused operated in these areas, will be led. It will be shown how the local population in each area was 'softened up' for recruitment, either by the propaganda material which was distributed there or by simplistic anti-government history lessons which had been taught to some of the accused abroad.

The Soweto unrest in June 1976 provided a golden opportunity both for recruitment for these cells and for the conspiracy viz. recruitment for military training. Evidence will be led to show that the conspirators were all members and/or active supporters of the ANC or Umkhonto we Sizwe (Spear of the Nation), the military wing of the ANC, which is under the overall political guidance of the ANC. The State will show that the ANC is a front or cover organization used as a tool to achieve the objectives of the South African Communist Party; that this involves the subjugation of the black national revolution to Marxism-Leninism, and that the net effect of a successful ANC revolution would be that a white-dominated Russian-Marxist government would replace the present government. It will thus be argued that the twelve accused, as well as being terrorists, were in the process of 'selling-out' black national liberation to Russia.[30]

Statement from the dock before sentencing by accused number one, Mosima Sexwale: Now that I have been convicted – and I knew from the beginning that I would be convicted – I want to explain my actions so that you, who must sentence me, should understand why I chose to join the struggle for the freedom of my people. Looking back, I now see that it was during my primary school years that the bare facts concerning the realities of South African society and its discrepancies began to unfold before me. I remember a period in the early 1960s, when there was a great deal of political tension, and we often used to encounter armed police in Soweto. I remember particularly vividly a slogan reading 'Free Nelson Mandela and others' painted on the walls of a building I passed each day on my way to school. I remember the humiliation to which my parents were subjected by whites in shops and in other places where we encountered them, and the poverty.

All these things had their influence on my young mind then, and by the time I went to Orlando West High School, I was already beginning to question the injustice of the society in which we lived, and to ask why nothing was being done to change it. In this, too, I was not unusual. Throughout the universities and high schools of South Africa, the South African Students' Organization (SASO) and its subsequent high school equivalent, the South African Students' Movement (SASM), were very active in conducting meetings to preach the philosophy of Black Consciousness. I rapidly appreciated, however, that this activity was all very well, but these were only student organizations. Our efforts were small and ineffective and had no influence on government policy. I realized that it was only political organizations which could hope to play a part in changing the situation.

The oldest and largest political organization was the African National Congress. There were many former members living in the townships, and the ANC was a common topic of discussion. I talked to former members, read whatever literature I could lay my hands on, and generally informed myself about its ideals and activities. The ideals appealed to me as authentic, rational and highly democratic. I learnt, too, of the history of the ANC, of its formation in 1912 as an organization working for a peaceful solution. I learnt that these proposals for talks had been summarily rejected out of hand; that the ANC escalated its efforts, and that the government replied to these further peaceful efforts with violence and by banning the organization. I learnt that this, in turn, led to the end of the ANC's non-violent policy and to the decision in 1961 to turn to the use of force.

I sympathised with this decision: the non-violent struggle seemed to me a relic of the past, a myth which was suicidal in the 60s and the 70s. And I supported the policy as set out in the Freedom Charter: a democratic South Africa, belonging to all its people, black and white – a society in which all, and not just the select few, participated in deciding how the country was to be run. And so it was that I decided to join the ANC, and offer it my services.

It is true that I was trained in the use of weapons and explosives. The basis of my training was in sabotage, which was to be aimed at institutions and not people. I did not wish to add unnecessarily to the grievous loss of human life that had already been incurred. It has been suggested that our aim was to annihilate the white people of this country; nothing could be further from the truth. The ANC is a national liberation movement committed to the liberation of all the people of South Africa, black and white, from racial fear, hatred and oppression.

My Lord, these are the reasons why I find myself in the dock today. When I joined the ANC I realized that the struggle for freedom would be difficult and would involve sacrifices. I am married and have one child, and would like nothing more than to have more children, and to live with my wife and children with all the people in this country. One day that may be possible – if not for me, then at least for my brothers.

I appreciate the seriousness of my actions and accept whatever sentence may be imposed on me. That is the sacrifice which I must make and am willing to make for my ideals. There is no doubt in my mind that these ideals will triumph: the tragedy is that it seems possible that there will be continued conflict and resultant bitterness before those ideals are achieved. As I look back, I cannot honestly say that I believe the decisions I took, which led me to this position, were wrong: what I regret most was that it was necessary and inevitable that those decisions had to be taken.

Pretoria Supreme Court Justice Myburgh: Having had regard to all the relevant considerations, accused number one is sentenced to eighteen years' imprisonment.

Can you spot plant trouble before it starts?

Are you prepared?

In these volatile times tight security is a vital necessity.
Sharp Surveillance Security Systems can be tailored to your specific needs to give peace-of-mind and strategic point protection. Plus a high powered public address system to provide vital communication.
Remember, continual surveillance and a PA facility gives you the time and the means to de-fuse a panic situation. Your security is in your own hands, but Sharp can put the systems that you need into your hands — safety is as close as your telephone. Ring us.

SHARP
Surveillance Security Systems Division

Sowetan, 19 August 1981: The three Sasol-Booysens treason trialists were yesterday found guilty of high treason in the Pretoria Supreme Court. They are Anthony Bobby Tsotsobe (25) of Dube Village, Soweto, Johannes Shabangu (26) of Mhluzi township, Middleburg, Transvaal and David Moise (25) of Sebokeng township near Vereeniging. Their charges were a sequel to the bombing of Sasol Two, Dube railway station, West Rand Administration Board Offices in Diepkloof, a house belonging to Constable Mayeza Malaule in Malelane, the attack on Booysens Police Station and the gutting of Uncle Tom's Hall.
Mr Justice C.D.T. Theron found the three had a common purpose of furthering the aims of the banned African National Congress. Soon after they had been found guilty, drama erupted outside the court. During a demonstration in which people chanted and raised their clenched fists, four black men, three black women, one white man and one white woman were arrested. The demonstration by about 40 people started with a song, 'Somlandela' ('We shall follow Mandela'). Minutes thereafter, riot police in camouflage uniforms, armed with batons, quirts,[32] and four dogs, arrived to control the situation. Earlier in the courtroom, prior to the arrival of the judge from tea break, the three accused had led the public gallery in a freedom song, 'Abagana Bomkhonto Balwelizwe' ('Boys of Umkhonto, Fight for the Land').

Soweto Post, 7 June 1980: A young white schoolboy playing a role in an 'anti-terrorist' exercise nearly fell victim to the new fear of guerilla attacks that has swept the South African white community since the bombings of Sasol on Sunday. André Niemand, 13, came to school this week in Klerksdorp wearing a stocking cap over his face and carrying a plastic machine gun. The boy took his class 'hostage'. The school principal, who had not been told that this was all an exercise arranged by the boy's teacher, called the police. They encircled the school and, through a megaphone, the local Security Police chief asked the hooded figure who he was. The boy – evidently carrying out his instructions to the hilt – replied: 'A terrorist.' The teacher was able to intervene in time to prevent sharpshooters, who had taken positions around the school, from gunning down the boy. The incident illustrates the new 'state of siege' mentality that has become current among many of South Africa's 4.4 million whites. They were shocked when ANC guerillas blew up the government-run-oil-from-coal refinery at Sasolburg. It was the first time the whites had been confronted with such evidence of organization by the banned African National Congress, which claimed responsibility for the attacks.

The Johannesburg *Star*, 5 April 1980: Police have launched a nation-wide hunt for the terrorists who yesterday attacked Booysens Police Station in Johannesburg. Lieutenant-Colonel Leon Mellet said at a press conference last night that in the attack RPG7 rockets were used for the first time against an urban target. About 150 rounds of AK47 automatic rifle fire also peppered the building and at least one hand grenade was thrown. Afterwards, ANC pamphlets calling for the release of Nelson Mandela and Walter Sisulu from Robben Island[31] were found at the scene. The attack is seen as a violent demonstration to highlight the 'Free Mandela' campaign.
Crowds from all over Johannesburg flocked to Booysens Police Station yesterday to see the damage terrorists had done. Mr T. Ecksteen (60) of Melville Street, Booysens, said: 'They're getting cheeky. This is getting just like Rhodesia.' Mr Zia Mezes of Southdown Mews said he heard a loud bang during the night. When we got up to investigate, all his neighbours 'were running all over the show waving guns'. Mr E.J. Norden of 2nd Avenue, Melville, said: 'These incidents are happening much too frequently.'

THE ANC: MOSCOW'S SERVANT

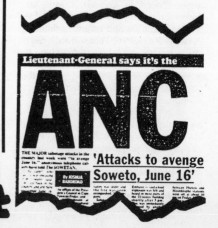

ANOTHER POLICE STATION ATTACKED

THREE MEN armed with automatic rifles and hand-grenades attacked Soekmekaar police station in Lebowa at about 7 pm on Friday night. The men escaped by car.

Lieutenant-General says it's the

ANC

'Attacks to avenge Soweto, June 16'

SABC, 19 August 1981: All three members of the banned African National Congress accused in the Sasol Two/Booysens treason trial were sentenced to death in the Pretoria Supreme Court this afternoon. Passing sentence, Mr Justice Charles Theron said that, from their evidence, the accused, Bobby Tsotsobe, Johannes Shabangu and David Moise, had emerged as very intelligent people. They should have known that their actions could have caused the deaths of innocent people. Nevertheless, Mr Justice Theron said that they had committed their deeds with premeditation and with total disregard to the safety of the public. He said he had no alternative but to impose the utmost punishment.[33]

RED ARMS IN ATTACK ON SADF BUILDING

By RIKA van GRAAN

Brigadier Stanley Schutte, Divisional Criminal Investigation Officer, Eastern Transvaal, addressing the South African Security Association annual meeting, 26 June 1980: Urban terrorism is one of the primary weapons in the arsenal of those who seek the downfall of the Republic of South Africa. It is, in fact, the pet child of the revolutionaries. With this weapon, they can reach those weak spots where it hurts most. With this weapon, they can persuade and condition the population to that level where there is no resistance, with a resulting total capitulation to the demands and prescriptions of the terrorists and their manipulators. There are two groups involved in this action, namely, the group that does the fieldwork – that is, the true terrorist, who has already been identified as the lackey of the Soviet Union – and the manipulators of this terrorist, namely the Soviet Union itself. The ranks of the urban terrorist are swelled by the intelligentsia, students, layabouts, whores, criminals, politicians, men, women and children. Their claim that they act on behalf of the community, the proletariat, and the less privileged provides the terrorists with an inexhaustible source from which their ranks can be filled.

Sowetan, **22 March 1982:** A powerful bomb destroyed the cells behind the Langa Commissioner's Court, where thousands of pass (mandatory identification document for blacks) law offenders have been sentenced, at the weekend. The blast, on the eve of the anniversary of the 1960 Sharpeville shootings, ripped away almost the entire asbestos roof of the cell block and damaged the courthouse across the narrow yard. No one was hurt by the explosion, which occurred at 2.05 a.m. on Saturday. The Langa Commissioner's Court was the scene of the first major confrontation between the Nyanga squatters and police last year. Professor Martin West, the head of the Department of Anthropology at the University of Cape Town, said more than 16,000 people were arrested in the Peninsula on pass offences in 1980 – and most of them passed through the Langa Commissioner's Court. Tight security was imposed at the site of the blast. Reporters were forbidden to inspect the damage or take photographs.

Who do you think is behind these bomb explosions that have disrupted the Republic Festival celebrations?

Sophie Swart, high school student participating in the 1981 Republic Day Festival in Durban: It's people who don't agree with it, who are deliberately trying to stop it. They're trying to ruin everything we love; they're people who are just negative about everything we have in this country, everything we try to build up and everything we try to do. But we mustn't get nervous about their actions. We should just go on and show them that we are not interested in what they do.

What do you think could be their motivation?

Sophie Swart: These people are not interested in anything we do for them in this country. They have this communistic and Marxistic interest. They're terrorists, that's all.

Soweto students, Jabulani: I remember when I was first told of this Terrorism Act,[34] I wondered, who is a terrorist? And I decided that these were the black leaders who were not given a chance to speak politics freely, so they went into exile. And that, in fact, why they keep on infiltrating this country with violence is because they really want to bring about change in South Africa.

Ben: At first, I thought these were people who were coming from Russia or other communist states, but then I came to know that it was the people right from this country, because they were being deprived of their rights. So they went away from this country, skipped the borders, and then gathered themselves to become well-equipped militarily in order to penetrate the country so that they will gain their rights. And my parents told me that those are the people who are trying to bring about change through bloodshed, because they've been trying all the years to speak in a polite way, but there was no change. Because the government is threatening us with prisons and torture, we have to threaten them in another way. The only solution is through violence.

45

Exhibit in State vs. Duna terrorism trial, Zwelitsha, 1982, Umkhonto we Sizwe's 'An Elementary Handbook on Explosives':[35] The people must be able to understand why you have attacked a particular target (which) must symbolize the people's hatred for the government. Great care should be taken to avoid loss of life or injury to our own people. Military action should take place within the context of mass activity and participation.

The Star, 3 November 1981: The African National Congress has confirmed in a statement from Lusaka that a unit of its military wing, Umkhonto we Sizwe, mounted the raid on Sibasa police station on Monday last week in which two policemen were killed and one civilian seriously wounded. Sources close to the ANC see the killing of the two policemen at Sibasa and a similar attack recently on the Mabopane police station just outside Pretoria as representing no shift in ANC armed policy of not attacking those it deems 'innocent' civilians. The sources point out that those 'enforcing or legitimizing apartheid' are liable to attack by ANC guerillas. This includes civilians involved in military or para-military capacities.

Rand Daily Mail, 29 May 1982: Police suspect saboteurs used limpet mines to damage petrol storage tanks at the Hectorspruit depot in the eastern Transvaal near Komatipoort, on the border between South Africa and Mozambique yesterday. A police spokesman said in Pretoria that the damage caused by the explosion was serious but could not give further details. Nobody was hurt in the explosion. Mr Ken Wood, manager of the Press and Information Division of British Petroleum-Southern Africa, confirmed in Cape Town yesterday that the incident took place, but would not give details. 'At this stage, I cannot give you further information,' he said. 'Existing security legislation and arrangements prevent discussion concerning the situation.'

The National Key Points Act of 1980 empowers the Minister of Defence to declare any area or place a National Key Point if he considers it necessary for the safety of the Republic or in the public interest. Any person who furnishes in any manner whatsoever any (unauthorized) information about an area declared a National Key Point, or about any incident that occurred there, shall be guilty of an offence and may be fined up to R10,000 or jailed for three years or both.

Minister of Defence General Magnus Malan, opening the headquarters for the military commando at the ISCOR parastatal electricity plant, 15 August 1981: We must guard against an extremely dangerous false sense of security – that as long as things appear to be going smoothly, the war is being decided in our favour. In any revolutionary war, where the military constitutes but one facet of the onslaught, a feeling of complacency is fatal. As Minister of Defence, I therefore consider it my duty to warn the people of South Africa that the revolutionary effort against us has now reached an extremely dangerous phase. The primary aim of the enemy is to unnerve, through maximum publicity. In this regard, we will have to obtain the co-operation of the South African media in not giving excessive and unjustified publicity to terrorists and thus playing into their hands.

A public square was the target for this bomb blast.

Psychological impact their aim

TO win credibility as a "liberation movement" — both among the local population and in the eyes of the world   *The USSR-ANC-SACP revolu-*   bulletins dealing with acts of terrorist and sabotage.

Confidential circular minute No. 12/1982 to all departmental Receivers of Revenue, heads of sections, head office Inspectors of Inland Revenue, tutors, re: Deduction of expenditure on security, Section 24D of Income Tax Act, 1962: In consultation with the National Key Points Committee, it has been agreed that the following procedure for dealing with such claims will be adopted: (a) Taxpayers who are owners of National Key Points or any specified important place or area wishing to lodge claims in terms of Section 24D of the Income Tax Act, will do so by submitting a claim to the Officer Commanding SA Army Command; (b) The OC SA Army Command will examine the claim and, if satisfied that the security measures stated therein have been carried out, complete Part IV. The claim will then be transmitted to Army HQ by secure means; (c) Army HQ will despatch the completed claim to the Head Office of Inland Revenue in Pretoria by secure means.

Post, 7 June 1980: A white university researcher, Dr Renfrew Christie, was sentenced yesterday to ten years in prison for having passed information on South Africa's Energy and Nuclear Programme to the banned African National Congress. Dr Christie was accused of passing on to the ANC a plan of a nuclear power station being built by a French consortium at Koeberg, near Cape Town, and of passing on information about two electrical power stations and an open-cast coal mine. Judge Frits Eloff said: 'The ANC wanted to use the information to strike at South Africa and cripple certain industries, to endanger the safety of South Africa's inhabitants and to endanger the distribution of light, power and fuel.' When Christie was led from the court, people in the gallery sang, 'Africa shall be free someday.'

Cape Times, 20 December 1982: The banned African National Congress last night claimed responsibility for four explosions at the Koeberg nuclear power station near Melkbosstrand at the weekend. Police investigators have disclosed that the blasts were caused by 'explosive devices'. The ANC statement, issued in Dar es Salaam, Tanzania, said the sabotage was carried out by a unit of Umkhonto we Sizwe, the ANC's military wing. The movement said the attack was intended 'as a salute to all our fallen heroes and imprisoned comrades, including those buried in Maseru this afternoon'. Thirty ANC members killed in last week's South African Defence Force raid in Maseru were buried in Lesotho yesterday.

A virtual news blackout was imposed during most of yesterday as local and foreign newsmen tried to ascertain the cause and extent of the explosions. The nuclear plant site was completely shut off to visitors and the press. News of the explosions was broken by a foreign news agency with contacts among contractors at the Koeberg site.

TERRORISM IN SOUTH AFRICA

WHAT WE MUST DO ABOUT IT

THERE CAN BE NO COMPROMISE TO TERRORISM

THEY'RE WATCHING US ...AND WAITING FOR THE MOMENT TO STRIKE

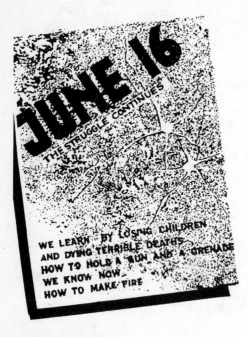

JUNE 16
THE STRUGGLE CONTINUES

WE LEARN BY LOSING CHILDREN
AND DYING TERRIBLE DEATHS
HOW TO HOLD A GUN AND A GRENADE
WE KNOW NOW
HOW TO MAKE FIRE

Cape Times, **21 July 1982:** Sabotage blasts took place in South Africa in January and February this year and the press was unaware of them. Repairs were done in secret to avoid publicity, according to a United States Government intelligence document marked 'top secret'. The document says the South African government is considering 'even stricter' press restrictions, in the belief that press reports benefit the banned African National Congress.

SABC, 17 August 1981: The Commissioner of Police, General Mike Geldenhuys, says that in spite of a shortage of staff and an infiltration of the country by communists, the police are still able to protect South Africa's internal security. Opening a new police station at Great Brak River in the southern Cape, General Geldenhuys said that the so-called liberation movements did not have the interests of South Africa at heart. They were being misguided by cunning promises on the part of communist countries. However, he said South Africa was now more sensitive to the threats which it faced, and there was still respect for law and order.

The Citizen, **28 December 1981:** Terrorists killed one policeman and wounded four in an attack on the Wonderboompoort police station in Pretoria late on Saturday night. In the sixth terrorist attack in six months on Pretoria, residents of the suburb of Mayville told *The Citizen:* 'We thought war had broken out!'

The Citizen, **25 June 1984:** Damage caused by ANC acts of terrorism and sabotage has been conservatively estimated at R600 million since 1976. This figure emerges from a document recently circulated by Major General Frans Steenkamp, chief of the Security Police. The figures also indicate a fairly dramatic increase in the number of acts of terror since the end of 1980. Out of a total of 217 incidents since 1976, 149 took place in the period from 1981 to the end of 1983.

Natal Mercury, **27 October 1983:** Blacks rated ANC leaders first and second when given a choice between Chief Gatsha Buthelezi, Dr Nthatho Motlana, Bishop Desmond Tutu, African National Congress leaders and Black Consciousness and homeland leaders, in four surveys on the Witwatersrand between 1977 and 1981. 'The ANC, which is committed to overthrow the government by promoting revolutionary change in which it sees the workers as a crucial element in a mass mobilization action, certainly has a foothold among black South Africans,' Professor Deon Geldenhuys, of the political science department of the Rand Afrikaans University, said yesterday. 'It maintains that the phase of armed propaganda, evident in terrorists attacks, has ended. It is now embarking on a full-scale guerilla or people's war, involving the mass involvement of people in the armed struggle, using a variety of means to intensify its revolutionary onslaught.'

Freedom songs:
We're going to take over, take over,
Take our country in the Mugabe way,
They call us kaffirs and they gave us
passes,
Take our country in the Castro way,
They took our country and they gave us
homelands,
Take our country in the Mugabe way,
They took Mandela and they gave us
Gatsha,
Take our country in the Castro way,
We're going to take over, take over,
Take our country in the Mugabe way.

Run away, run away, Botha,
Umkhonto has arrived,
We are the soldiers of Luthuli,[36] led by
Mandela,
Even if it is bad, we are going,
Move aside and give us way.

ANC men sing as they get death

The coffin of an ANC member — killed in the raid by South African commandos — is lowered into a grave at Maseru. Picture: RAYMOND PRESTON

SOUTH AFRICAN

Black Politics

ANC has the most support, says expert

ANC wants to 'win minds, not mutilate bodies'

THE primary aim of the African National Congress — in its the campaign of industrial sabotage, attacks on police ~tions and assassina-

and Mr Oliver the subsequent tween the two o

Referring to public antipathy two organisation adds:

"But both side

FROM LODGE ~of a ~~ politics

Richard Loring, SABC actor: Well I suppose that they've got to make some kind of stand. I suppose they've tried all the talking, and they're trying now to make themselves heard in a different form – in other words, urban terrorism.

It seems that guerilla activity is escalating; does that worry you?

Richard Loring: Well, I suppose, unfortunately – without wanting to ignore it – it's rather like when you hear of somebody having a car accident, and you say, 'Oh, I'm sorry to hear that.' But unless you're actually involved, it's very difficult to put your finger on it and say it actually scared you.

Since any contact with the ANC involves a big risk, has that lessened support for the ANC amongst the people, in your view?

Tshediso Matona, Congress of South African Students organizer: No. You know, the masses of the people know the relevance of the African National Congress. They know the ANC is their organization, the organization that is going to bring their liberation. But they cannot come out openly saying they support the ANC, because they know the repercussions. People know that this is the organization that is fighting for them, even though there is a propaganda campaign against the ANC. The government says it is a communist organization and it kills innocent people, but this does not deter the people. They don't believe it.

But civilians do die in some ANC attacks.

Tshediso Matona: Anyone knows that there can never be a revolution without casualties. It is going to happen somewhere that people are going to die, but the ANC says it is not their policy to kill innocent people. They say their targets are those institutions and instruments that are used to defend the South African government, and if there are any people who find themselves in these institutions which are used by the system to defend the status quo, that is, to oppress the people, they are unfortunately going to fall victim to attack.

What is the reaction in the black townships when the ANC launches a successful attack?

Tshediso Matona: It acts as a great booster of morale, people really rejoice. You know the situation: people are harassed when they attend mass meetings, there's a lot of detentions and so on, so there is now this very popular feeling amongst people that only armed struggle will solve their problems. People think that the only way they are going to realize their liberation is by armed struggle. I've heard a lot of people say this, that they believe action speaks louder than words.

'Time Has Run Out', Mongane Serote: [37]

Alas —
time has run out:
too much blood has been spilled. please my
countrymen, can someone say a word of
wisdom.
it is too late. blood, no matter how little of it,
when it spills, spills on the brain – on the
memory
of a nation– it is as if the sea floods the
earth. the
lights go out. mad hounds howl in the dark;
ah,
now we've become familiar with horror. the
heart
of our country, when it makes its pulse,
ticking time,
wounds us. my countrymen, can
someone,
who understands that it is now too late, who
knows that exploitation and oppression are
brains which,
being insane, only know how to
make violence;
can someone, teach us how to
mount the
wound, and fight.
time has run out —
period.

3. Reform

P. W. Botha's four statements express the essence of the state's response to the post-1976 economic and political crisis: apartheid will not be overhauled, but rather fine-tuned. The reform strategy aims to defend – not change – the status quo, by broadening the government's base of support to include Coloureds, Indians and some urban blacks. The reform era has brought a new kind of segregation: it is no longer black versus white, but whites and 'qualified' blacks versus the 'unqualifieds'. A small core of blacks whose labour is required in the urban areas is now recognised as having permanent urban resident rights. These blacks qualify to live in the cities, while all other blacks are disqualified and deported back to their poverty-stricken rural homelands. The goal is to phase out the mass arrests of blacks for violations of the 'pass' laws requiring all blacks to carry an identity document – to take influx control 'off the streets' and into the workplace[2] by providing much stiffer penalties for employing and housing unqualified blacks. The result has been a widening of the gap between qualifieds and unqualifieds, as the number of blacks who can live in the urban areas is limited by the numbers of jobs, houses and facilities the government is able or willing to provide.

To the government, the apogee of reform is its new constitution, in which Coloureds and Indians are represented in separate chambers of a three-tiered Parliament: a white-dominated body (with a 4:2:1 ratio of whites, Coloureds and Indians) which selects the executive State President, who in turn appoints his own cabinet, with any deadlock between the white, Coloured and Indian chambers resolved by a white-dominated President's Council.

The new constitution was successfully marketed to the white electorate through a sophisticated advertising campaign for a 'yes' vote in a referendum held in late 1983. Big business contributed handsomely to the R5-million campaign via a Reform Fund that canvassed support for what white executives

A. Selling the System

SABC, 31 October 1983: The Republic of South Africa Constitution Bill has now been minutely scrutinized in one of the longest debates ever held in Parliament. It was the culmination of an unprecedented exercise in political negotiation and deliberation, in the service of justice and security.

Opening clauses of the Republic of South Africa Constitution Bill: In humble submission to Almighty God, Who controls the destinies of nations, and the history of peoples; Who gathered our forbears together from many lands and gave them this their own; Who has guided them from generation to generation; Who has wondrously delivered them from the dangers that beset them; We declare that whereas we are conscious of our responsibility towards God and man; we are convinced of the necessity to stand united in pursuing the following national goals:
— To uphold Christian and civilized standards, with recognition and protection of freedom of faith and worship;
— To safeguard the integrity and freedom of our country;
— To secure the maintenance of law and order therein;
— To further the contentment and the spiritual and material welfare of all in our midst;
— To respect and to protect the human dignity and the rights and liberties of all in our midst;
— To respect, to further and to protect the self-determination of population groups and peoples;
— To uphold the independence of the judiciary;
— To further private initiative and effective competition;
We are prepared to accept our duty to seek world peace in association with all peace-loving nations; and are desirous of giving the Republic of South Africa a constitution which provides for elected and responsible forms of government and which is best suited to the traditions and history of our land.

South Africans who vote Yes vote for:

1. A secure future for ourselves and our children.
2. Peaceful co-existence and equality of opportunity.
3. Orderly reform and reason.
4. The protection of group interests through self-determination.
5. The promotion of common interest through co-operation.
6. Strong and purposeful leadership.
7. A united and resilient South Africa.
8. Economic, political and social stability.
9. The maintenance of orderly government and civilised standards.
10. Fairness, freedom and prosperity through justice.

If you're considering voting No, answer this quiz.

saw as a vital means of protecting their interests. The campaign was directed by the South African associate of Saatchi and Saatchi, the advertising agency that packaged and sold Prime Minister Margaret Thatcher to the British electorate. The managing directors of the Johannesburg agency, Klerk, Marais and Potgieter, re-charted the political spectrum, and placed their product – reform – smack in the moderate middle, between the 'crazy conservatives' on the right and the 'dangerous liberals' on the left.[3] Had this custom-made political spectrum included black opposition, it would have been moved so far left as to dwarf any criticism from the tiny white right, but it suited the advertisers to portray the reformist government as courageously battling against an archaic racism that threatened South Africa's economy.

Klerk, Marais and Potgieter managing director Jannie van Rensberg: The people opposed to this reform are themselves in opposing camps. On the one hand, you have right-wing extremism, which wants to take segregation to the most frightening conclusion. Then, on the left, you have those advocating one man, one vote for all population groups in the country, which will mean the demise of the white man overnight. So what we're doing is we're taking the road of moderation.

You know, in advertising terms you have a 'positioning' of your product. You have to swing people on to your product. So, we're looking for support for our product like any other classical advertiser would want to do, for any product, be it motorcars or soap with pink bubbles.

KMP director Derek Carstens:[4] You must always meet a need for the consumer, you must always position your product competitively. We've positioned the constitutional proposals as the right solution at the right time, for your future. We believe people are looking for change, evolutionary change, and we are promoting the new constitution as change from a position of strength. Rhodesia – I mean, Zimbabwe – is the classic case: if Smith had listened ten or fifteen years ago, things might have been a lot different there. But when he finally decided to change, he was changing from a position of weakness.

Jannie van Rensberg: I think it was too late for ordinary change there, and that is what we are trying to prevent in this country. That is what this whole new constitution is about: broadening the base of democracy – now.

Could you explain what you meant by some of the phrases you used in your ads, such as 'maintenance of orderly government' and 'civilized standards'?

Jannie van Rensburg: I think, if we look at the way that governments are going in other parts of the world, where the change has been disorderly, what we're promoting is an insurance policy we're taking out, to assure that whatever development there is, it will be orderly, and to the benefit of the individual.

So who is your client?

Derek Carstens: The National Party.

But none of your ads actually state that.

Jannie van Rensberg: That's because of the fact that we're keeping this whole campaign above politics. It's for the sake of the country. We're not trying to promote party political interests.

The advertising campaign was a success: the government won the 'yes' vote it needed to demonstrate 'popular' (white) support for its reforms. The government did not even attempt a sales campaign for the Coloureds and Indians who it claimed would benefit from reform; instead of a referendum, their only choice was to vote for representatives in the new Parliament – or not to vote at all. Throughout the late 1970s and early 1980s, the black response to the government's elections for black Community Councils, Coloured management committees, and the South African Indian Council followed a similar pattern: vigorous boycott campaigns against the 'puppet shows' resulted in massive voter stay-aways.

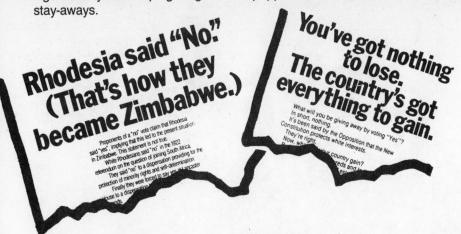

Rhodesia said "No." (That's how they became Zimbabwe.)

Proponents of a "no" vote claim that Rhodesia said "yes", implying that this led to the present situation in Zimbabwe. This statement is not true.

White Rhodesians said "no" in the 1922 referendum on the question of joining South Africa. They said "no" to a dispensation providing for the protection of minority rights and self-determination. Finally they were forced to say yes at Lancaster House to a dispensation...

You've got nothing to lose. The country's got everything to gain.

What will you be giving away by voting "Yes"? In short, nothing. It's been said by the Opposition that the New Constitution protects white interests. They're right.

Now, what will your country gain? ...

The African National Congress indicated its support for such boycotts by targeting 'dummy bodies' for guerilla sabotage.

Few whites were aware of the widespread black resentment against the government's reforms, for the election boycotts were attributed to 'intimidation', and ANC sabotage to 'terrorism'. The views of Hannie Nortje and Pieter Oberholzer, Afrikaner professionals from Krugersdorp, typify the total confidence of most whites that reform will secure their future and mollify the blacks.

Hannie Nortje: You have no idea how things are now changing. There's a lot of things being done, you know, to get the racial question normalized. It's gradually coming more normal, and I think before very long the world will see this.

Pieter Oberholzer: Not that anyone is forcing us to change. Things have been changing naturally in this country all these years. You know, even in the olden days on the farms, on Sunday the blacks would come down by the farmer's place and they'd read the Bible and sing a few hymns, and the black people would be sitting in the sitting-room on the floor with them, with the whites. So now it's just being normalized a bit further.

Do you think things will ever change to the point where they are in Zimbabwe now, where there'll be majority rule?

Hannie Nortje: No, No. Never. Because we've got a different approach here. We have this parallel – what do you call it?

Pieter Oberholzer: Parallel development.

Hannie Nortje: Right. We're giving the blacks their own portion of this country, where they will be able to develop right to the very highest posts, in their own territories. When they come here, to white South Africa, they come as labourers, to work here.

Pieter Oberholzer: Not labourers, people seeking employment. The same that's happening now in Europe: Frenchmen going to Germany, Germans going to France, you know, going over the borders and working there. And then, the Coloureds and the Indians, look what we're doing for them. They're even allowed to vote. So it's all being arranged, you see.

What about any objections to these arrangements, from blacks?

Pieter Oberholzer: The objections come from the communist side.

Hannie Nortje: Look, you have a few liberalists trying to egg them on, but you talk to your ordinary black man: he's satisfied with this change. You get the communistic kind that will always find fault with the government, but most of them, they're happy with the way things is going.

Pieter Oberholzer: Here, it's not going to go like Rhodesia, because we have this new constitutional dispensation. We'll sort things out if the world will just leave us alone to get on with it.

Albertina Sisulu, Federation of South African Women leader, addressing an Anti-South African Indian Council conference in Lenasia, September 1981: The Nationalist government has become crafty and sly over the years. Where the Freedom Charter said, 'The people shall govern', the Nationalist government has created Bantustans, representative councils, community councils, the President's Council and the South African Indian Council. Where the Freedom Charter said, 'Everybody shall have the right to vote for and stand as candidate for all bodies which make laws', the Nationalist government created dummy bodies to help it put into effect its racist and oppressive laws.

So let us not be fooled into believing that the government is meeting our demands – and let us tell the government that we are not fooled – by staying away, boycotting all the elections of dummy bodies. Those who participate in these mock elections are helping the government in its attempts to fool the people – and to oppress us all. Those true patriots who refuse to vote will be telling this racist and inhuman government that we refuse to be divided and governed along ethnic and racial lines.

Some of you may ask, 'But what can I do? I don't want to be banned, I don't want to be arrested, I don't want my children to be harassed.' Nobody is asking you to do any of these things. But there is still something you can do. You can boycott the elections. You can refuse to have this government oppress you. Simply by staying away from the polls, you will be telling the Nationalist government that we refuse to be divided and governed along racial lines. You will be making your contribution towards a free and just South Africa. You, too, will be adding to the numbers of the oppressed who have said, 'These freedoms we will fight for, side by side, until we have won our liberty!'

The Star, **3 November 1981:** Bombers struck in Durban for the tenth time this year, when an explosion ripped through the city's Department of Internal Affairs building early today in an obvious protest against tomorrow's South African Indian Council elections. The building at the corner of the Esplanade and Stanger Street houses the headquarters of the SAIC, the Directorate of Indian Education, and the regional representative of Internal Affairs. Windows were blown out all the way to the top floor of the building, only 500 metres up Stanger Street from the offices of the Department of Co-operation and Development, which were bombed on October 10.

The blast was obviously linked to the Indian Council election being held tomorrow, Mr Louis le Grange, Minister of Police, said today. He appealed to the Indian community to turn out at the polls to show 'those people' that they would not be intimidated in exercising their democratic rights. He gave an assurance that policemen would be available at all polling stations and voters would not be intimidated 'by any party'.

Reform
B. A Stake in the System

In late 1980, the government's symbolic representative of reform, Minister of Co-operation and Development Piet Koornhof, paid a visit to South Africa's biggest black township, where he was awarded the 'Freedom of Soweto' and declared an honorary citizen by the chairman of the Soweto Community Council, David Thebehali. The ordinary citizens of Soweto – the two million blacks forced to live in the segregated ghetto – were not impressed.

 Interviews with an angry crowd of protesters outside the Soweto Community Council Chambers, kept at bay by riot police, dogs and teargas, 15 October 1980:

What do you think about Minister Koornhof's visit?

First man: Koornhof is nothing. He's representing the very government we don't want.

What do you think about Mr Thebehali making Minister Koornhof an honorary citizen of Soweto?

Second man: Well, it's a pity Koornhof's been given citizenship by a man who happens to have none. So both of them are like mad people. As far as we're concerned, Koornhof is just trying to brighten up a non-existing nobody like Thebehali, who happens to be in the machinery of the racist regime, and we reject him as much as we reject the government itself.

First man: Thebehali claims to be a leader of the people: then why doesn't he come out here and address the people? Why does he have to hide in that big hall with the ministers of the racist regime? It just shows he's a nobody, a toothless bulldog.

Second man: Listen to the shouts from the crowd: he's a total reject, he's a sell-out.

What do you think about the incident of sabotage, the bombing of the railway line, that happened this morning?[5]

First man: Look, I didn't go to work today, because I wanted to show solidarity with our people, I wanted to be here. So I am only too happy if people don't get to work because the railway is bombed. Great!

Ceremony inside the Soweto Community Council Chambers, led by Chairman David Thebehali: Minister Koornhof, members of our executive, councillors, officials and other guests, it is with great pleasure that I stand before you today in order to bestow the 'Freedom of Soweto' on a great man. Although there are certain forces that were trying to create problems to disrupt this occasion this afternoon, I am convinced that the majority of people of Soweto really identify with the honour we are now bestowing on Dr Piet Koornhof.

Sir, never before in the history of Soweto has there been one man who has succeeded in opening vistas of a better life and a better city, as you have done. Sir, the people of Soweto look to you as their redeemer. We are being told again and again that the government, your department, is not responding to the needs of the people of Soweto. But I think the people of Soweto, Mr Average, is seeing what is happening. He is seeing that the streets of Soweto are being paved. He is seeing that telephones are being installed. He is seeing that job opportunities are being created. By the end of 1982, early 1983 at the latest, there will be electricity in every house in Soweto.[6] May God grant that the light Dr Koornhof brought to Soweto will also burn in the hearts of its residents! (Applause.)

Minister Piet Koornhof: His honourable Worship, the Mayor of Soweto, Mr Thebehali, all other councillors, friends, ladies and gentlemen, it is indeed a very great honour for me to have been invited to this memorable, indeed also historical, occasion. I see it not only as a friendly gesture, but also as a result of the process of mutual co-operation to which I have committed myself over many, many years. I will use this Freedom of the City of Soweto

in the interest of the people of Soweto, whom I can truthfully say I've over many, many years come to like and come to love.

Despite the difficult circumstances today, and the fact that some people wanted me not to be here on this occasion, I'm very happy that they haven't got their say, because I believe that only a handful feel that way, and by far the majority of the people of Soweto wanted me to be here because they know that I am their friend. I bring you a message of hope on this occasion, a message of hope to the youth of Soweto and to all the people of our country – the only trouble is that you cannot do all the things that are required to do before breakfast. Good and important things take a wee bit longer. You cannot have real reform in twenty-four hours. It takes longer, it takes dedication, it takes a lot of hard work, it takes tremendous planning, it takes money, it takes co-operation.

Over the years, I've got to know the black people well, and I got to respect the very things that they hold dear. The black people have always had a high respect for those that are placed in authority over them. They always had respect for their leaders and the children always had respect for their parents.

Now I plead with you: listen to your parents. Have respect for your parents, and not for these wolves who are leading you astray – who are at this very moment, some of them, outside these buildings – who will lead you to burn fires and to have very, very bad things coming your way. Respect authority – it's God's will that you must do it. And therefore, I want to plead with you: always be positive in your approach and do not break down. It's so easy to break down. If you should criticize – and it is your right to criticize - then try to do it in a constructive manner. Be mature and positive, and I have no doubt your contributions will yield dividends.

We are in the process of reform in this country. The road ahead is difficult and it is long, but racial relations will be normalized in South Africa, and I'm dedicated to that task. When I say I can bring real hope to the youth of Soweto, it's not idle words. They will experience it, if only they would be a wee, wee bit patient. If the young ones of Soweto will rally round their parents, and authority, around me and us, so that we can carry on with the constructive work and stop the nonsense of breaking down and of destroying things which cost millions and millions of rands to build up again, then we will succeed. May God bless this council, may God bless His Worship, the Mayor. May God bless the people, and especially the children of Soweto. Thank you. (Applause.)

SABC, 15 October 1980: The Minister of Co-operation and Development, Dr Koornhof, says three bills, to be published within the next month, will have far-reaching effects on the black community. The Minister was speaking at a banquet in Johannesburg, after receiving the Freedom of Soweto. He said one of the bills would deal with the new local government structure to replace the Community Council system. It would provide for city council status for black local governments. Dr Koornhof said the second bill would contain amendments to the Administration Boards Act. These boards would be completely restructured as Development Boards, and would no longer be called Administration Boards. The Development Boards would have smaller composition, but greater measure of involvement in the private sector. The third measure, to be known as the Black Community Development Bill, would amend or replace a large number of Acts, including the Urban Areas Act, which would be abolished along with the Black Labour Act.[7]

SUPPORT SOWETO CIVIC ASSOCIATION:

DOWN WITH THE
COMMUNITY COUNCILS

MASS RALLY

- •OSCAR MPETHA
- •DR MOTLANA
- •ZWELAKE SISULU

SUNDAY 27 November 1 pm.

AT: REGINA MUNDI

Issued by S.C.A. 12 de Villiers St. Jhb.

ASINAMALI
MASIHLANGANENI
attend

MASS
MEETING

NO! to high rent.
NO! to community councils

Guest Speakers: Dr. Motlana
Curtis Nkondo
Rev Frank Chikane

Venue: Roman Catholic Church,
Zone 12, Sebokeng, (opposite the Post Office)

Time: 1 pm

Date: Sunday 9 October 1983

Organise or be homeless

Issued by Action Committee, Box 2126, Vereeniging. 1930

VHA SO NGO
KHETA!
MUYSNHSNO
— GUTE

Vhadzuli vhothe vha wa Tshiawelo wha
khou rambiwa mutanganoni u sina tsaleli.

U khetha Vho-Nkhetheni vha Community
Council ndi u di-khethela u badela rennde
yo gonyiswaho!
Na ukhethela u shaya madi (cholera).
Di na u thelela mbya yau muthelo
wogonyaho electricity??
Gundo lashu li kha vhuthihi hashu.
Maanda a kha rine.

Fhethu: Lutheran Church (near Swiss
Mission) Tshiawelo .
Duvha: 20 Lara (Nqvamber) 1983
Tshifhinga: 2 p.m.

VHA SO NGO
KHETA!

The Urban Bantu Councils established in the 1960s were scathingly ridiculed in the black townships as 'Useless Boys Clubs'. Finally toppled in the 1976–7 unrest, they were replaced by the Community Councils. The reforms were unveiled with great fanfare by Piet Koornhof, who once more renamed the bodies 'Black Local Authority Councils' and slightly upgraded their powers. The catch is that the new councils, like their previous incarnations, are totally self-financing. Without black labour, taxes and spending power, there would be no Johannesburg or Cape Town, but those municipal governments provide only for the 'white' cities and suburbs – not for the black dormitory townships of Soweto or Gugulethu. The Black Local Authority Councils are supported by housing and trading site rentals, liquor and beer sale profits, dog taxes and loans (not grants) from the state – hardly enough income to fund new houses, tarred roads, health and recreational facilities. And when it comes to raising rents, evicting tenants, and raiding 'illegal' blacks, the white government is no longer responsible. Instead, any complaints are channelled to the black councillors, elected by minuscule mandates in boycotted polls.[8]

Congress of South African Students organizer Tshediso Matona: People have identified their enemies. The people do not want anything to do with these dummy institutions. It is widely accepted today that those who work within those institutions are committed traitors. Because you cannot say you are working within these systems and still speak against the oppression of the people. For you are thereby collaborating with the system in enforcing laws against the people. For instance, the raising of rents – you cannot hope to be part of these institutions and still agree to such things.

There are people who claim that they can change the system from within.

Tshediso Matona: Sure, many people claim that, but you soon find that they are not really doing that. They get swallowed up in the system and it becomes very difficult to defy the system from within. You see, one thing which causes people to be swallowed up within these institutions is the benefits they are given – like they get a beautiful car, live in a beautiful house. I mean, your whole political outlook, then, is going to change, because you'll soon be a petty bourgeoisie.

What do you mean by 'petty bourgeoisie?'

Tshediso Matona: Well, my understanding of a petty bourgeoisie is anybody who has a big house, a car and gets a good salary. He doesn't care about what's happening with the rest of the people, especially those who talk of liberation, and as a result, he starts getting afraid of the revolution because he thinks that the revolutionaries want to deprive him of his house and his car. Of course, these people do have certain political aspirations, but they are, you know, moderate. Like, they'll be talking against apartheid, how they want to share hotels with whites, whereas the masses of the people do not have the means to go to hotels.

Don't you think it's important when the government allows blacks to eat in multi-racial restaurants and hotels?

Tshediso Matona: No, that will not change the standard of living of our people. Apartheid can be removed tomorrow, but people will continue to be poor. The aspirations of our people go much further than that, you know: we want power to be transferred to the people, that the people should be the sole deciders of their destiny.

Why did you decide to get involved with the black local government system?

Gugulethu councillor Daniel Ngo: Well, I felt that it was an asset to get the African to do things for himself, or at least to get involved in what is being done for him. Before, we used to get things done for us, and you didn't have any idea what was being done. At least this way you are able, in a small way, to be able to get involved and see what is being done for you and maybe do it for yourself.

Why do you think it is that the government has embarked on a programme of reform?

Daniel Ngo: Well, some people have felt, I mean, there is a school of thought, that it was because of the 1976 riots.

Sowetan, **8 May 1981:** Mr David Thebehali, Soweto Council chairman, narrowly escaped death when a bomb ripped apart his car on Wednesday. A hand grenade exploded under his official car shortly after he left the council chambers that night. Mr Thebehali, who was behind the steering wheel at the time, was unhurt. Mr Thebehali said he had no idea who could be responsible for the incident.

'The people of Soweto know we are responding to the city's civic needs for electrification, housing, industrial projects, as well as the upgrading of various other projects. They realize this is meaningful change.' he said. 'However, there are others who are aware of what we are doing in Soweto and do not like it.'

Said Mr T W Kambule, prominent black educationist: 'It is time that Thebehali rethinks his stand. As chairman of the community council, I think it is advisable for him to sit down and think about all the risks involved, and whether it is worth it.' Mr Andrew Maronganye of Orlando West said: 'He is responsible for the trouble he is in. He must not expect sympathy from blacks because he is responsible for high rents and electricity bills.'

What would you say is better pressure on the government: the community councils or popular unrest?

Daniel Ngo: Well, I must say, reluctantly, I have to say it: it seems to me it is riots that have more effect. But I don't think that is a reason not to be involved on the council. I mean, because I cannot own a car, must I not try to get a bicycle to get around? Is that the argument? I mean, in other words, because I haven't got the vote, I mustn't move up to a position where I can ultimately get at a vote? I believe that we've got to talk to the white man, talk to him, and be a thorn in his flesh.

What could you point to that your council has achieved for the people of Gugulethu?

Daniel Ngo: Well, for years the black man has been clamouring for a right to say, 'This house belongs to me' and to defend that house at all costs, yet we were never allowed that privilege, to have a house which we could call 'my own', to say, 'I have built it, I have spent money on it, I will defend it, come what may.' And I could never understand why that could not get through to the white man: allow the black man to build his home and he will defend it. During the riots, you know, it was pathetic to see. You would see people destroying buildings, houses, but what could you say? Does it belong to you? No. Then why defend it?

Now, for the first time, we've got a leasehold system. I am sure this will be a forerunner for better things to come and we will hear less of the continual riots we have had in this country. At least I must say 'thank you' to the white man for that little concession which he has made. Accommodation here in the Western Cape for the black has been very, very scarce, and whilst people haven't a place to live, they can never be satisfied. But if you can satisfy them in place of worrying, so that they are now going to start worrying about what they are going to put in their houses, you keep them off the streets, you keep them out of mischief. That is our policy: give them houses, and then of course they will be busy, they will be happy.

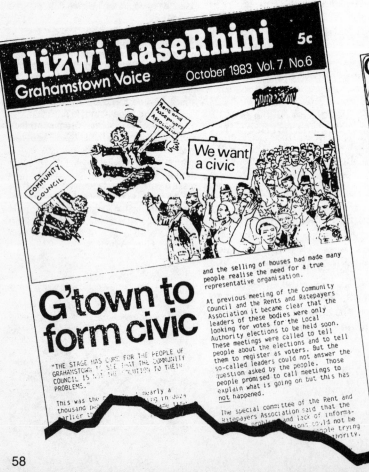

Selection Park housing scheme

One of the Urban Foundation's top priorities is giving better-off blacks a choice of housing. That's the idea behind Selection Park, an elite township in Pimville, Soweto, where houses like these are going up.

The inside of a Selection Park home. According to the Foundation, the idea was to cater for those people who could afford something more than the standard four-roomed township house.

Soweto's elite suburb

Selection Park is a major showpiece project of the Urban Foundation, an organization formed by top business leaders in response to the 1976 unrest. The Urban Foundation makes tempting offers to fund projects, but its motives are so suspect in the black community, that such offers are hotly debated and often rejected.

Judge Jan Steyn, Urban Foundation Executive Director: I cannot see any thinking businessman declining to participate in South Africa's future through the Urban Foundation. His dividend will be the emergence of a black middle class and a greater stability in our urban societies. I am convinced that there is a new appreciation on the part of commerce and industry of the gravity and urgency of our situation, not only as far as the maintenance of the free enterprise system is concerned, but in regard to the survival of everything we hold dear.[12]

How do you respond to criticism of the Urban Foundation from blacks?

Judge Jan Steyn: The Urban Foundation has been criticized for embarking upon housing programmes which allegedly cater only for the thin layer of affluent blacks. The provision of better class housing, such as the projected 500 houses which we are developing under the umbrella of local authorities, and in co-operation with building societies, in Selection Park, Soweto, has in my view, been unjustly criticized. I say this because it is one new choice people are offered. It is a freedom – albeit a circumscribed freedom – which is being given content.[13]

Selection Park should be living proof of the success of the joint strategy of the government and the private sector: to co-opt a black middle class that will act as a buffer between the disenfranchised black majority and the white ruling class. Yet the residents of this buffer zone bristle at the term, 'black middle class'.

Bus tour of Soweto conducted by Community Council chairman David Thebehali:[9] Ladies and gentlemen, we're coming now to Selection Park, the new area where elite housing is in progress. Now the average price of these houses varies from R15,000 to about R28,000. They are two- and three-bedroomed houses and they're built according to the same standards as any middle-class European home. They are fully serviced with electricity, water and sewerage and there will be tarred streets here as well. Now, Selection Park is a complete departure from the traditional four-roomed 'matchbox' house system. This is part of our home ownership scheme, through the leasehold system.[10] The people who live here were involved in the designing and planning of these houses. For example, that house you see there, that belongs to an employee of Anglo-American. He's a very important black official at Anglo, and he came with a plan himself for that house to be built, and since he could afford it, he was actually able to get a double stand to build that very big house. And that's typical of who lives in these houses: executive types of business and professional people, businessmen and so on, they all live here.

All right, ladies and gentlemen, let's move on now. We are going to have tea in a place that is called the Oppenheimer Tower. This tower and park was built in recognition of the contribution that was made by Sir Ernest Oppenheimer,[11] who provided a loan of six million rands for the building of houses in Soweto. Now, on our right, ladies and gentlemen, we have the Total (petroleum corporation) golf course. The golf course forms a buffer strip between Soweto to the left and the Coloured township of Eldorado Park, down to our right. This golf course is very important because in the near future, Soweto will be having a few millionaires. Golfing is going to be very important to them because, you know, golf has become such an important sport to the well-to-do people, especially businessmen.

South African Panorama (government publication), September 1984: Established in 1976 by public-spirited businessmen and community leaders, the Urban Foundation has changed its approach in recent years. No longer does it merely sponsor scores of projects to alleviate the most pressing needs of poorer black communities, it has become an agent for structural reform. The Urban Foundation has been most successful in bringing change to housing. Indeed, the housing situation has altered almost dramatically for the better in the last few years.

Today, almost every block in Soweto boasts at least one improved dwelling, and a former mayor of Soweto, Mr David Thebehali, can safely predict that the city will be almost unrecognizable in the next decade or so (and it will soon have been completely electrified.) The same thing is happening in other black towns like Katlehong, where owners are converting hundreds of tiny, formerly state-owned houses into fine homes. What better way of gaining a stake in the free enterprise system!

Entirely financed by the private business sector, and in particular by large firms, the foundation has been particularly successful in raising funds. Much of the loan capital was raised in Europe and the US, where the Urban Foundation has won considerable support for its efforts to improve the quality of life of poorer urban communities. The foundation's chairman, Mr Harry Oppenheimer, one-time head of Anglo-American Corporation, says: 'South Africa is on the road to meaningful and fundamental reform, largely directed by government, but the private sector also has an important part to play.' This arm of the private sector has in a short period done much to catalyze peaceful reform and socio-economic upliftment, thereby aiding urban black communities in particular to pluck the full fruits of the free enterprise system.

Selection Park Residents, Ben Motsuenyane, Anglo-American Corporation personnel manager: This will never work, to try and alienate a certain sector of the community from its roots. I consider myself to be part and parcel of the black community. I don't even see myself as being economically better off than other blacks in Soweto, because what I own, it is on paper. I do not actually own it for it is somebody else's capital and somebody else's land. I feel I am just an ordinary worker, getting a salary like any other black. This term, 'black middle-class', it's sickening.

Richard Molewa, Anglo-American Life Assurance administrator: I would say that the living conditions may be different with us here in Selection Park, but we are still swimming in the same waters with every other black. We have the same rent increases, we ride the same buses, and we carry the same pass book (mandatory identification document for blacks.)

Lizzie Motsuenyane, nursing sister: I feel I am the same patient with the same disease – like any other black.

The Urban Foundation is responsible for the houses you are living in; how do you feel about its role in the community?

Pullen Moeki, Anglo-American Life Assurance administrator: I feel that their actions are like those of trapped mice. They are trying to look for stopgap measures to bridge the dissension among blacks. They give us houses, roads, even TV, whereas in reality, they have not touched the core of our needs and of our aspirations. The Urban Foundation is one of those organizations which is trying to promote the so-called 'buffer' between the privileged blacks and the unprivileged ones. It is only because they are aware that, collectively, blacks can dent the economic system that they want to protect.

Richard Molewa: They try to promote the free enterprise system, but there is nothing free about it. Even those very few blacks who think they own businesses, like Kentucky Fried Chickens, they are merely black fronts: you'll find that the capital is white. As a black man, I have no control of my affairs. I do not own land, whereas free enterprise says there should be ownership of property. I do not sell my labour where I wish because there are constraints such as influx control. Big corporations like ISCOR (Iron and

Steel Corporation) and ESCOM (Electricity Supply Commission) are state-owned, almost every trading site belongs to the state, and lately, even my birthright has been stripped of me. If the South African government really believed in free enterprise, I should be trading downtown in Eloff Street.[14] How can they talk about building up a middle class when we are being denied so many opportunities? How can they legislate the suppression of communism when their economy has so many constraints on the black man that it almost seems socialistic?

There is an ongoing debate as to whether the capitalist system is serving the needs of all South Africans, and whether a socialist system might be adopted in the future. Where do you stand on that question?

Ben Motsuenyane: If there is ever going to be change in this country, the majority will not opt for capitalism, because it is seen as bringing the very suffering we are enduring now.

Richard Molewa: I might prefer capitalism, but I know that most blacks would opt for socialism, so I will have no option but to align myself with my people. I am going to align myself with the masses in such a situation because right now, I am part of them. I don't consider myself owing any allegiance to this so-called black middle class, but with the masses. That's where I have to throw in my lot.

The government often speaks of the black middle class as a stabilizing factor. Do you see it that way?

Pullen Moeki: What they mean by that is that during the riots, there was all this anti-government activity from the black people, especially the high school students, when they burnt government buildings and vehicles. Now the thing we noted when they opened these so-called middle-class black areas, they were all centred near high schools. So when they talk about a stabilizing factor, they are hoping that if I got finance from my company to build my house, I am not going to let anybody throw stones around it. I will try to stop it. That's the hope.

Ben Motsuenyane: But how can I protect property that does not actually belong to me? Say there is suddenly an uprising – is it my capital? Was I involved in the structuring of this so-called middle class? What are my priorities here? I think what rates highest, in our opinion, it is the vote – nothing else. How can you say that you are building a stable middle class from a community which is denied such a basic right?

How do you think that the rest of the black community views you?

Beatrice Kubheka, market research manager at Bates, Wells and Kennedy advertising agency: Everybody talks about us being 'token' blacks. There is resentment. Looking back, I wish I hadn't moved to a middle-class area, because of this credibility problem. I am seen differently from when I was living in a regular neighbourhood in Soweto.

The government thinks it is creating its own stooges, people who, when the struggle comes, they'll say, 'No, no, we are comfortable, we don't want to lose all our materialistic things.' And the government has been saying it over and over: 'We're creating this black middle class.' So that we are already being seen as something special, something attached to the government. I think it is very sad, because the fact that I've got now more money hasn't changed me from what I've always been.

Eric Mafuna, director of Consumer Behaviour (his own advertising agency) and chairman of the Black Management Forum: The likes of me are living through hell every day. If you think about it too much, you could go crazy. People start saying things about you, so you end up spending all your energies trying to justify the perception that you are a middle-class person.

Ben Motsuenyane: It seems it's the government's intention to create this so-called black middle class in order to protect the status quo. It's a sort of black laager,[15] if I may put it that way, an enclosure of so-called affluent blacks, with the masses, who run into the millions, wanting to come into this laager. Can you imagine the position this puts us in?

Community Arts Project Newsletter, November 1979, 'Urban Foundation: Benefactor or Bogeyman': The Urban Foundation has two basic aims. The first is to entrench a black middle class. One of the ways of doing this is revealed in the efforts of big business and the Urban Foundation to get security of tenure for Africans. This is the much publicized 99-year-lease, which they claim they won from the government. Their motivation has been quite simple: the Urban Foundation feel that giving a number of blacks the possibility of owning their homes will give them 'a stake in the system'. They are aware that only the small black middle can ever have the chance to own their own homes. But their aim is to strengthen this class by giving them a few crumbs of equal rights, in the hope that they will be a moderating influence on the mass of the people, and that they will suppress antagonism towards big business.

The second aim of the Urban Foundation is to make propaganda for capitalism. The main aim of businessmen, the force which drives them, is the need to make large profits. To do this, it needs a capitalist system (they call it 'free enterprise'). The 1976 uprising gave big business the jitters because they began to fear for the future of the profit system in South Africa. They quite correctly saw the events as an attack, not only on the government, but on the system as a whole – including them! A large part of the function of the Urban Foundation has been to rectify the widespread belief amongst the people in South Africa that the capitalist system is bad. The Urban Foundation thus tries to distance itself from the state, and is trying to get a good name for big business by showing it is on the side of progress. The Urban Foundation must be revealed for what it is; its approaches deserve to be treated with the utmost suspicion.

..for the better

McCann Erickson advertisement, 1980: At McCann, we utilize black people to create advertising on behalf of our clients, to help in defining and understanding who may be our best customers, to select models and voices to match the personality of the product, to produce our commercials, to originate our copy in the relevant vernaculars and to act as regular consultants to creative, media and client service departments, as well as to clients. And we use black personnel to conduct research amongst consumers to ensure that we are on target. We encourage our white personnel to maintain close and frequent contact with the black people through monthly group visits to Soweto and through periodic get-togethers at which black dignitaries in the fields of commerce, media, research and politics air and exchange views. The importance of the black people to the South African advertiser is increasing at a tremendous rate. McCann-Erickson is aware of this and is in constant contact with them, and we aspire to grow with them.

With the government's attempt to build an affluent, though voteless elite – however half-hearted and insincere it seems to those inside the 'black laager' – came the private sector's mad scramble to corner the 'black market'. The black market really opened up in 1982, when the SABC launched separate television channels for blacks in Nguni and Sotho languages to complement the Afrikaans and English language TV channel catering for whites and, since the new constitution, for Coloureds and Indians.[16] Grant Shakoane, Pearl Luthuli and Tom Bailee produce commercials for TV-2 and TV-3 at the South African subsidiary of the American J. Walter Thompson advertising agency.

Grant Shakoane: Since TV-2 and TV-3 started, all the agencies want blacks, and there are not nearly enough. I know of agencies where they still have no blacks, so when they write an advertisement, they just bounce off the copy to some of their staff and messengers to get a black point of view.

Tom Bailee: When the SABC announced that they were opening a second and third channel, we realized we were into a whole new ball game with regard to the production of black ads. We had to do market research to find out how sophisticated we should make our ads. Grant, you remember when we were making the Lion Lager commercials? You see, on the white market, the ad depicted a group of macho guys climbing on a jeep, their portable refrigerator full of Lion Lager Beer, with their bush hats and their cameras, trekking off

'We don't mess around anymore...'

"We enjoy living well. That's why we buy everything we need from the OK!

The OK has everything, from spacious supermarkets to furniture, carpeting, bedding and gardening departments. Also, you'll find all the well-known housewares and appliances – big and small, as well as a complete range of family clothing! In fact, the OK offers the widest selection of merchandise – at value-for-money prices.

So, if you want to enjoy the better things in life, come to the OK. Don't mess around anymore – shop where South Africa shops."

OK

Kenyon & Eckhardt OK/6564

'Advertising to Soweto: Marketing and Advertising Strategies,' issued by *Soweto Today* advertising supplement, 1982: For the purpose of marketing and advertising strategies, the population of Soweto can be divided into two broad levels: the 'more traditional' and the 'more Westernized'. The 'more traditional' group consists generally of labourers, industrial and domestic 'blue collar' workers, and the unemployed. The 'more Westernized' group are a young and rapidly emerging African middle class of clerks, salesmen, teachers, skilled workers, journalists, entertainers, businessmen, and women and professionals. They are urban, through and through, and have no ties with tribal homelands, though some are the offspring of the 'more traditional' group. The group is materialistic; they aspire to a white lifestyle and the quest for more money has become their basic motivation. They are greatly influenced by the American Negro, but feel proud that they themselves are 'true Africans'.

Members of this group have accepted Western standards of success and status. They tend to speak with exaggerated eloquence, and dress more fancifully and colourfully than their white counterparts. They are the township elites, who enjoy what they term as 'freaking' at discos, parties, international hotels and high-class shebeens (black speakeasies).

into the bundu, getting away from the city, getting back to the sticks, you know, for real enjoyment.

Whereas the black commercial we made was very much a disco scene, bringing in the centre of man-made relaxation, with sophisticated cars, that sort of thing. The intrinsics were the same – relaxation and getting away from it all. But getting away from it all in the black commercial meant something totally different from what it meant in the white context.

Grant Shakoane: You see, we're from the rural areas, and to us it's advancement, you know, developing, to be in the city. The whites have been there already, and to relax, they just get out the door and leave town.

Tom Bailee: It has to do with different aspirations and different backgrounds.

What about the details of those aspirations? Where is that house with the disco music?

Grant Shakoane: We make it a house in one of Soweto's fancier neighbourhoods. And the people, they are up-market people – you can tell from their clothes, their hair, the kind of women they go out with, the kind of cars they drive. It will all tell you that this is where everybody wants to go – it's Johannesburg, where the action is. There's more jobs, more money, you know, everything is here, the buzz is in Joburg.

Tom Bailee: Whereas the dirty old khaki shirts that the guys wear in the white Lion commercials would be totally misconstrued. We've got to watch out, we've made mistakes before. I remember a beautiful ad for Joko tea. This black guy, working far from his family in the centre of Johannesburg, climbs on this rickety little bus and he travels, through the night, beautifully shot, obviously travelling some great distance away from the big city. He's going home, which is what the Joko platform was all about.

They'd used that very approach for the white market: a returning serviceman coming home to his parents' home, out in the country on a smallholding farm. It was all pure nostalgia, you know, beautifully shot, very evocative, very right for the Joko position at the time: 'coming home to Joko'. They transposed the concept almost unadulterated into the black market, but it bombed out totally. Why? Because it had no aspirational element in it at all. It didn't work. It didn't sell. Very bad rub-off for Joko tea.

Grant Shakoane: No, it was all wrong. It said 'Go back to the farms, those used to be the good old days, that's the good life for those people.'

It probably also smacked a bit of homelands.

Grant Shakoane: Exactly.

Pearl Luthuli: You know, people want to be better. They want to have a better style of living. They want change. So taking them back from where they came from, where they don't want to be – that's not helping them in any way.

Do you think that with this evolving black market you are moulding a new consumer consciousness?

Tom Bailee: It's possible. I'm thinking of some of the products we've had to sell to blacks that required a whole kind of education process: products like Vim and Handy Andy, those sort of scourers and cleaners. We had to try and make the purpose of these products understood before we could begin to convince anyone that there was a purpose in buying them. Because there are traditional ways of cleaning pots and pans and things which were perfectly effective, so why buy this expensive thing in a plastic container?

Grant Shakoane: We had to educate blacks about things like germs and bacteria, and teach the people that it's better to use these products because it is safer, it kills germs.

Tom Bailee: The tricky one, of course, was always toothpaste, because so many blacks don't brush their teeth, and yet most of them have better teeth than we whites do. And deodorants, that's another new concept we're working on.

Grant Shakoane: Another area where we've just begun to educate blacks is with wine. Blacks drink a lot of beer and liquor but they haven't yet been brought into the wine market in a big way.

André du Toit, chairman of KWV Wines, speaking at the 61st annual general meeting, Paarl, 6 July 1982: The approach of the Bantu Administration Boards, after many liquor distribution points were burned down during the riots, was tragic. It was as if they wanted to prove to the black people that they would not be able to burn down the new distribution points, and subsequently built unsightly forts where liquor could be bought. Very little was done to present liquor to black people in a decent, sophisticated way.

Black people should be granted every opportunity to become acquainted with wine as a beverage of moderation. The swing of urban black consumers from sorghum beer, with its privileged distribution set-up, to other liquor types, as well as their social and economic progress, meant a completely new liquor distribution dispensation to black consumers. This was not only unavoidable but also highly desirable.

When the SABC's Radio Bantu began broadcasting in the 1960s, the first advertising agency to set its sights on the untested but promising black market was an Afrikaans-owned company, VZ, Ogilvy and Mather (affiliated to a US multinational), which has produced more ads for black radio than any other agency. Its director, Nick Tredoux, is aiming for the same lucrative distinction with black TV.

Nick Tredoux: Wherever television has come into the marketplace, there has been an increase in the level of marketing expenditure. This goes hand in hand with the rise in per capita income of the blacks, which has been quite dramatic, as well as the general buoyancy in black consumer spending. Most of your big advertisers in this country are in fact very keen and sophisticated marketers. Many of them are parts of overseas international groups, people like Unilever, Beechams, Chesebrough-Pond's, you know, they're all here. And when an opportunity like this occurs, they climb right in. I mean, it's just there for the taking, as it were. And I think in developing the market they will in fact stimulate the size of the black market. That is inevitable.

You mean you'll encourage black consumers to buy more?

Nick Tredoux: We're introducing new lifestyles, new products, to consumers who've not been that effectively exposed to it before. You take, for instance, the electrification of Soweto. You cannot have television if you're not electrified. Now, with it goes all the electrical equipment which can now be put into their homes, which they've never had before – things like washing machines, fridges, toasters, electric stoves. There's a whole burgeoning market out there which will be supplied through the medium of television. All those goods will be advertised through the medium of television. Blacks already have that aspiration, they're exposed to the goods that the whites use, and they want it all. I mean, what they want is what we have, what we whites have.

Congress of South African Students President Wantu Zenzile at Heroes' Day meeting, Soweto, 23 March 1980: The government has set out to buy us, the so-called urban blacks, to become a buffer zone. We are being fooled with permanent urban residence rights, we are being fooled with the 99-year-lease, we are being fooled with all these so-called privileges. When the government tells us it is out to improve the quality of life for the black man in the urban areas, we are being led down a blind alley. The government is out to create a so-called middle class, in order that those who have a stake in the system may begin to protect their masters! Amandla!
Crowd: Ngawethu!

Educationist Dr Neville Alexander:[17] The government is taking a calculated risk if it sees the creation of a black middle class as a policy instrument to avert revolution in South Africa. They believe it is a viable strategy to give enough black people enough of an economic stake in a slightly altered status quo by way of higher salaries, small businesses, professional opportunities, homes of their own and so forth. They believe that these people would use their economic and intellectual power to prevent the black workers from engaging in extreme forms of protest, persuading them to try gradualist, constitutional means. The strategy can only work if the potential and actual middle class allows themselves as a group and as individuals to fit into the scheme. Let there be no misunderstanding: economic and political developments necessitate the creation of a black middle class. Such a class, though tiny at this stage, already exists. But it does not follow at all that the black middle class will behave as the government hopes that it will.

How do you know so much about the black consumer?

Nick Tredoux: We've done surveys, market research. The black consumer is in a state of flux, a state of development. Among blacks you've got the whole spectrum of westernization. You can go into Soweto and you can get a man who is a lawyer, a doctor, a marketing executive – very sophisticated, has a house as good as any white man has. But you can also get the man who's just arrived from the platteland (the countryside). You know, he's literally a black guy who's wearing clothes, that's all. He's had very little schooling, he's just here to get a job – but he's still part of the market. When he earns money he's going to buy cigarettes, he's going to buy beer, he's going to buy Coca-Cola.

Do you think blacks will begin to take on new values as a result of all this advertising geared towards the black consumer?

Nick Tredoux: Sure, they'll be much more aware of the values of our society in materialistic terms. They will aspire more strongly to have what white people have.

They'll become middle class?

Nick Tredoux: Yes, that's terribly important. It seems to be important everywhere in the world that you should have a stable middle class. And what is a stable middle class? People who're earning good money, living in rather decent homes, and using the products which their peers use. I think that through advertising, the values of the capitalist society are transmitted to a much greater degree than through any other medium except, perhaps, educational institutions.

Do you believe that encouraging the blacks to enter the consumer market will in any way help to defuse conflict in South Africa?

Nick Tredoux: I suppose you could philosophically argue for both sides. You could be saying: 'This is what our society has to offer and those of you who are successful and are earning money and being productive, this is what you can acquire, in terms of lifestyle.' But you could also probably say that if you continuously bombard the conscience of people with things they aspire to but are unlikely to get, you'll only breed more discontent. I personally feel that you'll always have the poor amongst the blacks, but I think more and more of them are becoming richer, and I think more and more of them are gravitating into that middle class that we are talking about. But whether the discontents at the other end will eventually burn the place down, that is not for me to say. That can happen. People who want to make fire will make fire.

Look, if South Africa fails to bring blacks into the capitalist society, it will fail as a society. It's as simple as that. And then they'll just be anti. And in the end, they'll want to destroy that society. But if they can successfully be part of it and enjoy the rewards of it reflected through the products which they can use and buy and have for themselves, then I think we have a chance of making them part of it. I mean, if black aspirations cannot be accommodated in a capitalist society, where are they going to go? They're going to go to a communist society – the choice is very simple. And television, in my opinion, is a key medium in bringing that message to the blacks – showing them what the capitalist society has to offer, and hopefully doing it in such a way that they can identify with the aspirations which are involved. So, in that sense, you know, it's more than just selling toothpaste and detergent!

One issue that concerns all young white men of your age is that of the military. How do you feel about serving in the South African army?

Pretoria University students, James van Zyl: I think it's a positive thing. You must do your bit for your country. Of course, it's not very nice to have to go away for two years, but we know what it is about and what it is for, and we think it's a good thing.

Etienne Scheepers: I think it has to do with our education. We've learned of so many battles in our history so I think that from a very young age we are trained to cope with any demand our country may ask us.

Stiffening up for taste of life in the army

through
started
ZYL

WHY EVERY SOUTH AFRICAN SHOULD SERVE HIS COUNTRY

When you go to the army, what are you fighting for?

Jaap du Plessis: We are actually fighting for Christianity, because communism doesn't allow you to practise your own religion.

Do you ever think about what the other side is fighting for?

James van Zyl: The terrorists are only the instruments that the Russians use to fight Christianity, so that they can take over the world and implement their own beliefs. I don't think the terrorists worry or analyze – they're only trained to use guns and kill. I think they are just indoctrinated into believing that only the gun can bring change. I know you might say that, well, Christianity doesn't say we must kill, but the enemy, he is not a religious man and he is going to shoot you if you don't shoot him first, you see.

Benny Viviers: It is a Christian war. We are not the aggressors; they are the aggressors. We are only defending our property and our people.

So who do you think is going to win the war?

Etienne Scheepers: I think we, as Christians, believe that if God wants us to win the war, we will win. And I think we will win because we are defending His name here in South Africa.

James van Zyl: That goes for South West (Namibia), but as far as South Africa itself is concerned, I think there will be change in this country and the change will be peaceful – that's why we're fighting the war.

Vanessa and her sash

JUST the thing for the boys on the border: 19-year-old Vanessa Harris of Marina Heights, Durban, is into ice-skating, surfing and horse-riding and, of course, looking good for the camera. She is the latest entrant in The Daily News Girl of the Month competition which offers a monthly prize of R100. Anyone who wishes to enter should send a black and white or a colour photograph to The Daily News Girl of the Month Contest.

SABC, 1 August 1981: Well, it's on with 'Forces Favourites' on this Saturday afternoon. Our first greeting goes out to Rifleman Kevin Geoff, somewhere on the border: 'Love you, honey, and miss you stacks. Counting the days, look after yourself, and God bless. From your loving wife, Bridgit, and baby son.' This next message goes out to Gideon Bezuidenhout in Potchefstroom: 'Darling, wonderful having you with me on your last visit. Remember, I love you stacks and always will. Waiting for you faithfully, from Connie.' Now I have a return greeting to you, Connie: 'Thank you for the wonderful time you gave me on my seven-day pass. You have left me with some wonderful memories. Not long and you will be my fiancée. From your one and only Gideon.' Now here's a greeting for Mike Gibb: 'Best wishes on your birthday. Shoot straight and keep your head down. Looking forward to seeing you back in the States (South Africa). Love from Aubrey, Brett, Patrick and the Maritzburg gang.' And we will be repeating that greeting tomorrow in case Mike was out on patrol. And now let's listen to this tune, which might inspire us all to think about our boys on the border, as some of them are coming home.

The South African police state of the 1960s and 1970s – etched into international consciousness through photographs of police shootings at Sharpeville and Soweto – has become the military state of the 1980s. The military is everywhere: at school, at work, at the movies, on TV, in advertisements, in comic books. The country is led by a former Minister of Defence. Parliament is no longer the most influential decision-making body; it has been replaced by the State Security Council, which is dominated by top military personnel.[18]

It was the defence establishment's demand for 'militarily defensible' policies that spurred reformist political restructuring. According to the new rhetoric of the military, South Africa is no longer defending white, Afrikaner supremacy, but rather 'free enterprise' and economic growth. The alliance between government and big business is reinforced by ever-increasing militarization. The para-statal arms production industry, ARMSCOR, is the third largest corporation in the country, and at least 2,000 other companies benefit from the skyrocketing defence budget. The South African Defence Force ensures economic control through laws that force major factories to spend millions on security and compel industries to supply SADF with 'vital goods'.[19] From this evident insecurity, born of guerilla sabotage and industrial unrest, the private sector has built a new booming business: security.

Give your country a LIFT

RIDE SAFE
Where you see this sign.

While the government's long-term military priority is inevitably the escalating guerilla war inside the country, the SADF has so far concentrated its sights beyond South Africa's borders. South Africa has occupied the neighbouring territory of Namibia (also called South West Africa) since World War I and has been fighting the South West African Peoples' Organization (SWAPO) since the movement launched an armed struggle for Namibian independence in 1966. When neighbouring Angola gained its independence from Portugal in 1975, and the new socialist government offered SWAPO support and military bases, South African forces invaded Angola, but were repulsed before reaching the capital, Luanda. For the next decade, tens of thousands of South African troops occupied northern Namibia, launching constant raids into southern Angola. The 'boys on the border' have become a permanent and inescapable part of South African reality.

(Song translated from Afrikaans)

He is just a troopie, standing near the main road,
He's got a weekend pass and he wants to go home,
Pick him up, take him with,
He's still got a long way to go,
That troopie who stands by the 'Drive Safely' sign,
His hair is short, his shoulders broad and strong,
And his arms are tanned brown,
With pride he does his national service,

Respected wherever he goes,
He's more than just a number, he's a man's man,
Even if this song is never a hit, all that I want to ask,
Is that everyone of our motorists will also do our bit,
Pick him up, take him with,
He's still got a long way to go,
That troopie who stands by the 'Drive Safely' sign.

South Africa's occupation of Namibia is a study in contradictions. South Africa claims to be there at the request of the Namibian people, yet forces thousands of civilians off the land and breaks up communities in the name of defence. South Africa says it wants peace, but continually stalls the ceasefire negotiations. The South Africans claim to win every battle, yet the war escalates. While the war is costing South Africa $1 billion a year,[20] making peace will also have its price, in cutting off the lucrative supply of Namibia's diamonds and minerals, including uranium indispensable to the nuclear power and arms industry. Withdrawal from Namibia would also mean the loss of a valuable testing ground for SADF weapons.

ATTACK ON SWAPO

'There were dead terrorists everywhere. .

ATTACK ON SWAPO

SABC, 10 August 1982: Good evening. Another 113 SWAPO terrorists have been killed in continuing Security Force operations aimed at SWAPO bases in southern Angola. The Prime Minister and the Minister of Defence have expressed the government's sympathy with the families of the fifteen South African airmen and soldiers killed. They said events like this shook the people of South Africa, but comfort should be drawn from the fact that the deaths were incurred in maintaining civilization, something which was of the utmost importance to South Africa. Now for news comment.

It is the essential paradox of civilized society that, while its measure is its regard for the sanctity of human life, its survival depends on its determination to act ruthlessly against forces which may deny that ultimate value. There is no common basis, no mutually agreed ethical code, for negotiating with aggressive barbarism that recognizes only the right endowed by might. That is the broader context of the killing this week of fifteen young men of the South African Defence Force, when a terrorist rocket struck their helicopter over southern Angola. The incident itself shocked South Africans by the magnitude of the tragedy. It was the worst single casualty in the long, drawn-out war against SWAPO terrorism.

Through the condolences to friends and relatives has run a common theme: the fifteen died for a cause. They sacrificed their lifes in the preservation of the norms and values of a Christian community. In the modern world, the barbarian at the gates is the terrorist. His aim is to take over society and to change it to his prescription, and his instrument for doing so is a remorseless onslaught on its moral foundation of reverence for human life. The South African and South West African people and their leaders have stood firm against the barbarian onslaught filtering across their borders, and while they have energetically pursued the goal of a just and stable order, they have not ignored the nature of the adversary. The terrorist has given notice that he has no intention of changing his nature or abandoning his methods. The only appropriate response, as Israel discovered after years of suffering terrorist depredations from Lebanon, is to employ sufficient strength against him to render him innocuous. SWAPO bases on the Angolan border, therefore, must be taken out. The aggressor, the barbarian, dictates the grim and gruesome form of terrorist warfare. Those who fall in the battle against it are, in the most tangible sense, martyrs of civilization.

SABC, 23 February 1981, Bea Reed reporting from Namibia: This was the first time the South African Defence Force has extended an invitation to a party made up solely of women of the media, to see the operational area. I am sitting here now at a braaivleis (outdoor barbeque). The hospitality is wonderful, and the outstanding feature of the party is that every man here is wearing a uniform of the South African Defence Force, and the party, believe it or not, is on the banks of the Okavango River. As I stand here, I look across this wide and very beautiful river in the moonlight and I am looking at Angola, though I cannot tell you the exact spot where I am because of security reasons. As somebody who has come up from the Republic for the first time to South West Africa, I did not really believe that I would sit calmly with a glass of wine in my hand, a chop in my fingers, looking at the land of the MPLA (Angola's ruling party) and SWAPO – yet I am quite unconcerned. I suppose if I really looked into the bushes I would find young men of the armed forces, guns across their shoulders, quietly watching for our safety and security. There is no sign of fear here, there is an incredible calm and really a feeling of peace in what is not a very peaceful world. I am very affected by it.

I came up here with feelings that I suppose many South Africans have, of, well, there are our lads up here on the borders of South West Africa and Angola, but why are they there and what are they doing there? But after a few days with the military forces, without any sort of obvious propaganda, simply by talking to them and having them talk to us, you suddenly realize that there is a meaning in it, and they are defending a border, and if they were not defending this border, they would be defending a border much closer to home. (Sound of troops singing in the background.) This is Bea Reed, on the border for 'Radio Today'.

SABC, 1 September 1981, Minister of Defence General Magnus Malan: In less than a decade, a wide number of new weapons systems have been successfully designed, developed and produced in South Africa. Most of these weapons systems are now battle-proven, and I do not hesitate in saying they are not only successful, but in some cases, superior to those manufactured in countries which are far more advanced than South Africa.
SABC: Some of South Africa's latest weapons systems were used under battle conditions for the first time during last week's military operation in southern Angola. How successful were they, in fact?
General Malan: Well, the one that I can name here that was very successful, and was used for the first time, is a 127-millimetre artillery rocket system. I think the South African Defence Force is very, very happy at this moment with the result they achieved with this weapon, and I foresee that in future, this will be a very important part of our armoury.

Even more important than the testing of the arms in Namibia and Angola, has been the testing of political and military strategies and tactics, for future use within South Africa's borders. The tortuous attempt at installing a controllable version of black rule is a trial run for reform at home: the costly and complex system of separate ethnic governments in Windhoek (Namibia's capital) has obvious parallels in South Africa's ethnically segregated Parliament.

From Namibia – via the lessons of past counter-insurgency campaigns in Rhodesia, Vietnam and Malaya – comes the oft-repeated maxim that guerilla war is only 20 per cent military and 80 per cent political.[21] On the battlefields and in the villages of Namibia and Angola, South Africa is figuring out the formula for that crucial 80 per cent.

General Charles Lloyd, South West Africa Territorial Force Commander, at a Windhoek press briefing, 5 February 1981: We can win this war through military means. We could actually destroy our military enemy. But that is not to say that we will destroy SWAPO, which is a political thing as well, that is in the minds of the people. As you know, bullets kill bodies, not minds. So we can destroy our military enemy, but that is not to say that we have destroyed the ideology of SWAPO. I would not say that we will solve the problem of South West Africa in a military way. That cannot be done, as I see it. What you really need for counter-insurgency warfare is good government.

SADF 'Civic Action' manual on counter-insurgency warfare, issued on a confidential basis to national servicemen in 1980: Nowhere in the world do we find circumstances more favourable for insurgency than in the RSA and SWA. All the following factors would seem to count against us:

a) The whites, despite the fact that they are in the minority, are in a position of control due to their advanced technology.

b) Few countries have as cosmopolitan a society, with so many divergent cultures, as SWA and the RSA. There are so many obvious differences within the various ethnic groups (Bantu) that no signs of mutual harmony exist. No Zulu would be prepared to live under a Sotho government any more than Indians or whites would. The position in the RSA and SWA is thus potentially one of conflict, and an ideal breeding ground for insurgency.

South Africa, however, has the solution for thwarting the Russian expansionist ideals. That solution lies within her people as bearers of the Christian faith, basic humanity, and the recognition of the principle that separate development offers the only logical solution to the threat of cultural and racial conflict.

The struggle to gain the support of the population can be compared to a rugby match. He who wins the scrum and controls the ball scores the try. Gaining this support requires on the one hand, strong action against the terrorist, and on the other hand, maximum friendship with the population. This is the winning way. No soldier will be able to influence the black man if he does not know and respect the black man for what he is. Whereas the success of our struggle depends on how well you know your target group, an appeal is made to high integrity and humanity at the same time. The aim of this pamphlet is to provide the soldier with a background knowledge of his target group, as well as the techniques that will enable him to reach the target group in order to obtain and maintain its support; thus to achieve a balance in our efforts to counter and prevent insurgency.

Therefore, in your daily contact with the black man, reach out and communicate with him. Tell him convincingly of the disadvantages which the communist ideology holds for him. Bear the following statement, made by an Ovambo who is well-disposed towards us, in mind. Asked why he still listened to a certain terrorist organization, he answered: 'They speak to us but you Boers say nothing to us. How then can we believe you?' Here are a few examples of how, as a result of irresponsible actions, the efforts of the Security Forces can be thwarted by the population:

a) Withholding information concerning the enemy from the Security Forces, or revealing it at such a late stage that it cannot be followed up anymore.

b) Intentionally providing the Security Forces with incorrect information, and thereby leading them astray.

c) Furthering the cause of the terrorists by hiding and accommodating them and providing them with supplies and medicine, etc.

Relations can easily be harmed by all persons involved in the struggle. Do not:

a) Say something rash to a member of the local population and thereby cause feelings of hostility.

b) Drive your vehicle through a spring, thereby turning what is possibly the only available waterhole of a kraal and its cattle into a quagmire.

c) Scare herdboys and their cattle by chasing them with your vehicles. It will take days to round up the cattle again.

d) Drive away if you have run over a cow or a goat.

e) Drive through a kraal without permission of its chief.

f) Search huts without permission.

g) Summarily demand cultural articles or commodities. They may have magical uses.

h) Lose a hand grenade. It may later be picked up by children, explode, and cause death or maiming.

i) Assault members of the population.

j) Fire weapons at random.

k) Neglect greeting. In most cases, the black man expects his superior (the white man) to greet him first.

l) Make discriminatory remarks about the black man or swear in his presence.

m) Unnecessarily rush the process of getting answers. The black man is seldom in a hurry.

The non-application of these rules is sometimes the most important reason for the sympathy the population has for the enemy. We can forget about ever winning a counter-insurgency campaign if we do not guard against actions like these. Remember also that a limited number of Civic Action members cannot win the struggle for the 'hearts and minds of the people' on their own. It requires correct action, acknowledging human dignity, from every member of the South African army.

Though soldiers are thoroughly trained to track down and destroy the enemy, it may occur that during the period of several months' service the soldier does not see a single terrorist. This causes the soldier to become frustrated and to act in a way that suits the terrorist down to the ground. Instead of committing thoughtless actions because of frustration, the soldier must devote all his energies to educating the population, and in making them immune to enemy influences. Thereby, 80 per cent of the struggle will already be won.

The soldier as a ruthless fighter and the soldier as a friend of the population are reconcilable. A balanced soldier, who knows his enemy and their methods, and who realizes that the role played by the population is critical to the struggle of our time, has the key to victory. Apply this in the interests of our country and all her population groups.

'Civic Action' was the theory: the reality emerged from the litany of alleged atrocities committed by South African soldiers and their black recruits. With the SADF heavily committed to operations into southern Angola, the South African Police assumed more and more responsibility for the 'maintenance of law and order' in Namibia, and in 1978 formed a special counter-insurgency unit known as 'Koevoet' – Afrikaans for 'crowbar'.[22] Composed largely of black members of the majority Ovambo ethnic group, Koevoet claimed the highest 'kill rate' against SWAPO of any South African unit, and was accused of mounting 'pseudo operations', wherein members of the unit dressed as SWAPO forces and committed atrocities in an effort to discredit SWAPO with the local population. Despite the greatest proportion of military forces to civilians in the world, with 80 per cent of the population under martial law, South African troops met such resistance from the Namibian people that the 'hearts and minds' approach soon gave way to more straightforward repression.

REFORM

DEFENDING THE SYSTEM

Windhoek Advertiser, **8 November 1983:** The manual roasting of a man by soldiers of the South West Africa Territory Force, and the torture of three Kavango schoolteachers by Koevoet members, were among allegations made at a press conference here on Friday. Representatives of the Namibian, South African and foreign media first heard of how three teachers and a farmer from west Kavango were detained, beaten and shocked. Their unemotional and matter-of-fact rendering of how they felt it to be their duty to feed marauding guerillas, and their subsequent detention and assault, was a poignant and sad sketch of the life of those caught in the crossfire of this country's 17-year-old bush war. Despite their fear of SWAPO because they were armed, they said, 'SWAPO only kill puppets. As long as you give them food and water, you are alright.' Had any of them heard of atrocities committed against civilians in their area by SWAPO? 'No,' they said.

Mr Ndara Kapitango, 63, who was allegedly roasted and then tossed into a fire, could not be present. He was still recovering in hospital in Kavango from injuries inflicted in June. One of his arms had to be amputated after his hellish ordeal.

A spokesman for the SADF in Pretoria said yesterday: 'We have nothing to add to the scores of statements already made about alleged atrocities.' In the past, the SADF has reacted similarly to such allegations by either saying they will be investigated thoroughly by a commission of inquiry, or by dismissing them as 'SWAPO propaganda'.

A spokesman for the SWA Police said in Windhoek: 'It is disturbing generally that people exploit allegations of maltreatment to discredit the Security Forces and to undermine the trust between the police and the public.' When asked about the scars shown at the conference, he said: 'It occurs sometimes that policemen do assault people, but they are in a minority. We will do anything possible to stop so-called atrocities.' The police spokesman said he could not understand the motive of the men for making the allegations. 'Why do they not relate atrocities that have been committed by SWAPO, if they support humane causes?'

Bar Council of South West Africa memorandum to a government commission of inquiry into security legislation in the territory, May 1984: It seems clear that the norm of the 'policemen' of Koevoet and the Police Special Task Force is to shoot first and ask questions later, even if the person in front of them is outwardly an unarmed civilian. There is no need for any police unit with instructions to kill in the first place, instead of to arrest and bring to trial. Recently a photograph was displayed of a senior member of this unit wearing a vest with the motto: 'Killing is our business and business is good.'

Cape Times, **24 November 1983:** The motivation of, and concept behind, the police special counter-insurgency unit, Koevoet, is 'barbaric', a top psychiatrist told the Windhoek Supreme Court yesterday. Dr Charles Shubitz, a Johannesburg neurologist and psychiatrist, was giving medical evidence at the trial of Johannes Paulus, 23, a Koevoet member convicted of murder, rape, attempted murder and robbery with aggravating circumstances. On January 2 this year, Paulus murdered headman Robert Amunwe in the Ovambo war zone, in what the court earlier heard was a 'rape and robbery spree', while disguising himself as a SWAPO guerilla.

Paulus said that one of the ways in which Koevoet operated was to interrogate villagers at kraals when they suspected that SWAPO guerillas were in the area. 'If they won't give us information, then one of our group assaults them, slaps them with his open hand, or beats them with a rifle butt.' Paulus said that, as a member of Koevoet, he was paid R350 a month, but they were paid bonuses according to how many guerillas they killed in a month. 'If we wipe out the freedom fighters, we get this

money. The more we kill, the more we get. This is called kopgeld (bounty).' He said Koevoet officers had told him he had to 'wipe out SWAPOS, because we don't like them because they support communism'.[23]

Windhoek Observer, **24 July 1982:** An inquest was held into the death of Mrs Caulilikekwa Mwingona, 35, who died with her baby on her back, together with another woman who also carried her baby and child. SADF Platoon Commander Mark de Backer said in a sworn statement, supported by several other affidavits, that he and his men were doing operational duties in the war zone and laid an ambush when night had fallen. They had definite information that insurgents were operative in a specific region.

It was about 20.30 hours, said Platoon Commander de Backer, when three people later identified as two women carrying their babies and a child came walking in their direction. He had given his men instructions to open fire the moment he, as a Platoon Leader, commenced firing. This was done. He recalled that one of the adults tried to run, but was shot down. After the ceasefire had been given, they found the two women shot and the child, and the next morning at daylight, that both women had babies on their backs who had also been struck by the bullets. Mr G. J. Retief, of the Ondangwa inquest court, said that he could not find criminal liability because the soldiers had acted bona fide, and in terms of the Proclamation that no nocturnal movements were allowed in the Ovambo-speaking region.

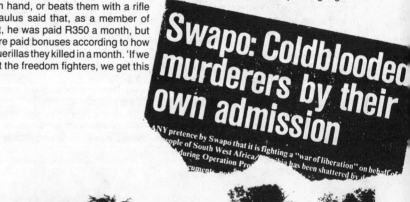

Swapo: Coldblooded murderers by their own admission

ANY pretence by Swapo that it is fighting a "war of liberation" on behalf of the people of South West Africa/Namibia during Operation Pro... has been shattered by...

74

How do you respond to recent reports of atrocities committed by SADF troops?

Brigadier Rudolph Badenhorst, officer commanding SADF Sector 10, Ovamboland, at a press briefing, 19 March 1982: Well, you must always underline good manners. If I visit your house with my kids and they are rough, beforehand I must always tell them: 'Listen, behave yourself, please do this, please don't do that.' And then, of course, when they arrive at your house and break down your rose bushes in spite of my warnings, well, we always underline the fact that we must apply good manners. We must treat the people like human beings. We must not destroy their property, we must not kill them unnecessarily, we must not kill innocent people.

And about those alleged atrocities?

Brigadier Rudolph Badenhorst: Ja, in any family you get naughty children, in any family. I believe in my family I've one. I believe in your family you've also got naughty children, and that is my answer to you, okay?

The formation of black counter-insurgency units is an example of yet another strategy that the SADF perfected in Namibia, with an eye toward further use in South Africa.

Major Erroll Mann, officer commanding the black Caprivi Battalion, at a press briefing, 4 February 1981: The best people to fight blacks with is with other blacks. And they are very good in the bush. In many ways they're hardier than white troops. They're used to living hard. And economically, at the moment the blacks in this area have no real economic incentive, and taking a black out of circulation of the economy won't do any harm. You take a white out of circulation in the Republic, it must ultimately affect the Republic's economy.

So these black troops are part of the South West African Territorial Force, and you are with the SADF?

Major Erroll Mann: I'm a Rhodesian, actually. I was with the Rhodesian army for ten years. Now I've got nowhere else to go because I won't fit into Europe, so I've got to fit into Africa. Besides, I enjoy soldiering and there's a war here that needs soldiers.

How would you compare your black troops here with the Rhodesian African Rifles (Rhodesia's black battalion)?

Major Eroll Mann: We are achieving in a very short space of time what the RAR took a long time to achieve. We've got a positive black development programme here. We've got to do it – it's the only way to win this war.

Namibia's first ethnic unit was the 'Bushmen Battalion', formed of the Kalahari San people in the early 1970s. These isolated hunter-gatherers managed to survive into the twentieth century, only to be forced into reserves by the South African military, who first organized them into para-military tracking units, and then recruited them into special counter-insurgency battalions. The San people in Angola suffered a similar fate under the Portuguese colonialists. Some joined guerilla armies that opposed the revolutionary movement that ultimately came to power,[24] so after Angola's independence they fled to Namibia, where they were immediately recruited by the SADF.

Lieutenant Ben Wolff officer commanding 'Bushmen Battalion', at a press briefing in Rundu, 4 February 1981: We decided that, having this population here, we could use them, and it was decided to start the base with bushmen. They are fantastic in the bush, as far as tracking goes, bushcraft, and seeing things in the bush which I doubt we can see. We've got about 4000 people at this base: 250 whites, 850 bushmen troops, 1500 bushmen children and 900 bushmen women.

Now let me explain to you this badge we wear, the badge of our unit. You know, the bushmen fled from Angola and then we decided to use them as soldiers, but if it should ever happen that they want to go back to Angola, they won't be able to — they'll immediately be in trouble for being our soldiers. So it was decided to use a crow on our badge because in the time of the Bible, when Noah had his ark, the very first bird he sent away to see if the land was drying up was a crow. And the crow never returned, so the bushmen left Angola and they'll never return. And if you have a closer look at our badge, you can see it's got a little white chest, which means the white leadership amongst the black bushmen. And the white circle around the crow is the western influence on the bushmen.

One of the reasons why this base was started was to save them from extinction in other words, no bushmen being left over. Our aim here is not to try and westernize them, but to try and make a better bushman.

When the bushmen are sent out on operations, will they always be under command of a white?

Lieutenant Ben Wolff: That all depends. If the bushman can reach a stage where he can command his own unit, where he can start reading, writing and understand things like that, maybe. But at this stage it's impossible.

They've got their own facilities, their own bars, where they drink. Their sergeant is entitled to six beers a night, full corporal or lance corporal gets four beers, and a troop gets two beers a night.[25]

What alternatives do they have to joining the SADF? Is there any other way they could make a living in this area?

Lieutenant Ben Wolff: At this stage, basically you could say, basically nothing. Except going out into the area and hunting, going back to their original nomadic way of life.

Are they at all political? Do they realize what the war is about?

Lieutenant Ben Wolff: Politics to them is basically their commanding officer. He's got the last say, and that's that.

You mean they don't know why they're fighting?

Lieutenant Ben Wolff: Ja, basically you could say that.

Like the whites in Rhodesia, the South Africans in Namibia cultivated the image of a black versus black war, of soldiers of all races joining forces against the communist threat to Christian civilization. In 1980, black Namibians began to be conscripted into the 'independent' South West African Territorial Force. The exercise was a dismal failure and did more to recruit for SWAPO than for the South African cause.

In transposing the Namibian experience to the South African context, the SADF was desperate to avoid the kind of opposition it was encountering among black Namibians. Thus the 'Civic Action Programme' was devised – an attempt to win the 'hearts and minds' of potential black South African conscripts by imbuing a positive image among the black youth.

Parents of young black Namibian men, speaking at a meeting protesting against conscription, Katatura Township, 12 July 1981: Despite its apparently unassailable power, the South African Army is also stupid. Everything they do makes the people angry. Before people are called up for military service, there should be a general election to test the will of the people. The so-called enemy is your own brother, who was forced to leave the country because of repression. The enemy of the South African army is said to be SWAPO. Who is SWAPO? SWAPO is the people. We cannot fight our own people.

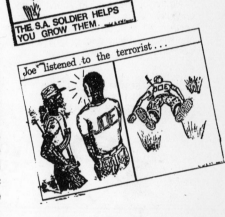

Major Gert Brits of Western Province Command Civic Action: All the lessons and principles and know-how have been and are being applied in South Africa.[26] One of our main aims is to build up good relations with the population – to be seen to be helping and defending them. Winning the confidence of the people is the main factor in countering insurgency. We've got to show people – or rather, teach them to decide for themselves – what is better for them. And therefore we must supply them with teachers. We send trained teachers to the schools; there are hundreds of teachers in the SADF. People here accept the man in uniform. We take educational films and go out into their areas. We make contact in schools and with community groups and committees. There's also a very close diplomatic co-operation with the homelands. There's a big demand for Defence Force teachers.

What are the political aims of the SADF?

Major Gert Brits: You cannot divorce the Defence Force from politics, but its political aim is a broad one – you could call it the Christian democratic system, harmony and development. The way I look at it is that in South Africa there is enough sun for everyone to give everyone his place. What we in the army are doing is working for evolutionary change against revolutionary change, but it's a politically neutral way of action. The army is neutral, it's everybody's army. We are trying to make people realize this and win their trust. And we are succeeding in doing so.

To what extent has there been opposition in the black communities to your activities?

Major Gert Brits: If I was an agitator I would also be very opposed to Civic Action because it destroys what they're trying to do. But despite all these problems, we've had tremendous success. There has been a huge demand for youth camps and we just don't have the manpower to maintain contact. But we keep in touch through our education development programmes, and these need to continue, which is why we have started the Civic Action magazine, *Contact.*

KONTAK CONTACT

Contact – Civic Affairs News is one of many free publications aimed at South Africa's black community.

The Warrior, **free SADF publication, 30, 1981:** The South African revolution is on – now. It did not start yesterday and it will not end tomorrow, for it is a revolution that does not destroy and overthrow, but rather builds foundations for a better future and lifestyle. It is unique – a revolution that is speeding up evolution. That South Africa is on the forefront of the Third World in quality, quantity, and variety of educational facilities enjoyed by its black people is beyond dispute. There can also be few countries in the world that are trying harder than South Africa to eliminate overcrowded living conditions and provide modern housing.

The rest of Africa has realized the folly of Nkrumah's 'seek ye first the political kingdom and the rest shall follow'-philosophy. In South Africa, the quest for the economic kingdom is well underway and advanced, even though it is often buried under a mass of double talk and criticism. The conclusion is that there is no 'quick-fix' solution. It remains a problem of modern society. A problem which is not being simplified by the multi-racial South African society, where so many people of so many different backgrounds, cultures, living standards and standards of education are living together. A problem not only for the state to attend to and certainly not caused by the state, but a problem which involves the whole society and which will take a lot of time, a lot of work and a lot of goodwill to solve.

The SADF not only infiltrates government schools with its teachers and publications, but runs Civic Action youth camps, in conjunction with black administration boards, community councils and churches.

THE SOUTH AFRICAN ARMY
IS THE GUARDIAN
OF THE PEOPLE

Atlantis News **(Cape Coloured township government publication) 1 May 1981:** 'The 52 youngsters had a marvellous time. It was a weekend they will never forget,' said Sister Mary Josephine of the Roman Catholic Church. Once a year, the Youth Club of their church goes on a weekend camp. This year, it was the Civic Action of the Western Province Command of the South African Army who took them on a weekend trip to Soetwater. According to Major G.N. Brits, who organized the whole outing, it was more an education weekend camp. 'The emphasis was on leadership, and by way of lectures, slides and literature, we tried to have a well-balanced programme for the youngsters,' he said. 'We hope we will be able to do the same thing in the near future. The army would like to be of service to the whole community. In fact, we would like everyone to feel it is their army,' he said.

The response of the black community to these camps has been fiercely negative, for they are seen as psychological preparation for the conscription of Coloureds and Indians, in line with the government's constitutional reforms.

Grassroots community newspaper, April 1984: 'SADF stay out of our area. We don't want our children to go on your camps.' This was the message of a meeting in Hanover Park (Coloured township) recently. 'We were never informed that our children would be going on a camp with the SADF. We cannot allow our children to go on these camps because the SADF upholds apartheid and all its injustices,' said one parent at the meeting. Speakers outlined the role of the army in apartheid society and spoke about how the SADF had taken children from Mbekweni on a weekend camp, without the parents knowing, and how the parents went to fetch their children from the camp. 'The SADF will increasingly be fed to our people like this. Because of the new constitution which the government wants to sell to us, the SADF will try to build up a good image in the community. But we know the real image of the SADF. We know that the SADF is used against our people in protests and whenever we stand up against apartheid. We refuse to be fooled and we refuse to send our children to SADF camps to fight in the SADF,' said another parent.

Ela Ramgobin, executive member of the Natal Indian Congress, at an anti-conscription meeting in Phoenix, Natal, 30 October 1983: Mothers, sisters and wives must get together and reject the new constitution for the Republic of South Africa, as the acceptance of the constitution means that husbands, sons and fathers will be taken into the army to protect and give credibility to the apartheid system of this country. We must stand together and fight till the last drop of blood. Our sons and husbands would not be soldiers but murderers. Our brothers and fathers will have to take orders from their white counterparts and shoot to kill their own kind. And if they don't take orders, the boys will be put into jail. Every time the children go on boycott to demand better education, or every time fathers go on strike for better wages, members of our family will be called with guns to shoot their own fathers and brothers. They will have no option but to shoot. We will not allow our children to die for an unjust cause!

Cape Action League Bulletin, **December 1983:** One of the main aims of the 'new deal' is to get our children to join the South African Army. They want our sons and our daughters to go and fight on the borders in defence of apartheid and 'free enterprise' (capitalism). Now it is clear for all to see: the 'New Deal' is a graveyard for our children. We cannot let our children go to war to defend this rotten system against their own comrades! Those Namibian and Azanian freedom fighters whom they call 'terrorists' were sitting in the same school benches as your son and your daughter just a few years ago. They are as much our sons and daughters as are our own children. They are fighting to free this country from racial oppression and economic exploitation. You may not agree with their methods but you cannot send their own brothers and sisters to go and kill them. If we do this, we do Botha's dirty work for him.

Every boy wants to be a Muhammad Ali. Here is our chance to turn every one of our children into a Muhammad Ali. He refused to go and fight for America against the colonially oppressed people of Vietnam. He was prepared to spend five years in military prison. Dare we follow his example? Let us organize our youth in their millions to fight against conscription. Let us ruin their plans. We won't join the army! Let us make war on their unjust wars in South Africa! We refuse to kill our brothers and sisters!

South African Panorama, **February 1984:** Inspired by the ululations of a gathering of women at Soweto's Civic Centre, the men of 21 Battalion recently marched into the city that is so close to their hearts with drums beating and colours flying. This training school for black soldiers had received the Freedom of Entry to the City of Soweto at the insistence, among others, of the then Mayor, Councillor David Thebehali.

'Their families inherit the discipline of the members,' said Councillor Thebehali, as the Scroll of Freedom was presented to the Commanding Officer, Commandant L. Kotze. 'This can only have a stabilizing effect on family life, and contribute to the people's sense of security,' he added. Nearby, as if to prove the point, a number of posters adjured the citizens to 'Get that feeling of permanence: buy your own home.'

Says 21 Battalion's second-in-command, Major C. J. Kruger: 'Today the black man has a place as a soldier in the defence of freedom. If South Africa wants to survive and curtail communist expansionism, it will have to rely on each and every one of its inhabitants to take up arms and be trained as a guardian on the walls. These men are motivated. Not only are they making a career of soldiering, but they are aware of the Red threat against Africa.'

Hundreds of blacks have already graduated from the battalion's soldiering classes, and have gone on to man battalions and armies in countries which were formerly part of the Republic of South Africa, as well as the self-governing national states. Lenz Base trained the nucleus of the Transkeian Army, and performed the same service for Bophuthatswana, Ciskei and Venda, all independent countries today. Colonel P. Faure, officer commanding the Venda Defence Force, has on behalf of President Patrick Mphephu of Venda, offered the army's services to the South African Defence Force to curb communist expansionism.

The ultimate goal of the Civic Action Programme is to groom soldiers for the SADF, but in typical South African government fashion, a different agenda is planned for each ethnic group. Coloureds and Indians are to be conscripted, on the assumption that their newly acquired constitutional rights carry an increased responsibility to do their bit in defending the country and meeting the SADF's stretched manpower needs. Rural Africans, on the other hand, are recruited on a voluntary basis to homeland armies, designed as a first line of defence against guerilla incursions, and as a means of quelling internal unrest. Urban Africans, too, have a place in the military, as the SADF made clear in a propaganda exercise at the military base where black soldiers are trained in Soweto.

THE BLACK MAN'S VIEW

A Black journalist, Mr David Masango, speaks to his own people after a recent visit to the Operational Area. . .

OUR SOLDIERS ARE NOT ONLY FIGHTING MEN. . .

MANY of our people do not know what Black soldiers do for [...] interesting thi[...] bout the soldiers is that they do not [...] are many other things which [...] ticularly for the

The performance of the 21 Battalion Band is definitely Number One.

IT is true that men cannot live on br[...] other things that maketh a man. [...] the Chaplain of 21 Battalion [...] spent thr[...]

Our Black soldiers are keen to go to the border

21 Battalion, the Black unit at Lenz, has accepted its first intake for voluntary training this year. Many of the volunteers at Lenz arrive with no idea of what military life is like. For this reason they are put through a very tough selection course which separates the men from the boys.

A Black volunteer to 21 Battalion must be a South African citizen with no criminal record. He must also be h[...] n 18 and 35 years old [...] h [...] ination of Stand[...]

◄ That glowing report failed to mention the heavy police presence needed to shield the black soldiers from crowds of demonstrators, who jeered and sang freedom songs before being arrested. Like black Namibians, black South Africans rejected the carrot of Civic Action because, for them, the stick of state repression was far more real. By 1982, the SADF had admitted that its military and political experience in Namibia was not directly applicable to the very different kind of war it was fighting at home.

Chief of the Defence Force, General Constand Viljoen, *Financial Mail*, 15 January 1982: In South West Africa, SWAPO has only fought in the border area, with 90 per cent of incidents happening within 20 to 30 kilometres of the border. In South Africa itself, we expect a different approach. They, apparently, do not have a border war in mind. They are going to fight an area war. In manpower terms, this means we must be able to call on sufficient manpower so that no area in South Africa will be vulnerable to attack. If we had to deal with this using the full-time force, the demands on the system would be too great. But we are going to deal with it by using area defence, which means we are going to raise the defensibility of all the people.

In practice, 'area defence' means the mobilization of the white population into military and para-military structures: police reserves, civil defence organizations, school cadets, rural, urban and industrial commandos. In order to supply all the manpower needed, the government drastically increased the mandatory military commitment so that all white men are required to do two years of national service, twelve years in the Citizen Force, five years in the reserve, and further service in local commandos until the age of 55.[27]

Meaning that people living in a particular area will be liable for military service in that area?

General Constand Viljoen: Meaning people living in an area must be organized to defend themselves. They must be the first line of defence. Our full-time force must be a reaction force. The first line of defence will contain any terrorist attack, and the better equipped and trained reaction forces will deal with insurgents.

DISSENSION IN THE RANKS

CIVIC ACTION SOLDIER OBJECTS

SABC, 24 October 1983: The amendment to the Defence Act last year provided for the establishment of local commandos to be responsible for local area defence, and a start is now being made with the priority areas, which are, of course, the eastern and northern borders. These have already formed their commandos and been put through the army's six-day intensive training course. I joined the Nelspruit commando on it's final day.

Colonel Doep du Plessis, of Pretoria military headquarters: People from all walks of life from this local area have been taken up into the commando now. They vary from bank managers to farmers and the whole spectrum in the economic activity of the area, so obviously they have a very good knowledge of the area concerned. Most of them said, 'At my age, no bloody corporal is going to chase me around on the parade ground or is going to tell me left, right, now you must go and wake up at two o'clock in the morning – I'm not going to take that from any corporal.'

SABC announcer: The mayor of Komatipoort, Wynand Viljoen, who'd come over to see how his men were getting along, said the prevailing opinion was now very different.

Mayor Wynand Viljoen: Being called up, I think it was a tremendous experience. I thoroughly enjoyed it and I think they've knocked us down to size.

SABC announcer: Most of the instruction during the course concerned the actual nature of the physical threat, and in the course of this, the commando was shown how easy it is to do extensive damage with landmines. The final briefing came from Sergeant Frans Malan.

Sergeant Malan: The idea now is that from here you will be phased in with an existing section, in the area where you live. And you will from now on be going into the regular training programme, so when you leave from here you will be given a programme for the rest of the year. (Sound of army drill fades).

Not every white South African responds enthusiastically to the call from the SADF. Each year, some 4,000 men fail to report for service, by evading the military or leaving the country, and a handful have served time in prison rather than undergo military training. One of the first conscientious objectors was Richard Steele, a Baptist and universal pacifist who was sentenced to a year in military detention barracks in 1980 for his beliefs.[28]

Richard Steele. The first thing people always want to know is: why am I different? After all, there's so much pressure on young white men in this country to accept the military, so why didn't it affect me. I think that I just came to a point in my Christianity where I felt it would in fact be antithetical to my beliefs to go into the army. It was a very difficult decision to make, though, because of the whole conditioning process to make you go into the army. Defending your country is supposed to be a good thing, a Christian thing, and it's the manly thing to do. This is quite an important factor in young men's lives, that you have a kind of macho understanding of what the army is, that you somehow become a man through miliary training. It's like playing on the first rugby team, in terms of manliness and also the way girls respond to you. One of the things that happens in basic training that some of the guys in detention barracks told me is that you are told to refer to your rifle as your wife! That is just straight perversion. It's quite frightening to me just to think of the correlation they're making, in terms of sexuality and violence.

And the really dangerous part is that it so happens that in our situation the enemy is black. And all the evil images of the terrorist enemy that they project automatically generalize to one's views of blacks. Like when you are taught to salute, you are told that you must hold you hand flat and firm, the same way as you would when you slap a kaffir. So it all combines to confirm the stereotypes about blacks.

I remember during these so-called 'chaplain's periods' they used to have in detention barracks — which was usually just straight propaganda — one time they had a talk on the national anthem. Now you remember the last line: 'We'll die for you South Africa'? Well, they were getting into this whole thing of dying for your country, what a glorious thing that would be. I just couldn't believe it. I mean for me, no government or particular authority is ultimate in any sense, but particularly for this government, I can't imagine dying to protect a system which is so totally unjust and violent. One of the ironies was that some of the officers used to say to me, 'you know we're fighting to defend religious freedom.' And there I was sitting in jail because of my religious beliefs! It was absolutely pathetic!

Billy Paddock was also imprisoned for a year (1982–3) as a conscientious objector, but out of opposition to South Africa's role in what he regarded as a civil war.

Billy Paddock: I don't believe that a pacifist stance is possible. I believe that we are all involved in institutionalized violence. The minute I earn money and pay taxes, I am contributing to violence, because our taxes go directly to the police and the SADF. So when a policemàn fires into a crowd of black demonstrators, you're standing behind him. And every time that people try to protest to the government with non-violence, they face violent repression. The ANC proved the lack of effectiveness of the non-violent position in affecting change in this country with about fifty years of non-violent struggle, before they went into violence and sabotage and took up arms.

How does this relate to your opposition to the SADF?

Billy Paddock: I believe that South Africa is unjustified in fighting this present war. I'm not prepared to try and defend the oppressive and unjust system that prevails in this country. Right at the core of this society is injustice, and everything that flows from that is unjust. So I ascribe to the 'just war doctrine',[29] if you want a label for it. For me, Christ's command is that I take sides with the poor and the oppressed, and that clearly means that I cannot support the status quo in this country. I believe that SWAPO and the ANC are more justified in this war than South Africa. Their cause is just: they want freedom.

Do you think your stance threatens the government?

Billy Paddock: Yes, clearly. I believe that the few of us who have chosen this road threaten the most important battle that has to be fought, and that's the psychological warfare. Even the military says that the battle is only 20 per cent military and 80 per cent socio/political/economic, so I think it's incredibly important to fight to undermine the propaganda.

The Defence Amendment Bill: 'Resistance Continues', pamphlet distributed in Cape Town, 1983: Resistance, born of increasing questioning of the SADF's role in our society, constitutes a major threat to the SADF's ability to deploy a well trained force. As the SADF points out, only 0.18 per cent of conscriptees object. However, the effects of their objection go far beyond their small numbers.

Why do their ideas and arguments pose such an ideological threat? Firstly, they represent dissent from within the white privileged group. This opens up cracks in the state's control of its white support group – a crack which helps to develop organized white opposition, able to challenge from inside the notion that our future depends on total support for the state initiatives. Secondly, they add their voices to the chorus of opposition to the SADF, and stand together with the South African masses struggling for political change, and through this participation forge the future non-racial society.

A range of positions have been taken up, from pacifist to entirely political arguments for objection. However, all those objectors who questioned the role the SADF plays in society have linked this to the critical position the military occupies within the state.

Public support for conscientious objectors is severely constrained by laws forbidding any encouragement of a decision not to do military service.

Despite the legal constraints, a Conscientious Objectors Support Group was formed to offer objectors moral support and to spread the anti-militarist message through literature, newsletters, seminars and national speaking tours. When Brett Myrdal announced his decision to object to military service – the most militant political stance to date – the Support Group geared up to publicize his case. Copies of the statement Myrdal planned to make at his court martial were circulated to student, church and community organizations all over the country.

Section 121(c) of the Defence Act: Any person who uses any language or does any act or thing with intent to recommend to, encourage, aid, incite, instigate, suggest or otherwise cause any other person or category of person or persons in general to refuse or fail to render any service to which such other person or a person of such category or persons in general is or are liable or may become liable in terms of this act shall be guilty of an offence and liable on conviction to a fine not exceeding R5000 or to imprisonment for a period not exceeding six years, or to both such a fine and imprisonment.

Statement by conscientious objector Brett Myrdal to his court martial, set for November 1983: I address this court as one of the thousands of young South Africans who have been morally and physically prepared for war in defence of the South African government. Along with all white South African schoolchildren, I was taught to stand and sing 'Die Stem' with pride, to respect the South African flag and the leaders of our government. At Grey High School in Port Elizabeth, I attended school camps, at which we played 'Nats (National Party members) versus Terrorists' instead of cowboys and Indians. But our game was more than a game. It presented us with a picture of our government, justly defending itself against violent terrorists.

School cadets were important in training us for the army – training us to be leaders amongst men. We were taught to shoot, to drill with R-Is. We saluted uniformed teachers, and on cadet camps were trained in 'counter-insurgency warfare' and 'attacks on mock terrorist bases'. Nor were girls unaffected. While we route-marched to our sister school, Collegiate, they performed fire drills, coming out proudly to watch us drill: a rehearsal with us playing future war heroes, and them, the girlfriends, sisters or wives, keeping the homefires burning.

I was fortunate to be able to defer my call-up by attending university. Many of my friends went to the South African Defence Force to 'get it done with'. They are still trying to get it done. When they came back, many from the border, they carried with them forever the scars of what they had been forced to do. At university, I realized that I had escaped neither the dilemma of conscription nor the reality of war. Rhodesian students who were close to me spoke of the futility of the sacrifice they had made in an unwinnable war. I was

The day before Myrdal's scheduled court martial, the SADF suddenly dropped all charges, and announced that he would receive another call-up after new legislation took effect, which would recognize religious objectors only and carry a six-year (instead of the previous two-year) prison sentence for all other objectors.[30] The new law widened the focus of war resisters beyond conscientious objection: a nation-wide campaign was launched against conscription itself.

Where does this leave the resister who refuses to serve in the SADF, yet is not prepared to serve six years in jail? A group of young white men got together to discuss their options. Chris, Barry and Will did their military training straight after leaving school, as the army recommends. Joel and Mark have avoided the military, through student deferments.

Chris: I was in the infantry and we landed up on the Namibian border and I was 17 years old. And, like, the rifle's in my hand, and here it is – it's war. It was then that I realized I just couldn't go through with it – it, meaning killing the 'enemy'. It was from that point onward that I started resisting what the army was putting out.

Barry: I went straight from school to the army, with the idea of getting it over with. I remember this officer giving us a speech during training: he held up his rifle and he said 'See this here in my hand? This is the only thing that talks to a kaffir.' And the other thing he said was 'Gentlemen, have a look at your hands. You'll notice, they are white. That is your privilege, and that is what this war is all about.' And then he went on and said, 'We are actually here to win the hearts and minds of these people, so treat them nicely – but remember, a kaffir's a kaffir.' To me, that was my point of no return. I've been called up for camps since then, but I've managed to avoid them.

Will: My turning point came when I was posted to the Namibian border, through seeing what actually was done to the civilian population. It really scared the hell out of me, realizing what role the army actually was performing, and how totally different it was from what's put across in the press and on television in South Africa. Just all the lies being told, about how we were there to protect those people. I couldn't imagine how the other guys handled it, until I saw that they legitimized the system by rationalizing what they did. It was sickening. I remember this story of a 'terrorist' who was shot in the head and he kicked around for about ten minutes before he actually died. And the guy who shot him was saying things like, 'This goes to show that a kaffir can live without a brain.' And this was a guy who wouldn't have said something like that beforehand, but he had to rationalize what he was involved in, he had to play their game.

Chris: I don't mean to apologize for that kind of attitude, but you can't underestimate the emotional toll of the border experience. I remember coming back from the border, realizing exactly what I had been involved in, but not being able to talk to anyone about what had happened. I just clammed up. It took a long time to come to terms with it all. That's why I think it's really incumbent on white South Africans to come up with a clear position – politically, on the military – otherwise, the next minute they'll be on the Namibian border shooting the shit out of villages and not knowing why.

Barry: I later took a non-combatant stand, or at least I tried to. They put a lot of pressure on me to conform, made me seem a total outcast, carrying a pole instead of a rifle, hitting me with the business of 'Aren't you a man?' But at the same time, they'd rather deal with that tactic and not make waves, than deal with another CO. Anyway, it was what I did at the time, but now I see it as a concession that the army can cope with, this business of allowing for 'non-combatant' status. I don't think you can get away from the fact that any sort of participation in the SADF is, in fact, contributing to upholding the South African system.

Will: I think it's part and parcel of the army's campaign to 'win the hearts and minds of the people'. It doesn't really matter who fires the gun; you're helping the fighting machine just as much. I figure that you either accept the status quo for what it is and you defend it, or you resist it and fight against it. And the way I think that white South Africans can best fight against it is by not offering themselves to the SADF.

Mark: The only response is resistance, total non-collaboration. I mean, the answer is aligned with the liberation struggle in South Africa. You can't divorce the army issue from that. The liberation movement has clearly indicated that whites must resist the army on all levels. It's a personal question as to how you're going to do that. Some people are strong enough to sit in jail for a couple of years and they have Christian values to support them. Others decide to live in exile, and others evade.

Joel: For example, I haven't been at all yet, and I don't intend going. My intention is to keep studying as long as possible, so that I can continue to stay in the country and do political work. In the worst event, I would consider leaving, but I'd try and avoid that as long as I can. I've seen the effect that exile has had on my friends, the massive gaps that result in leadership, and how demoralizing it is for those who are left behind, so I'd like to avoid that option as long as possible.

Barry: There are some people who've been to the army years ago, like me, who then try to say that it's okay to do a camp, but more and more, that sort of thing is considered unacceptable. People sometimes try to say that their political position inside the country is so important that they should try to stay, even if it means fulfilling their continuing military obligations, but to me, that's a double standard; why should the leadership be allowed to go into the army, while the members of various organizations have to evade or leave the country?

Will: I feel very strongly that the issue of the military epitomizes the white position in the struggle in South Africa. Whites have a choice – all the time. They can side with privilege, with the status-quo – that's the easy option – or they can take the hard position, they can make the decision to resist. Sure, it's hard, it requires sacrifice and all that. You might have to live with fear and tension if you evade. You might not see your friends and family for a while, if you decide to leave. Or you might even end up in jail. But when you weigh it against the fact that freedom fighters who enter this country are hanged for not even committing a crime, it's nothing. I think if one sees it in that context, it's a minimal sacrifice.

also deeply saddened by the loss of many friends who chose to go into exile rather than serve in the SADF. My rejection of apartheid grew. I saw how the government dealt with resistance. I realized that, as a South African, I had to choose where I stood in the struggle against apartheid. At the end of my studies, I knew that I could not go into the SADF.

As a soldier in the SADF, I would be called on to defend a system based on the violence of apartheid. Life under apartheid, for most South Africans, is a battle for survival against the combined oppression of poverty and the laws of the government. South Africans seeking an end to these injustices face the bannings, detentions, shootings and imprisonment used to crush any form of resistance. I cannot defend a society based so inextricably on violence against its citizens.

Throughout my life, one of my fundamental principles has been a desire to serve South Africa and its people. Going into the SADF would so blatantly contradict my ideals, that I could not reconcile this with my conscience and at the same time remain committed to the struggle against apartheid. The consequences of my stand are but a small price to pay when it is compared to the suffering endured daily by the majority of South Africans. My ideals have led me to strive, with many other South Africans, for a new South Africa, free from the hatred of apartheid. The Freedom Charter, drawn up in 1955 by the representatives of millions of South Africans from all walks of life, best reflects these ideals: of a non-racial and democratic South Africa in which the people shall govern. I see my decision to conscientiously object as the best way in which I can serve South Africa and its people.

Untitled poem by Steve Kromberg, read at 'Conscription Action Focus Week', University of Cape Town, May 1984:

Finger curled tight –light squeeze
Upon the hell bent terror bearing down on me
As I lie in the dirt
With my corporal behind me.

It's not until you've had to kill that you understand
he says
Once you've understood, there's no return.

The hell bent terrors bears down on you
from every wall that clothes you and your square bed and shining
floors and screaming corporals.

Who sit with you on Sundays watching rugby.

We love one another, work together, sneak through the grass together
Save each others lives from the hell bent terror bearing down on you.

And soon the night descends with every cigarette glow drawing death
With every careless move
With every doubt which shadow your eyes drawing death from
the hell bent terror bearing down on you.

And if you ever feel drawn to the sound of kwela (township jazz music) on the streetcorner
You're supposed to remember the hell bent terror
You listen no longer
You turn up your memories of the cigarette glow, drawing
death from the black of the night where the cocking of a rifle
travels 500m to the ears of the hell bent terror bearing down on you.

And if you travel through the dry starvation of the homeland homeless
You ought to remember the hell bent terror
But as the terror fades and you re-adjust you may find yourself
listening to the kwela on the streetcorner with the nostalgia of a child crying for a mother removed by the lack of a dompas

And if you walk through the ghetto
On a kwela-living evening
you may well remember
The red glow of a brazier warming the hands of a cold nightwatchman

And you realize
that the hell bent terror is bearing down on you

And you realize
that the hell bent terror is bearing down on you

You may ask yourself
Who is the hell bent terror

And you realize
that the hell bent terror was a poster on the wall of your bungalow

Then the postman arrives
with a brown envelope
You tear it open
You notice the red stamp
You recognize the camp
Your heart quickens
The words glow brighter
The letter swirls
The nation calls
The night descends
You hear the cocking of a rifle
Your cigarette butt glows
and you realize
That the hell bent terror
is bearing down on you.

And you realize
that the hell bent terror was a cardboard cut-out target on the shooting range.

And you begin to wonder
if there isn't someone sitting in Pretoria cutting out hell bent terrors
And posting them on the walls
to scare the children into believing
that if you don't sit tight
when you hear the kwela

The hell bent terror is going to leap off the wall and bear down
on you.

PEACE

THE ROLE OF THE CHURCH

stop the call-up

END CONSCRIPTION CAMPAIGN PEACE FESTIVAL 1985 / TOWARDS A JUST PEACE IN SOUTH AFRICA

NO CALL FOR CIVIL W

End Conscriptio

OH, MY GOD!

AS DICK STANDS IN THE DEVASTATED KRAAL, HE SUDDENLY REMEMBERS **HIS** HOME + **HIS** LITTLE SISTER...

THAT BEEN AS MA EARTH

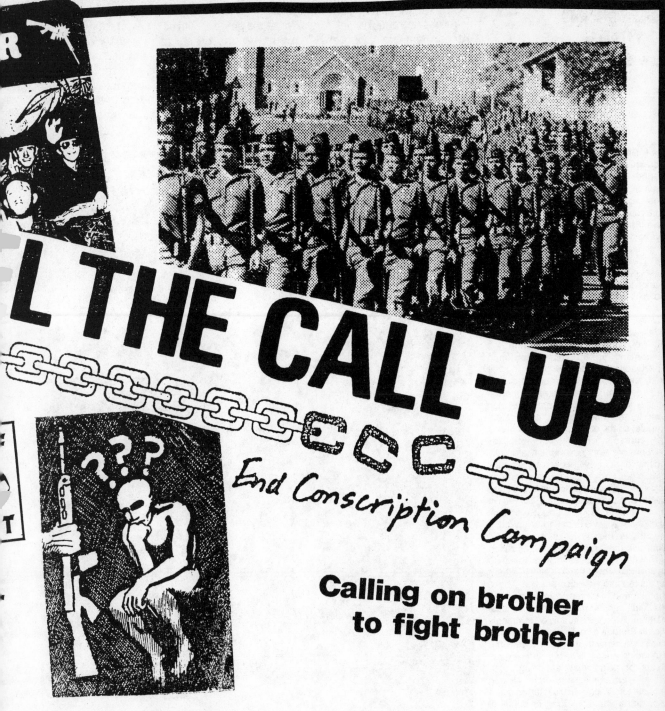

L THE CALL-UP

End Conscription Campaign

Calling on brother to fight brother

Reform
D. Within the System

The potential jail term for 'furthering the aims of a banned organization' is enough to prompt a frantic denial from anyone the government accuses of supporting the African National Congress. Yet there is one organization whose leader has flaunted his alleged ANC links: Chief Gatsha Buthelezi has announced on many a public platform that his mainly Zulu cultural movement, Inkatha, represents the ANC inside the country. As Chief Minister of the KwaZulu homeland, Buthelezi was criticized for 'working within the system', but he claimed that his 'multi-strategy approach' to liberation was sanctioned by none other that the imprisoned ANC leader, Nelson Mandela.

Chief Gatsha Buthelezi, speaking at Jabulani Amphitheatre, Soweto, 21 October 1979: There is an expression which my opponents parrot ad nauseam about 'working within the system'. I want to invite you to look with me at what that great son of Africa, Nelson Rolihlahla Mandela, says on this question. In a book of articles, speeches, and trial addresses entitled *No Easy Walk to Freedom,* Mandela states: 'It is a serious error to regard the boycott as a weapon that must be employed at all times and in all conditions. In this stand there is also the failure to draw the vital distinction between participation in elections by people who accept racial discrimination and who wish to co-operate with the government in the oppression and exploitation of their own people, on the one hand, and participation in such elections, not because of any desire to co-operate with the government, but in order to exploit them in the interest of the liberatory struggle, on the other hand. The former is the course generally followed by collaborators and government stooges, and has for many years been consistently condemned and rejected by the liberation movement. The latter course, provided objective conditions permit, serves to strengthen the people's struggle against reactionary policies of the government.

Ours is the voice of the masses. Inkatha is the largest black organization this country has ever seen. It has taken up the struggle where the ANC left it, after it was forced into an exiled position. Those who demand that I resign my post in the KwaZulu government are political charlatans who are wittingly or unwittingly allies to Pretoria's horrible divide-and-rule tactics. Wherever I go, I hear the resounding voices of the blacks telling me to carry on doing what I am doing. From jail, I hear a message from Nelson Mandela and Walter Sisulu[31] telling me to go on doing what I am doing on behalf of millions of black people. From my brothers in exile I get that same message, all the time. Its ring is not lessening, but is increasing in its crescendo.

In fact, Buthelezi was quoting Mandela totally out of context, for the ANC had never sanctioned participation in the homeland governments. Throughout the 1970s, the ANC had refrained from public criticism of Buthelezi's attempts to boost his own credibility through an implied association with the ANC. The ANC hoped to encourage support from Inkatha's powerful constituency – Buthelezi claimed a membership of 750,000 – without seeming to embrace the homeland leader or his 'non-violent' strategies. But after Buthelezi unashamedly tried to make personal political capital out of a brief private meeting with the ANC in London in 1979, misrepresenting the encounter as a wholehearted ANC endorsement, the ANC responded with a stinging repudiation of Buthelezi as an uninvited 'interlocutor' between the oppressor and the oppressed.[32]

Buthelezi sniped back, branding the ANC as 'opponents of the people', his ire reminiscent of the SABC's anti-'terrorist' jargon.[33] Although Buthelezi continued to exploit ANC tradition – Inkatha's colours were the ANC's black, green and gold – P.W. Botha himself made it clear that Buthelezi poses no threat to the government, describing him as 'a product of policies made possible by this government', and Inkatha as 'his own type of Broederbond for the Zulu people.'[34] And if the government tolerates Buthelezi, the private sector adores him.

Tertius Myburgh, *Sunday Times* **editor, introducing Buthelezi at the 'Sunday Times Businessman of the Year' award banquet, 10 November 1979:** The chairman of the Anglo-American Corporation, Mr Harry Oppenheimer, said only last week: 'As leader of the largest tribe in South Africa, Chief Gatsha Buthelezi is crucial to the future of the business system in this country, as indeed to the political system and the country's future as a whole. One of my reasons for optimism about our future is the calibre of this man and the fact that he has the stature and the backing to prevent fragmentation of black leadership and to uphold evolutionary change without degradation into Marxist decay.'

We, too, place great store on the leadership of Chief Buthelezi and we salute him for his commitment to peaceful change, for his opposition to the deployment of trade as an international political weapon, and for his commitment to the ideal of free enterprise.

Chief Gatsha Buthelezi, delivering the keynote address at a conference on 'Free Enterprise and the Individual', 20 November 1979: I want to make one point quite clear, which is that I personally do not know of any other economic system which man has invented which stimulates development, as development, better than the free enterprise system. This is so, despite the exploitation which this system has entailed for us blacks. There is a role for the free enterprise system, and yet to date Inkatha has received no financial or moral support from organized commerce and industry in South Africa. This fact is an indictment of South Africa's free enterprise system. I am asking simply that free enterprise backs Inkatha to the hilt, as Inkatha rallies behind me and supports me doing that which I am able to do in the performance of my duties.

The Star, **5 November 1979:** Hopefully, an increasingly impotent ANC will turn away from Marxist domination and return to its nationalist cause, adding to Chief Buthelezi's base from which to negotiate without violence. He can speak as a moderate without threats, yet be seen to have the muscle. It may be the last chance to find a peaceful solution.

When the South African government embarked on its process of constitutional reform, Buthelezi formed his own commission of inquiry, an alliance with Natal provincial business interests, in pursuit of a formula for the stability required for the development of the KwaZulu homeland. To the business community, and white liberals worried that the government's cautious reforms were no long-term solution, Buthelezi looked like 'the great white hope': a moderate black who coupled the rhetoric of mass-based – but anti-ANC – politics with the reality of respect for property and investment.

The rapproachment between Inkatha and these liberal whites has a certain logic and inevitability. Both define themselves as opponents of the government while working within government structures: Buthelezi is based in a government-created homeland, while the political home of most white liberals is the Progressive Federal Party. Outspoken criticism from the official white opposition in Parliament is sometimes a source of irritation to the government, but it is far outweighed by the party's role in legitimizing South Africa's 'Western-style Parliamentary democracy'.

The Progressive Federal Party exerts more influence than its small minority in Parliament would indicate, for PFP-supporting mining and industrial concerns own South Africa's English language press (which competes against the government supporting Afrikaans-language press). With heartrending accounts of the brutalities of black resettlement and outraged editorials against discriminatory racial policies, the opposition press has won itself a reputation as a crusading and courageous critic of apartheid – and South Africa the reputation of boasting 'the freest press in Africa'.

However, to the journalists who work for the Anglo-American Corporation-controlled companies that publish South Africa's English language newspapers, the liberal press merely represents the interests of a certain sector of big capital as against the interests of Afrikaner and black nationalism. Three journalists drew on their personal experience in working for the liberal press to illustrate the hypocrisy behind its claims to be a true force of opposition. They represent South Africa's largest-circulation Sunday newspaper, the *Sunday Times;* the major black daily (backed by the same financial interest that controlled the white liberal press),[36] the *Sowetan;* and the now-defunct Rand Daily Mail.

Paratus (SADF magazine), May 1982: The support of all parliamentary parties for South Africa's defence effort was confirmed during the recent Defence Debate in Parliament, as spokesman for the ruling party and opposition parties aired their views, asked questions and made suggestions. The South African Parliament's united front on defence contains sufficient room for the parties to approach the issue openly and critically and, as in any debate in a democratic society, the latest Defence Debate was no exception. The official Opposition's chief Defence spokesman, Mr Harry Schwarz (PFP Yeoville), said the world conflict was not between capitalism and communism, but between democracy and total-itarianism. Democracy meant that people could change their minds about the government they chose, whereas this could not be done in a totalitarian state.

Frederik van Zyl Slabbert, leader of the Progressive Federal Party, at the 1981 party congress: As a party, we believe that military action is necessary to preserve stability, to create a shield behind which we can pursue the goal of a peaceful constitutional change. As a political party operating in Parliament, we accept the necessity for stability in order to bring about constitutional and evolutionary change. Such change has never taken place anywhere in the world under conditions of instability and chaos.

When a young white man comes to me as a politician and asks me, 'Must I do military service?', my answer to him is, 'Yes, you have to do military service so you can prevent those who wish to bring about violent change from being successful, in order that we, behind the protective shield which you can create through your military action, can bring about evolutionary and peaceful change in South Africa.' If I didn't believe this, and if I didn't think this was possible, then I would have no right to be leader of the opposition in Parliament, or to ask people to support me to pursue peaceful and evolutionary change.[35]

Sunday Times reporter: Whenever I wanted to do even just a mildly political feature story, the question that would always be asked in the editorial meeting was: 'But would the lady on the Kensington[37] bus care about this?' If you were writing about the rising cost of living, you wouldn't deal with the cost of mielie meal; you'd start out with the assumption that your audience lived in a white middle-class suburb with two kids and a maid. To the editors of the *Sunday Times,* the lady on the Kensington bus was someone who was apolitical. Her only conception of politics was white politics, and she probably supported the PFP, though not necessarily very enthusiastically. She was more concerned about making sure that her kids got a good education and having a perm and living comfortably and listening to Billy Joel albums – those were her priorities. The whole thing about the *Sunday Times* is that there supposedly is no ideology. The idea is that you can take tea with a member of the Broederbond and with Bishop Tutu; you can hold a conversation with anybody and you never sink to the level of politics or ideology. That's what they claim, you see, but the point is that they're reinforcing the ruling ideology in everything they publish.

What about black politics? How is that covered?

Sunday Times reporter: It isn't seen as relevant; it was certainly not seen as a burning issue for the lady on the Kensington bus. Therefore, it wasn't supposed to intrude too prominently in the paper. Often, if you wrote a piece on labour or on township unrest, they'd tell you to take it to the 'Extra' edition, the black edition. There wasn't space for that kind of thing in South Africa's Number One Family Newspaper.

Sowetan reporter: It's sad to say that even in these times, the white editors of our papers for black readers still think blacks are only interested in sensational news: blood, stabbings, rapes, and then a bit of social events, music and sport.

What happens if you try and write something more political?

Sowetan reporter: I find I often can't even report just the facts of what blacks are saying in political meetings. The editors say it's propaganda, it's heavy, it's against the government, it may clash with this law or that security legislation. The Tutus and Motlanas, they do get coverage, but the more militant people in the trade unions and the student movements, their statements don't make it into the papers because they're too hot.

And then there's the more subtle political bias: most of the liberal press, it's pro-Black Consciousness and anti-Charterist. You see, they know there's little harm in the BC organizations. They're just young groups which have little history of hard struggle, as opposed to the other groupings, which come from a long history of struggle. Even the police, they know that little real action will come out of those BC groups. You can notice this bias in the kinds of slogans that are quoted in the press: you'll see many supporting black power, but we aren't allowed to report it when a meeting opens with ten minutes of slogans and songs praising Oliver Tambo or Joe Slovo. I'm not saying that's totally wrong, because you can get people into trouble with such reporting – or even yourself. You'll find yourself being forced to be a state witness in a court case about what you wrote. Many journalists have suffered that way, spending months and months in jail for refusing to testify. And I have to admit, I do a bit of self-censorship. For example, after a big bomb blast, I had to go to AZAPO for some reaction. I couldn't go to the Charterists for a quote, because I know what the editors would say: 'They're just pro-ANC.' And also for their own benefit, their statements could be seen as being pro-ANC and that could put them into problems.

Where do you find that you get the most valuable information for your stories about black politics?

Sowetan **reporter:** Well, if you are involved with the people, if you make yourself part and parcel of the struggle, you will always get information. You must become involved if you want to get good, strong news. I know what you'll say: 'But journalists are supposed to be objective.' But let me ask you, who is objective? It's just a myth to say that journalists must be objective. I believe that, as a black journalist, I must be in tune with the feelings of the people, and carry out their wishes. As a black journalist – or any journalist who wants to see a change in the system in this country – you do play a role, and that's how you must approach your work, knowing that you could get banned, you could get detained. We have no option; everything in South Africa is politics. You can't run away from politics, and you can't run away from writing politics.

Rand Daily Mail **reporter:** For me, the biggest eye-opener as regards the true nature of the liberal press came when I was covering the mine strikes in 1982.[38] The liberal press portrayed the whole thing as these thousands of black miners going on a 'rampage' and rioting – forcing the mine security guys to shoot in self-defence, a lot like what they see as happening in the black townships with the police. But in fact, the issue was low wage increases. It was a labour matter, a strike. And ten miners were killed in the unrest. And it just so happened that I interviewed a miner in hospital who had twelve bullets in him, three of them in his back. I spoke to another miner who was paralyzed; he'd been shot in the back with buckshot. Which certainly indicates something more about the dynamic of the unrest than had been portrayed in the liberal press, which tended to reproduce the mine owners' version of the events.

So I went back to the newsroom, really keen to break the story of this guy with twelve bullets in him. But the news editor wasn't interested and neither was the deputy editor. And it seemed pretty clear to me that the main reason they wouldn't touch the story was out of a desire to protect the mining interests. Although the reasons they gave were things like: 'This man could have been burning a building or throwing stones. We don't know what circumstances he got shot in.'

It just points up the basic problem with the liberal press: there's an ideological identification with the mine owners. Everyone knows that Anglo has a certain ownership of SAAN (South African Associated Newspaper group) and Argus (newspaper chain). I mean, you rarely read an exposé of mine conditions in the liberal press. There are hundreds of potential stories about mining to be done, in terms of safety conditions and migrant labour. And the fact that those stories are not done is, I think, a reflection of the fact that the liberal press is not prepared to take on the mine owners, the big financial interests, in any big way. Whereas they would go for it on a story about resettlement or detainees, because that's addressing government policy. For the liberal press, their opposition is the government – not big capital. If anything, they identify with big capital.

The impotence of liberal rhetoric is shown up most starkly in the increasing government control over press coverage of guerilla attacks. The government not only defines and restricts the contents of sensitive news stories, but dictates the style as well. A jibe at the pervasive linguistic bias in press reports came in an anonymous black reporter's tongue-in-cheek account of a police counter-insurgency operation.

Sunday Post, **7 April 1980:** Have you ever noticed how so many newspapers go out of their way to convince us all that the commies are coming every time there's an ANC attack in the country? 'Terrorists armed with Russian communist-made AK-47s', etc. Last week I received this report from one of our erstwhile reporters, who shall remain nameless. The objectivity, you will note, is exactly the same:

Policeman armed with capitalist machine guns of European origin and travelling in American capitalist-made vehicles were yesterday conducting a massive manhunt for the men who attacked the Booysens police station on Thursday night. The gang of apartheid law-enforcers – believed to be members of the pro-Western South African Police – vowed to 'get their man'. The leader of the highly-trained band of policemen issued a free enterprise pamphlet calling for the return of Jimmy Kruger[39] as the 'only true, authentic leader of our police force'.

The massive manhunt staged by the SAP is seen as the latest in a series of incidents designed by the organization to gain maximum publicity for its aims. Eyewitnesses described the cops as determined, highly-trained and extremely dangerous. The SAP receives most of its funding, arms and training from countries and organizations under the domination of Washington.

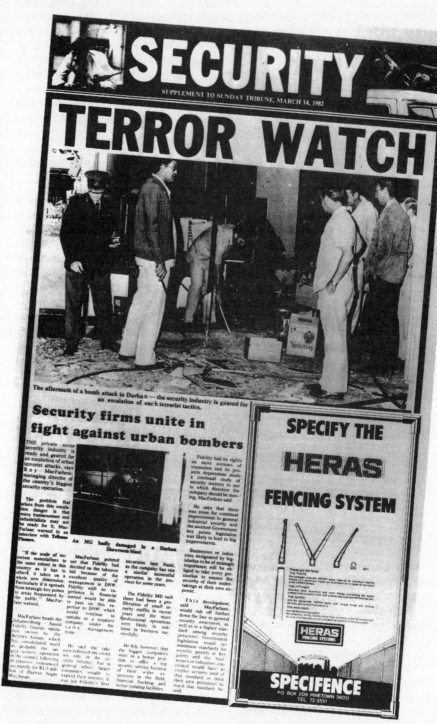

The government could not afford to rely solely on public exhortations about 'objectivity' and 'responsibility' to keep the press in line; confidential guidelines were issued and enforced – not only by the police, but also by the army.

'Guidelines on Statements in Respect of Incidents of Sabotage and Terrorism: The Need for Security Consciousness and Responsible Reporting', confidential memo from the Chief of the Defence Force, August, 1981: While the need exists for the general public to be informed and reassured concerning acts of terrorism, keeping the public informed must be weighed against providing the enemy with intelligence. As a general rule, 'the least said, the better' applies. The stage has been reached, in this escalating war that is being waged by various terrorist organizations against both the infrastructure and the population of the RSA, when everybody concerned, including the public, must be made aware of the vital need for security. The attention of all possible agencies who might be called upon to make public statements with regard to terrorist attacks must be pertinently drawn to this vital need, and they must be given guidance on how to react.

Effectiveness of Security Systems: In order to deny the enemy this type of intelligence,

a) Don't mention how the intruders entered or left the premises concerned (e.g. through unguarded gates, by cutting the fence, etc.)

b) Don't give any information on the effectiveness of the guards, whether they are armed or not, or whether or not they have guard dogs.

c) Don't mention whether the entry had been discovered by accident or not.

d) Don't mention whether the attack was made from inside or outside the security fence.

The Attack Itself: The enemy must not be allowed any intelligence concerning the effects of his attack on the target. Therefore,

a) Don't tell the public what would have happened if some other item had been attacked within the target area, or some other more vulnerable target.

b) Don't tell the public what results the attack achieved, i.e. don't say what specific thing has been damaged or destroyed or the cost of repairs.

c) Don't give information on the effectiveness of the enemy's weapons.

d) Don't give details of enemy casualties, especially if anybody is captured.

e) Don't tell the public what has been mobilized or activated. (Say only that the SA Police are investigating – the SADF must not be mentioned.)

f) Don't publish the fact that the fire brigades from different places had to be called for assistance.

g) Don't publicize the fact that what was attacked was a National Key Point.

h) Don't mention how difficult or easy it was to restore the facility.

i) Don't mention that 'we are not impressed with the enemy's efforts'. This type of intelligence will spur the enemy on to improve his methods.

j) Don't mention the possible access routes that the terrorists followed, e.g. that 'We know that they came through Swaziland from Maputo.'

k) Don't mention exactly where roadblocks have been set up.

The Media: Keeping the public informed is important, but denying the enemy useful intelligence is essential for the safety of the RSA. All the agencies of the media must realize that to provide the enemy with intelligence, either knowingly or unknowingly, is treasonable.

Conclusion: The time has arrived when every citizen, of all races and affiliations, must be made aware of the urgent need to be more security conscious, along with the need to deny the enemy the intelligence that would assist him to replan his strategies and methods in an effort to attack the RSA more effectively. All who receive these guidelines are urged to apply them conscientiously for the benefit of all the inhabitants of this country.

With laws like the Protection of Information Act, the Police Act, the Official Secrets Act, and the Internal Security Act, the South African government has almost every conceivable legal means to control news and information. In this era of reform, the government is no longer looking to further expand its legislative arsenal to silence its opponents.[40] On the contrary, the credibility of the government's reforms depends on the image of a healthy opposition from within the system – expressed in the context of what the government has called 'consensus journalism'.

Minister of Constitutional Development and Planning, Chris Heunis, *Sunday Times*, 26 August 1984: The new South African constitution represents a development away from the traditional Westminster - style 'winner - takes - all' democracy, towards a new kind of politics, with the emphasis on consensus and co-operation between the different groups in South African society. In other words, politics must not be perceived as zero-sum ('the one's gain is the other's loss') ethnic competition, but as competitive co-operation based on common grounds, from which all can benefit. In this kind of society, the media should contribute towards this perception. This means that more emphasis must be placed on commonalities and co-operation than on differences and conflict. A new media style is necessary to complement and reflect the new political style. The media in South Africa played a big role in bringing about necessary reform. I believe that in future they will continue to probe, to question and to help the peoples of South Africa to reach consensus.

PRESS IS GAGGED

READ LEAFLETS, POSTERS THE WALL—NEWSPAPER

Reform

E. The System Looks West

Sunday Times, **20 January 1984:** The worse the news, the higher the gold price. The nastier the Russians, the richer we get. A revolution in Iran is worth, say, a billion rands. An invasion of Afghanistan sends the gold price up another $100 an ounce, and that's worth another billion or two. The basic principle of life in South Africa is best summed up (oddly enough) in the old Marxist slogan: the worse, the better.

When all goes well with the world, South Africa has a miserable time. The newspapers are filled with abuse. The United Nations votes against us 150 to 0 and people all talk about sanctions and write books asking how long can they survive. But when times turn sour, things look up. That's when South Africa gets even. So, as the clouds of war gather, we must remember to make hay while the sun shines. This is our day, the day of the polecat.

US President Ronald Reagan, in a television interview, 14 March 1981: As long as there's a sincere and honest effort being made, based on our own experience in our own land, it would seem to me that we should be trying to be helpful. Can we abandon a country that has stood behind us in every war we've ever fought, a country that strategically is essential to the free world? It has production of minerals we must have, and so forth. I just feel that if we're going to sit down at a table and negotiate with the Russians, surely we can keep the door open and continue to negotiate with a friendly nation like South Africa.

'They need us more than we need them' – that is the brave public face, but the reality is that South Africa craves approval and support from the West. While the South Africans spent the 1970s concocting ambitious and illicit international influence-buying schemes (ultimately derailed by the Information Scandal revelations),[41] by 1980 the conservatives were in power in Europe and the United States, and South Africa was back in favour as a strategic western ally. Shortly after taking office in early 1981, Ronald Reagan gave South Africa the most enthusiastic public endorsement it had ever received from the US government.

Ronald Reagan had his facts a bit confused: far from supporting the US in World War II, many of South Africa's leaders were interned for their pro-Nazi sympathies. Behind the President's hazy sense of history lay a calculated anti-Soviet counter-insurgency strategy for the subcontinent, based on patient support for Pretoria's reforms – euphemistically known as 'constructive engagement.'

SABC, 2 December 1981: There is clear evidence today of a more consolidated and constructive western approach to South Africa. The trend was initiated by the Thatcher government in Britain and strongly reinforced by the Reagan government in the United States. Now it is being followed by other leading members of the western community. There would appear to be two reasons for the development. First, there is the realization that stability in this region, access to its raw materials, and protection of the lines of communication which it commands, are necessary for the security of the West. Secondly, there is greater appreciation today of South Africa's problems, and of the measures being undertaken to resolve them.

Last month, America's United Nations Ambassador, Mrs Jeane Kirkpatrick, charged the world body with using the human rights issue as a bludgeon, particularly against South Africa, Israel and non-communist Latin American states. On Monday, the American representative, Mr Kenneth Adelman, criticized the General Assembly for having refused, since 1976, to allow South Africa to take part in its deliberations. He spoke of the futility of isolation, and declared that the world body was shying away from, instead of facing, the political realities in South Africa. He told the Assembly that the United States supported people inside and outside the country who supported peaceful evolution. He referred to the labour reforms that had resulted from the Wiehahn Commission, to the removal of many discriminatory measures, and to the creation of the President's Council, and he called for an honest dialogue.

On the same day, the British ambassador in South Africa, Sir John Leahy, spoke in Johannesburg. He said that in his two years in the country he had learned that the internal situation was far more complex than it appeared from a distance. It did not fit into any familiar political pattern, but was a part Third World and part First World. A great deal had been achieved in South Africa, and he expressed the view that it had much to offer the rest of the continent. He echoed the opinion of Dr Chester Crocker, America's Assistant Secretary of State for African Affairs, that the Republic is the key to the development of the region. This is the evidence of a more consolidated and constructive western approach to security and progress in the subcontinent, and to the protection in this quarter of the globe of vital western interests.

South Africa proudly claims credit for shaping this revisionist western view of the apartheid state, in large part through the intensive lobbying efforts of organizations like the quasi-government, private sector-funded South Africa Foundation.

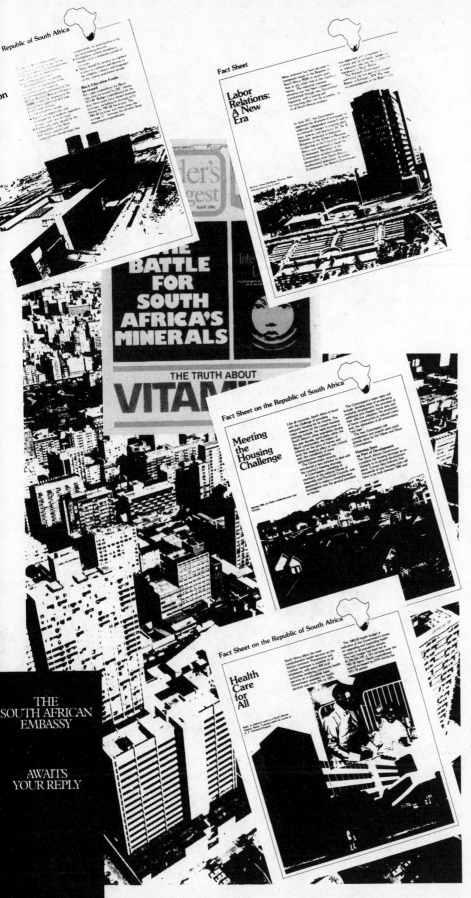

THE SOUTH AFRICAN EMBASSY

AWAITS YOUR REPLY

SABC, 21 March 1982:

Announcer Cliff Saunders: What is it that the West wants of South Africa, specifically? Is it a one man, one vote system?

South Africa Foundation Director-General Peter Sorour: In our experience, it is not. I cannot say that I have ever come across anybody in a responsible political or economic position who has asked for that.

Cliff Saunders: Well, then, what do they expect?

Peter Sorour: I would say that the term that they would use would be to see 'greater justice' in South Africa. They see a lot of injustice in the racially discriminatory laws that are on the statute book in South Africa. We get it stated in so many words: 'If only we can see a steady progress towards an elimination of those human injustices, we would not ask any more of you.'

Cliff Saunders: John Chettle is Director of the Foundation's Washington office. Mr Chettle, how do you interpret the American policy towards South Africa, which has been described as one of 'constructive engagement?'

John Chettle: One of the exciting things about this policy is that, for the very first time, I think, an American administration has decided that it is in American interests to have a relationship with South Africa, which is one way South Africa can emerge from the isolation in which it has been.

Cliff Saunders: This question of constructive engagement, does it presuppose pressure on South Africa to produce a one man, one vote system in the country?

John Chettle: No, it doesn't. There is a fairly clear recognition that South Africa is going to have some kind of government which is either federal or confederal, that there has to be some kind of different structure to adjust to the realities of South Africa.

Cliff Saunders: The Foundation's policy has alway been one of identifying future policy-makers. To what extent have you been successful over the past years?

John Chettle: A great triumph, really, has been how successful we were in identifying the policy-makers that have taken high office in the Reagan administration. Every single significant major policy-maker in the Reagan administration, from the President on downwards, was in contact with the Foundation in the year before Mr Reagan's election. So this has been one of the things that we have been most happy about.

Cliff Saunders: How extensive is future anti-apartheid action likely to be?

John Chettle: It will be quite extensive, but one of the things that I am trying to emphasize is that this is very dependent on perceptions of deterioration in South Africa. Our opponents have a vested interest in seeing South Africa as continuing to deteriorate, continuing to apply measures that are unappealing to the Americans, and so on. And we can, by reform, undercut a good deal of that opposition. The thing that they really fear is the signs of reform in South Africa, because it makes them irrelevant.

Western investment in South Africa totals nearly $30 billion, and provides technology vital to the country's economic development and military security. Twelve hundred British firms, 375 US companies and sixty-five transnational corporations account for 85 per cent of South Africa's foreign investment, while earning profit margins among the highest in the world.[42] Foreign banks play a vital role in bailing South Africa out of economic and political crises: in 1982, the US helped South Africa borrow $1.2 billion from the International Monetary Fund. If any of these ties were suddenly cut, the effect would be far more damaging than either South Africa or the West care to admit.

Classified cable from the US Consulate in Johannesburg to the US State Department in Washington DC, revealed by the black American lobby, TransAfrica, 30 July 1983: According to information we have recently obtained, US financial involvement in South Africa is much greater than we previously believed. The total is probably in excess of $14.6 billion. This includes direct investment, bank lending, and portfolio investment, particularly in gold mining shares. The magnitude of this involvement places the current disinvestment debate raging in the US in a new perspective. US investment in South Africa is probably much more significant than the 20 per cent of total foreign investment in South Africa that we generally quote. All of this suggests that the potential for US disinvestment could be more important to the South African economy than we had previously assumed.

Under mounting pressure from anti-apartheid lobbies, western investors justify their lucrative involvement in South Africa with claims that they promote western-style equality and opportunity for their employees, regardless of race. Less than half the American and European corporations in South Africa subscribe to codes of conduct said to guarantee fair employment practices and desegregation of the workplace, so in 1984, the Reagan administration began urging endorsement of the 'Sullivan Principles' (the American equivalent of the EEC Investment Code) in a bid to counter growing demands for foreign investors to pull out of South Africa. Another justification for the western role in the apartheid economy is that disinvestment would hurt blacks more than whites. This is also the South African government's line, although it prefers to let the argument be advanced by blacks.

The Star, 7 September 1981: The Deputy Vice-President of the black-led Trade Council of South Africa, Mrs Lucy Mvubelo, has appealed to Australia not to seek the isolation of the Republic from the world community. Mrs Mvubelo is in Australia as a guest of the Australian-South Africa Association, an organization of local businessmen who want to strengthen ties with South Africa. Australian firms, she said, should not withdraw from South Africa. ' That would be unfair to the black man who has nothing else to do but sell his labour.' The Association's secretary, Mr Allan Dexter, a public relations consultant whose clients include South African Airways and the South African Broadcasting Corporation, interrupted a stormy press conference in Sydney at the weekend to assure journalists, 'Lucy is not an Aunty Tom.' Mrs Mvubelo said she was 'not a puppet of the South African government'.

The response of the black majority in South Africa to that line of reasoning is hard to gauge, for publicly opposing foreign investment is a crime punishable by a minimum five-year prison sentence. Nevertheless, Mvubelo and others who identify with the pro-investment line come in for heavy criticism from fellow blacks.

By 1984, the ferocity of the attacks against Mvubelo's anti-disinvestment campaign had escalated: her home was petrol-bombed twice by the 'South African Suicide Squad', a Soweto group that has repeatedly attacked government 'collaborators'.

The loss of foreign investment would be a blow to South Africa, but cutting international trade links could be far more damaging, as the South African economy depends on the export of gold and the import of oil. The threat of economic sanctions against South Africa – periodically endorsed by the United Nations General Assembly, then vetoed by major western powers in the Security Council – is chilling, for the international oil and arms embargoes have been costly enough. Since the Arab-controlled oil and petroleum exporting countries refuse to sell to mineral-rich but oil-poor South Africa, it is obliged to buy all its oil at inflated prices on the spot market, through multinational middlemen, or via clandestine deals with countries which officially ban sales to the apartheid state. By the same token, the South African military devotes much of its budget to circumventing the UN prohibition on weapons trade with South Africa.

South Africa responds to the sanctions threat with bravado, claiming that the arms embargo has actually been a boon that has spurred the development of a self-sufficient domestic arms industry, now capable of manufacturing world class weapons like the 155-millimetre G-5 gun.

SABC, 30 March 1982: The international arms embargo against this country has achieved precisely the opposite of what it was intended to achieve. The remarkable story of the development of the G-5 partially reveals the technological consequences that the arms embargo has had. Among the achievements have been this field gun, the R-4 rifle, and electronically advanced navy strike craft fitted with guided missiles, which have been described by military experts as making South Africa a world leader in artillery design and manufacture. Overall, the country is now ranked tenth in the world in weapons production, and last year became a net exporter of arms. In fact, the boycott has been, according to no less an authority than Dr Chester Crocker, an utter failure. He believes its only effect has been to turn South Africa into what he calls 'an important regional military power in global terms'. In virtually every sphere of military operations in which the country may realistically expect to be involved at any time, it is more or less self-sufficient in its requirements, and vastly better prepared than before the boycott.

While South Africa billed the G-5 as a totally indigenous product – 'battle-tested' in the Angolan war zones – the gun was actually foreign-made. The required technology, high-powered artillery shells, and the licence to produce the guns were all supplied by a weapons plant that straddled the US-Canadian border, in a sanctions-busting operation assisted by the CIA.[43] What is more, the G-5 was no fluke: South Africa produces missiles based on Israeli models, armoured cars manufactured under French licence, and tanks modelled on British designs, as western powers continue to supply South Africa with security equipment, electronics and computers, in defiance of the arms embargo. In some areas, such as sophisticated aircraft, missile guidance systems, and precision data-processing equipment, South Africa is completely dependent on foreign imports.[44] The full extent of South Africa's arms trade may never be known, because the military-industrial complex is shielded by a barrage of legislation: the Defence Act, the National Supplies Act, the Armaments Development Act and the Arms and Ammunition Act.

Another international forum from which South Africa is barred is competition in the Olympics and other world sporting events. Sport may not seem as important as arms or investments, but the effect of ostracizing this sports-mad country cannot be underestimated. The government has stepped up lobbying for readmission to the international sports scene on the basis that sport in South Africa is now completely integrated. With the aid of private capital, South Africa tried to buy its way back into international sport, by paying sportsmen and women huge sums of money to break the anti-apartheid boycott and tour the country. The response of the government's opponents, expressed through the non-racial South African Council on Sport, is that there can be 'no normal sport in an abnormal society', so all international sporting links should be shunned.

South African Council on Sport pamphlet opposing the 1983 West Indian Cricket Tour of South Africa, entitled 'Halt All Apartheid Tours – 10 Questions to You "Honorary Whites" ':[45]

1) Who invited you? (oppressors/oppressed)

2) Why did you defy the UN and the international boycott and blacklist, your own governments, and the wishes of the oppressed?

3) Is money the root of all evil?

4) Are South African black children dying of malnutrition?

5) Do blacks have any social, political and economic rights?

6) Will you guys, as black as you are, be willing to: carry passes, live in any South African slum, travel 20 kilometres to work in a stuffy bus, study gutter education, get imprisoned if you open your mouth, be called an 'agitator' when you demand basic human rights, be a migrant worker in your own country, be separated from your family by influx control?

7) Have you ever heard of the South African Cricket Board? (SACOS-affiliated, which condemned the tour)

8) Have you ever thought of what your fat cheques could be used for: building houses, feeding hungry children, creating jobs, better education?

9) Have you ever heard of these terms: herrenvolk (master race), blood money, oppression and exploitation, bridge-building?

10) What are your priorities: cricket mania, justice and equality, exploitation, nice times, nothing?

The quest for western approval extends beyond the sports field, to the stage, as South African entrepreneurs entice entertainers with big financial incentives to break the cultural boycott and perform in South Africa and its homelands. The government also sponsors free tours for foreigners, although these are usually shunned by all but fellow members of the international 'Pariah Club': Israel, Taiwan and Chile. The biggest catch, however, is the permanent settler. Immigrants lured by high wages and generous settlement allowances are warmly welcomed – as long as they are white – for they ease South Africa's skills shortage and boost its credibility. Britain has been the traditional source of immigrants, but the 1980s brought new waves of settlers, from Rhodesians fleeing black rule in Zimbabwe to Polish refugees recruited by the South African government and by industry.

Sunday Times **magazine, 5 February 1984:** Around 30,000 white Zimbabweans and 3500 Poles have settled in South Africa during the past two years. They have come with different objectives – the Poles in search of a new world, while the Rhodesians hope to revive their old life in more promising surroundings. For many of them, South Africa is attractive because of, rather than despite, her internationally unpopular political policies.

'South Africa is very far away and very anti-communist,' one Polish refugee told a reporter in Europe. ('We listened to the BBC and the Voice of America. We had heard that South Africa was a beautiful country and that it was a paradise for white people).'[46]

'There is at least a chance here that white people can go on living in Africa, even if we have to fight for that right all over again,' says a young ex-Rhodesian, who went straight from school into the army, in the land of his birth.

Lieutenant-General Peter Walls, former commander Rhodesian army, is a regular guest at Polish community functions in South Africa. 'We think he is one of the greatest living soldiers,' says Edward Devirion, chairman of the Polish Association in South Africa. Walls is equally complimentary about the Poles: 'They make excellent citizens, and can never be accused of looking back and whining about the past,' he says.

Like Walls, most Rhodesian immigrants are tight-lipped about South African politics. The recent constitutional referendum created an overwhelming sense of déjà vu and a weary cynicism about moderate reform. 'If anything short of one man, one vote satisfies South African blacks, I'll be the happiest man alive,' says a former Rhodesian businessman. 'But I fully expect to go through the whole thing again – the call-ups, the fear, the daily death lists – until eventually, we all face the crunch of having nowhere to go'.

Administrative Memo Number 1 of 1982, from the Department of Finance, Office of the Director-General, to Commissioners, Secretaries and heads of the departments of: Customs and Excise, Inland Revenue, Financial Policy, the Treasury and the Mint: Recruitment of Trained Foreign Personnel: Polish Refugees. The Commissioner for Administration has indicated that he is possibly in a position to acquire the services of Polish citizens who have left Poland. In light of these circumstances, it would be appreciated if you would indicate if you have suitable vacant posts available.

The fact that white immigrants are enthusiastically recruited while blacks born in South Africa are deported to barren homelands, and that the West imposed sanctions to help anti-communist whites in Poland, but not on behalf of blacks in South Africa, is all too much for many blacks to stomach.

Letters to the *Rand Daily Mail,* **3 February 1982:** When I first heard of the Polish uprisings and tribulations, my heart was filled with sympathy towards these people, but now I envy them. These people, I feel, deserve any black man's sympathy, as long as they stay there in Europe, or fly over to America or Australia, but once they come to South Africa, they come to make worse the 'white problem' which we blacks are already faced with. Little do these queueing people know that their destination is a country of 25 million voteless, voiceless and powerless people, a country where a strike like the one they have successfully staged in communist Poland would put them all behind bars. Not one of them would reach an embassy gate to ask for a travel document to some merciful country. – Polelo Mavule, Durban.

It has become almost a way of life for South Africa to help Polish immigrants and offer them good jobs and comfortable housing. With this goes almost R3000 for them to 'settle down' in this country. The irony of it all is that blacks, born and bred in this country, are not given such opportunities. Under the present state of affairs, where there is such an acute shortage of housing and employment for blacks, how can this country still manage to offer housing and employment to the outside world, whilst people who actually belong to this country are denied these basic rights? – Leeto Wilfred Semenya, Atteridgeville.

No matter how great South Africa's success in wooing immigrants, investment, sporting or cultural ties, the government still needs a moral argument to counter critics of apartheid. There must be an explanation for the visiting businessman, rugby player or pop star when unrest erupts after a squatter settlement is razed or when guerillas attack a police station. The government's simplistic rationalization, proclaimed incessantly on the SABC and parroted by whites, can be summed up in six words: 'It's happening all over the world.'

SABC, 12 May 1981: The recent unrest in the Coloured township of Reiger Park is a situation which is by no means unique to South Africa. The black community that rioted in the London suburb of Brixton last month was protesting essentially over its powerlessness in the face of what it sees as official callousness and private white exploitation. Similar motives were attributed to the rioting in Miami last May, over an influx of Cubans. In multi-ethnic societies everywhere, the pattern grows increasingly familiar. Minority communities, feeling their living space and standards to be threatened, demand political redress in the only manner available to them in the unitary state, by having recourse to violence. For the past several decades, all over the world, community insecurity has been the chief cause for national civil unrest.

White man interviewed after 1983 Durban bombing: It's urban terrorism, it's happening all over the world. You've got the same thing going on all over the world, so it's nothing unique. I suppose it will continue to happen, let's hope it doesn't get much worse. But I don't think it's any worse than what's happening in the rest of the world.

SABC interview with President P.W. Botha, 22 June 1981:
SABC announcer: Would you describe the South African situation as a revolutionary one at the moment?
P.W. Botha: It is exploited by revolutionary elements. The same elements are operating in other countries of the world. They exploit the situations which they can apply for their own purposes, and we know that subversion and terrorism are the products of Marxist expansionism in the world.
SABC announcer: But is the situation completely under control?
P.W. Botha: It is under control, but that does not mean that we won't have repetitions. All countries are experiencing problems to maintain order and orderly government, and South Africa is no exception in this regard.
SABC announcer: What do you say to statements that the unrest has been partly caused by a so-called unjust society and misuse of power?
P.W. Botha: No, I don't agree with that. There is no just society in the world. This side of the grave, there is no just society. South Africa is a society in which you have religious freedom, in which you have an independent judicial tradition, in which you have, to a large extent, a free press, in which you have many other privileges of a well-organized society. So I cannot agree with that statement that we are experiencing problems because we are an unjust society. And let me say, even in other societies like America, you have your Miamis. In London, you have bomb explosions as well. Now, surely these are not proofs that America or Great Britain are unjust societies?

The South African government tries to have it both ways: it claims that its light is not unique, yet in response to calls to end apartheid, it argues that its nique and complex problems require a uniquely South African solution. The fact at the West is willing to let this contradiction go unchallenged is not lost on the overnment's opponents inside South Africa. While South Africa's white rulers ay be looking West, the black majority is beginning to look in another direction.

Soweto students, Siphiwe:
I think that people regard the West as an enemy, because they believe that the West has invested in this country and the West is enjoying the fruits of apartheid. So the West has made up its mind that it will protect and in fact support the status quo and uphold the system. As a result, people are inclined to see the East as an ally.

abulani: When arms caches are found somewhere in the country, always the press and government will speak in terms of 'Russian-made' grenades or 'Eastern bloc' arms, with everything coming from the East. So people generally interpret this as the East supplies us the arms to resist with – so the East therefore must be good.

eter: In fact, the West is killing our struggle. For instance, Americans, they are having so many investments in South Africa, and that means they won't want to see a dramatic change in this country. They'll always try first to secure their investments. And this is a factor that delays our struggle. It's a pity, because I think the only other thing that shall bring change in this country – besides, of course, the armed struggle – is if these outside countries can start boycotting South Africa in sports and economy.[47] But so far, it seems that they are not too keen. They would rather keep their investments secure.

en: The people see the United States and Britain as having a hand in their oppression because South Africa always goes to these countries for help. And, of course, people know that the West supports South Africa with arms and that type of thing. So that people regard the West as a friend of their enemy, and you know that a friend of your enemy cannot be your friend.

4 Repression

A. Aliens

South Africa's new 'tri-racial' constitution mentions its black majority only once. The sole reference to the Africans who make up nearly three-quarters of the country's population is contained in this clause: 'the control and administration of black affairs shall vest in the President'. Thus the government's reforms entrench control of the black majority not only by denying Africans any power in the central government, but by maintaining that they have no right to demand any power. The constitution simply refines and enshrines long-standing apartheid policy: whites dominate, Coloureds and Indians are now incorporated, Africans employed in the urban areas are tolerated, while the homelands serve as dumping grounds for the millions of South Africa's people who will never be accommodated by the government's reforms. Africans must still carry the hated 'pass' that proves they have permission to be in the city to sell their labour, and hundreds of thousands of yearly pass-law prosecutions ensure South Africa the continued distinction of having the highest per capita prison population in the western world.[1]

Rand Daily Mail, **13 April 1984:** Pitched somewhere between a whisper and a murmur, the pass laws grind their way inexorably through the lives of those who come to the Commissioner's Courts at Number 15 Market Street on any weekday. Benches are packed with anxious relatives and friends bringing cash for the fine, the reference book or 'pass' to show the commissioner, or to take 'custody' of a relative who must return to his place of origin.

There are 118 cases today, in about four and a half hours – about 26 cases an hour, one every 2.3 minutes. A name is called. 'William Mane!' His case is real – his name has been changed. Now the accused is in the dock. The wheels of Section 10(4) of the Blacks (Urban Areas) Consolidation Act of 1945 and Section 1(a)(II) of the Blacks (Abolition of Passes and Co-ordination of Documents) Act of 1952, roll once more in the rapid, whisper-murmur of the Commissioner's Court. Mane has pleaded guilty to being in the area for longer than 72 hours without a permit, and to failing to produce his reference book. The Commissioner delivers his verdict: I find you guilty on both counts. Have you anything to say in mitigation of sentence?

Mane: 'I was in South Hills to see my mother.'
Commissioner: 'Where was your pass?'
Mane: In my jacket. In another room.'
Commissioner: 'Did the police give you a chance to fetch your pass?'
Mane: 'No, they took me by the belt and pushed me into the truck.'
Commissioner: 'Cautioned and discharged.'

Mane's plea, conviction, evidence in mitigation and caution takes two and a half minutes. He now has a criminal record.

Annexure B to BA-403 (additional conditions) from an official contract labour form: Any inservice registration of a person mentioned in Annexure A will be refused or cancelled if:
a) Such a person does not occupy accommodation approved by the Labour Officer;
b) Such a person's wife or family accompanies him to the (Cape) Peninsula;
c) Such a person's wife or family is found to be illegally present in the Peninsula;
d) Such a person travels to the Peninsula by means of unauthorized transport;
e) It is found that such a person did not return to his home address after the termination of his previous contract of service.

Dr Piet Koornhof, Minister of Co-operation and Development, at a Johannesburg Press Conference, 30 October 1980: If you haven't got a measure of control over undue squatting, then there would be no way in which you can maintain order, and the point is that without a measure of control, you would not be able to maintain stability and peace. The fact of the matter is it cannot possibly be in the black man's interest if there is not a measure of control so that you can accommodate people properly, because otherwise they will be subjected to squalor and it will not be possible to improve the quality of life. Is that clear? This is not a problem specific to this part of the world. This is a universal problem. There's a lot of squatting in other parts of Africa, a lot of squatting in other parts of the world.

The homelands evolved as labour reserves for the mines and farms, and a means of subsistence agriculture for the migrant worker's family, to supplement his low wages. In this era of reform, the homelands serve less of an economic function – importing labour – than a political one: exporting unemployment from the white areas. The granting of 'independence' to underdeveloped, impoverished and remote rural areas improves South Africa's black social welfare statistics by transferring (on paper, at least) embarrassingly high rates of joblessness, infant mortality and disease on to the black governments of the homelands. Eight and a half million Africans lost their South African citizenship when Transkei, Bophuthatswana, Venda and Ciskei gained 'independence', and millions more would meet the same fate if Pretoria cut its ties with the rest of the homelands. The only legal means of escaping the deprivation of the homelands is through contracted labour, which allows a migrant (usually male) to see his family for only a few days each year. The women and children from the homelands who defy these laws and attempt to join their husbands in the cities are seen by the South African government as 'squatters'.

Despite the government's efforts to apply the 'It's happening all over the world' thesis to the squatter problem, the reality is that South Africa's squatters are unique. Their illegal migration to the cities is a logical development of – and protest against – the unparalleled policy of influx control. The women and children in the country's oldest and largest squatter settlements in Cape Town did not flee the homelands of Transkei and Ciskei, travel hundreds of miles, build plastic tents and tin shacks, and brave constant police raids out of a vague attraction for the bright lights of the city. They saw that course as their only means of survival.

Squatters at Cape Town's Crossroads and Nyanga Bush shantytowns, Gxidi Ziphumele:
I wouldn't like to go back to Transkei because there are no jobs there, no jobs at all. I've got six children, all schooling. It's useless to go to Transkei when you haven't got money. Useless. All you can do is steal from other people, because people are starving there. To a man who has got his children, his family, it's very bad to just go and sit there.

But the government says that things are changing.

Gxidi Ziphumele: I know, that is an old story. They always give some promises and then don't fulfil those promises. Nothing has changed except that it's worse now.

Mama Luke: Every bus from Transkei is full of these people escaping (President) Matanzima. Why should they come to town if there was any change for the better there? I am not interested in Transkei because that 'freedom' over there is only for the ministers and their families. It is not for us.

Miriam Ntloye: In the Transkei we will only starve. The children will become ill and the medical facilities there are not enough to help them. They put sick children four to a bed at the hospitals there, and a friend got her dead baby back in a cardboard box.[2]

Edward Mini: There is nothing there in the homeland – no factory, just dusty roads. There's no food, the sun is too hot, and there is no rain. I think I better forget about my homeland and look for my future.

Johnson Ngxobongwana: If the government says we should go back to the homelands, why don't the Afrikaners go back to Holland? This is our country where we were born and bred. We will not move.[3]

The government's response to the Cape Town squatters – burning their shelters, jailing women and children, and blaming outside agitators – was no aberration, but part of a process of repression and control that lay at the heart of the apartheid system.

The government's barriers against 'illegals' had traditionally been administrative, from pass law prosecutions to bulldozing of shelters. The 1981 Cape Town squatter camp raids saw new kinds of barriers erected for the first time, as thousands of residents of Nyanga Bush camp were 'deported' to the homelands under the 'Regulation of Admission of Persons to the Republic Act', and prevented from returning by police roadblocks.

By 1984, this trend towards treating 'illegal' blacks as 'aliens' had been made into law. Under the Aliens and Immigration Laws Amendment Act, blacks must pay a passport control officer to obtain a temporary permit to enter 'white South Africa', and any 'alien' who is deported is forbidden to re-enter the country. Any South African who offers a job or a place to live or does business with an 'alien' is subject to a two-year prison term or a R5000 fine. With this new weapon, the government declared war on all the defiant squatters of the Cape.

SABC, 26 August, 1981: The Minister of Co-operation and Development, Dr Koornhof, said the government was facing an organized threat to law and order with the squatter situation at Nyanga. In an interview with the SABC, Dr Koornhof said it was a confrontation situation and the government had no alternative but to take firm action. He said there were already 20,000 blacks who were legally in the Cape Peninsula,[4] but who were all out of work. Squatting was a complex problem and the government had been trying for years to find a solution, using the best modern and scientific means at its disposal. The Prime Minister said the squatting at Nyanga would not have occurred if it had not been organized and orchestrated by people who were trying to exploit the plight of the squatters.

Argus, **21 August 1981:** Transkei's borders with South Africa have been sealed off to prevent the Nyanga squatters, who were sent back to the homeland this week, returning to South Africa. More than 1000 squatters arrested in a massive dawn swoop by police at the 'No Name' camp at Nyanga on Wednesday were put into 17 railway buses and transported back to Transkei. The police set up a roadblock at the usually uncontrolled border crossing into Transkei near Queenstown and stopped every bus, truck and car coming into South Africa from Transkei. The buses were met by a large contingent of police, railway officials and border post personnel. Railway officials referred to the squatters as 'prisoners'. The buses were escorted as far as the border by police vehicles from Cape Town, including two lorries carrying a contingent of police in riot dress.

Residents of 'Old Crossroads' squatter settlement: They can bring in the army and shoot us and then take our dead bodies to Khayelitsha and bury them there. We are here for the purpose of seeking work to be able to live. That place is just like a chicken run, with barbed wire all around it, and it's too far out of town. We will not move, even if they bring soldiers to force us out.[5]

Dr George Morrison, Deputy Minister of Co-operation and Development, at the September 1983 Cape National Party Congress: Crossroads has become a symbol of provocation and of threatening the government. That symbolism must be destroyed at all costs. We will not allow or tolerate the erection of illegal squatter huts anywhere in the Cape Peninsula. We are always on the lookout for squatters erecting illegal huts, and we are trying to eradicate this dismal facet of our life as far as we can. A full unit of riot police is deployed at Crossroads day and night to try to stop this sort of thing.

Mogopa villager: They did not discuss with us. They just come. They come in the middle of the night, all armed with revolvers. They come and surround your house as though you killed somebody. Then they force you to leave your house without you knowing why, how you must go. But you must accept because they already break your house. They must be great cowards to come and surround people when they are all fast asleep to do these things.[8]

After years of suffering police raids, demolition of their camps and deportation from Cape Town, squatters developed a new tactic of building shelters each night, then dismantling them in the early morning before the police arrived to burn them. The government responded in late 1983 with a surprise midnight blitz on the Cape shantytowns using spotlights and teargas to aid the demolition and arrests. Then the government announced what came to be known as its 'final solution': all Africans in the Cape – 'legal' squatters as well as blacks in existing townships – were to be resettled in a single, sprawling commuter township intended to house some 300,000 blacks by the turn of the century. This mini-homeland for Cape Town's African workers was dubbed 'Khayelitsha' (Xhosa for 'our new home'), but those who were told to move to the desolate settlement – bordered by the sea and an army camp, with only one road and railway link to Cape Town, 40 kilometres away – have vowed to resist the biggest single removal in South Africa's history.

Squatters are not the only people forcibly moved by the government's army and police: Africans whose labour is no longer needed on white farms, as well as settled black communities living on freehold land, are also targeted for expropriation and removal. More than 3.5 million people have been uprooted and resettled by the government since the early 1960s, with another two million still threatened with removal before Pretoria is satisfied that all 'black spots' have been erased from the apartheid map.[6]

While the government claims that its reforms have brought a new policy of 'consultation' and 'voluntary removals',[7] the experience of the 300 families of Mogopa village in the western Transvaal shows that coercion is still the chief tactic. When the villagers refused to be moved to a dusty, far-away patch of the Bophuthatswana homeland, the government simply destroyed their schools, churches and clinics, poured diesel into their water pumps, suspended their bus service, and stopped paying pensions. Some families moved 'voluntarily', rather than watch their village disintegrate, but two-thirds of Mogopa continued to resist removal. Declaring Mogopa an 'operational area', armed police cordoned off the village with barricades, warned people, over a loudhailer in the dark, not to leave their homes, and beat those who ventured outside.

The South African government's reforms are specifically designed to nurture a class of blacks with 'something to lose', yet removals have not spared the relatively privileged class of black landowners. The transformation of a man named Saul Mkhize, from moderate to martyr, is one such case of alienation and radicalization. Mkhize's ancestors bought a farm in the eastern Transvaal before the 1913 Land Act barred blacks from buying white land, and had successfully farmed several plots (with the help of tenant farmers) for generations. When the government announced that the farm was to be demolished and the landowners dispossessed and deported to their respective homelands, Mkhize did not mount a protest – he wrote the government a series of polite letters.

Two days after writing his final plea to the government, Mkhize was dead — shot by a policeman at a meeting called to discuss the threatened removal. Mkhize's killer was acquitted of murder, but to thousands of people who flocked to Driefontein for Mkhize's funeral, he was killed because he would not be co-opted by the system.

Another example of the government alienating the very people it is trying to woo is seen in the nearly one million removals of Coloured and Indian people, conducted under the Group Areas Act. This law determines where the different racial groups can live and trade, and is in no way repudiated by the new constitution, with its separate ethnic Parliaments. The Group Areas Act has destroyed racially integrated neighbourhoods in the city centres, and forced Coloureds and Indians into segregated townships far out of town.

Last in a series of letters sent by Saul Mkhize to P.W. Botha, 31 March 1983: Your help is needed because we are being forced to move by the Department of Co-operation and Development. Dr Koornhof has been known to say, 'There will be no removal of black people from black areas', and yet here we are, without any real discussion, being told by his department that we will move. This is not humanitarian or, in God's name, proper. Why should we consider leaving our land at all? Why should we give up our legally-owned property? Your Honour, we have suffered for many years due to the uncertainty of our position. We have heard rumours, we have been told to obey, but we have never been properly informed or had proper discussions regarding the 'whys' and 'wherefores' of our situation. In God's name, Your Honour, is this merciful? We are, as all South Africans are, a proud people, and all we ask is to remain so. We do not wish to be rebellious in any way, but only to continue to live our lives out in our own environment.

'Tell me if I'm Wrong', **pamphlet circulated in Reiger Park in 1981:** Tell me if I'm wrong if I say the Group Areas Act was specifically passed in order to uproot families that have been settled for years in other areas and dumped on a limited space of ground. Tell me if I'm wrong if I say that the South African apartheid law prevents families from getting a house because of the colour of their skin. Tell me if I'm wrong to say that shelter is without question a basic human right, and that white immigrants who arrive in this country are housed overnight, while we who were born and bred here and who have contributed to the wealth of the country are hassled by hurtful discriminatory laws. Tell me if I'm wrong if I say that the housing shortage is a government-created problem which can be attributed to the high divorce rate. Tell me if I'm wrong to say overcrowding leads to a high rate of teenage pregnancies, alcoholism and insecurity. Tell me if I'm wrong if I say South Africa is the only country in the world where, when a boy or girl approached you and told you that he or she was going to get married, your first response would be, 'Where are you going to live?' instead of 'Congrats, who is the lucky boy or girl?'

Reiger Park is a Group Areas ghetto for Coloureds removed from the East Rand. In mid-1981, violence flared in Reiger Park, after a trader began renovating a shop on land intended for desperately needed housing. The government and the commercial press saw the fact that the trader was Indian as proof that the 'riots' were racially motivated, but the people of Reiger Park maintained that frustration over lack of adequate housing had sparked the unrest.

The forced relocation of millions of black South Africans has been described as the most staggering example of social engineering attempted by any government since World War II.[9] The government's efforts to give a more positive image to this policy are echoed by the campaigns of private entrepreneurs to win credibility for their homeland investment schemes. The most expensive non-governmental public relations exercise on behalf of the homelands has come in the form of the R30 million pleasure resort, Sun City, located in the middle of the Bophuthatswana homeland, beyond the reach of South Africa's Calvinist sex and gambling laws. South African multi-millionaire Sol Kerzner found the turnover from his casino and hotel large enough to allow him to use Sun City's 'Superbowl' purely for prestige and publicity, so money has been no object in his effort to entice world class entertainers to the barren Bophuthatswana bush.

Sunday Times, **9 August 1981:** Frank Sinatra has put Bophuthatswana on the map in the United States like nothing else before. Glowing press reports from American reporters travelling with Sinatra have marvelled at the wonders of Sun City. They have also dwelt at length on the existence of Bophuthatswana as a black homeland where segregation is unknown. And they have been full of praise for Sol Kerzner in luring Frank Sinatra for his nine-day show. The mass-circulation magazine, *People,* headlined its story: 'For $2 million, a South African homeland gets Frank Sinatra and some priceless credibility.' The article said 'Sun City is surely the world's unlikeliest tourist mecca. But in three years, Sol Kerzner has transformed this impoverished backwater – where the annual per capita income averages $700 – into the Las Vegas of the dark continent.' Frank Sinatra said: 'The whole government is black, and is an equal partner of Sol Kerzner. Bophuthatswana gets 50 cents on every rand that goes into a Sun City slot machine or roulette game. Furthermore, Sol has given much needed employment to 3000 black Tswana tribesmen.'

The homelands have been nicknamed 'casino states' for their all-out efforts to attract investment through tax concessions, the abolition of restrictions on whites acquiring land or operating businesses, and even allowing the employment of minors in industry and on farms.

Chief Minister of the Lebowa homeland, Cedric Phatudi: We belive in the creation of a strong middle class, in a capitalistic culture, with a stake in the land – people who will be a pillar of the society they live in.[10]

Life-President of the Ciskei homeland, Lennox Sebe: As our commitment to being a true free market and tax haven gains the attention and confidence of the world, we can predict an accelerating movement from being one of Africa's poorest countries to being Africa's first economic miracle – or, one might say, the world's new Hong Kong. We are not unaware of the fact that when the white man leaves an African state, he takes his money with him. We have been quick to notice that Marxism seeks to fill a man's mind and not his stomach. It is only when my people have as much to lose as the white man that they will be committed totally as a brother with the white man in defending this country.[11]

"The best tax dodge this year is to start a factory in my homeland."

South African Industrial Week, 6 December 1983: Scores of inquiries from Israeli companies are flooding into the Republic of Ciskei, following a visit to the Jewish state by President Sebe. The latest addition to Ciskei's burgeoning industrial sector, Israel's Ciskatex, will manufacture high quality underwear for the southern African market. A spokesman for the Ciskei People's Development Bank, Frans Meisenholl, says: 'The Ciskei government is ready to assist and welcome fresh industrial investment and is confident the success that will be enjoyed by Ciskatex will influence future decisions by Israeli industrialists to establish businesses in Ciskei.' Nat Rosenwasser of the Ciskei Trade Mission in Tel Aviv says that numerous inquiries are being received at the mission's offices.[12]

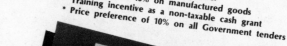

THE COMPETITIVE EDGE

That's what an industrialist needs — and that's what an investment in QWAQWA gives

Besides having the advantage of being situated halfway between the markets of Johannesburg and Durban, Qwaqwa also offers a lucrative package of incentives to industrialists who relocate their factories or start new ones in Qwaqwa.

Check them:
* No capital outlay for factory land and buildings
* Relocation allowance for existing factories from Durban, Pinetown and the PWV area
* 75% rental and interest subsidy for 10 years
* Labour incentive of up to R110 per worker per month
* Housing subsidy for key personnel
* Rail rebate of 40% on manufactured goods
* Training incentive as a non-taxable cash grant
* Price preference of 10% on all Government tenders

There's Gold in Transkei

Among the few international investors to show interest in homeland tax havens is Israel, which has invested $15 million in ten factories in Ciskei. The greatest incentive to homeland investors is what is discreetly referred to as a 'stable labour pool', meaning that desperate job-seekers have no choice but to accept exploitative wages and poor working conditions. Since the contract wages of migrant workers are the homelands' chief source of income — aside from Pretoria's hand-outs, which provide nearly 83 per cent of Ciskei's budget — homeland governments have come to regard their labour force as a commodity to be marketed competitively and when necessary disciplined by the security police and ethnic chiefs.

The inevitable clash between homeland government and workers has been seen most starkly in Ciskei, where the independent trade union movement dared to challenge the alliance between the Ciskei government, the South African state, and big business. The eastern Cape, where Ciskei is centred, has the highest rate of unemployment, infant mortality and population density in South Africa, for it has been the dumping ground for victims of squatter camp raids and black spot removals. The eastern Cape also happens to be the cradle of black resistance, dating from the eighteenth and nineteenth century wars against white settlers, ranging through the twentieth century campaigns of the African National Congress and Pan-Africanist Congress. In mid-1983, the partly state-owned Ciskei bus company raised its fares by 11 per cent and commuters launched a bus boycott in protest. The Ciskeian police, army and vigilantes moved in to crush the boycott: assaulting, detaining, and torturing hundreds of people. As many as ninety people are believed to have died in the bloodiest confrontation in any homeland to date.

Ciskei Manpower Minister Chief Lent Maqoma, speaking in the Ciskei Parliament, 21 May 1983: Contract-breaking Ciskeians are irresponsible and unpatriotic. They are breaking down bridges Ciskei is trying to build with Pretoria. Our 25,000 migrant workers in South Africa are Ciskei's main source of income. They're our black gold. We are in continual competition with workseekers from their national states (homelands), as well as those in South Africa, and employers can afford to be selective. A few bad apples are enough to prejudice the chances of hundreds of other dedicated workers finding employment and, in some instances, virtually starving Ciskeians who are only too willing to earn a living in order to keep the wolf from the door.

Statement to the Centre of Applied Legal Studies, University of the Witwatersrand, investigation into the violation of human rights in Ciskei:[13] My sister was shot by the police when they opened fire on the commuters who were proceeding to the train station in preference to the buses of the Ciskei Transport Corporation, which they were boycotting. A day after the funeral of my sister, at approximately 2 a.m., vigilantes came to my house. They knocked on the doors and windows and demanded that I accompany them. They accused me of using a white Golf to transport workers who were refusing to catch the buses to their places of work. In fact, I have no car at all.

Nonetheless, they took me to the Sisa Dukashe Stadium, where I was assaulted. I was suspended, while handcuffed, and whipped on my body and feet with sjamboks and sticks for several hours. Thereafter I was left in a changing room with approximately thirty-five other persons who had been brought there by the vigilantes. I was left there until Tuesday. During that time, many other persons were assaulted by the vigilantes. We were given no food or water. There was no toilet in the room. By Tuesday, there were approximately eighty persons in the room, which was approximately eight metres square. Faeces were piled along the edges of the room and in the corners. At one stage, two vigilantes came into the room and took out a young woman. They raped her in the adjoining changing room.

On the Tuesday, I was taken to a police station and handed over to the police. I had no idea what charge I was to face. There was no docket at court and I was taken back to my police station cell. The following day I was taken to court and charged with 'public violence'. Apparently I am alleged to have commited the offence at the time at which I was being assaulted in the stadium.

111

South African Allied Workers Union President Thozamile Gqweta: The determination of the people is based on the loss of many friends and relatives in the wake of the boycott. They say the buses smell of blood, of detention, and everything else they despise, and they may not ever be prepared to ride the buses at all – whether the fares are lowered or not. The people have shown their determination and unity. They have braved torrents of rain, they have had to walk long distances to and from work, they have had to face Sebe's guns and vigilantes. But they are not prepared to ride the buses anymore. That is why we feel the Ciskeian government should, at this point, be prepared to negotiate with the leaders of the people in the region, instead of using violence as a solution.

We therefore appeal to democrats throughout the world, but particularly South Africans, to turn their attention not only to putting a stop to the atrocities committed by the Sebe government, but to oppose the entire Bantustan (homeland) system. If we are to avoid similar situations happening elsewhere, we must remove the cancer which causes the conflict – the apartheid system which is based on the bantustanization[14] of our land.
— We call on all democrats to oppose the ban on SAAWU.
— We demand the release of all detainees.
— We call for a united and democratic South Africa, free of exploitation and oppression.
— We call on democrats to support us in united action.

SAAWU songs sung by Ciskei workers:
Thozamile, Thozamile, we are going to die in jail,
We go in, we go out, we shall surely die in jail.

The workers shall succeed,
We are being led by Gqweta,
Exploitation and oppression
Shall be done away with,
The homeland system
Shall be done away with.

SAAWU is our union,
They kill our leaders in prison,
They tried to kill our union,
Gqweta is ours,
SAAWU is powerful,
It will conquer Sebe.

Don't be afraid, your day has arrived,
Today the workers sing,
Don't be afraid, workers,
The day we have been waiting for has arrived,
We are going forward to freedom.

The resilience and determination of the boycotters grew as the government's brutality pushed the people beyond tolerance. Trade unions became the vehicle of communication and organization, offering an opportunity to share accounts of assaults, to boost morale and to sing freedom songs. When the eastern Cape's key trade union, the South African Allied Workers Union, was banned at the height of the boycott, the workers concluded that the government was actually using the protest as an excuse to smash their organization.

Nearly a year after the boycott began, the Ciskei Transport Corporation was forced to rescind the fare increase that had spawned the protest. Life-President Sebe tried to save face by calling the concession 'a triumph for negotiation and dialogue',[15] but he had clearly lost this battle in the ongoing war. For many white South Africans, the Ciskei nightmare was the first public evidence that homeland governments could not exist without fear and force. For many black homeland residents, that fact had long been painfully clear.

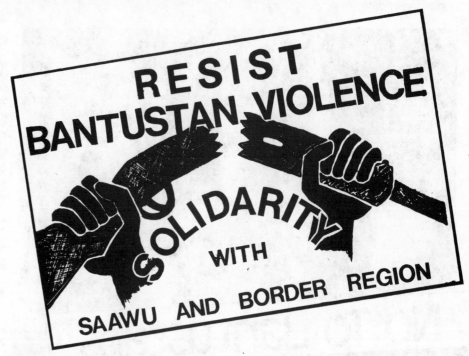

Madoda, Transkei resident:
If you think that people seem to be supporting Matanzima, it is only because of fear. We had hoped to get some real freedom from this independence, but now we have seen that it is the same kind of oppression, only it is black against black now. So, support for the government comes out of fear, and also because of money. You'll find that if you work with the government, you'll get everything you want, but the minute you stop supporting, you lose everything you have.

What are people afraid of?

Madoda: They can take you to jail at any time. They call it a detention, but it's really just being beaten up. And they can kill. We don't even know how many have died in detention in Transkei, but we believe they are plenty. Because people are taken and nobody knows where. If the family goes to find out what's happened, they will be chucked in jail, too. So people must keep silent. And people are afraid.

What is the government afraid of?

Madoda: They are afraid that people will be rebellious and they will try to help South Africa get its freedom. That's why Transkei is so negative against the ANC. The government also feels it must keep such tight reins so it will not lose the economic exploitation. But it's hard to talk about these things, there are so many of Matanzima's spies. Out of five people, you may only trust one. So you must just keep quiet.

Despite the harshness of repression in the homelands, rural resistance is building. The militancy bred in the villages of Soekmekaar, where the Batlokwa and Makgato people have been twice removed from their ancestral land, is a warning to the government that its policies have a price. When a delegation of church leaders visited the northern Transvaal community, they sensed a seething resentment.

South African Council of Churches report on a journey to Soekmekaar, October 1979: The Makgato village looks like a town that has experienced a bomb attack during a war. Only the walls of the houses are standing. The village is completely deserted. The ruins of several larger buildings can be recognized as the remnants of buildings that only a few weeks ago were still in use as churches and schools. It is reported that the feelings of the people are deeply hurt. Mention was made of four people who have died, obviously as a result of the shock and the uprooting which they have experienced.

After the families of the Makgato village who had refused to be moved to Vivo had found refuge in the homes of the neighbouring Batlokwa villages, the two chiefs of the Batlokwa tribe were called by the commissioner, Mr Pieterse, to Pietersburg. They were told that they were expected to persuade the Makgato people who were now staying in the Batlokwa villages to move to Vivo. The two chiefs are reported to have replied that they have the same right as the South African government to grant shelter to refugees.

On the part of the officials, objections were raised against the use of the term 'refugees' to be applied to the Makgato people, since this term only applies to situations of war. The officials were then told by the representatives of the Batlokwa tribe that they, the South African government, had made war on the Makgato people. The only difference to other wars was that in this case only the one side, namely the representatives of the South African government, had weapons, whereas the other side is without arms. During our visit to the Batlokwa area, the fear was expressed that serious unrest will arise, if the South African authorities should decide to evict the refugees by force.

These predictions of both the government's force and the people's resistance came true: the Batlokwa and Makgato fled into the bush rather than be moved to the Lebowa homeland. An unexpected twist came with a guerilla attack on Soekmekaar – the first major African National Congress attack on a rural outpost.

Post, **18 October 1980:** The January 1980 AK-47 and grenade attack on Soekmekaar Police Station was an 'armed propaganda' attack in protest against the removal of black residents from the area, one of the accused men told the Pretoria Supreme Court yesterday. Mr Petrus Mashigo was giving evidence at the trial of himself and eight others. He said he and five others returned to Mozambique in August last year, after undergoing military training in various parts of Africa. He said during a briefing they were told of the removal of the people of Soekmekaar from their residence to a place unknown to them, which was in a dry area.'

'We were told that the people were not satisfied about what was happening and that the police from Soekmekaar Police Station were assisting in the removal of these people,' said Mr Mashigo. He said the notion of 'armed propaganda' in relation to Soekmekaar meant the attack was intended to show the people of Soekmekaar that the ANC sympathized with them, and to demonstrate to the police that what they were doing was wrong. Mr Mashigo said it had been explained to them that people joined the police force believing they were assisting their community, only to find they were involved in doing things against their community. Staging such propaganda was to show such policemen that what they were doing was contrary to the wishes of their people.

The success of 'armed propaganda' in drawing the links between forced removals and ANC opposition was made more evident in the reaction of whites to a rocket, grenade and rifle attack that killed two policemen in the Venda homeland in 1981.

After the Venda attack, a spate of detentions focused on the Lutheran Church, the only voice of opposition to survive in the homeland. No one was ever brought to trial in connection with the ANC attack, but a prominent lay preacher, Tshifiwa Muofhe, was beaten to death by Venda police during interrogation (a fact confirmed by an inquest, though a Venda court acquitted his assailant). One missionary was quoted as saying that the ANC should be 'thrilled' with the politicizing achieved by the police on the movement's behalf.[16] However small and seemingly ineffective, the ANC's attacks serve to demonstrate solidarity with the millions of South Africans who, under the government's reformist policies, remain 'aliens' in their own country.

Cape Times, **28 October 1981:** The attack on a police station at Sibasa, Vendaland is a grave development and confirms the new trend towards rural terrorism, on the classic pattern of guerilla insurgency. The sporadic bomb attacks in some urban centres will no doubt continue, as will sabotage aimed at symbolic targets. But the Sibasa outrage, bearing marks of a somewhat more sophisticated approach than has hitherto been in evidence, suggests that a new style of rural subversion is in the offing in border districts, which may in time assume the proportions of a second front and require the opening of a new operational area.

A worrying thing about this upsurge in rural subversion is that it takes place at a time of apparent stagnation in reformist initiatives. The Cape squatter crisis and the deportation of so-called aliens to the Ciskei were hardly calculated to capture the hearts and minds of the rural African masses, who provide the ocean for the proverbial Maoist fish. If the local populations are going to welcome the ANC gunmen as liberators from an oppressive yoke, and give them hiding, food and shelter, the job of eradicating this scourge will be a formidable one. Military preparedness in dealing with insurgency is a relatively small part of the battle, which is essentially political. On present form, the Botha administration is faring poorly indeed on the political front. A thorough reassessment is overdue.

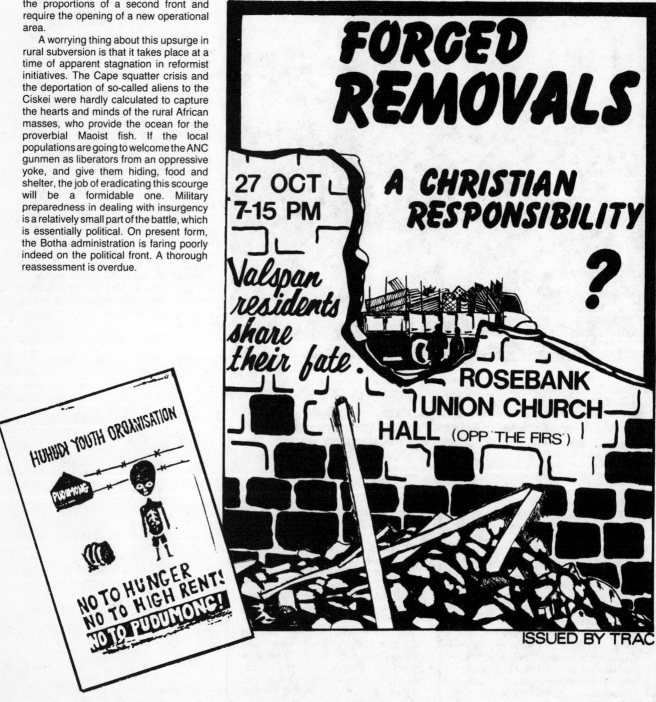

The reasons for the widespread disillusionment with the government's much-vaunted reforms can be clearly seen in the labour field. The reformist labour laws were designed to allow unions to develop outside a political context that might lead to strike action and community involvement. The plan did not work. So the government responded in 1984 by proposing tough new labour legislation, which would require the state to monitor and approve all recognized agreements between unions and employers, force unions to prove they have no link with political parties, and curb consumer boycotts and solidarity strikes in support of workers' demands.[17]

Such laws alone did not seem to satisfy the government's desire for control of the independent trade union movement. The exposure of a secret government document, outlining a plot to smash the growth of non-racial unions in the eastern Cape, made it clear that the security police were authorized to conduct their own clandestine union-busting campaign.

solidarity with detained workers

their struggle is ours

Repression

B. No five-star hotels

**'Repression in a time of 'reform',
pamphlet issued by the Johannesburg
Democratic Action Committee, 1984:**
State propaganda would have us believe
that we are living in an era of relaxation.
Yet the extent of repression is, if anything,
increasing. This harsh reality is being
hidden from the public by the use of new
tactics of repression. Why the new tactics?
— The government is desperate to win
support for its constitutional initiative. To
do this, it has to convince people,
particularly the Coloured and Indian
communities, that the hated bully has
turned into a kind uncle. Highly visible acts
of repression make this sleight of hand
very difficult to pull off.
— Reagan and other supporters of
'constructive engagement' in South Africa
need to justify their claim that apartheid is
reforming itself. Attention focused on
detentions and the systematic use of
torture has frustrated the government in its
attempts to project an image of reform,
both at home and abroad.
— The security police have realized that
the old method of detaining and banning
the leadership of organizations, apart from
being embarrassing, has been insufficient
to render mass-based organizations
ineffective. The state has now turned to
new tactics to cripple progressive
organizations.
P. W. Botha is like the emperor who was
convinced that he had a new suit of
clothes, whereas in fact, he had nothing at
all. Like the emperor, apartheid is bare for
all who want to see it, despite the elaborate
attempts to dress it up in the transparent
finery of 'reform'.

**Confidential document circulated to
East London employers in 1981 by a
security police officer, who was
defended by the Minister of Police as
having acted 'in good faith and towards
the maintenance of law and order':[18]**
What is seen as a possible solution to
break the power of the South African Allied
Workers' Union and unregistered black
unions, and to normalize labour unrest?
One would have to think of a short-term
solution to act as a millstone around the
necks of SAAWU to prevent the
acceleration of its successes. Here one
must think of the success which SATV (an
East London employer) achieved in
preventing a strike, because the firm was
in possession of a list of names of about
800 unemployed people who could start
work at very short notice, if required.

The success of the action of SATV was
mainly attributed to the fact that the
workers or prospective strikers were
aware of the authenticity of this list, and
that it was not only a rash threat. SATV
conducts interviews regularly throughout

the year with unemployed people and they
are told that they will be kept in mind when
posts become vacant.

Industry should be encouraged to keep
such lists of employment seekers, instead
of just turning them away at the gate
without taking down any of their
particulars. To take down the bare
essentials and keep this on record would
help firms not to give in to ridiculous
demands when their present workforce
goes on strike. The big worry of firms today
during labour unrest is the loss of
production and time which normally goes
hand in hand with strikes. Confrontation
and the refusal to work can continue for
days on end until the weaker of the two
parties gives in, and normally this is
management because time is money and
the longer the confrontation, the more
management will be apt to give in to the
demands as set by the strikers. With such
a reserve list on record at any firm, it would
be easier not to give in to pressure from the
workers, if they demand that SAAWU be
recognized as a union.

For all the talk of reform, repression remains the chief means of government control, and the most effective means of repression is still detention without trial. Every trade unionist, community organizer, student activist and church leader knows that the security police can come at any time, and that he or she can be locked up, interrogated, and abused for as long as the government deems it necessary for the 'maintenance of law and order'. The Internal Security Act of 1982 – the fruits of a reformist 'revamping' of security legislation – gives the authorities powers to arrest and detain a person indefinitely and incommunicado, without going through the courts and other normal procedures of law. The 'preventive detention' provision of this legislation allows the Minister of Law and Order to authorize the detention of a person, not for interrogation or potential court action, but simply to remove him or her from society. Even more frightening than detention itself is the conspiracy of silence that surrounds it, for the Protection of Information Act, the Defence Act, the Police Act and the Prisons Act all hinder the reporting of security matters in the press.

Trade unionist Tom Mashinini remembers the night his wife, also a trade union leader, was taken away from their home in the middle of the night, at gunpoint. Emma Mashinini was detained in a nationwide security crackdown on trade unionists (and other activists) in 1981, which saw scores of leaders and supporters of the independent trade union movement imprisoned for months in solitary confinement. Most were eventually released – except for one young white medical doctor who had forsaken his professional career for an unpaid post as a regional organizer of the African Food and Canning Workers Union. Dr Neil Aggett was found dead, hanged from the barred door of his cell, on 5 February 1982. The security police said it was suicide. His friends and fellow trade unionists called it murder.

One hundred thousand black workers in factories all over South Africa downed tools for half an hour to protest against Dr Aggett's death in detention, in the first general political strike the country had witnessed in over two decades. His funeral saw 5000 blacks and whites march through the streets of Johannesburg in an overwhelming show of trade union unity.

Among the thousands of mourners at Dr Aggett's funeral were two people who would normally have shunned such a gathering: his elderly parents. Aubrey and Joyce Aggett emigrated to South Africa in 1964, after the former British colony of Kenya gained its independence.

Tom Mashinini: Several vehicles pulled up at our home, and policemen surrounded the house, brandishing guns like we were terrorists. I let them in and then the children were awoken and were very shocked. The white lieutenant in charge was very arrogant and told me to get out out of my own house. My children were witnesses to all this. What will they think? I was told not to speak to Emma, and then they took her away. Must we be treated like this? I have committed no offence, and Emma is the mother of my young children. Things are going from bad to worse.[19]

Aubrey Aggett: I wasn't very keen on staying in Kenya under a black government. South Africa was the obvious place for us to come. Verwoerd (South Africa's then-Prime Minister) did everything he could to welcome us. We got £60 to help settle in.

Joyce Aggett: The South African government paid our fares down, too. It's very sad, in a way, because we've been very happy in South Africa up till now. It's ironic that we left Kenya because of a black government, and now we feel so bad about this present white government.

Have you voted for this government in the past?

Aubrey Aggett: I have. I must admit it. I'm ashamed of it.

Would you vote for them again?

Aubrey Aggett: Never. Because I think they're totally dishonest. You take the (Steve) Biko affair. I heard about Biko, I thought he was probably a bad fellow who got what he deserved. Since our troubles I have read a lot about Biko, and to my mind, there's no argument: Biko was murdered. But I've only come to feel this way about things since this tragedy happened to us.

Did you ever think, before Neil died, that you'd be saying anything so anti-government as that?

Joyce Aggett: Never, never.

Aubrey Aggett: I considered myself a very loyal South African and I still think I am, but I think the security police are exactly the same as the Gestapo were. They are doing in this country what the Gestapo were doing in Nazi Germany.

Dave Lewis, General Workers' Union General-Secretary, speaking at Dr Neil Aggett's funeral, 13 February 1982: The democratic trade unions and other democratic organizations have been leading a strong fight against the system of detention without trial. And now one of those leaders who was detained without trial is dead. Maybe there's a lesson in that. Maybe the lesson that we must learn is that whenever we are protesting against detention without trial, we are protesting against the government killing our leaders.

We must look at why Neil was in jail in the first place; we must look at what Neil's 'crime' was. Neil was a man who believed that workers in South Africa were oppressed and exploited and he believed that the only way they could end their oppression was by organizing together, so he joined the trade union movement. And in this country, where the police don't allow the workers to belong to the trade unions they want to, then Neil was a criminal for wanting that. Neil saw that the workers' lives didn't end at the factory gate at five o'clock. He saw that there was no democracy anywhere in South Africa, and he saw that for democratic unions, there must be a democratic country, so Neil fought for democracy in South Africa. And in a country ruled by a minority, anyone who fights for majority rule is a criminal. So if Neil is a criminal, so is everybody in the democratic trade unions. And we're proud to be criminals like Neil!

Comrades, I think that Neil's death is a grave price to pay for the unity of the trade union movement, but I think that Neil's work and Neil's death is what is going to bring us together. The trade unions must see now clearly who the common enemy is. We must start to think about uniting the trade union movement. And that must be the monument that we must build to Neil Aggett. We must show the government that while they sit in Parliament passing new laws about the trade unions, their hands are full of the blood of our heroes!
Crowd: Amandla! Ngawethu! An injury to one – is and injury to all! Detention to one – is detention to all! Dismissal to one – is dismissal to all! Organize – or starve! Aluta continua.[20] Neil was not a terrorist! He is a hero! Botha is a terrorist! Neil is a hero!

SABC, 29 June 1982: The inquest court investigating the death in detention of the trade union leader, Dr Aggett, has heard evidence that Dr Aggett allegedly supported Marxist ideology. An unsigned, typed document, allegedly prepared by Dr Aggett before his death, was read to the court by Mr Peter Schabort, for the Minister of Law and Order. The police officer in charge of interrogation at John Vorster Square Police Headquarters in Johannesburg, Major Arthur Cronwright, said he was withholding from the inquest many pages of statements written by Dr Aggett. He said the documents contained secret information which could not be released to the court without the permission of the Minister of Law and Order. It was believed to relate to the activities of the Communist Party of South Africa, and Major Cronwright said it could lead to another major investigation.

Sworn statement dictated by Dr Neil Aggett to a police sergeant, led as evidence in the inquest into his death: I was arrested on the 27/11/81 by a Captain Crouse of the Security Police and am detained under Section 6(1) of 83/1967 at John Vorster Square cells. On the 4/1/82, a black member of the force called Chauke came to fetch me at the cells and took me to the 10th floor, room 1012. In the room Lt Whitehead, the black policeman, Chauke, and a railway police security sergeant called Schalk were present. I was interrogated by Lt Whitehead and every time he asked me a question and I denied it, he accused me of calling him a liar. Then this Schalk would assault me. He hit me with his open hand through my face and I fell against the table with my back, and I could feel a scab on my back. He also assaulted me with his fists by hitting me on the side of my temple and my chest. He also kicked me with his knee on the side of my thigh. This Schalk wore a watch which cut my right forearm and it was bleeding. Later this Schalk went to wash off the blood that was on him. While I was assaulted by him he grabbed me by the scrotum and squeezed my testicles.

I was kept awake since the morning of the 28/1/82 to the 30/1/82. During the night of the 28/1/82, Lt Whitehead and another security sergeant whose name I don't know, and another black male, also a policeman, were present when Lt Whitehead blindfolded me with a towel. They made me sit down and handcuffed me behind my back. I was shocked through the handcuffs. I don't know what they used to shock me. I was shocked a few times. I have a scratch on my left pulse (radial nerve) where I was injured whilst being handcuffed.

I complained at the cells to Warrant Officer McPherson about my back. I was not seen by a doctor. I was visited by Magistrate Wessels on 18 January 1982 and I reported to him that I was assaulted by the Security Police. I know and understand the contents of this declaration. I have no objections to taking the prescribed oath. I consider the oath to be binding on my conscience. Signed, N.H. Aggett, 4 February 1982.

At least fifty security detainees had died before Dr Aggett,[21] but he was the first white to die in detention. The state inquest into his death aroused great public interest and took nearly a year to complete. The security police contended that Dr Aggett took his own life after confessing to being a 'communist'.

Nothing was subsequently heard of these alleged Communist Party links, which the security police refused to reveal to the inquest court, but the testimony of six former detainees corroborated Dr Aggett's own claims – made in a sworn statement fourteen hours before his death – of security police torture.

At the end of the inquest, the magistrate found no one responsible for Dr Aggett's death, and dismissed the evidence of the former detainees, while accepting the testimony of the security police. Even when another security detainee, Ernest Dipale,[22] was found dead in his cell just six months after Dr Aggett's death, the Minister of Law and Order continued to defend the policy of holding political prisoners in solitary confinement, without charge or trial, for months on end.

In response to the 1981 security crackdown that included Dr Aggett's detention, a group of political activists and ex-detainees in Cape Town published a manual on the political, legal and personal aspects of detention. The booklet featured a letter, based on the experience of four detainees subjected to security police interrogation, written to a young activist, in an attempt to help her and other potential detainees cope with the trauma of interrogation.

Letter from an ex-detainee from Cape Town manual on detention:

Dear Zoliswa,

I have watched your political development in the last few months, as we worked together, side by side. I know it will not be long before your commitment to the struggle will take concrete form, in that you will decide to give your active support to the democratic movement. Realizing this, I am both filled with joy and saddened. I am filled with joy, because I know that we will gain a comrade. But I am sad, because I also know what personal suffering this way of life will bring you. There can be no easy walk to freedom.

When my friends were being detained all around me, I didn't even think that I might be detained. I did not realize that a number of my activities could be regarded as subversive. I was so used to reading banned books and participating in discussion groups, that it did not occur to me that the state would disapprove strongly of such activity. I know now that I must always fully understand what I am doing. I must know what I have done and what my reasons were for doing it. This is very important because the purpose of interrogation is twofold: to extract information and to reinterpret the detainee's reality. Interrogators don't only try to find out what you have done – they also suggest to you why you have done it.

For example, you may have helped a matric pupil study history. As far as you are concerned, you tutored the pupil because you wanted to help her pass her exams, and you also wanted to give her a broader understanding of the subject. Your interrogators will say that you were trying to indoctrinate the pupil for the purpose of politicizing her further in the future. You were trying to influence the pupil to view the activities of banned organizations in a favourable light. And in so doing, you were furthering the aims of those organizations. What you must always fight against is internalizing their interpretation of your reality. Be firm in what you believe and do not allow them to cast doubt in your mind.

When the fans were turned on me that first night, I had no idea that that was only the beginning. I thought that I would be taken to the cell the following day, where I could at least lie down on a mat. But no! For many days and nights, my home was to be a tiny room furnished with only a table and two chairs. And then it was one tormentor after another, each asking the same questions, but using different forms of pressure. The lack of sleep, the long hours of standing, were taking their toll. I could no longer think clearly. Every nerve in my body was tensed up and I could not will myself to relax.

'You are going to have a heart attack, you won't be able to hold out much longer,' they said to me. 'You are going to die.' And when I felt my body hit the wall as they struck me, I was beginning to believe that myself. But it wasn't only the violence that was breaking me down. It was the constant abuse of my dignity. Their harsh words systematically chipped away my pride. I was made to feel subhuman. I had used people, they said, abused their confidence, and allowed people outside the country to use me. I was also nothing but a whore. Only fit to be raped. The verbal assault was never ending.

I felt terribly humiliated, but was beyond crying: my tears had dried up on the third day, when the terror fully gripped me. I was convinced that I would die soon. Everything was becoming very hazy. My heart was beating so rapidly that I thought it could burst through my chest, or perhaps I would burst a blood vessel in my head. They wouldn't let me sit down or close my eyes. Oh, how I longed to faint. When would this end? I thought. I still have a contribution to make. Why should I suffer so, when I know that other people have done far more serious things and are walking about outside? Why me? All these thoughts flashed through my mind as I battled to resist.

Detention and interrogation are part of the struggle, and if you are committed to fight, you must be prepared for the consequences. If you break down and divulge information, the movement will suffer some setbacks, but will not be defeated. You must always be ready to take up the fight again, and not be pulled down by memories of how you were humiliated and temporarily defeated. In the words of Ho Chi Min, 'Those who protest at injustice are people of true merit. When the prison doors are opened, the real dragon will fly out.'

Yours in the struggle, Thandiwe.

Minister of Law and Order Louis le Grange, 9 August 1982, in a speech to the Foreign Correspondents Association, Johannesburg: I know that South Africa is being blamed for the number of deaths in detention. I know it is a particular point of debate, but the fact of the matter is, ladies and gentlemen, that one must also look at these matters in perspective. I am not trying to say that one should take these things for granted – not at all! It is a very serious matter when anyone dies in detention. But, is this now so exceptional in the world? I can quote you figures of countries from where some of you come which is much higher than any figure that South Africa has had for the last ten years. Much higher. I don't think it is necessary for me to go into too much detail, because I don't want to embarrass any of you, as much as you don't want to embarrass me about those matters. All I am asking is that one should also keep one's perspective and not point such a long finger at South Africa whenever we have a death in detention.

Foreign correspondent: But what we'd like to know, Mr Minister, is why it is necessary in the first place to keep a man in such conditions, in a cell by himself?

Minister le Grange: The man is being detained to obtain information from him and I don't think you will obtain much information from a man if you accommodate him in a five-star hotel!

Freedom song heard at protest meetings in South Africa:
Akanatyala, akanatyala,
He is not guilty, she is not guilty,
Release those detainees
Whose only crime
Is to work for the freedom
Of all people in our time,
Mandela/Mpetha/Gqwetha/Zenzile/
Mkhize/Joseph[23] is our comrade,
His/her only crime,
Is to work for the freedom
Of all people in our time.

South African Police Profile (official police publication), 1982: Since the early days of police work, the informer has played a major part. Without information received, the task of the policeman would almost be impossible. An informer passes information to the police about other people, or incidents which are going to occur or have already occurred. Quite often the informer has reasons why he informs against another person, but equally often, he is a citizen doing his duty by telling the police of what he has seen or knows.

The identity of the informer is normally kept secret. He is known to the policeman to whom he is passing information. The police rely largely on the support of the public for passing on information and wish them to know that their identity will be protected at all times. Remuneration for informers is based on the following: the seriousness of the case, the risk involved, the time spent gathering the information, and the personal inconvenience.

'Informer', by Nhlanhla Paul Maake
happy birthday
star of the auction
block
born in the ghetto
bred in the brick
and mortar pillars

who can forget
your ubiquitous
ear
that can hear
whispers in a
tremor

none
so dull as
to miss your forked
eyes
that cut through the dark
to look at things
they cannot
see

perverted seller
of human
souls
diseased with deceit

feet
nimble with tales
and mouth talented
in lies

in darkness
your shadow
becomes blacker than
blackness
while your purchased soul
remains pale

State repression is not confined to police cells and court rooms. Activists are intimidated, and communities demoralized, through a range of 'dirty tricks', from smear campaigns to physical violence. The most common method of disorganizing opposition movements is through the use of paid informers.

In the black community, the view of spies is uncompromising. The exposure and punishment of a 'sell-out' was one of the first political lessons for Thandi, a community activist, Robert, a trade unionist, and Hassan, a student leader.

Thandi: When I was at boarding school, we had a small group and we used to get together for political discussions, things like that. We didn't know it, but apparently we had a spy who went to the police and told them about the group. So the police came and they had a whole list of everybody in the group, and everybody was taken in. The spy, she was one of the girls in our class. She came out of the van with the police, and when the police took us away she was there standing next to them, as if she was standing next to her father or something. So after we got out, what we did was we waited for her back at school, till she got to the bathroom, then everybody took their wet face rags and when she came in, we beat her. She ran out of the gate, naked. She never came back to school. She couldn't. Everybody hated her, because of what she'd done. I'm not sorry for her. People have got to learn such lessons.

Robert: A sell-out is anyone who collaborates with the system, but I can think of two categories of sell-outs. Firstly, there are those individuals who, for financial gain, or because of intimidation by the security police, decide they have no option but to get what they need from the government in this fashion. Then the second category of sell-outs is those who opt out of the general democratic struggle and decide that they can force change from within institutions that have been established by the racist government. That would be the Buthelezis, the Hendrickses,[24] those involved in the homelands, the community councils, and those ethnic Parliaments.

Hassan: At one stage I was approached by the security police and they said, well, I seem to be a very responsible character and if I could assist them to maintain law and order, I would be rewarded. They said I must just look around the campus and report to them on people who are trying to cause some commotion so that then they can deal with them. And in return, I would get some kind of bonus. This type of thing is happening throughout South Africa, and with most of the students and community leaders, you find that the SBs (security branch) do approach people and ask them to do such favours, and if you don't take a stand early on, you might find yourself in fact agreeing to such gestures.

What was your response?

Hassan: Well, I completely rejected their offer, and I suspect that's where the clash between me and them started. You see, if you've been approached and you've said no, they can make life difficult for you.

Robert: I remember one time, two security police arrived at my house, one black and one white. They didn't actually come into the house, they sent somebody to come and call me. And when I came outside, they requested me to get into their car, but I said, 'I'm not going to get in unless I know exactly what you want me for.' Finally, they persuaded me to just talk with them, and I sat in the car, but my legs were outside, just in case they decided to drive off.

They said they wanted me to go to meet them at John Vorster Square on the following Monday. So I said, 'What do you want to talk about there that you can't talk here?' And then the black security policeman said, kind of angrily, 'Don't make yourself stupid, you know exactly that we want you to help us catch others like you.' Being as they knew I was politically involved, for them it was a question of using a thief to catch a thief.

That's when I jumped out of the car, banged the door, and pointed at the cop, saying, 'I haven't lost my conscience like you have done!' But before I could finish, they'd driven off. And later I found that they had been to the offices of my employer and told them that by employing me, they are employing a communist and there is likelihood of labour unrest.

How are people treated who are known informers?

Hassan: They are regarded as lepers in the community, though there are no fast rules in terms of treatment. But many times they can be liquidated by unknown assailants, and then later on, word will get out that the reason this was done is that the person was in fact a sell-out.

Thandi: It is a big problem in the black community, these spies. I think that must be the easiest job to get. Because, you know, there is a lot of unemployment and people are always in need of money, and the system is taking advantage of this. The system can say, we'll give you so much money, we'll get you a car, and people find it very easy to co-operate. They are told that all they must do is attend a meeting, put on those tape recorders or simply inform on what is happening in the community.

Robert: I can remember being taken in for questioning, and the security cops would be boasting, saying we have all this information on you, kind of implying that your closest friends are informers. It's very easy to start getting so worried that you trust nobody, out of fear that anyone could be an informer.

The question always asked, especially by those trapped by police informers, is: how could anyone live the double live required in order to compromise one's political colleagues? Security Police Major Craig Williamson, a double agent who infiltrated student politics as well as the international anti-apartheid movement before being exposed, admitted that he relied on a kind of personal schizophrenia.

Whatever the motives for informing on their friends, 'sell-outs' receive no mercy when they are exposed. All are ostracized, some are killed.

Major Craig Williamson: Like any good actor, you've got to play a part. You've got to psyche yourself into the role. To an extent, you've got to be what I always call – I'm probably cutting my own throat here – a controlled schizophrenic. It's a very delicate process, the whole thing. The farther you are away from your base, the greater your problems are: the problem of maintaining your morale and all that sort of thing. You build up an entirely fictitious existence, and you keep a core group of people who fulfil a very important function because they are your link with reality.

Perhaps the most vital tool of the agent is supreme self-confidence. But on the other hand, you've got to be very sure that your supreme self-confidence is balanced and won't let you become over-confident. You have to have total faith in the person who's in charge of the operation. If that person does one thing to upset the equilibrium, it can mean big trouble.[25]

Sowetan **19 April 1982:** An executive of the Soweto Committee of Ten saved the life of a man who was attacked by angry mourners after he was pointed out as a Security Policeman during a funeral service for former ANC man Elias Tsimo at the weekend. The kicking and punching drama, which brought the funeral service at the War Memorial Chapel in Dube to an abrupt halt, began when a weeping woman rose from the audience and pointed out three men who she said were Security Policemen. The woman also displayed a 'recording transmitter' which she said was given to her by a youth who confessed to the *Sowetan* that he was planted among the mourners by 'the system'.

When angry mourners converged on the three alleged Security Policemen, two of them managed to escape. The one who was surrounded by mourners and kicked and punched all over the body was saved when Mr Leonard Mosala, master of ceremonies, intervened and ordered that the attack be stopped. Mr Mosala said there was no liberation struggle that had not been infiltrated by spies and informers. He said they should not be killed, but left to live long enough to see liberation and to realize that their work can not stop the march to freedom. 'Jomo Kenyatta had spies planted among his men. Machel had them, and Mugabe had them,[26] but nevertheless that did not stop their countries from attaining their liberation, and South Africa can not be an exception,' he said.

The other side, too, has its spies: those who work within pro-government bodies to effect anti-government ends. The few that are exposed are such an embarrassment to the government that their cases are hushed up in secret trials. In 1983, South Africans were shocked by the disclosure that the commanding officer of the South African Naval Dockyard, on the strategic Cape sea route, had been transmitting military secrets to the Soviet Union for over twenty years; Commodore Dieter Gerhardt was sentenced to life imprisonment for treason in a trial held totally in camera. A less publicized, but just as damning spy case, was that of an ANC 'mole' in the Coloured Labour Party in Cape Town who was exposed only after his death.

A favourite government technique to confuse, divide and demoralize opposition is the distribution of fake pamphlets aimed at smearing the reputations of anti-government organizations and individuals. The frustration, for those victimized by smear campaigns, is that it is usually impossible to prove that such operations are government-sanctioned. The exposé of a secret 'inter-departmental action committee', created by the Cabinet in 1980 to combat the Cape bus and school boycotts, provided a rare opportunity to prove indisputably the connection between the government and a smear campaign. Minister of Foreign Affairs and Information Pik Botha was forced to admit publicly that the

Sunday Times, **3 May 1981:** The secret life of a 'spy' was revealed when he was given a hero's burial under the flag of the banned African National Congress as 5000 mourners watched. Till then, no one knew that John Hennie Ferrus – a top official of the Labour Party – was really an ANC agent who had infiltrated the party in 1977. Mr Ferrus's double life came to light last Sunday, when members of the ANC came out of hiding and 'hijacked' his funeral and distributed specially printed pamphlets to thousands of mourners, in tribute to 'Comrade Hennie'. Labour Party members were snubbed at the mass funeral. Most of the people present wore rosettes in the ANC colours of black, yellow and green. The hall was also decorated in ANC colours and, at the graveside, the ANC flag – which was held aloft during the march there – was also displayed.[27]

Foreign Minister Pik Botha, in a statement released on 1 August 1980: The Cabinet instructed the committee in question to plan and implement actions designed to combat the unrest and violence which was building up, inter alia, as a result of the schools boycott earlier this year. In some cases, anonymous pamphlets were prepared and disseminated by the committee, because the committee considered this the most effective way to counter unrest and subversive plans, and of helping to maintain order. The pamphlets reflected the opinions and attitudes of a considerable proportion of the general public. If it should again prove necessary, similar methods will be utilized to combat the actions and false propaganda of the nameless agitators and the proponents of violence to promote peace and calm in the country.[28]

committee, run jointly by his ministry, the security police, the Department of Co-operation and Development, the Department of Coloured Affairs and the Department of Indian Affairs, had sanctioned the production and distribution of crudely written anonymous pamphlets. The secret government committee issued – among others – a bogus pamphlet aimed at stopping taxi owners from assisting commuters in the bus boycott.

The independent trade unions have been frequent targets of smear campaigns aimed at sowing disunity in a movement just beginning to unite. In 1980, a series of pamphlets distributed among workers in the east Rand attacked the Metal and Allied Workers Union, and urged workers to join the Engineering and Allied Workers Union.

Nobel Laureate Bishop Desmond Tutu must hold the record for the most smear pamphlets produced against one individual. When the Bishop returned from an overseas trip in 1981, on which he once again called for international pressure against Pretoria, Soweto was inundated with thousands of anti-Tutu pamphlets.

The total lack of credibility of the anti-Tutu pamphlets was due in part to the fact the the organizations which purported to issue them were known to be non-existent. Smear pamphlets aimed at sabotaging the 1980 Release Mandela campaign were distributed in the name of the ANC, but were rejected as frauds because of the use of the word, Azania, a Black Consciousness and PAC name for South Africa that is not used by the ANC.

Pamphlet produced by the government's 'inter-departmental action committee' during the 1980 Cape Town boycotts: Taxi owners: we are fools. We are hurting ourselves. We are sacrificing our pride over self-respect! We are neglecting our families! What for? For the sake of a few intimidators who are forcing us and our families into starvation? What are these enforcers and intimidators contributing to the boycott? We are cutting our noses to spoil our faces. No. I say: let's stand together and put an end to this senseless boycott!

Phony pamphlet from the 'United Trade Union Council': This is the man who wants us to suffer through boycotts. He lives in tycoon style. We slave for our daily bread. Boycotts will make us jobless. Boycotts will not make Tutu lose his job. We will suffer – he will not! He lives in luxury. He rolls in money. He says, 'People would gladly suffer for their principles.' Will he suffer? Even his children study overseas. It is we and our children that will suffer. He will always have bread. We will have nothing. Who pays for his luxuries? Tutu gets money overseas to help the oppressed, but he just helps himself.[29]

Pamphlet purportedly issued by the ANC in 1980: People of Azania: Beware. People signing the petition for the release of Nelson Mandela are being closely watched by the Security Branch. Beware, several names and addresses have been collected by SB spies. Azanians, the white oppressors will never free Mandela; they will only detain or ban the people supporting the petition. The loss of your freedom is not worth signing the petition. Azanians, let us not waste time with petitions, let us support our free leaders. The past learned us that we are helpless against the Security Branch. Our struggle for liberation is hampered by the childish fights among leaders of Black Consciousness movements. Divided as we are at present, we will never win victory over our oppressors. This pamphlet was issued by the African National Congress.

Kate Philip, 22, is the newly elected president of Nusas.

The liveliest media war has been waged on the campuses of South Africa's English language universities, as a tiny core of right-wing students has tried to answer the popular publications of the liberal and left-oriented Student Representative Councils with smear pamphlets. The 'moderate' students are led by Russell Crystal, a National Party organizer on the University of the Witwatersrand campus for nearly a decade, who has never denied having links with the security police. Crystal's clique has far less support than the democratically elected student organizations, but it has far more money, most of which seems to be ploughed into the preparation of slick, right-wing publications.[30]

The most damaging smear pamphlet was one laid out in the same format as the National Union of South African Students' newsletter, and distributed widely at the universities of the Witwatersrand, Cape Town, Natal and Rhodes. Using crude revolutionary language, it linked NUSAS with the ANC – in direct contradiction to the NUSAS policy of non-violence.

The damage caused by smear pamphlets paled in comparison, however, with the effects of activities apparently aimed at intimidating anti-government activists, trade unionists, lawyers acting in political trials, student and church leaders, and journalists. Incidents have ranged from malicious pranks to death threats, from slashed tires to shots fired. The most worrying aspect of these 'dirty tricks' is that nothing – neither police probes nor press exposés – seems to stop them. In 1983, white journalists in the eastern Cape city of Port Elizabeth were the target of a particularly vicious and systematic intimidation campaign.

'Campus News', fake pamphlet distributed in 1983: Although conscientious objection has hitherto played a significant role in frustrating the ability of the fascist army to organize itself, the possibility of active service in favour of MK (Umkhonto we Sizwe) has not previously been seriously explored by the student movement. Yet if students are not to sit on the sidelines of history, surely this is the only logical step which they can undertake. All South African students must realize that the attitude of the inevitable victorious African National Congress after the revolution toward whites in South Africa will depend entirely on their own behaviour during the next three to four years, or so. They will deserve no mercy for their past sins, and indeed will receive none, unless they demonstrate in the clearest possible terms, by their actions, which side they are on.

Do not imagine that any last-minute, see-which-way-the-wind-is-blowing lukewarm commitment will impress Comrade Tambo when the time comes. Comrade Mugabe's patience, even with renegades from the Rhodesian Front such as Ian Smith, is not likely to be repeated in South Africa. The only logical conclusion one can draw from this situation is the necessity to participate actively in the work of MK. Although NUSAS has hitherto followed a very careful strategy of remaining just within the limits of the law, and yet conscientizing students in favour of the ANC, the time has come to depart from this strategy, despite the considerable risks involved. At this point, two questions must be addressed to students: are you prepared to die for the liberation struggle? More to the point, are you prepared to kill for the liberation struggle?

You are a POTENTIAL TARGET OF THE ANC!! Through events on this campus have y[ou] already [been] part o[f a] campa[ign] destroy y[our] of life[.]

THE CHAIN OF TERRORISM

SWAPO — A.N.C. — ? — P.L.O.

? THE MISSING LINK ?

NUSAS ON SWAPO: RESOLUTION: 65/78 NUSAS N.S.A.
1. TO EXTEND ITS SOLIDARITY TO SWAPO AND THE PEOPLE OF NAMIBIA IN THEIR STRUGGLE FOR TRUE FREEDOM FROM COLONISATION AND EXPLOITATION.

HAS NUSAS CHANGED?
HEAD OFFICE REPORT: DURBAN CONGRESS 1982:
"WE MUST RECREATE SOME OF THE MILITANCY WE HAVE HAD IN PREVIOUS YEARS."

THE STUDENTS' ACTION FRONT CONDEMNS THIS NUSAS STANDPOINT!

IS NUSAS RELEVANT TO STUDENT POLITICS?

S.A.F. CHALLENGES NUSAS TO PUBLICLY CONDEMN ITS PREVIOUS POLICIES IN CONNECTION WITH S.W.A.P.O. AND A.N.C. VIOLENCE.

ISSUED BY THE STUDENTS' ACTION FRONT.
UNIVERSITY OF NATAL, PIETERMARITZBURG, P.O. BOX 375, 3200

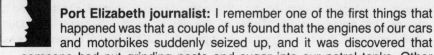

Port Elizabeth journalist: I remember one of the first things that happened was that a couple of us found that the engines of our cars and motorbikes suddenly seized up, and it was discovered that someone had put grinding paste and sugar into our petrol tanks. Other journalists received a series of telephoned death threats, quite heavy ones – 'we're going to get you, we're going to kill you' – from different people each time. Another journalist flew to Johannesburg from PE and found that his luggage had been diverted, and when his luggage finally got to him, it had obviously been gone through. Then when he put on his jacket, his eyes started tearing up terribly and he found that tear gas powder had been put in the lining.

Another journalist had the brakes of her car cut, and then discovered four fired bullets in her car radiator. And another journalist was driving with a friend in PE and someone started following them. The guy pulled up alongside them – it seemed he wanted to squeeze them off the road – and then he threw a brick through their windscreen and nearly killed the person in the passenger seat. So all these things do seem to add up to a well-co-ordinated campaign of intimidation.

Why do you think that white journalists were the target of this campaign?

PE journalist: I think an important factor is that the white population in PE has traditionally been a very conservative one. The English-speaking settler population lacks any tradition of liberalism that you find in, say, Cape Town. PE was also an historical centre of Nazi sympathizers during the Second World War. Yet at the same time, the eastern Cape has been one of the centres of black resistance, dating back to the last century, and more recently, this area has had a history of militant union and community activity. In response to this, the security police have been particularly brutal in the way they've tried to suppress any kind of black opposition. Steve Biko and Lungile Tabalaza both died in security police detention in PE, and Siphiwe Mtimkhulu, a COSAS organizer, had thallium poisoning administered to him while in detention and then mysteriously disappeared. There definitely seems to be a willingness by the authorities in PE to use any means possible to maintain the status quo.

So, in 1980, when some progressive and liberal-minded journalists started working in PE, that was really unusual, historically. Information is a key area, especially where you're dealing with a situation that's highly charged, politically. And suddenly you had reporters who had some insights into the true dynamics of what was going on, who were writing stories that

---

Untitled poem by Ben J. Langa:[32]

i heard small children ask:
where's tiro
mdluli
mohapi
saloojee
haroon.
they asked where's
ahmed timol
biko
and the answer came from
the birds
the leaves of plants
and from the earth itself
they're gone,
they are no more.
the hand that slays in the dark
has removed them
only from the face of the earth.

i heard children ask:
what happened to mandela
to sisulu
mbeki
gwala
the list was long
i lost count.

they asked about sobukwe
about mahlangu
they were asking about the heroes
of their times.
they wanted to know about mama ngoyi
and all the heroines
whose sweat had brought hope
for the young and old.
maybe they would have forgotten
had mxenge
not been added to the list.
but now they shall ask:
where's g.m.
when history books are rewritten
the answers to these questions
will be in
black on white...
no longer whispered in corridors
but spoken
openly.
and when the story is retold
about g.m.
it shall be said:
scavengers
murderers
beasts

reflected more than the managerial point of view on strikes, and the police point of view on disturbances, and I think that was regarded as a threat.

Those journalists were also making contacts in the community, helping people in the townships establish a community newspaper, making contacts across racial barriers which had rarely existed before in PE. Because no one was acting illegally, there was no way to bring those journalists to court, so I guess it seemed the only way to dampen their enthusiasm for progressive work was to intimidate them on a level at which they couldn't strike back.

Normally, one would think of calling the police to have such incidents investigated.

PE journalist: Well, we did, eventually. The Criminal Investigation Department took statements and fingerprints, but we got no indication that they were particularly keen on apprehending the people involved. They told us it was people working professionally and said they couldn't pin anything on them. We felt it was a bit like asking the people who are attacking you to investigate themselves, although we couldn't say publicly that we thought it was the security police.

Do you think that perhaps the culprits were some kind of right-wing fanatics?

PE journalist: That's how the CID and our editors at the newspapers wanted us to see it, that these were isolated incidents of right-wing thugs who were pretty fanatical and had decided to launch their own personal vendetta. But the systematic nature of the campaign, and the fact that the attacks involved quite sophisticated techniques, showed that this couldn't have been pulled off by just a few, isolated right-wing vandals. They were professional people, operating a professional campaign, with a lot of resources.

Although the government passed an 'Intimidation Act' in 1982, the only people ever prosecuted under this law have been striking workers and community activists. The Intimidation Act has never been used against the perpetrators of the intensifying campaign of violence aimed at liberal and left-wing government opponents, which spread to Johannesburg in 1984, with even more vicious attacks on individuals, homes and property. The South African Police Force, which claims great success in apprehending 'terrorists', has had little success in solving the estimated 2000 incidents of right-wing terrorism reported over the past twenty years.[31] Even when the violence escalates to the point where political activists are murdered, the police rarely arrest any suspects.

Post, **23 November 1981:** The brutal killing of leading Durban civil rights lawyer and former Robben Island prisoner, Mr Griffiths Mxenge has been condemned as politically motivated by East Cape residents, lawyers and black organizations. Mr Mxenge, originally from Rayi Location, near King William's Town, was found on Friday morning at the Umlazi Stadium, Durban, with his throat slit and body badly mutilated. The secretary-general of the Port Elizabeth Black Civic Association, Mr Sandile Manase, said: 'We strongly condemn and deplore the terrorist killing of one of our black brothers. It reminds us of what recently happened to the family of the leader of the South African Allied Workers' Union, Mr Thozamile Gqwetha, whose mother and uncle were burnt to death when their home was set alight.' He added that what had happened to Mr Mxenge and to Mr Gqwetha, and others in the past, was what had come to be expected to happen to black leaders in the liberation struggle.

Mr Mxenge's wife, Victoria Nonyamezelo, also an attorney, said today she believed her husband had been murdered by a person or people opposed to what he stood for, politically. Mr Mxenge was an instructing attorney in many political trials, including the cases of Mapetla Mohapi, of King William's Town and Joseph Mdluli, of Durban, who both died while detained by Security Police. Mrs Mxenge said that when she identified her husband's body at the mortuary she could not believe it was his. 'One of his ears was cut off, his stomach was ripped out, his head was bashed in, and his whole body was full of stab wounds,' she said.

masquerading under the dark of night
in cowardly manner
ambushed a lone warrior
slew him
and threw him into the dumps
trying to disguise their
dirty dastardly crime.
they may have smiled and joked
because they are beasts
with sick minds.
did they not start with the dogs...
sordid minds
poisoned the dogs
as a prelude to their macabre game.
as they cut him to shreds
they satisfied
their gruesome sense of humour.
and the son of the soil
lay on the soggy grounds
his blood
washed into the soil
in final enactment

of his belongingness to the earth
the final
marriage
and return in soul
and blood to the land he loved
so dearly
so totally
... and his return to his roots
was made complete.
and as torrents fell
the earth rejoiced,
plants swayed merrily
as their roots
for so long thirsting
drank their fill.
Where the drops of blood fell
a monument shall emerge
and a fountain
from which africa shall drink
shall open
and griffiths' blood shall not
have been shed in vain.

Shortly before midnight in May 1984, Ben Langa answered a knock at the door and was shot dead.[33] "Late at night in August 1985 Victoria Mxenge was assassinated as she arrived home from a political meeting.

Repression

C. Never on Our Knees

East London *Daily Dispatch,* 9 April 1981: A trade unionist, detained for over seven months before he was called to give evidence in a security trial, was sentenced to a year's imprisonment when he refused to testify in court yesterday. Mr Philemon Bonisile Norushe, 34, local secretary of the African Food and Canning Workers Union, was called as a state witness in the trial of Mr Mandla Gxanyana, 26, charged with being a member of the ANC, but said he could not 'betray' Mr Gxanyana.

'I cannot testify because his contribution is great to me and my nation. I cannot testify against anyone who fights for our nation. Secondly, this case is a Congress (African National Congress) case and the Congress kills people who testify. Thirdly, there are people who have testified once, but they are leading bad lives today, because no one wants to associate with such people – they are called sell-outs. Some never drank liquor but today they are drunk. Why? Because of frustration, as no one wants to know them,' said Mr Norushe, when asked for his reasons for refusing. Mr Norushe had been called to testify about certain banned literature allegedly given to him by Mr Gxanyana, who is also charged with furthering the aims of the ANC, by helping a Mr Bubule Boya to flee the country, following his role in the school boycotts last year.

South Africa projects its political system as a western-style democracy based on an independent judiciary – a far cry from some 'tin pot dictatorship' where government opponents mysteriously disappear in the night. Detentions and interrogations of those suspected of being a threat to state security are conducted according to laws, and when the state amasses enough evidence to take to court, detainees are charged and tried. Although such 'crimes' are often no more than possession of banned literature or the display of anti-government views, the trials are never described as political. Those who violate South Africa's security laws are 'criminals', a label aimed at depoliticizing their opposition to unjust laws.[34]

Often interrogation is not aimed at eliciting a confession or evidence to be used against detainees in their own trials, but rather at coercing them to give evidence in the trials of fellow detainees. The outcome of many political trials hinges on the testimony of state witnesses. While many detainees succumb to the pressures of solitary confinement and security police torture and agree to take the witness stand for the state, an increasing number do not. The court room has become a theatre of resistance, as detainees brought to the witness box by security police choose to return to their cells rather than testify for the state against their friends and colleagues.

In 1983, a white priest was sentenced to six months in jail for refusing to testify in the trial of a young student charged with treason.

Father Thomas Stanton of St Peter's Priory, Johannesburg, in a letter explaining to the judge why he refused to testify for the state in the trial of Carl Niehaus: Your Worship, I am a member of the Community of the Resurrection, which is an Anglican Order. We live together in obedience to a Rule, giving priority to prayer and worship, and we serve the Church in various ways, according to our gifts and resources. In the Rule of this Community, there is a sentence: 'Nothing shall be finally required of any brother which violates his conscience.' I believe that to make a statement, or to give evidence against Carl Niehaus, would violate my conscience.

Carl Niehaus has stayed at our Priory in Rosettenville occasionally. We value our contact with him, especially because he is a member of the Dutch Reformed Church. I can say that he is my friend, though in fact I don't know him very well. I have no idea what he has done, to warrant this charge. But I believe in him. I believe that he is concerned to bring about a more just ordering of society than exists here at present. I would wish to support him in this; to give evidence for the state in their case against this young man would be a thing of which I would be deeply ashamed for the rest of my life. It seems to me that it would be a form of betrayal and I cannot do it.

I do not mean to be contemptuous of the court, and I do not wish to impede the course of justice. I believe that the police, in fact, already have the information which they want me to give under oath. I am told that I shall go to jail, and that going to jail will be an empty gesture – that it will do no good. Your Worship, I would rather live in jail as a result of an empty gesture made in good faith than outside it with a guilty conscience of having said or done anything to further the conviction of this young man.[35]

Former security detainee who refused to serve as a state witness: Unless you've thrashed through this issue before you get detained, there's no way you can work it out for yourself inside. There's the problem that once your interrogators tell you they want you as a state witness, there is a sort of feeling of relief: 'Whew! I'm not going to be in the accused box.' Whereas before, you were the detainee, and they're hammering you, now you've actually got a bit of leverage behind you because they need you as a state witness.

Fortunately, I had dealt with the issue before, and I had told people outside, before I'd been picked up, that if I was ever called to be a witness I wouldn't do it. So in a sense it was off my chest, knowing that the people outside, whom I couldn't communicate with, at least knew that was the position I was going to take. But then you have to start gearing yourself for a prison sentence. Because you know then that it won't be just a few weeks till you're out, but it'll be a few years – that's the kind of sentence you get these days for refusing to testify, and it will probably get worse and worse.[36]

Not that I didn't go through doubts. It seemed that they had found so much on the accused, in terms of evidence, that I really didn't see that they needed me as a witness. So that led me to thinking, well, they've actually got it in for me and they want to intimidate me at this point. And then, of course – I'm sure everybody thinks it – I'd think, one person is going to jail anyway, so why should two go? I'd think, maybe I would be more effective outside; if I'm stuck in jail, I can't make any contribution at all – so that's another

reason to cave in and testify. But I'd keep coming back to the principle of the thing. It would be such a betrayal of whoever you worked with. I mean, you have to be able to assume that people are going to refuse to give evidence when you do political work with somebody, because that's the basic minimum of trust that you have to develop. And then there's also the fact that to be a state witness you're giving evidence for a state that we actually regard as being illegitimate anyway, because it doesn't represent the people. So to be a state witness would be to just totally sell out your principles and those of the people you worked with.

But maybe the most important to me is the personal aspect. I knew that I was in a far more advantageous position to serve a prison sentence than a lot of other people who would also choose to refuse. I had no dependents, I was young, I was healthy, I had a whole life ahead of me, and a four or five year prison sentence was not going to kill me. I mean, if I wasn't prepared to make a small sacrifice, who would be? And, of course, my personal relationship with the accused was a big factor. I can't imagine how he feels about the people who did give evidence against him, because of the betrayed trust. I mean, for one of your friends to stand up in court and contribute to your prison sentence! You just don't do that to people who are involved in the same struggle as you, the same cause, who are your friends.

The pressures on security detainees who refuse to serve as state witnesses have perhaps been best articulated in a poem by a former political prisoner, written about a fellow inmate at Pretoria Maximum Security Prison, John Matthews.

'Walking on Air' (excerpt), by Jeremy Cronin:[37]

White and 52
so they treated him nice.
They only made him stand

On two bricks
for three days
and three nights and

When he asked to go to the lavatory
they said:
Shit in your pants.

But the State needed witnesses
So they changed their tune.
Tried sweet-talking him round.
Think of your career
(that didn't work)
Think of the shame of going to jail
(That thought only
filled him with pride)
You really want kaffirs to rule?
(like you said)
Think of your wife
(Dulcie. Dulcie.
7 kids. Dulcie.
She's not political at all.)

And there they had him
On that score he was worried, it's true
And they promised him freedom.
And they pressed him for weeks on end
until finally he said:

Okay, agreed.

— But first I must speak with my wife.

Barely an hour it took them to find
and rush Dulcie Matthews
out to Pretoria Jail.

Then looking nice, because they let him
shave,
let him comb his hair, looking nice then,
chaperoned by smiling, matrimonial
policemen, shaven and combed, John
Matthews
got led out to his wife, and holding her
hand, they let him hold her hand, he said

— Do you know why they've brought
you?
And she said
— I do.
And he said
— Dulcie, I will never betray my
comrades.
And with a frog in her throat she replied
— I'm behind you. One hundred per cent.

So back they hauled John Matthews then
and there,

Back to the cells,
that was that, then, but
all the way down the passage
toe-heel, heel-toe, diddle-diddle
ONE HUNDRED PER CENT
I mean, he was high
off the ground, man.

He was walking on air.

South African security legislation defines a range of offences, from 'furthering the aims of a banned organization' to High Treason. Until recently, though, the only non-wartime treason trial in South African history was the prosecution of 156 leading members of the Congress Alliance (comprising the ANC, Congress of Democrats, South African Congress of Trade Unions, Indian Congress and Coloured People's Congress), a marathon trial that began in 1956 and ended in 1961 with the state's failure to prove the defendants' involvement in a communist conspiracy to overthrow the government. Throughout the rest of the 1960s and 1970s, the state charged its opponents on various counts under the Internal Security, Terrorism, Riotous Assemblies, Suppression of Communism and General Law Amendment Acts, but never for High Treason. Even ANC leader Nelson Mandela was sentenced to life imprisonment in 1964 under the Sabotage Act – not for treason.

In the late 1970s, the state's tactics changed. The children of the 1976 Soweto uprisings were back in the country as trained guerillas and those the police arrested needed to be made examples of. When twelve Soweto men were charged in the Pietermaritzburg Supreme Court in 1979, the government decided the time had come for another treason trial.

The circumstances of this case – with the first evidence of running gun battles between insurgents and security forces, plots to assassinate police and government officials, and huge arms caches throughout the country – represented a greater threat to state security than any political activity since the 1960s. Yet it was the drama that unfolded daily in the courtroom that won this treason trial its place in the history of South African resistance. Tension between the defendants and the judge had been building since the twelve men were first marched into their specially constructed glass dock, but it was a ruling by the judge, ordering part of the trial to be held behind closed doors, that sparked off a confrontation unprecedented in South Africa's courts.

Rand Daily Mail, **2 August 1979:** Policeman armed with automatic shotguns were at Pietermaritzburg Supreme Court yesterday, as 12 suspects appeared on charges of High Treason and conspiracy to commit murder. As Mr Justice Hefer and two assessors took their seats, the accused filed into a dock specially constructed of shatter-proof glass. The accused are Mr John Selete, 24; Mr Tladitsgae Molefe, 23; Mr Jeffrey Legoabe, 30; Mr Thibe Ngobeni, 27; Mr Andrew Mapheto, 20; Mr Bennet Komane, 46; Mr Titus Maleka, 25; Mr Sydney Choma, 23; Mr Mandlenkosi Hadebe, 27; Mr Mandla Mthetwa, 22; Mr Vusumuzi Zulu, 28; and Mr James Mange, 24.

The state alleges that the accused recruited people, trained them in the art of warfare, armed them, and deployed them in South Africa for the purpose of overthrowing the government. Training of the accused took place at the Engineering camp, the Benguela camp, the Nova Gagenga camp and the Quibaxe camp in Angola, the Mambeshe ZAPU camp in Zambia, and the Pirivalie camp in the Ukraine, Russia. The state claims that the men attempted to bring AK-47 rifles into the Msinga area and that they established arms caches in Natal in the districts of Ndumo and Nongoma and reconnoitred pipelines at Merebank, near Durban, in order to sabotage them.

Statement by the twelve treason trialists: We have decided that the nature of High Treason is a crime affecting society, and by excluding the public, it would be defeating the purposes of this trial, of what the ANC wanted to achieve. We are charged as members of the ANC, and we perceive the crime of High Treason as the violent overthrowal of the white South African government. We therefore wish to take no further part in this trial and would rather the trial proceeded in our absence. If we are accused of bad things, the public is entitled to know how bad we are, why we are bad, and who says we are bad. If the trial is in camera, the public won't know what bad things we have done, or have in mind. That is why we refuse, under all conditions, to take part in this trial while it is closed to society.

Justice Hefer supported an application by the state that the testimony of certain of the 144 planned state witnesses be heard in camera. Quoting from the official ANC publication, *Sechaba,* he said the aim of the ANC was clearly to 'eliminate' police informers, witnesses who testified for the state in terrorism trials, and the security police. The twelve accused then announced that they no longer wanted to take part in the trial, and dismissed their lawyers. From that point onwards, it was no longer twelve black 'terrorists' who were on trial, but the South African system of justice itself – which had never before been confronted with such explicit and determined defiance.

Justice Hefer: In the interests of justice, the dignity of the courts has to be preserved. If we lose control of trials, then we lose control of the administration of justice.

Natal Mercury, **13 November 1979:** Twelve suspected terrorists, who repeatedly broke into song, gave Black Power salutes, and shouted ear-splitting war cries, were warned by a judge yesterday that further outbursts would not be tolerated. The warning from Mr Justice Hefer came after the men had paraded into the court at the start of proceedings and burst into song. They had clapped their hands, danced in the dock, and then given the members of the public Black Power salutes, before taking their places in the specially-built dock. After the men had shouted war cries, their leader, Mr James Mange, shouted 'Down with capitalism, down with fascism!'

Yesterday afternoon, Mr Justice Hefer told the men they would be punished if a further outburst occurred. 'You may think it will not make a difference at this stage what you do in court,' he said. 'I warn you for the last time, particularly accused number 12 (Mr James Mange), who is the leader of these little sing-songs, that what I do will make a difference,'

The Supreme Court had the look of an army headquarters in a war zone yesterday. As judgment began, some of the strictest security measures ever seen at a South African trial went into operation. Squads of police armed with riot gear, rifles and submachine guns, guarded all entrances and exits to the court building. All vehicles entering the court grounds were searched, and members of the press and public were body searched before being allowed into the courtroom.

Tears, jeers and song as 11 begin 184 years in jail

Terrorist sent to the gallows

The trial ended with South Africa's first convictions for High Treason outside wartime, and defendant James Mange – whose singing, chanting and general contempt of court most angered the judge – received the death sentence.[38]

Durban *Daily News,* **16 November 1979:** A Russian-trained terrorist was sentenced to death and 11 of his comrades were jailed for a total of 184 years, when South Africa's first treason trial in 20 years drew to a close yesterday. James Mange (24), who was sentenced to death for plotting to exterminate the magistrate and police sergeant at Whittlesea in the Cape, sat impassively in the dock while Mr Justice Hefer pronounced sentence. He then leaned forward, threw up his arm in the ANC power salute, and screamed 'Amandla!' before settling himself comfortably in the corner of the specially constructed dock.

'All were South Africans or owed allegiance to the country, and have been found guilty of what is, in a sense, the ultimate crime against the state,' said the judge.[39] The court could not allow people who had a grievance, and no constitutional means to rectify it, to resort to unconstitutional means to achieve their aims. 'By allowing this, society would destroy itself and the courts could not be party to it,' he said. Mr Justice Hefer referred to the men's behaviour during the stormy seven-week hearing, and said they had displayed 'the most blatantly provocative defiance' he had ever experienced. Mange, 'who had been the instigator of most of the unpleasantness,' later again led the accused in song, and chanted, 'Long live Bram Fischer, long live Joe Slovo, long live Fidel Castro!' Giving reasons for passing the death sentence on Mange, Mr Justice Hefer said: 'How far is a traitor to be allowed to go before the death penalty is imposed?' He added that he took into account 'the times in which we are living, when the ANC has so often proclaimed it is at war with South Africa.'

Sunday Post, **18 November 1979:** The storm of anger that howled through Soweto and other parts of the country in 1976 reverberated in the Pietermaritzburg Supreme Court during the first treason trial to be heard in South Africa since 1961. Twelve men who left South Africa about the time of the 1976 uprising, to receive military training in Russia, East Germany, Angola, or Zambia were in August this year charged with High Treason. Each man's background, as sketched by the court, includes a period lived in Soweto, with a subsequent absence from South Africa during which he received military training. During judgement, the prisoners displayed placards smuggled into their specially constructed shatter-proof glass dock, proclaiming, 'Apartheid is High Treason' and 'Never on Our Knees'. The 12 sang battle hymns sporadically throughout the hearing, sacked their defence counsel, refused to participate in the trial, gave ANC salutes while chanting political slogans, and, again this week, sang in court after Mr Justice Hefer pronounced them guilty of High Treason. And still they sang. Even as the Black Maria (police van) drove them away from the Pietermaritzburg Supreme Court, and the small group of family and friends who huddled together in the rain waved encouraging clenched fist salutes.

For many black South Africans, the judge's statement – that the ANC is at war with South Africa's rulers – was probably the only aspect of his verdict that they accepted. Of all the sensational media accounts of the landmark treason trial, only a Soweto newspaper recognized the escalation of the South African conflict represented by the case, and the direct link it drew between the Soweto uprisings of 1976 and the ANC of the future.

Rand Daily Mail, 8 December 1983: Words scratched on a tin mug have earned a Dobsonville man 18 months in jail under the Internal Security Act. Mathews Thomas Ntshiwa, 23, of Mmutle Street, was given a further 18 months suspended sentence for advocating, advising, defending or encouraging the achievement of the objects of the banned African National Congress. In the Krugersdorp Regional Court yesterday, the magistrate, Mr W. Aucamp, accepted evidence that Ntshiwa had engraved on the mug: 'Amandla Gowethu' (sic), 'Release Nelson Mandela', 'Remember our leader', 'Those who are trying to destroy apartheid in our land', 'Umkhodo we siswe' (sic) and 'P.W. we want our land back'. He said that it had to be taken into account that Ntshiwa had used his mug in the factory canteen, which was used by many workers who could have been incited. Mr Ntshiwa told the court he had not thought the engravings would 'lead to such seriousness. I only used to drink tea out of my mug,' he said.

Rand Daily Mail, 3 June 1983: Two Rastafarians were each sentenced to an effective four years' jail yesterday after being convicted by the Johannesburg Regional Court of furthering the aims of the African National Congress. Joseph Charles, 24, and Rufus Radebe, 18, were found guilty of singing ANC songs and chanting ANC slogans at a music festival in Roodeport on February 12. They had pleaded not guilty. According to Constable Nel, Radebe and Charles, who are members of the reggae band 'Splash', had performed songs entitled 'A Tribute to Martyrs' and 'Freedom to Mandela' and had chanted 'Jah Nelson Mandela', 'Jah Oliver Tambo', and 'Amandla'. Before sentence was passed, Mr G. Dyson for the defence, said that as members of the Rastafarian cult, Radebe and Charles did not advocate violence. 'They don't seem to be people who would actively stir up support for a banned organization. Anyone who did what they did is clearly not a calculated, cunning opponent of law and order,' he said.

Rand Daily Mail, 12 November 1983: The three people acquitted by a Krugersdorp magistrate of furthering the aims of the ANC yesterday said they were thrilled to be reunited with their families and friends. But they all said they believed there had been no reason for their arrest. Mr George Moiloa, 29, Miss Amanda Kwadi, 31, and the Reverend Molefe Tsele, 27, accused of taking part in the activities of the ANC and also of trying to overthrow the government, said in interviews at their homes that this was a test case, because if they were found guilty, it would have set a precedent. The Reverend Tsele of the Lutheran Church said their acquittal reaffirmed their rights to celebrate those days which blacks were proud of. Miss Amanda Kwadi, an executive member of the Federation of South African Women, said as far as she was concerned, organizing a Women's Day commemoration service was not an offence. She said this was a historical event which blacks were proud of. 'I am happy to be free, but I think of those still in jail and in detention. Apartheid and oppression are still intact.'

Since the Pietermaritzburg treason trial, this ultimate political crime has become a common offence. Between 1980 and 1983, the state mounted fifteen different treason trials, involving thirty-seven people. Mange's death sentence was eventually commuted to twenty years in prison, but the appeals of three ANC cadres later convicted of treason were rejected, and they were hanged in 1983. A similar trend is seen in the government's efforts to charge and convict political activists on minor and technical breaches of security laws, in an effort to discourage the new wave of support for the ANC.

With these trials, the government has succeeded in 'criminalizing' even the paraphernalia and ephemera of resistance. It has even gone one step further, attempting to make events and commemorations criminal. Three political activists who had organized a commemoration of South African Women's Day – a holiday historically identified with the ANC – were arrested more than a year after the meeting, held for months, and then prosecuted. Although they were ultimately acquitted, the state had succeeded in deactivating three prominent organizers while 'justice' took its course.

Funerals of former ANC leaders draw thousands of people who seize the opportunity to march through the streets singing freedom songs and chanting slogans, since open-air gatherings (except for religious services and meetings of recognized political parties) have been banned since 1976. When Rose Mbele, an ANC activist in the 1950s, died on the ANC's seventieth anniversary in January 1982, her coffin was draped in an ANC flag and escorted through Soweto by singing, chanting supporters. Security police filmed and photographed the funeral, but made no arrests until more than a year later. The ensuing trial was yet another attempt by the state to make criminal any event at all related to the ANC.

Rand Daily Mail, **25 February 1984:** Albertina Sisulu was yesterday sentenced to an effective two years' imprisonment for furthering the aims of the banned African National Congress. The case arose from the funeral of Mrs Rose Mbele, of the (formerly ANC-affiliated) Federation of South African Women, in Soweto in 1982. Sisulu (66) and her co-accused, Thami Mali (25), were charged with singing ANC songs during the funeral service, distributing pamphlets and stickers, displaying the ANC flag, praising the organization, and draping the deceased's coffin with the ANC flag. The magistrate said Sisulu, wife of the imprisoned ANC leader, Walter Sisulu, was an elderly women and a grandmother, who had spent many lonely years because of her husband's incarceration. However, he said, it was the court's opinion that the ANC had escalated its activities, and the offences had been part of ANC strategy.

Rand Daily Mail, **5 November 1983:** The leader of the extreme right-wing Afrikaner Weerstandbeweging (Afrikaner Resistance Movement), Eugene Terre'Blanche, was carried shoulder-high down the steps of the Pretoria Supreme Court yesterday by flag-waving supporters, after being given a suspended jail sentence as an accomplice in the unlawful possession of firearms. The fiery arch-conservative then gave an impromptu speech in Church Square, before a crowd of about 100 AWB members and journalists, saying, 'The battle for the survival of a white, Christian nation will continue.' Terre'Blanche. the AWB's secretary, Jan Groenewald, and former member Jacob Daniel Viljoen, were found not guilty by Mr Justice Henk Van Dyk on charges of terrorism, or alternatively, participating in terrorist activities. The judge found them guilty of possession of firearms, among which were four AK-47 automatic rifles, and more than 4000 rounds of ammunition. But, he ruled, Terre'Blanche was only an accomplice. Groenewald was found guilty of possessing a missile and a smoke grenade. All are former members of the South African Police. Before passing sentence, Mr Justice Van Dyk said he found the accused to be 'civilized and decent people. The fact that they were in possession of these articles was an unfortunate concurrence of events. The community would certainly not expect me to send them to jail,' he said.

Reuters News Agency (Johannesburg bureau), 30 May 1984: A white youth who battered a black man to death with karate sticks was ordered to serve 1200 hours in prison on weekends (less than six months). According to trial testimony, Ronnie van der Merwe was walking down a street with a girlfriend and bragged that he was going to kill a 'houtkop' (blockhead), a derogatory term for blacks. He beat to death the next black man he met. The judge said van der Merwe (20) could be partly excused since he was upset because his parents were on the verge of divorce. 'This is totally demeaning to us,' a black journalist complained privately after the sentence. 'The judge treated the case as if someone had wantonly killed a dog.' In another case, three young white men who kicked a black man to death because they thought he was tampering with their car were sentenced to five cuts with a cane. A Johannesburg newspaper quoted one of the defendants as saying he laughed after the caning, as he got off so lightly. Lawyers say a black is more likely to be sentence to death than a white. Out of 100 people sent to the gallows in 1983, 99 were black.

The same system of justice which can send a black grandmother to jail for attending a friend's funeral and pass a death sentence on a black youth who has taken no life can show remarkable mercy where white criminals are concerned – notably those with strong right-wing and racist views – and an apparent lack of compassion for their black victims.

One of South Africa's most wanted criminals, bank robber André Stander, was a former police lieutenant and the son of a high-ranking police officer. When Stander was shot dead by American police in a hideout in Florida in 1984, after escaping from a South African prison, evading a police dragnet for months, and finally fleeing the country, Stander's father blamed the police for turning his son to crime.

Police shootings are the most chilling form of state repression, and the number of people shot by police in South Africa has risen markedly during the recent years of 'reform'.

Although the vast majority of people shot dead by police are blacks in townships,the numbers of whites killed by police have also risen in recent years. In Johannesburg in1983, a young white family man was gunned down by police in unmarked cars who claimed they thought he was a car thief. The Minister of Law and Order responded to calls for a judicial inquiry into the case with a reminder that the Criminal Procedures Act gives policemen the right to shoot and kill a suspect.

The city of Pietermaritzburg, the provincial capital of Natal, lost two young men in police shootings within six months – one black and one white. The sharply contrasting reactions of the black and white communities to the two killings underscore the differing realities of police violence for blacks and for whites.

Repression
D. No Warning Shots

Rand Daily Mail, **23 February 1984:** Retired Police General Frans Stander believes that the drastic personality change which turned a top policeman into a dangerous robber was brought about by his experiences in the police force. Stander, who joined the police in Rustenburg when he was in Standard 9, completed his matric with four distinctions in the same year he was nominated Police Student of the Year. Stander's dissatisfaction with police methods came to a climax during the 1976 riots when, his father said, he killed 22 blacks. 'André loved blacks and always got on very well with his black colleagues, but as a policeman he was forced to shoot kaffirs,' General Stander said.

South African Press Association, 16 February 1984: A total of 211 people were shot and killed by the South African Police in the execution of their duties during 1983, the Minister of Law and Order, Mr. Louis le Grange announced yesterday. Mr le Grange revealed that of the 211 people shot dead by police, nine were juveniles. He said that 169 were black adults, 29 coloured and four white. An analysis of shootings by the police conducted by the Natal University academics, Professor Lawrence Schlemmer and Ms Marisa Fick, last year showed that 1300 people were killed by the police between 1972 and 1982. The figure in 1972 was 92 killed and 299 wounded. Five years later, this had increased to 163 killed and 495 wounded. The analysis showed, they said, that compared to statistics in western Europe, the number shot by police in South Africa was high.

Natal Witness, **30 September 1982:** Hundreds of black youths, angered by the death of a Sobantu teenager shot during a protest on Tuesday, marched through the township again yesterday and at one point were set upon by riot police with dogs. The youths were preparing to march on the Drakensburg Administration Board offices with placards protesting against a R3.90 rent increase, when they heard that Graham Radebe (17) had died. News of his death provoked many youths to create new placards asking, 'Why did you shoot us?' The protesters then marched toward the DAB offices but were dispersed by riot police who arrived in police vans and ran at the youths with Alsatians on leads.

Mrs Nancy Radebe, Graham's mother: One would have expected the police to let his soul be laid down in peace and dignity, considering how he died, but his grave was turned into a riot scene.

Natal Witness, **19 February 1983:** The telephone hardly stopped ringing at the Christie Road home of Mr Brian Eudey and his wife Margie yesterday. They were calls offering condolences at the loss of their son, Bryn, who had returned for the weekend from a three-month army camp. Bryn was shot dead at the wheel of his bakkie (pick-up truck) in College Road at about 2.30 a.m. on Thursday. Among those present was Mr Alain Currie, a close friend of Bryn's who was sitting in the passenger seat when the police opened fire. Retracing the events leading up to the tragedy, Mr Currie said he first saw Bryn that day at about 1.50 a.m. at a party, and he asked Mr Currie to go for a ride to see how the bakkie backfired.

'At about 2.25 a.m. we drove down Longmarket Street, then turned right into West Street. As we went down the hill, there was a lot of backfiring and we laughed a lot,' said Mr Currie. 'As we turned into College Road, I heard what I thought was more backfiring and I thought it was strange as we were accelerating at the time. The next thing I knew, Bryn slumped sideways over me. I jumped out immediately and a police van drove up. I shouted to them to call an ambulance, but all I heard was someone saying in Afrikaans: "Why did you shoot at the Supreme Court?" Then a policeman said, "Hou jou bek." (Shut your mouth.) Mr Currie said that at no stage had he seen any policemen or a police vehicle before the shooting. 'There was no warning – no sound. There was no possible reason for the shooting.'

However, according to Brigadier W. van Wyk, a senior police spokesman, a uniformed policeman, standing under a light near the bridge, had both signalled and shouted at the driver to stop. The policeman opened fire after the bakkie had driven away after the first slowing down. Mr van Wyk said College Road was a 'sensitive area'.

Daily News, **31 January 1983:** A bomb exploded at mid-day yesterday at Pietermaritzburg's College Road Supreme Court, damaging the historic, red-bricked venue of many terrorism trials and the Air India (Seychelles) hijack trial.[40] The blast hurled stones and bricks more than 300 metres. A schoolboy playing cricket nearby was reportedly grazed by flying mortar, but no one was hurt by the explosion, which was heard by people as far as 12 kilometres away. Uniformed, plainclothes and reactor unit policeman were at the scene of the blast within minutes. The area was cordoned off and roadblocks barred traffic and pedestrians from the area. A senior police spokesman said the region had been declared a restricted area and the public as well as press were prevented from entering the area while dogs sniffed around and police carried out investigations.

After a seventeen-year-old blackman was shot by police in the township of Sobantu, police feared a further display of outrage and militancy at Graham Radebe's funeral, so a ban was placed on all protests, political speeches, songs, placards and pamphlets, and a court order even dictated the route to be followed between the church service and the cemetery. Despite all these restrictions, armed riot police found it necessary to teargas the burial, arresting thirty-nine mourners and forcing the rest to flee.

There was a certain predictability to the events surrounding Radebe's death, from the protests that prompted the police shooting to the inevitable inquest finding no policeman to blame. The sequence of events that led to the fatal shooting of an unarmed 21-year-old white man in downtown Pietermaritzburg was anything but predictable.

Constable fined R3 000 for shooting

Three weeks before Bryn Eudey's killing, a blast shook the Natal 'Sleepy Hollow', as Pietermaritzburg is nicknamed. 'Terrorism' had always been confined to the dock of the Supreme Courthouse: now it was shattering the court's very foundations. It was no wonder, then, that when Bryn Eudey's truck backfired in front of the courthouse three weeks after the blast, the police were feeling a bit jumpy – at least, that was the defence lawyer's argument when Eudey's killer was prosecuted for culpable homicide in that same courthouse.

At his trial, Constable Barnard admitted that he had shot and killed people before, during the course of his duties as a policeman. He agreed under cross-examination that he had shot a black man in the head and killed him, while investigating a case in which a shirt had been stolen off a washing line, and said he did not believe in firing warning shots, as there was a danger of ricocheting bullets hitting others or himself. Constable Barnard was never prosecuted for killing that black man; it took the murder of a white man to get him into the dock.

There were no angry demonstrations after Bryn Eudey's death, no marches, no placards, and no need for teargas at his funeral. A few friends and some students from Pietermaritzburg's white university sat in on Constable Barnard's trial to show support for the Eudey family, and perhaps register some vague sense of injustice at the 'senseless killing'. Bryn Eudey was not mourned with freedom songs; his death fuelled no struggle. The contrast between the effect of Bryn Eudey's death on the white community, and the effect of Graham Radebe's death on the black community, was stark, as is seen from the views of those who live in Pietermaritzburg's white suburbs and black townships.

Black: A lot of people were saying, after the Eudey killing, 'If they shoot their own people, can you imagine what they'd dare to do to us?' We've seen this hardening on the part of the police. We know they respond violently. White policemen have been turned into ardent racists, in order to do their job, so even with the new reforms coming in from the top, you still have this repression underneath. The only positive thing that comes out of it, from our point of view, is that ordinary people are beginning to see clearly the role played by the police in this society, whose interests the police are actually protecting – because of their own bitter day-to-day experience.

White: Bryn's death should have been a major issue, at least on campus with the (white) students, but it wasn't, really. It was front page newspapers for a few days and that was it. Even Bryn's parents didn't seem to want to push the issue, as if they were afraid of taking on the police or something. I know a journalist who wanted to interview them and do a story on what the whole tragedy had done to their lives, and they said no, they didn't want to talk, and how they really supported the police and this was just an unfortunate incident. I'd like to think that my parents would make more of a stink if I was shot!

I guess you could say that the reason for the apathy is that everyone just knows nothing's going to happen, that the police will get off. But then, you know, when blacks are shot or arrested and there's a court case, blacks cram into court to show their support – and they certainly know that they're not going to win the case.

Black: There were some people in the black community who were relating the Eudey shooting to the bombing at the courthouse, saying that the whites had gone scared and trigger-happy, saying that the blast had had the desired effect if it made the cops so nervous.

White: The courthouse bombing actually made people quite scared, because you start wondering what your security's like if you can have bomb blasts at the Supreme Court.[41] So I think all these bombs are alerting the white population, especially because of the fact that they've been so well planned and well executed. I mean, it's not idiots who are doing these things –

there does seem to be a strategy of sorts behind these bombings. I remember I saw this grafitti after the blast: 'Rid the world of injustice – bomb a Supreme Court today!' Okay, that's a bit facetious but it certainly indicates that people are thinking about why these courts are being attacked.

Black: Black people know what those courts represent: they're part of the government which is responsible for the conditions that black people face every day. People identify those structures as being part of the system that is oppressing them. Every second black person has been through those courts at some point or other, for some petty or stupid offence: not having their pass, or trespassing or something. And then, of course, there are the political trials that are held in those courts.

People are starting to make connections between these kind of blasts and the repression of the system. People are aware that the government instigates this kind of thing, by leaving people without alternatives. People understand that violence is the only response to a violent system. When something like the Radebe murder happens, people may feel fairly hopeless against the power of the state, but when these blasts and other attacks happen, people begin to feel that they're not alone, that there's another force that's a much bigger force, which is supporting their resistance, and it boosts their confidence.

It was interesting, being at the scene after the courthouse bombings. People rushed to the place, just to get a look at what damage had been done. You hear whites standing around, saying, 'Oh, we must expect these things.' I think that indicates an acceptance of the violence, the fact that these kinds of bombings have been happening all over the country, and now they're happening in our town – that it's to be expected. The blacks didn't want to say too much, with whites standing nearby, but you saw lots of smiles, black people smiling at each other and giving the thumbs' up sign[42] – but also being very careful who they smile at. There's such tension, such polarization. It's on days like that you feel the war.

The Star, **3 June 1983:** The late Bryn Eudey and the man who shot him dead, Constable Marthinus Barnard, were both victims of urban terrorism, Barnard's defence counsel, Mr Jan Combrink, SC, said today. Had the Supreme Court building not been bombed about three weeks before Mr Eudey's shooting, this tragedy would not have occurred, Mr Combrink said. He said Mr Barnard's acts did not originate out of his own initiative. Mr Combrink said that Mr Barnard was remorseful because he thought he had shot a terrorist, only to find out he had shot an innocent young man who had served his country for two years on the border.

State counsel Mr John van der Berg said that police were in a state of tension because of the acts of terrorism in the country and that more shootings of innocent people were possible. The mere fact that terrorists were seeking out targets for attack was not justification for the police to grab their guns and shoot. They had to make sure a target was, in fact, being attacked and not risk the lives of innocents. He said that in 1982, 739 people had been shot by the police and of this number, 188 had died.

Rand Daily Mail, **4 June 1983:** Constable Marthinus Christoffel Barnard was yesterday sentenced to a fine of R3,000 and a suspended sentence of three years' jail for the 'tragic and senseless' killing of 21-year-old Bryn Eudey. In passing sentence on the 29-year-old policeman, Mr Justice Nienaber said the police force must be given the impression that they must make sure they are dealing with criminals before reverting to shooting to kill. The judge said he had decided not to send Barnard to jail because he had acted in the performance of his duties. He said there was no doubt that Barnard honestly believed the sound of the backfiring was gunshots and that a terror attack was being made on the College Road Supreme Court.

Repression

E. Détente Grows From the Barrel of a Gun

South African Army chief, General Jannie Geldenhuys, in 'Revolutionary Warfare and Counter-Insurgency', University of Pretoria Strategic Studies publication, 1984: Cross-border raids aimed at the elimination of insurgents in their bases are ten times more cost-effective in terms of Security Force lives than search-and-destroy operations conducted against insurgents on home ground.

From the soldier's point of view, killing of insurgents and destruction of their facilities at their bases is preferable to seek-and-destroy and/or hot pursuit operations launched after the insurgents have crossed the border. But cross-border operations aimed at destroying SWAPO bases in Angola have political implications which have to be weighed by the politicians in power. The commander will probably have a lot of pressure on him from the politicians and administrators to provide more and more protection, but he will simply have to resist that type of pressure. If he does not, he will end up with all his troops committed to defence in a war where offensive action is vital.

SABC, 26 August 1981: In this bulletin, we highlight an Angolan request to the Secretary-General of the United Nations to force what it calls the South African invasionary force from southern Angola, and news that twenty-nine more SWAPO terrorists have been killed by the Security Forces since last Thursday. In Cape Town, a spokesman for the Department of Defence said it was known that the South African Security Forces cross the border into Angola from time to time, for follow-up operations directed at SWAPO forces. This is done to protect local inhabitants in South West Africa against attacks by SWAPO terrorists. The spokesman said this morning that in carrying out such operations, the Security Forces try to adhere to a policy of avoiding contact with Angolan troops. He said the Angolan propaganda campaign could definitely be interpreted as a calculated blow before the UN Assembly session on South West Africa. The spokesman declined to make any further comment.

The commander of the South West African Territorial Force, Major-General Charles Lloyd, said that both the Prime Minister and the Minister of Defence had repeatedly noted that South Africa was doing everything she could to live in peace with her neighbouring states. However, those states had been warned that good neighbourliness was irreconcilable with support for terrorism. General Lloyd said that acts of terror against the local population could not be tolerated, and it was inevitable that terrorists would be pursued and the bases from which they operated destroyed.

The South African government's twin strategies of reform and repression have foreign policy counterparts. South Africa claims to seek regional peace and stability, yet from the mid-1970s it has worked to destabilize the subcontinent. Destabilization evolved as a response to the crumbling of the colonial buffer that had surrounded South Africa until the Portugese empire fell in 1974, and independent Mozambique and Angola began offering support to Pretoria's enemies, the African National Congress and the South West African People's Organization, fighting for majority rule in Namibia. Ever since South Africa's abortive invasion of Angola in 1975, it has launched countless raids across the border from Namibia, and occupied vast areas of southern Angola. South Africa's goal has been twofold: to stymie SWAPO's incursions into Namibia, and to hit economic targets in Angola, so as to cripple the revolutionary government which supports SWAPO and the ANC. South Africa's generals believe that offence is the best defence, and have persuaded the politicians that such a policy makes economic as well as political sense.

Thus South Africa has fought SWAPO, not only in Namibia, but in Angola.

For many white South Africans, these invasions of Angola were not unlike South Africa's efforts to compete in the international sports arena: anti-apartheid demonstrations are a bit annoying, but South Africa can be sure that international condemnation will be outweighed by the unflagging support of its western allies, in particular the United States. When the biggest mobilization of conventional forces by the South African Defence Force since World War II coincided with the boycott-breaking Springbok rugby tour of New Zealand in 1981, the SABC could not resist drawing the analogy.

SABC, 31 August 1981: As, over the weekend, South Africans rejoiced at the splendid victory of the Springboks in New Zealand, other of the country's representatives were returning from the battlefield in Angola. Their mission, too, was splendidly accomplished. There is, nevertheless, with one notable exception, an international outcry against the raid – by the Third World communist consortium, the United Nations Secretariat, and west European countries, led by the new socialist government of France. The notable exception is the United States of America, whose Secretary of State said on Friday that although the South African action was a disruption of the peace process, judgement of it must be linked with other aspects of the situation. These included the continuing presence of a large contingent of shipments of Soviet arms to that country, and their use by SWAPO to inflict bloodshed and terrorism against innocent non-combatants in Namibia.

The Security Council resumes its deliberations today, and these were the critical developments that were occurring as, at the weekend, South Africans celebrated the Springbok victory. There is good cause for pride in the performance of our men in New Zealand and Angola – and also for turning our thoughts and prayers to the families of the ten soldiers who will not return from Angola, and to all those who have suffered in the service of their country and civilized standards in the operational area.

It was this confidence in America's support that spurred South Africa to launch its first cross-border attack against the African National Congress on the eastern front. Guerilla attacks were on the rise and the government believed the ANC was infiltrating the country through Mozambique. Emboldened by the recent inauguration of US President Ronald Reagan, the South African military mounted a raid in January 1981 which killed twelve ANC members in their homes in the Matola suburb of the Mozambican capital of Maputo. The implications were not lost on the people at home. A Soweto memorial for those killed in Matola confirmed the scope of the battlefield.

Maputo sources give details of ANC raid

SA TROOPS USE RUSSIAN MADE VEHICLES TO STAGE THEIR DARING GETAWAY

● Details of the precision raid carried out by SA troops on ANC houses in Matola.

Matola commemoration service at Regina Mundi Church, Soweto, 22 February 1981; sermon by a local parish priest: We are gathered here today to mourn the provocation of Matola and the death of our brothers out there. The Lord no longer asks us to raise prayers to Him: He wants us to burst our chains. The dead have made their contribution. The task that remains faces those of us who are still alive. How do we continue our resistance? Each of us must regard himself as an apostle of resistance and we must go all out to recruit men and women who are ready to participate practically and actively in resisting oppression. We are in a situation where we are being forced, where we are being compelled by the sheer exercise of state violence to think, not in New Testament terms, but in the Old Testament terms, where we speak of an 'eye for an eye and a tooth for a tooth'.

Violence has reached full circle. If the state thinks it has a moral right to use violence, why should the oppressed then not resort to violence as a viable means of changing the status quo? It seems that in this country we always speak with two languages: the white government speaks about 'terrorists', but we shall always speak of 'freedom fighters', and the deceased we are honouring today, we see as our martyrs. Amandla!

Crowd: Ngawethu!

Soweto civic leader: For them, no linen for lining the coffin, nor carved casket do they lay in. No, strewn in their coffins, they lie with Makarov, with Scorpion, with Kalashnikov,[43] with Umkhonto. Mayibuye!

Crowd: i Afrika!

Mother of one of the Matola dead: Sons and daughters of the soil, our hearts are sore about what happened in Matola. Our boys were taken by surprise. I don't know what to call a man who does that ...

Crowd: Coward!

Mother: Exactly! At night, when our boys suspected nothing, the cowards came in, well armed, to finish our poor children. And let me say that our children did not leave the country because of frustration or for some small reason – they left this country determined to return and get our country back. They are not terrorists, our children who died in Matola. Amandla!

Crowd: Ngawethu!

Student leader: The worst injustice which we can ever do to our comrades is to sit down and mourn and not take up their battle where they left off. Let our motto be: 'We shall not mourn the dead', for if we concentrate on mourning, our eyes shall be clouded with tears, to an extent that we won't know where we are going, we won't be able to identify the enemy.

What did our comrades die for? They died in pursuit of a better South Africa for us. They died in pursuit of a non-racial and democratic society. And they died for those principles enshrined in the most democratic document ever, the Freedom Charter. They left the country, they left the protection of their parents, the comfort of their homes, the warmth of their loved ones, and made the most supreme sacrifice in the human struggle. They said to themselves, 'The struggle is my life', and they joined the people's army. Amandla!

Crowd: Ngawethu!

Student leader: Now we have got to take up this fight and then try to mobilize the masses and educate them about those principles that the comrades died for. I shall request everybody to repeat after me these words which were their guiding principles, from the Freedom Charter. These freedoms ...

Crowd: These freedoms ...

Student leader: We shall fight for ...

Crowd: We shall fight for ...

Student leader: Side by side ...

Crowd: Side by side ...

Student leader: Throughout our lives ...

Crowd: Throughout our lives ...

Student leader: Until we win our liberty ...

Crowd: Until we win our liberty ...

Student leader: Power to the South African people! Education to the illiterate! And houses to the squatters! Mayibuye!

Crowd: i Afrika!

SABC, 23 February 1981: In Cape Town this afternoon, Prime Minister Botha described as far-fetched the suggestions by some black leaders that blacks saw no justification for the recent raid into Mozambique and regarded the terrorists as heroes. Mr Botha said that some blacks might see things in this light, but there were tens of thousands of blacks who wanted nothing to do with the Soviet Union, the ANC or Marxism. Mr Botha emphasized that South Africa did not seek trouble with its neighbouring states, but it would not stand by silently and allow internationally orientated terrorist groups to undermine its stability without taking any action. He said that South Africa would carry out more raids if they were in the country's interest.

Minister of Defence General Magnus Malan, 21 May 1983: If we don't start taking (retaliatory) action now, we're sitting around and waiting for an atrocity to happen. So we've got to do something about it. South Africans must learn to realize that war does not start and finish at the country's borders. I would say that 95 per cent of the population is unaware that there is a war in progress.

The former British protectorate of Lesotho, entirely surrounded by South Africa, was next to be hit, as it was believed to be a 'springboard' for ANC attacks on South Africa. Thirty ANC members and twelve Lesotho citizens – including women and children – were killed in a midnight raid in December 1982 on houses in the capital city of Maseru.

The conflict continued to intensify: in May of 1983, the ANC's deadliest bomb blast to date, outside South African Air Force Headquarters, Military Intelligence and Naval offices in downtown Pretoria, killed nineteen military personnel and civilians. 'Oh God! It was like war!' shouted the headlines, and the South African Defence Force immediately threatened a Maseru-style counter-attack.

The SADF seriously botched its retaliatory raid into Mozambique, launched three days after the Pretoria bombing, then tried to cover up the fiasco with a feverish propaganda campaign. While the South Africans claimed that 'scores of terrorists' were killed when ANC 'bases', 'headquarters' and 'camps' were hit, foreign journalists who visited the devastated Maputo suburb of Matola saw only the bodies of three Mozambican workers, a Mozambican child, a FRELIMO[44] government soldier and a South African refugee, plus the bombed-out shells of a jam factory, a crèche and several private Mozambican homes. The South Africans tried to explain the discrepancy between their casualty figures and those quoted internationally by charging that the Mozambicans had 'rearranged the bodies'. When that line proved unconvincing, the propaganda focus shifted to an Air Force officer's warning allegedly radioed to Maputo's airport control tower just before Matola was strafed.

Mike Zero One calls Maputo and tells startled air control...

'Keep out of it or our planes will hit back'

By CHRIS OLCKERS and JOSE CAETANO

MINUTES before SAAF Impalas launched a blitz attack on ANC bases in Maputo yesterday morning, an Air Force officer warned the Mozambique Government not to interfere or else action would be taken against it.

A startled air traffic controller at Maputo's international airport heard the officer asking him on the radio to warn Frelimo to "freeze" during the operation.

More reports — Page 2

Convicts' saw bid fails

A CLASSIC bid by several long-term prisoners to escape — by sawing through their prison bars — was foiled when a warder spotted them.

A statement by a spokesman for the Prisons Service did not say how the men at Leeukop Prison, near Johannesburg, obtained the sawing instrument.

The potentially dangerous prisoners were transferred to another cell immediately after warder Mr M Thekiso saw them.

The prisoners involved are serving sentences ranging from nine to 24 years for murder, theft, robbery, and housebreaking.

The Prisons Service was investigating the escape bid.

This was one of the main points which emerged during a Press conference at Defence Headquarters in Pretoria yesterday in which it was revealed that the South African Government gave the go-ahead for the Air Force raid on Maputo only hours after a car bomb had killed 18 people and injured more than 200 in Pretoria on Friday.

A transcript of a tape recording of the conversation between the pilot and the controller was played to members of the Press at a conference in Pretoria yesterday afternoon.

The South African pilot, Mike Zero One, called the tower and this was what followed:

"This is Mike Zero One. I have an important message for you. Tell your military HQ that aircraft are conducting operations in your area. They are operating against the ANC. We have no quarrel with the Frelimo Government and any interference with these aircraft will result in immediate retaliation."

"Maputo Tower. Say again. Say first your call-sign.

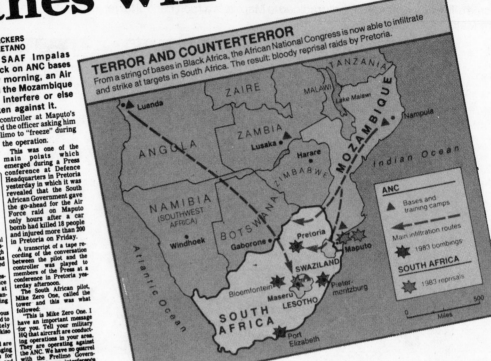

TERROR AND COUNTERTERROR
From a string of bases in Black Africa, the African National Congress is now able to infiltrate and strike at targets in South Africa. The result: bloody reprisal raids by Pretoria.

ANC
▲ Bases and training camps
← Main infiltration routes
✶ 1983 bombings

SOUTH AFRICA
✶ 1983 reprisals

Tape-recorded conversation between South African pilot and Mozambican air controller, played at a Pretoria press conference, 24 May 1983: This is Mike Zero One. I have an important message for you. Tell your military HQ that aircraft are conducting operations in your area. They are operating against the ANC. We have no quarrel with the FRELIMO government, and any interference with these aircraft will result in immediate retaliation. You understand?

What the South Africans neglected to report about 'Mike Zero One' 's cocky message was that it was recorded a full ten minutes after the raid had been completed, as the South African Impalas headed back to base. The trick was an old one, copied from the Rhodesian 'Green Leader' raid on Zimbabwe People's Revolutionary Army camps in Zambia, in 1979.[45]

Raids, however, represent only one factor of the destabilization equation. South Africa's goal is not only to hit the ANC but to sabotage the infrastructure of the neighbouring black states, thereby ensuring that they are in no condition to offer substantive military support to the ANC and SWAPO. A key means to this end has been support for surrogate insurgent groups like the Mozambique National Resistance, MNR, an originally Portuguese-funded and Rhodesian-trained army created to destabilize Mozambique's attempts to build a socialist society. South Africa took over the training, arming and resupply of the MNR after Zimbabwe's independence in 1980.[46] The MNR's radio station moved to the northern Transvaal, blaring out anti-Machel propaganda as the MNR cut power lines from Cabora Bassa Hydroelectric project, blew up rail links from Zimbabwe to the harbour of Beira, and terrorized the rural population with brutal attacks characterized by severed ears, noses and breasts.

While South Africa steadfastly refused to confirm or deny its support for the MNR, Minister of Defence General Malan conceded that South Africa would use any methods it deemed necessary to fight its enemies in neighbouring countries, 'even if it would mean that we would support anti-communist movements like the MNR to act against the ANC from our territory, we will do so.'[47] In contrast to the government's official ambivalence, the terrorist exploits of the MNR were brazenly encouraged in the South African media, and the SABC seemed to have privileged access to the shadowy movement.

South Africa has developed variations on this surrogate guerilla theme, backing the UNITA rebels in Angola, Lesotho's 'Liberation Army' and the Zimbabwe 'dissidents'.[48] This aggressive destabilization strategy seemed to give way to a new era of 'détente' in March 1984, when South Africa signed a non-aggression pact with Mozambique. The Nkomati Accord, so named for the venue of the signing ceremony, on the banks of the Nkomati River which forms the border between the two countries, was a tacit admission by South Africa that it had backed the MNR, and a pledge to stop doing so, in exchange for Mozambique's promise not to offer military support to the ANC.

While the western press dwelt exclusively on the military bludgeoning and the economic collapse that had forced Mozambique to deal with South Africa, less attention was focused on South Africa's motivations for pursuing détente. Skilled labour shortages, sluggish industrial productivity, the drought, the weakened rand and the plummeting gold price were all exacerbating South Africa's worst recession in fifty years, so both the government and the private sector saw great economic potential in recapturing the country's traditional markets and trade routes in Mozambique.

At the same time, destabilization had failed either to win concessions from the black-ruled states or to end the ANC's attacks inside South Africa. In fact, a few months before the Nkomati Accord was signed, after a clash between heavily armed guerillas and the South African army in the northern Transvaal, the Minister of Defence had admitted to a 'new tendency of internal support' for ANC cadres.[49] Destabilization had only succeeded in worsening South Africa's international image and putting its western supporters in a tough diplomatic position. It was for these reasons that Pretoria's diplomats had persuaded its generals that by relaxing South Africa's military stranglehold, its economic tentacles throughout the region would be strengthened.

Similarly, South Africa's apparent moves to pull out of Namibia represented an effort to lighten the financial drain of the territory's military and administrative budget, and to devise a watered-down Namibian independence that would satisfy western demands, while maintaining South African control.[50] South Africa also needed to ensure that Namibia did not become its Vietnam, for even the loyal *volk* were beginning to ask why their sons were dying in that faraway, soon-to-be-black-ruled desert.

SABC, 31 August 1982: The capture of six Bulgarians and the killing of ten Mozambican government soldiers by the Mozambique National Resistance movement is the latest incident in the ongoing battle involving pro- and anti-government forces in the Marxist state to the east of South Africa. The fighting has come at a time when the resistance movement has been stepping up its campaign to overthrow the FRELIMO regime of Samora Machel, which has been forced on to the defensive as the war has hotted up. After the exodus of a quarter of million Portuguese, Mozambique faced severe economic problems, and the country's twelve million blacks were left to pick up the pieces. President Machel's dream of a model state, based on a socialist economy, soon crumbled.

We have obtained exclusive interviews and behind-the-scenes material from the war front. Interviewed recently at his bushveld hideaway, the MNR's military commander, José Domingo, blamed Mozambique's economic plight on Machel's communist masters.

José Domingo: We want a constitutional regime in Mozambique and a free market economic system.

SABC: Yet, by President Machel's own admission, his country's Marxist economy is on the slides. As conditions deteriorate, FRELIMO will find itself under increasing pressure from the disillusioned populace.

newsfronts
Story and pictures: CLOETE BREYTENBACH

The Odds Are Undoubtedly Stacked Against The Fiercely Loyal UNITA Bush Fighter, But Somehow He Manages To Keep Going In his Quest For The Right To Be Master Of His Own Piece Of Africa . . .

UNIVERSAL SOLDIER

THE BUSH FIGHTER RULES, AK?

Columnist Willem de Klerk, *Rapport*, 15 January 1984: Why are we at war in the bush and swamps of South West (Namibia) and Angola? Four hundred young people have already died, and thousands have been maimed. Within South Africa, development plans for our own future stability will be expensive. Is South West really worth the life/money/difficulty? Is SWAPO really weakened after all these years of war, or do they remain the winning element that will still take over in South West? If 'experts' and the whole world community are putting their money on SWAPO's eventual coming to power, what are we fighting for?

Isn't it better strategy to let (SWAPO leader Sam) Nujoma take over? His disenchantment would be great, and his efforts to pull his chestnuts out of the fire would so burn his fingers that it might be just the thing to bring about stability through chaos. It will keep Russia busy. Why not draw the circle of defence round our own borders? Can't we hold back the Russians more effectively on our own borders? Are we sufficiently sensitive to Washington, London, Paris and Bonn? Vietnam? Wasn't Vietnam a piece of nonsense? Questions. The war of attrition has already gained one victory, which is that the public has begun to become irritated and even anxious. No, for God's sake, I am not playing into the enemy's hands. Rubbish. I'm trying to say: we have a right to be better informed.

***Sunday Times*, 18 March 1984:** The new alliances in southern Africa will have a valuable spin-off benefit in the international arena by making the prospect of economic sanctions against South Africa – ever-present for two decades – more remote. As UN member states such as Mozambique, Swaziland, Lesotho (and soon a newly-independent Namibia) become increasingly reliant on South Africa for economic succour, any injury to the Republic's economy will result in concomitant damage across our immediate borders. Pro-sanctions people, within South Africa and abroad, have always been careless of the hurt which would be inflicted upon our poorest communities by punitive economic measures. Do-gooders in distant committee rooms have always seemed willing to starve the blacks until the whites give in. Now they'll have to contemplate the starvation of our neighbours as well.

For South Africa, the most valuable byproduct of détente on both fronts – east and west, Mozambique and Namibia – was that it stood to win Pretoria more international acclaim than any propaganda fund could ever hope to buy. When P.W. Botha toured western Europe in the wake of the Nkomati Accord, South Africa neatly deflected anti-apartheid protests with the argument that, 'If white-ruled South Africa can talk to Marxist Mozambique, why can't Botha talk to Europe?' And when members of the government's ethnic Parliament were castigated as sell-outs, there came the retort: 'Why don't you call Samora Machel a sell-out? He negotiates with our government!'

Chief Gatsha Buthelezi quickly climbed on board the Nkomati bandwagon, announcing that the accord had 'vindicated my unwavering stand and argument that we have no chance at the moment of challenging the racist regime through the so-called armed struggle.'[51] South Africa's rulers were riding the crest of a wave of such confidence that their international isolation and the threat of sanctions suddenly seemed to be only a bad dream.

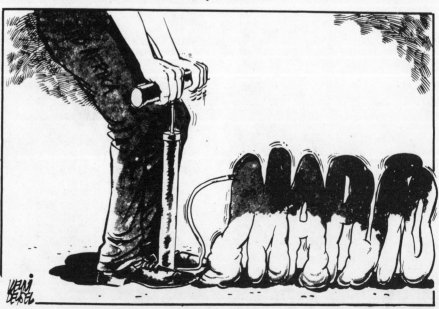

Mozambique upheld its end of the Nkomati bargain and, within weeks of the signing, the ANC's presence in the country was reduced to a ten-person diplomatic office. Since South Africa had never publicly admitted its support for the MNR, it did not announce any severing of the ties.[52] MNR attacks in Mozambique intensified throughout 1984 and 1985 with only the geography of the onslaught changing, as the supply routes and staging areas shifted to the borders with Malawi and Swaziland (which disclosed that it had signed a secret Nkomati-type non-aggression pact with South Africa two years before).

South Africa's success in forcing Mozambique to the bargaining table spurred moves to force similar negotiations on the rest of the region. Botswana and Lesotho complained that Pretoria was bullying them into signing accords, and Zimbabwe – the only frontline state which had staunchly refused any ministerial-level contact with Pretoria – came under increased pressure to make a deal.

South Africa's regional 'peace' moves prominently feature détente in the foreground, but destabilization still lurks in the background. Only days after South Africa signed the pact with Mozambique, it unveiled a military budget that was up a dramatic 21 per cent, and a Defence White Paper that credited 'forceful military action' and a 'successful strategy of deterrence' for paving the way to Nkomati.

Mozambique began publicly complaining in late 1984 that the accord was being violated, as the MNR closed in on the capital and paralysed transport links to neighbouring states. In September 1985, after Zimbabwean troops helped FRELIMO rout the MNR from its main stronghold in the centre of the country, the Mozambican government produced captured documents which proved South Africa's continued support for the MNR, forcing Pretoria to admit publicly that it had violated Nkomati.

P.W. Botha, speaking to the South African Institute of International Affairs, Johannesburg, 31 August 1984: I sincerely hope that those states in the region who still refuse to normalize their relations with South Africa will soon realize that they have chosen an impossible path, and that if they continue to give preference to a hostile and conflictual relationship, their peoples are the ones who stand to suffer most in the end.

Deputy Foreign Minister Louis Nel, in *Paratus,* **the SADF magazine, April 1984:** The actions of the SADF and the South West African Territorial Force have played a vital role in the current peace initiatives in southern Africa. The military presence of the Soviet Union and its surrogates in southern Africa remains a reality, and therefore South Africa cannot now relax its military preparedness, but must rather expand and consolidate its forces. The logic of military preparedness for the sake of peace is best expressed in the following maxim: If you want peace, prepare for war.

Rand Daily Mail, **23 June 1984:** The African National Congress was slowly but surely breaking down and the so-called armed struggle was becoming uncontrolled terrorism. This is the view of senior Security Policemen who supplied background information to the address of the Minister of Law and Order, Mr Louis le Grange, at the Police College in Pretoria yesterday. The recent attacks, in the words of Mr le Grange, could be regarded as a frantic face-saving effort by the ANC in the aftermath of the Nkomati Accord and the better understanding reached between the governments of South Africa, Swaziland, Lesotho and Botswana. Brigadier Herman Stadler said that, since the Nkomati agreement, the ANC was desperately trying to regain prestige. But there were serious divisions now within the ANC, he said. Security Police Major Craig Williamson said there was serious disagreement between factions inside the organization. There were those who believed the terrorist campaign was not a viable tactic, and that the emphasis should be on a political struggle. Another faction believed in action aimed at political and economic sabotage and destruction.

The Star, **24 April 1984:** What will the ANC do now? With its Mozambican support signed away, its operations closely limited all over southern Africa, the exile movement faces a drastic reassessment of its tactics. In response to its setbacks, the ANC in exile might opt desperately for some spectacular acts of violence. However, a more likely long-term strategy would be for it to intensify its operations within the country through existing organizations such as trade unions, black community bodies, and umbrella anti-apartheid groupings. Increasing politicization in these areas could lead – unless the government shows great restraint – to confrontation and fresh rounds of repressive action.

We would like to suggest another option. Might this not be an apt time to allow the ANC back into South Africa's political mainstream – to suspend the 24-year-old ban? Out in the open, it will be easier to identify the movement's true following and its lawful activities. South Africans would be enabled to know about its leaders and their objectives first-hand, instead of relying on third-hand official accounts filtered through a blanket of silence. The trade unions and the community bodies would be left more free to get on with bread and butter affairs. Should a legalized ANC turn to violence, incitement or sedition, there are certainly enough laws to deal with that. Eventually all anti-apartheid forces will have to seek accommodation if they want to avert the path of revolution – which has the potential for much disruption, if little foreseeable hope of success. The ruling party should assist these trends of reconciliation, not hinder them. Nobody can reasonably expect the consequences to be plain sailing, but letting the ANC back into the light may just prove a political master-stroke. It could help revive the movement's moderate trends of earlier years and promote the cause of non-violent change.

Thus peace has clearly not dissipated the national war psychosis.

The South African Police are also preparing for war while talking peace. The most important battleground is the field of propaganda, and the major focus, on discrediting the ANC. A post-Nkomati image of the ANC is being cultivated, of a desperate and isolated exiled group, abandoned by the frontline states, and split into a pragmatic, 'moderate' camp and a 'hard-line' communist wing.

This thesis of a divided ANC is a useful one for both external and internal consumption. The South African government started pressurizing western powers to deny diplomatic offices to the allegedly Moscow-controlled external wing, while cautiously initiating a process of legitimizing a supposedly moderate, internally-based wing of the movement. An editorial in South Africa's liberal press calling for the ANC to be unbanned would have been denounced by the government before the Nkomati Accord, but it now coincided with one of Pretoria's long-term hopes: the fostering of a non-violent, non-radical opposition with whom it could eventually agree to negotiate.

The murder of Tennyson Makiwani and then we hear that things are not well in the guerrilla training camps

The ANC recruit who came home disillusioned

Black South Africans and the government's white opponents are not convinced by the portrayal of the ANC as defeated and divided as a result of détente. They reject these efforts to encourage a transformation of the ANC from a liberation movement at war to a civil rights organization at the bargaining table – and are heartened by its continuing attacks throughout the country.

Robert, trade unionist: The government presented the signing of the Nkomati Accord as a victory, that it was able to neutralize the ANC and the armed struggle, and stem the tide of revolution. The gut reaction of blacks has been that it was not so much a victory for South Africa as a sell-out by Mozambique. That was how the whole thing was seen initially, but now that we've had time to see it in perspective, we see a different analysis. We realize that we've got to take the war home, we have to take the struggle back inside. We can't expect people outside to bear the brunt of our struggle. I can say now that we see Nkomati as a blessing in disguise, because it is going to precipitate an intensification of armed struggle. No more are we going to use other countries and other people as a protective shield. We initiate and carry out our own struggle and we'll carry our own shield. So I really feel that this accord will go some way towards galvanizing the people in our struggle.

With the government getting so much positive attention in the international media, didn't that demoralize people?

Robert: You know, people see through the lie of propaganda. If the government says something, people believe the opposite. If the government says this accord is good, people think there is something wrong with this accord.

Joel, war resister: I think the Nkomati Accord has had a positive effect because it makes people ask questions, like: If we're making peace with Mozambique and Angola, why do we still need this ever-expanding army? If there's no more 'total onslaught', what role is the SADF now playing? I'm not saying it didn't cause a bit of disappointment. I mean, the frontline states had a terrific impact on internal opposition – when they were fighting, when they got independence, when they defied South Africa – and now people are somewhat disillusioned. But there's been a maturing of people's attitudes towards struggle. People are saying we've got to be in a position to cope. So on the one hand, it was a blow, and on the other hand, it's been an incentive to consolidate, to work harder. On balance, I'd say that this reinforcing of our opposition outweighs any despair.

Rev. Allan Boesak, at a meeting in Laudium, Pretoria, 15 March 1984: The Nkomati Accord is a peace which has come out of the barrel of a gun. People must not blame us if we cannot understand how South Africa can set itself up as a peacemaker in the region when it remains the creator of destruction at home. While South Africa makes peace with Mozambique, our leaders still languish in prison, black people are still being forcibly removed from home and thrown into those concentration camps which are euphemistically called 'resettlement areas', and people here are still being banned and detained without trial. No matter how many agreements the government makes, or how well it subjects the frontline states to its will, the people of South Africa will not give up the struggle for democracy, freedom and human dignity. No matter how many pacts are signed, the final deal must be made with us.

BEHIND THE GLOSSY VENEER

images
of a
violent society

When JUSTICE rules, then will PEACE reign.

Printed by: Esquire Press (Pty.) Ltd., Vanguard Drive, Athlone Industria   Published by: Student Union for Christian Action P.O. Box 5 Athlone 7764

5 The War

There was no referendum to allow the Coloured and Indian population to endorse or veto the new constitution, in the way that the white electorate had been allowed to register its views. The government did not dare to put its plans to the test, for it sensed the growing opposition of the Coloured and Indian communities. So, in the traditional South African spirit of state-imposed political dispensations, the government proceeded, without a mandate, to hold elections in August 1984 for membership of the Coloured and Indian houses of the new tricameral Parliament. The resentment and contempt of the Coloured and Indian people was so great that the election candidates could barely campaign. Their election meetings were either boycotted, with pitifully poor attendance, or the speakers so badly heckled that they could not continue their meetings. Thus the government stepped in with a media campaign to advertise the elections, promote selected candidates and persuade Coloureds and Indians to register and vote.[1]

The election results showed that the Coloured and Indian people were as unimpressed with the tricameral Parliament as Africans have been with the 'independent' homelands: more than 80 per cent boycotted the parliamentary poll. It is abundantly clear to blacks, and the government's white opponents, that state bodies – the homelands, Coloured and Indian councils, and the white parliament – have never brought significant change. The new constitution had the unintended effect of providing a mobilizing base for government opponents, and creating unparalleled unity around a single, vital, national issue. In January 1983, the Transvaal Anti-South African Indian Council Committee met to assess its response to the government's reform schemes. The decision of the moderate Coloured Labour Party to participate in the new Parliament drew bitter condemnation. Reverend Allan Boesak, the president of the World Alliance of Reformed Churches and a respected Coloured leader, urged the meeting to translate its outrage into nationwide mobilization against the government's plans.

A. Freedom is Still Coming

South African Digest, **July–August 1984:** Industrialist, businessman and politician 'J.N.' Jayaram Reddy, is a man who believes in hard work and sincerity. From humble beginnings, he has become one of South Africa's leading businessmen and was responsible for establishing the New Republic Bank, the first black financial insitution, in 1971. Disinvestment, says Dr Reddy, is a hindrance to the progress and stability of a country.

The new constitution is a political innovation. 'One must firmly make use of all peaceful channels to ensure that the community's needs are fulfilled. Political utopia cannot be achieved overnight and boycott politics can be a retrogressive step'.

Born in Maitland in the Cape, Mr Peter Marais, leader of the People's Congress Party, devotes much of his spare time to the community in the form of social work. The party's top priority is the finding of a lasting solution to South Africa's social, political and racial problems. The PCP rejects statutory racial discrimination.

A businessman and member of various cultural and Islamic bodies, Mr Mohammed Begg of Crossmoor, Chatsworth, believes that all Indians should not follow a policy of rejection as far as the new dispensation is concerned. 'Despite certain laws that hinder our community, we still share the wealth, and have substantial freedom in this country. Admittedly there are problems, but name one country in the world that hasn't any.'

Reverend Allan Boesak, speaking to the Transvaal Anti-South African Indian Council Committee, Johannesburg, 23 January 1983: Working within the system, for whatever reason, contaminates you. It wears down your defences. It whets your appetite for power. All the while it draws you closer, blunting your judgement and finally exposing your powerlessness by your 'joining the system to fight the system'. And what you call 'compromise' for the sake of politics is in actual fact selling out your principles, your ideals and the future of your children. This situation calls for vigilance. We must not compromise the struggle we have been engaged in for well nigh a century. We must not betray the blood of our children.

There is, therefore, no reason why churches, civic associations, trade unions. student organizations, and sports bodies should not unite on this issue, pool our resources, inform the people of the fraud that is about to be perpetrated in their name, and expose those plans for what they are. This is the politics of refusal, and it is the only dignified response black people can give in this situation. We must continue to show South Africa and the world that there are black people who refuse to be intimidated by the violence of apartheid or tempted by the sugar-coated fruits of apartheid. So while we say 'No' to the hollow solutions built on personal gain and petty self group interest, we say 'Yes' to integrity and commitment.

FOSATU WORKER NEWS

Federation of South African Trade Unions

AUGUST 1984 NUMBER 31

As elections creep nearer FOSATU goes door to door

THE EYE

Vol. 3 No. 5   November 1983

Our organisations say:

Don't vote for APARTHEID

IS THE GOVERNMENT BEHIND

Price 20 cents

Inside

DOWN WITH COMMUNITY COUNCIL — page 3

CENTRESPREAD — YOUTH

SPEAK

THE VOICE OF THE COMMUNITY

Volume 2 Number 3   Non-profit Community Newspaper   15c July 1984

Elections
We tell it like it is

Big no to constitution as elections draw near

PEOPLE'S POWER

APARTHEID PARLIAMENT

DON'T SUPPORT APARTHEID

TVL ANTI-PC

WORK AGA

The formation of a national coalition of organizations opposed to the government's plans was clearly an idea whose time had come. Pretoria's claims to seek reform via 'consensus' had forced it to allow room for dissent, and political activists seized the opportunity to exploit this rare breathing space. Seven months after making his initial suggestion, Reverend Boesak was on a platform in Cape Town, addressing some 15,000 people at the national launch of the United Democratic Front.

Reverend Allan Boesak, Mitchell's Plain, Cape Town, 20 August 1983: I believe we are standing at the birth of what could become the greatest and most significant people's movement in more than a quarter of a century. We are here to say that the government's constitutional proposals are inadequate, that they do not express the will of the vast majority of South Africa's people. More than that, we are here to say that what we are working for is one undivided South Africa which shall belong to all of its people.

The time has come for white people in this country to realize that their destiny is inextricably bound with our destiny, that they shall never be free until we are free. People who think that their security and peace lie in the perpetration of intimidation, dehumanization and violence are not free. They will never be free as long as they have to kill our children in order to safeguard their over-privileged positions. They will never be free as long as they have to lie awake at night worrying whether a black government will one day do to them as they are doing to us, when white power will have come to its inevitable end.

To be sure, the new proposals will make apartheid less blatant in some ways. It will be modernized and streamlined, and in its new multi-coloured cloak, it will be less conspicuous and less offensive to some. Nonetheless, it will still be there. And we must remember, apartheid is a thoroughly evil system and as such it cannot be modified, modernized or streamlined. It has to be irrevocably eradicated.

Let me remind you of three little words, words that express so eloquently our seriousness in this struggle. You don't have to have a vast vocabulary to understand them. You don't need a philosophical bent to grasp them. They are just three little words. The first word is 'all'. We want all our rights, not just a few token handouts the government sees fit to give – we want *all* our rights. And we want all of South Africa's people to have their rights. Not just a selected few, not just 'Coloureds' or 'Indians', after they have been made honorary whites. We want the rights of all South Africans, including those whose citizenship has already been stripped away by this government.

The second word is the word 'here'. We want all of our rights *here* in a united, undivided South Africa. We do not want them in impoverished homelands, we don't want them in our separate little group areas. We want them in this land which one day we shall once again call our own.

The third word is the word 'now'. We want all our rights, we want them here, and we want them now. We have been waiting so long, we have been struggling so long. We have pleaded, cried, petitioned too long now. We have been jailed, exiled, killed for too long. *Now* is the time.

Not since the Congress Alliance, led by the ANC in the 1950s, had the government been confronted with such unified nationwide opposition. The formation of the United Democratic Front represented a new phase of legal mass resistance, both in the range and character of UDF affiliates and in the numbers of people from all over South Africa who converged on Cape Town for the national launch. Nearly four hundred organizations were initially represented, with more joining all the time: civic associations, trade unions, student bodies, youth

groups, women's organizations, churches, mosques, and sports clubs. The UDF aimed to bring together organizations that had been fighting campaigns around grassroots issues – rents, housing, transportation, education, as well as factory floor demands – and co-ordinate their isolated efforts on a national level to defy the government's reforms.

The numbers factor afforded some measure of protection against state repression; at the same time, it was not easy to unite the range of views represented by all the UDF's affiliates. As a result, the UDF purposely kept its stated goals broad, stressing its role as a front composed of different organizations which did not necessarily share the same ideology or ultimate intent, but had agreed to work together to fight the constitution aimed at co-opting Coloureds and Indians, and the laws that render Africans 'aliens'. While it was easy to fault the UDF's platform for a lack of specifics and a surfeit of rhetoric, the value of its role in challenging government strategy could not be underestimated. Before the UDF came on the scene, critical assessment of government policy had come mainly from the white parliamentary opposition and a few high-profile blacks who were accessible to the media. And whatever the UDF's weaknesses, the government saw it as a threat. Thousands of anonymous leaflets flooded the country, claiming that the launch had been postponed; the SABC avoided any mention of one of the largest and most significant political gatherings in South African history; and UDF supporters travelling to and from Cape Town were harassed by police.

MAKE YOUR MARK AGAINST APARTHEID!! JODAC JOINS THE UDF MILLION SIGNATURE CAMPAIGN

The United Democratic Front Million Signatures Campaign Organizer's Handbook: An ideal way of building organization is to be able to meet people in their homes so that both the UDF and the constitution/Koornhof bills (influx control reform laws) can be thoroughly discussed. Time can be spent answering individual questions, as well as recruiting interested people into the work. Door-to-door work is one of the best methods of conducting the campaign because it allows for the largest scope of educating and drawing in more people, and for volunteers to understand the people, know their level of consciousness, and be in tune with them through practical experience. Our responsibility is to involve the broadest range of people and organizations in the UDF. An important point to remember is that the process of recruiting never ends. Always find a space and role for anyone showing a keenness to join.

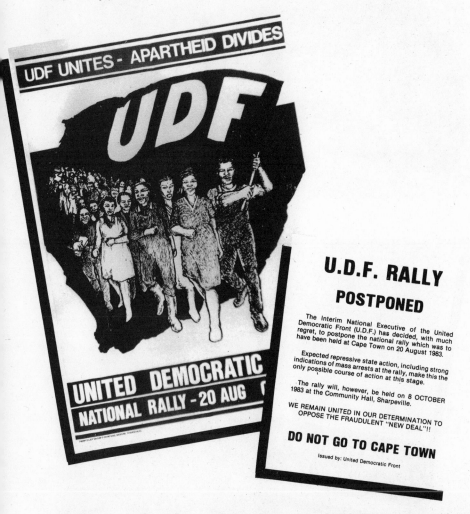

UDF UNITES - APARTHEID DIVIDES

UDF

UNITED DEMOCRATIC NATIONAL RALLY - 20 AUG

U.D.F. RALLY POSTPONED

The Interim National Executive of the United Democratic Front (U.D.F.) has decided, with much regret, to postpone the national rally which was to have been held at Cape Town on 20 August 1983.

Expected repressive state action, including strong indications of mass arrests at the rally, make this the only possible course of action at this stage.

The rally will, however, be held on 8 OCTOBER 1983 at the Community Hall, Sharpeville.

WE REMAIN UNITED IN OUR DETERMINATION TO OPPOSE THE FRAUDULENT "NEW DEAL"!!

DO NOT GO TO CAPE TOWN

Issued by: United Democratic Front

We are all aware that the democratic movement in South Africa has been and will be continually harassed and intimidated, and attempts will be made to disrupt whatever campaign it is involved in. We need to be acutely aware of this during the Million Signatures Campaign. We need to protect ourselves. Our most important defence weapon is discipline. We must not allow ourselves to be provoked either by police or people who have different views. We must locate a lawyer within our area who is willing to come to our aid in times of crisis, to assist when an activist is harassed or detained. We need to keep our publicity material and signed declarations in a safe place that cannot easily be found out. If any item is removed by the police, demand a receipt. If you are assaulted, you can lay a charge at the nearest police station. If a policeman assaults you, take his number down, if you do not know his name.

To get the most gain from the Million Signatures Campaign, we need to evaluate and assess our actions all the time. Each person should do this and signature committees should have regular evaluations. Evaluation must be honest and constructive – 'Tell no lies, claim no easy victories.' – (Guinea-Bissau guerilla leader) Amilcar Cabral.

While the UDF burst on to the South African political scene with an exhilarating spate of rallies, its members were well aware that its true effectiveness would be measured by its success in linking grassroots political issues with national political campaigns. The UDF's most ambitious campaign was the 1984 effort to gather a million signatures against the government's reforms. This goal was not approached as an end in itself, but as a vehicle to educate people about government strategy, to mobilize support for UDF, and to lay the basis for future resistance.

The Million Signatures Campaign was a failure in that only 400,000 signatures were collected before the exercise was overtaken by events in late 1984. But by other criteria, the campaign was a success. It provided a licence for UDF members to move into the communities and discuss issues on an individual basis with people who might never have ventured into a public meeting or mass rally. The campaign was not only a means of educating people about UDF, but of helping UDF members discover the grievances of their constituency.

The government certainly did not consider the campaign a lost cause. Scores of UDF members were arrested while collecting signatures, thousands of forms were confiscated, and the police issued unsubstantiated allegations – later picked up in smear pamphlets – that Million Signatures Campaign forms were being passed on to the ANC for use in recruiting new cadres.

'UDF: The Story Behind the Front', pamphlet issued in 1984 by the right-wing National Students Federation: On 22 January 1984, the recently formed United Democratic Front launched a well-publicized 'million signatures' campaign. Purpose? The bland explanation was given that the UDF wants to make it clear to the world that the majority of South Africans are opposed to the new constitution and the Koornhof bills, seen as further entrenching apartheid and white domination. This is pure whitewash. Some good brains are behind this million signatures drive, and the real intentions are far more sinister. Subsequent to the Nkomati Peace Accord, ANC ranks in some frontline black states suffered considerable upheaval. In the course of these upsets, photostats of UDF million signature lists were recovered – page after page with names underlined. It has been disclosed that these petition lists (requiring the signatory's printed name, address and signature) are being used as the basis of a major recruiting drive for the outlawed ANC.

Against the general background, it is also important to note that the ANC is currently striving to cultivate respectability; to portrays its leaders as good 'Christian gentlemen' rather than communists; to show itself as 'a legitimate political, nationalist force'. Certain radical left-wing quarters in Washington also seek to downplay the ANC's Soviet links, and present it instead as a 'purely national movement'. Similarly, this view is also being propagated in certain left-wing circles in South Africa.

Students who are still considering signing the million signatures petition should reject it if only to avoid the possibility that they could become priority recruitment targets – a prospect one is sure will disturb the majority of South African university students.

In reality, any overlap between the goals and ideals of the UDF and those of the ANC was purely a manifestation of the militant popular mood. Well before the emergence of the UDF, South Africa had witnessed a renewed consciousness of the traditions of 1950s resistance politics. The Freedom Charter was widely

accepted, ANC songs and slogans were heard at meetings, and its flags and colours flaunted. What did not come out into the open was the debate over the underlying issues at stake: class conflict and 'front politics', that is, the articulation of popular demands through a national front consisting of a range of different organizations and classes. This debate had to be conducted through a kind of code.

A group of influential trade unions, led by the nationally based Federation of South African Trade Unions and the Cape-based African Food and Canning Workers Union and General Workers Union, decided not to affiliate to the UDF, on grounds that their working-class demands might then be overshadowed by middle-class concerns. They preferred to direct their energies toward the formation of a national union federation, aimed at uniting some 300,000 organized workers under one umbrella grouping. Behind these unions' criticism lay the unspoken fear that to ally the unions formally with the UDF would lay the independent trade union movement open to government attack and internal splits, thus jeopardizing the shopfloor gains so carefully built up over the past decade. Other unions were willing to take that risk, and joined the UDF. To the South African Allied Workers Union, the General and Allied Workers Union and the Municipal and General Workers Union, the working class was not confined to the 15 per cent of the workers in trade unions, but included non-unionized workers, the unemployed, and homeland residents, who could all assert working-class demands through affiliation to the UDF.

South African Allied Workers Union Vice-President Sisa Njikelana: The community, women's, student, youth and other organizations based within working-class communities are also in a position to express the views of the working class, and are also legitimate organizations of the working class. Are workers' struggles for higher wages that unrelated to rent or bus boycotts?

Looking to other revolutionary experiences, such as those in Vietnam and Nicaragua, shows us that the progressive forces, unlike the 'left' sectarians, drew the broad strata of the population into the revolutionary struggle – and had to struggle for leadership of the democratic organizations of the peasants, small shop owners, professionals, artisans, students and other petty bourgeois strata. The only way the working class can lead the broad democratic front, as learnt in the experiences of other struggles, is through active participation within the organizations and structures of the front. The responsibility of the union leadership in this situation, if it has the interest of the working-class at heart, demands of them that they lead the union's membership into active participation within all its structures (regardless of their imperfections); to struggle for and ensure maximum working-class participation; and finally, working-class (not just union) leadership of the broad democratic front.[2]

Dr Ram Saloojee: One might expect that, being a professional man, having most of the material benefits of a well-ordered life available to me, with a fair type of education and other benefits available to my family, that I would be fairly satisfied. One would expect that I would be more satisfied than the person in a much lower socio-economic position, that such a person would be far more frustrated with the system. Yet I have found that I am possibly more dissatisfied than a lot of other people who are not as well off as I. I feel that this is because my expectations are not being fulfilled, and I am being prevented from achieving my full human potential. So I possibly feel more antagonistic to this system than many others in the lower strata of society.

Smear pamphlet issued in August 1983:
The National Forum Committee rejects the so-called 'United Democratic Front' for the following reasons:
1) Any black person genuinely committed to liberation from white oppression will reject participation by members of the white oppressor class in the liberation struggle.
2) The UDF is the old white-dominated South African Communist Party/ANC alliance dressed up in a new disguise. Admission of 'sympathetic' white organizations such as the National Union of South African Students and the Black Sash (pass advice office) is merely the pretext for continued white minority control under a different ideology.
3) The UDF is an obstacle in the path of the total liberation of Azania by blacks, for blacks.

The Manifesto of the Azanian People:
Our struggle for national liberation is directed against the system of racial capitalism, which holds the people of Azania in bondage for the benefit of the small minority of white capitalists and their allies, the white workers and the reactionary sections of the black middle class. The struggle against apartheid is no more than the point of departure for our liberation efforts. The black working class, inspired by revolutionary consciousness, is the driving force of our struggle. They alone can end the system as it stands today, because they alone have nothing at all to lose. They have a world to gain in a democratic, anti-racist and socialist Azania. It is the historic task of the black working class and its organizations to mobilize the urban and rural poor, together with the radical sections of the middle classes, in order to put an end to the system of oppression and exploitation by the white ruling class. The oppressed and exploited people of Azania demand immediately:
1) the right to work,
2) the right to form trade unions that will heighten revolutionary worker consciousness,
3) the establishment of a democratic, anti-racist worker republic in Azania, where the interests of the workers shall be paramount through worker control of the means of production, distribution and exchange.

The UDF and the 'community' unions felt a responsibility to forge alliances across class lines, arguing that to ostracize those in the black middle class was to offer them without contest to the government, which is hoping to co-opt them through participation in its tricameral parliament. Dr Ram Saloojee, a prominent member of the Indian middle class, is an example of a man the government would have liked to have on its side. Until the mid-1970s, he was a member of the government-created management committee for the segregated Indian living area of Lenasia and could have been a prime candidate for the Indian Chamber of Parliament, had he not quit the Lenasia committee in exasperation over its impotence. The wealthy medical doctor became increasingly involved in opposition politics and in 1983, he helped revive the Transvaal Indian Congress – one of the oldest political organizations in South Africa, with origins in the resistance campaigns of Mahatma Gandhi[3] – and was elected to the national executive of the UDF.

The South African government did its best to stir the debate over front politics, via an anti-UDF smear pamphlet allegedly produced by the improbable coalition of the pro-UDF South African Council on Sport and the newly formed Black Consciousness association, the National Forum Committee.[4]

The authors of that smear pamphlet were slightly out of date in their pseudo-analysis. In the 1970s, Black Consciousness stalwarts would have rejected a class alliance simply because of the inclusion of whites, but by the time of the founding of the UDF, Black Consciousness had veered left to keep pace with the militant times. Thus the National Forum dismissed UDF as an unprincipled, ethnic coalition with no true commitment to socialism. Black Consciousness supporters had always rejected the ANC and its Freedom Charter, but had never come up with any document to replace it – until the 'Azanian Manifesto' was drafted by the National Forum in mid-1983.

The United Democratic Front accepted criticism from the unions and conceded that they had raised legitimate working-class demands, but this attempt to replace the venerated Freedom Charter was denounced as arrogant and presumptuous. Nelson Mandela's daughter, Zinzi, fired the first volley, lashing out at 'ideologically lost political bandits who rejected the people's constitution and diverted the struggle'.[5] A more co-ordinated response came in an angry repudiation of the Azanian Manifesto by five UDF-affiliated organizations.

The opposition press seized on this ideological debate and translated it into a contest for power. The UDF was pitted against the National Forum Committee, the Freedom Charter versus the Azanian Manifesto, without attempting to weigh the influence and popular base of support for each point of view. The National Forum was merely the organizing committee of a weekend conference in July 1983; its leaders spoke for no defined constituency. The UDF, on the other hand, represented hundreds of affiliated organizations. As for the flawed analogy between the Freedom Charter and the Azanian Manifesto, few reporters bothered to compare the mandates behind the two documents. The Freedom Charter was the product of months of nationwide canvassing, culminating in its adoption by a national Congress of the People, while the Azanian Manifesto was drafted by a handful of unknown authors and ratified by unelected representatives.

A senior black reporter at the *Soweto Sunday Mirror,* Zwelakhe Sisulu, son of imprisoned ANC Secretary-General Walter Sisulu, and a long-time activist in Black Consciousness circles, had a theory to explain the media bias against the UDF.

Statement by the South African Allied Workers Union, the General and Allied Workers Union, the Congress of South African Students, the Azanian Students Organization and the Federation of South African Women, 23 June 1983: The Freedom Charter is the only democratic document ever to be drafted in the history of the liberation struggle of the oppressed people of South Africa. It stands out in history from all alternatives for change in South Africa, not only because of the demands reflected in it, but also because of the manner in which it came in to being. It can therefore never be substituted without the will of the majority. Any attempt to undermine the Freedom Charter by substitution can only be regarded as an act of betrayal of the aspirations of all the people of South Africa.

Zwelakhe Sisulu: I think the media has always tended to feel more comfortable with a strong Africanist, Black Consciousness approach; it felt it could control the type of demands made by those guys. They don't want to change society, they want to fit into society, whereas the progressives want to make fundamental changes in society. And of course, you know that in the South African context, any black-white alliance is seen in a very suspicious light, because more often than not they tend to go beyond political demands against apartheid to make economic demands.

It's more than just that traditional thing of the press saying that blacks are fighting amongst themselves: what the press is now saying is that you cannot conclude that the Freedom Charter enjoys broad support because there is, on the other hand, the Azanian Manifesto. So the Azanian Manifesto becomes the weapon given to the media to fight the Freedom Charter. It's an old trick used by whites trying to hold on to power in Africa: in Rhodesia, for example, they wouldn't say that Mugabe enjoyed broad support because there were people at Muzorewa[6] rallies. What they're building up to say in the near future is that you can't only negotiate with Nelson Mandela because there are others who you should talk to as well, like AZAPO and the National Forum guys.

Because, you see, all that's happening today is a prelude to negotiations. South Africa is going to try to do the same thing it's done in Namibia: to create all kinds of strange organizations purporting to have certain constituencies. Already, people are very suspicious of the government's motives in its dealings with black politics. For example, why were the Black Consciousness guys the first politically significant people released from prison and not banned? This is interpreted as a government policy of trying to destabilize the non-BC organizations. The BC guys immediately went to work trying to resuscitate the BC organizations. Then the government lifted the bans on all kinds of other people, so you suddenly had all these political activists coming back onto the scene, and the result was increasing divisions in the community.[7]

Would you say that the National Forum is a more radical group than the UDF?

Zwelakhe Sisulu: It's a very confused situation. On paper, the BC guys, with their Azanian Manifesto, seem to be trying to present themselves as left of left: left of the Freedom Charter, left of the ANC. But in reality we know that they are not. It's all an effort to build political credibility. They claim that they don't object to socialism or to communism, but to white participation, but we don't believe that they're real socialists. We know that they can afford to talk that way because the system knows they have no concrete programme for change. So it would seem that these BC guys are basically moving toward a situation where they are gearing themselves for negotiations, not for revolution.

For all the basic ideological differences between the UDF and the NFC, there was one issue on which they wholeheartedly agreed: they would never seek nor accept support from those operating within government structures. That ruling excluded parliamentary political parties, township councillors and homeland government officials, in particular, Chief Gatsha Buthelezi. The Inkatha leader had, at one time or another, formed alliances with all those blackballed groups, from the white Progressive Federal Party to the Coloured Labour Party.

The ire aroused by the KwaZulu homeland leader transcended ideology. Non-racial progressives and Black Consciousness supporters alike reviled Chief Buthelezi as a 'collaborator' and a 'sell-out'. They charged that the enormous membership claimed by Inkatha was mainly due to the fact that KwaZulu residents could not get housing, work or schooling for their children without an Inkatha membership card. Worse, they maintained that Inkatha fostered an extreme form of ethnicity: Zulu nationalism.

When students at the University of Zululand heard that Buthelezi was to hold an Inkatha rally on their campus in October 1983, they staged a peaceful protest demonstration. Just two weeks before, two people had been killed when Inkatha members invaded the Durban township of Lamontville in an effort to force the residents to accept incorporation into the KwaZulu homeland, so the students feared another violent confrontation. At dawn on the morning of the controversial rally, Inkatha supporters brandishing traditional Zulu spears and fighting sticks charged on to the campus and led a bloody attack that left six students dead and more than a hundred others seriously injured. The nationwide revulsion was enough to bring UDF and Black Consciousness leaders onto the same platform for a first-ever show of unity.

Buthelezi made no attempt to heal the wounds from the massacre. Instead he issued an edict in January 1984, ordering all students receiving KwaZulu bursaries to sign loyalty pledges to the KwaZulu government and Inkatha, so as 'to ensure that the government would not pay for the education of people who would one day turn against it'. Further venting his rage, Buthelezi denounced every organization that had criticized Inkatha.

Johannesburg memorial service for students killed at the University of Zululand, 3 November 1983, Muntu Myeza, General-Secretary of the Azanian People's Organization: Chief Gatsha Buthelezi is the Frankenstein of Pretoria, and the weekend's violence has only served to demonstrate the need for black solidarity and unity against forces of division such as Inkatha.

Reverend Frank Chikane, theologian and Transvaal UDF Vice-President: Inkatha is non-violent when it has to face the government, but very vicious when facing the oppressed people. Now we know where they stand: on the side of the oppressor.

The aftermath of the University of Zululand killings marked a new low in Buthelezi's relations with the ANC. He responded to its strongest denunciation of him in recent years with typical bravado, proclaiming that it could be the 'final nail in the coffin', in terms of future co-operation between Inkatha and the ANC. Buthelezi even accused the ANC of setting up the UDF in order to destroy Inkatha.[8] But if Buthelezi regarded all members of the UDF and the ANC as enemies, his opponents refused to write off Inkatha's considerable following, instead directing peace-making overtures at Inkatha's rank-and-file.

If the UDF could extend its hand to Inkatha members, if the UDF, the unions and the National Forum Committee could collaborate on specific issues, was there a chance that eventually all opposition groups would be able to resolve their differences and unite against the government? The central and seemingly insurmountable obstacle to unity stemmed from differing historical perspectives on South African resistance. The UDF was the only contemporary, legal political movement that stated explicitly, and in its founding principles and publicly at meetings, that it did not purport to replace 'the accredited liberation movement of the people'. Neither the National Forum nor Inkatha would make such a stipulation.

Patrick 'Terror' (a football nickname) Lekota was a leading member of the Black Consciousness movement, who was sentenced to six years in Robben Island prison after being convicted under the Terrorism Act in the marathon 1976 'Black Consciousness trial'. His co-defendents came out of jail to join the Azanian People's Organization, and to found the National Forum, but Lekota underwent a 'political metamorphosis' in prison, and on his release became an ardent advocate of progressive non-racialism, and the National Publicity Secretary for the United Democratic Front.

Terror Lekota: You have to remember that those of us who were involved in the Black Consciousness movement in the late 60s and early 70s came into our own at a time when any meaningful political activity had gone with the banning of the people's organizations in 1960. We were deprived of the wealth of the heritage of struggle which others who had gone before us had already amassed. So we moved into the arena of fighting apartheid as virgins, and we were bound to make mistakes in terms of judgement.

The era of the founding of Black Consciousness thought is in total contrast to the situation we now find ourselves in. The formation of the United Democratic Front must be seen in the broad context of the historical struggle of our people. Those of us who participate in the UDF as an initiative of the 80s do so fully aware that the struggle of our people does not begin today. We see ours as an initiative which merely complements a struggle which had already been waged for a long time before we came on to the scene.

What were the factors that changed your political perspective?

Terror Lekota: One very important factor had to do with our trial. We were arrested with men who were blacks like ourselves, men with whom we had shared platforms and campaigned together against apartheid. But it was precisely from among those men that some took the witness stand, side by side with the South African security police, and condemned us and sent us to jail. Now that became a crucial moment for reflection. If black men like ourselves could abandon the struggle against apartheid and oppression and side with the security police, how correct was it to say that only black people have the right to struggle against injustice?

Also, it just so happened that a white man, Anthony Holliday, was arrested at the same time that we were, for distributing illegal pamphlets. He was arrested along with a black man, and that black man abandoned him, joined sides with the security police and testified against Holliday.[9] So this again made me reconsider my Black Consciousness views.

There were many other cases: Bram Fischer, a white who died a prisoner for opposing apartheid, Beyers Naudé, who was ostracized by his own people and banned for his courageous stand.[10] All these cases made me feel it was high time to decide whether the struggle for justice in this country could be pursued only by blacks or whether in fact, this was a struggle of

Press statement released by Chief Buthelezi, 10 November 1983: With its small band of weedy followers, the Azanian Students Organisation had the temerity and audacity to accuse me of causing disunity! If those in AZASO have not yet learnt the errors of their ways and corrected the stupidity of their thinking, they will find that the Inkatha lion has up to now only growled ever so softly. We have not bared our fangs and I pray to God that AZASO never makes us do so. I ask you, my brothers and sisters, will you tolerate the continuation of these insults? I am actually asking what you, the people of South Africa, are going to do about this band of uncouth, lying, deceiving, plotting scum. You say we must deal with them. Well then, let us deal with them at every opportunity and let us do so with valour and with honour.

Chief Buthelezi at a rally in Soweto, 4 December, 1983: The United Democratic Front seems to be another force of disunity, which seems destined to destabilize the black political struggle in this country. The National Party, the ANC and the PAC cannot succeed in their aims without Inkatha or without a Zulu contribution. Inkatha believes in what it is doing, and from now on it will adopt the attitude of 'an eye for an eye and a tooth for a tooth'. If some would spit on us, we would spit back. If some would abuse us, we would abuse them in turn. If some would beat us with a stick, we, too, would pick up a stick and beat them. (At the University of Zululand) our youth did no more than defend my honour and the honour of our king. I must warn South Africa that if the kind of provocation we experienced continues, Inkatha youth will demonstrate their strength and prowess. Continuing labelling me as a sell-out is going to have ugly repercussions. We know just how powerful we are.

Azanian Students' Organization President Tiego Moseneke, at a memorial service for the slain students, 3 November 1983: We must have sympathy for rank-and-file Inkatha members. Those are *our* people, misled by Gatsha and Inkatha for their purposes. Our ranks are always open to them to join us.

those committed to justice – never mind the colour of their skin – against those committed to injustice.

I also had to face the fact that, although the majority of the capitalists in our country do come from the white race group, and the majority of working class people come from the African section of the population, it is also true that within the black community there are people who are middle-class elements, as well as even some black capitalists. Fortunately for me, I was sent to Robben Island, where I was able to meet Nelson Mandela and Walter Sisulu and many of the other freedom fighters of our people, and question them more deeply on all these issues. That was the highlight of my political metamorphosis, because it was through these discussions that I came to develop and embrace the non-racial progressive line.

And when you came out of prison?

Terror Lekota: When I came back from jail, I found that there was much more popular support for non-racialism, and much more awareness of the African National Congress. I found that talk of the ANC had become our daily bread, so to speak. An increasing number of young people in the townships are now saying openly that the ANC was formed over seventy years ago, as the first liberation organization of our people, and by that fact alone, the ANC is our natural political home. You go to any political meeting today, and if they're not singing about Nelson Mandela, then they're singing about Oliver Tambo, or they're singing about Joe Slovo. It wasn't like that before I went to jail, but now people talk freely about the ANC, especially the young people, they're head over heels in love with the ANC. The ANC is a reality, it's everywhere, and it's here to stay. The Nats themselves admit it. As a matter of fact, the Nats now are accusing the UDF of being a front for the ANC, in spite of the fact that we have said quite clearly that we are a particular initiative committed to opposing the constitution, the Black Local Authorities laws and other related legislation. But so conscious is the government of the ANC today, that any voice of opposition is perceived as pro-ANC.

What this all proves is that many people have come to regard the ANC as synonymous with the liberation of South Africa. We of the UDF are bold enough to concede that we are not the only factor that will determine the final outcome of the South African liberation struggle for a free, non-racial and democratic future. We are aware that the activities of others, for example, trade unions, political organizations and other groups – including liberation organizations like the ANC – amount to a simultaneous struggle against apartheid.

If Terror Lekota is a born-again convert to the non-racial, historical school of resistance, another UDF member, Helen Joseph, has been a true believer for decades. Since she first entered resistance politics in the 1940s, she has been detained, jailed, house arrested (the first South African to be so victimized), banned, listed (therefore unquotable in South Africa), threatened and physically attacked. Joseph was elected a national patron at the UDF launch, and as she stood on the platform in Cape Town – an ageing white figure in a throng of mainly young, black faces – her thoughts took her back to 1955, when she saw the Freedom Charter adopted at the Congress of the People in Kliptown, Soweto.

Helen Joseph: It was like history come to life again – that's what made it so exciting. It was just like Kliptown all over again. I think it's important that people are looking back to the fifties, with a view to understanding the resistance of that time, to take what was good from it, and to ignore what can't be repeated. I think we're learning the importance of decentralizing and motivating the people, educating the people, making them aware of the nature of the struggle, and preparing them for what will inevitably come in the future: increased violence against us. We have to teach people not to be afraid of the future, not to be afraid of jail, and when bans and jail are over, to come out and fight again.

What's so important is what's going on at the grassroots level, the strengthening of people's determination, their resistance to the kind of life they've been condemned to live. They're fighting. As they get given what appear to be better conditions, they don't sit back and accept it – no, they want more and more and more, and they are determined to have more and more and more — not just a slice of the cake.

While UDF is an open, legal, non-violent organization, there is increasing talk these days that violence is inevitable. How do you feel about that?

Helen Joseph: You can't preach it, obviously, you can't proclaim it, but I think people are aware deep down in their hearts. The Nats are more aware than anyone else of what's coming. It's being shouted at us all the time from the media, isn't it? I mean, the 'total onslaught' of the 'terrorists' and all that. Look, not even UDF can exclude the possibility of armed struggle. The UDF is committed to a non-violent solution, but I think everyone understands that to mean, as long as possible. Nobody believes that things will ever change in this country without some kind of pressure. I remember Solly Sachs, the old trade union leader from years ago,[11] I remember him constantly saying, 'There'll be no change in this country until the whites have to tighten their belts.' That's why I hope for a strengthening of economic boycotts, sports boycotts, cultural boycotts, because these kinds of things actually do hit the whites where it hurts.

Have you seen a resurgence of support for the ANC since the 1950s?

Helen Joseph: Oh yes, definitely. I see it like an iceberg: at the moment, you can't see the mass of the iceberg, but it surfaces every now and then, and you see the tip of the iceberg – in trials, in the attitude of the people. You know, I went to the trial of two young men who were tried for terrorism in Pretoria. I met their parents, and I was trying to prepare them for what was going to come. They were prepared for a ten-year sentence, and I had to say to them, 'Look, it may be longer than that, but this is part of the price we have to pay, and this was your son's decision.' And there was no doubt about it on their part, they were very proud of their sons. In fact, one of the mothers said to me, 'From now on, every mother must carry a soldier in her stomach!' And as for the young men, as they were going down to the cells, when they said goodbye to me, one of them whispered as he shook hands with me – he said, 'Freedom is still coming!'

The War
B. So Who's the Enemy?

For black South Africans, it is anger that breeds rebellion; for white South Africans, alienation comes first. Apartheid is scorned – though not necessarily challenged – through a lively white counter-culture. Nadine Gordimer and J.M. Coetzee have written prophetic novels set during the final stages of the war. Roger Lucey sings about police spies and bulldozed squatters. Paul Stopforth sculpts dead detainees. And alienation reigns supreme at non-racial discos like Johannesburg's 'D-V-8' and Cape Town's 'Scratch'. For those white South Africans who manage to confront their alienation and translate it into action, the English-language university is often the catalyst.

Leaflet produced by University of Cape Town students, 1983: At school we are taught that history in South Africa only starts in 1652, when a few Dutch settlers kis out (take time to relax) in the Cape of Good Hope, and that the black indigenous population are only the background against which Simon van der Vat and Barney Barnato[12] lay the way for apartheid today. But more than grammar and guidance, we are also taught to obey commands: principals boss teachers who boss prefects who boss the rest at the bottom of the pile. Cuts and detention to discipline us. Conform and be docile. Learn to accept that life is naturally hierarchical and apartheid is a fact of life.

So we leave school, find a job, and don't ask questions, live in our Group Areas, watch SATV and 'die rooikomplot' (the Red conspiracy) to fill our minds with a good dose of Pee Wee propaganda and fear of ko-mo-nisme (communism). And if we get to university, we are trained to be engineers, teachers, doctors – professionals who staff the Apartheid Machine. Co-option dee luxe. Apathy keeps us very cosy but it asks no questions – and it's exactly how they want us to be: meek and manipulable. Mindless, ek sê (I say).

Whites had been excluded from involvement in black student politics since 1968, when Steve Biko led a walk-out of black students from the white-dominated National Union of Students, and blacks formed their own student organization. It took more than a decade before non-racialism again took root among the youth; but by the early 1980s, black and white students were plotting joint strategy in anti-government campaigns. In areas where blacks lacked resources, progressive white students stepped in and applied their skills and university resources toward the production of political pamphlets for the black communities. These whites, like white activists before them, soon learned that when it came to political involvement, their privileged racial and class positions afforded them little protection against police harassment. Even totally legal activity, such as a 'pamphlet blitz', could get a white into trouble.

By the time the United Democratic Front was launched, progressive whites had proved – not only with their skills and resources, but with their commitment – that they formed a small but vibrant component of the growing nationwide non-racial alliance. Whites found their support actively solicited by black leaders.

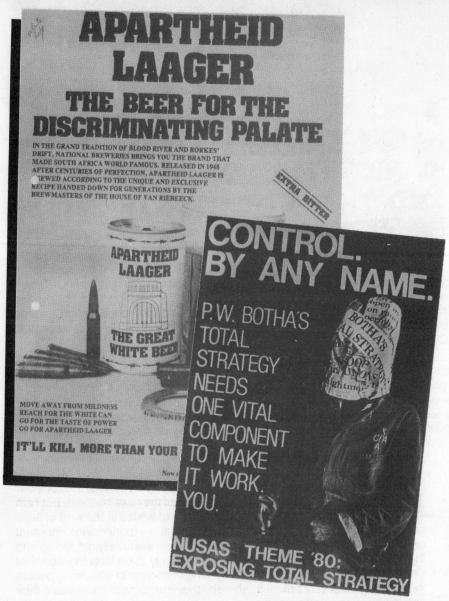

Instructions for pamphlet distribution from the University of the Witwatersrand Students' Representative Council 1981: Make sure you pamphleteer singly, but keep in sight of at least two colleagues. This is absolutely essential for your own well-being. If the police approach you and ask you to move on, you must do so, but you are in no way obliged to stop handing out leaflets. If a policeman tells you he is arresting you, you must go along – but try to have a witness who will testify that you were arrested. If your leaflets are confiscated by the police, you should ask for a receipt. The Riotous Assemblies Act makes it an offence to distribute leaflets in groups, but if you stay at least 15 metres away from the next person distributing, this should not be a problem. At all costs, keep moving when handing out pamphlets. If you are arrested, or need help, phone 39-1541.

Letter from the Natal regional UDF, 21 June 1984: Dear friends, The UDF has been heartened by the positive response of members of the white sector over the last year to the challenge of developing progressive organizations in their communities. This letter serves as a broad appeal to all progressive whites who share the objectives of the UDF, to come to a meeting in order to discuss the extension of the Million Signatures Campaign, and to share thoughts on how this might be organized; also to look briefly at the crucial anti-election campaign facing all democratic-minded South Africans. It has become clear that the white sector has an increasingly important role to play in the struggle towards a non-racial and democratic South Africa.

If the emergence of the UDF had vindicated the right and duty of whites to join in the fight for democratic rule in South Africa, it had also redefined the role of whites in that fight. With the resurgence of the resistance traditions of the 1950s, whites re-examined the achievements of the separate white branch of the ANC's Congress Alliance, the Congress of Democrats, and concluded that the best way to work for change in a racially divided society was to begin from within those government-imposed racial divisions. Thus 'Democratic Action Committees' and 'Area Committees' were formed in the white suburbs, affiliated to the UDF, but devoted to the 'conscientization' of the white community.

While it had often been fashionable in the past for whites on the left to spurn even white liberals, the focus was now on attracting all potential white opposition, from the women volunteers of the Black Sash pass advice offices to businessmen disgruntled with the soaring tax bill caused by the government's burgeoning bureaucracy.[13] When the white parliamentary opposition Progressive Federal Party agreed to participate in the tricameral parliament, betraying a pledge to oppose it, the new white committees castigated the move – but did not stop there.[14] They set about trying to educate whites to the understanding that the true forces of change in South Africa would not come from parliament, but from those who are excluded from political decision-making.

Jeremy Cronin, poet and ex-political prisoner, delivering the Academic Freedom Lecture at the University of the Witwatersrand, 4 October 1984: We are now seeing the downgrading of the role of the traditional white opposition parties in Parliament, with the advent of an executive president, and adjunct ethnic parliaments. In this situation, with the legitimacy of the official political institutions in tatters, we need to take a fresh look at the democratic political traditions outside parliament that the majority of South Africans have all along been obliged to pursue, if for no other reason than exclusion. What may be our growing scepticism in regard to parliament, the sickening spectacle of horse-trading, pseudo-oppositions, the switching of parties, the total absence of any principle, other than the pursuit of salaries and a dubious prestige – all of this should not lead us into a disgust with politics per se. Politics in South Africa is not synonymous with parliamentary politics. In a very real sense, the participants in those crisis-ridden structures are the boycotters. They are boycotting another political tradition which clearly has widespread legitimacy and support of an overwhelming majority of South Africans.

So who's the enemy? ANC guerillas were not born in Havana. They are the people who grow up under the violence of apartheid in Langa and Soweto. Shanty houses and nothing to eat, pass raids and mother in jail, force-fed the lies of Bantu Education, and in 1976, when their placards and songs were met with bullets and teargas, there's no choice left but to go across the border and the war is a civil war. A civil war in which a few powerful men expect us to fight, kill, maim and die to defend a system that defends their privileges. To get us to sacrifice our time, our limbs, and our lives, Botha's men are forced to present us with a set of lies. Lies about the war, the 'enemy', the system. They tell us that South Africa is threatened by a foreign enemy – Russians, Cubans, Palestinians, Muscovite agents. So it's natural the South African Defence Force must protect the Namibian people and us from Fidel Castro and his lot. And it's natural that we must give up two years of our lives to fulfil our patriotic duty.

But hang on. Check, is assisting apartheid's resettlement policy defending us against foreigners? Is conducting house-to-house searches in townships during a schools boycott protecting us from foreigners? Protector of the people? No, for most South Africans, the SADF is simply the fist of apartheid. And for most Namibians (and for most of the world), South Africa is an illegal occupier depriving Namibia of its freedom.

Okay, so when our turn comes, we stop and think about what choices we have: to defend a government which represents less than 10 per cent of the people, or to think about what alternatives we have. There is a call to oppose compulsory conscription into apartheid's army. Where do we stand? Let's make it our decision: it's our future! 'Would you let the system make you kill your brother?' – Bob Marley.

The most potent issue for mobilizing extra-parliamentary white opposition is that of military service, for it affects all young white males and their families – even immigrants.[15] Spurred on by a survey of English-language universities showing more than 60 per cent of students opposed military conscription, a range of white opposition groups endorsed the nationwide End Conscription Campaign.

Veteran organizers who saw the government thwart the incipient conscientious objectors movement in 1983 with tough legislation punishing resisters, are pessimistic about the scope for legal opposition to conscription, especially given the looming threat of Coloured and Indian resistance. Among young white activists such as Joel, Mark and Will, there is a growing expectation that the anti-conscription movement will eventually be forced underground.

Joel: So far, the white community has been very reluctant to consider any kind of extra-legal option, because of the risks involved. But I am confident that through the involvement of whites in the kind of legal political work that they are doing, as they continue experiencing consistent repression and harassment by the state, they will eventually get fed up and then consider such an option. In fact, you could say that a lot of the work that we're doing with people right now in fighting conscription is allowing people to go through that very process, whereby they are going to consolidate their commitment and understanding of the situation so that when they get so angered by the repressive measures that they themselves are experiencing, when they reach that stage, they will then become open to this very different strategy.

You see, there's a reason that people move into extra-legal activity. It evolved, not because people enjoy that kind of work, but as a response to concrete conditions. And what I'm saying is that we, as whites, have to experience those conditions in order to appreciate fully the need for extra-legal activity.

Mark: When we say 'extra-legal activity', well, I'm not going to spell it out here, but let's just say that it means no longer depending on the mass meeting, on open distribution of literature. You work on a different level, clandestinely. There are just no other effective means of opposing the military and staying in the country, and, more and more, people are deciding that they want to try and stay in the country as long as possible, to oppose from within – not just skip as soon as their call-up comes. These are not choices we make lightly – obviously not, given the personal risks involved.

Joel: You see, this is really the one important issue that directly affects whites and, especially in the eyes of the non-racial movement, we can't fall short – otherwise what kind of credibility do we have, what kind of claim can we make

as to the non-racial nature of the struggle? So as far as we're concerned, it's absolutely crucial that this issue be approached on a principled stand. There can be no compromise.

Mark: A lot of whites refuse to get involved in this campaign, or any other political activity, and then justify their position by criticizing the movement. They'll criticize the kind of non-racial alliance we're working so hard to build up. And the net result is that they don't get involved, they never put themselves on the line. I think it's quite a calculated position.

Will: If black people have been prepared for so long to suffer the consequences of their actions, then if we want to have an equal say in determining not only the nature of the struggle, but the nature of a new society, then we have to be prepared to make similar sacrifices. Otherwise people are going to say afterwards, and rightly so: 'What did you do? What right have you got to participate in decision-making processes now, when you weren't prepared to make the sacrifices that were necessary at the time?'

In late 1981, scores of white trade unionists, students and community organizers found out exactly what those sacrifices entailed when they were detained in the widest security police swoop on whites to date, and trade unionist

163

Dr Neil Aggett[16] became the first white detainee to die in a police cell. His death shocked the 'white left' and forced this small, tight-knit community to come to grips with the fact that a white skin offered no security when the security police took charge. A group of whites who weathered the 1981-2 detentions – two ex-detainees and two activists who lent support during the year-long ordeal – spoke about how the experience shaped their political development.

Sue: I used to think quite a lot about the possibility of being detained and I wondered vaguely how I'd respond, but when I woke up at four o'clock in the morning and there were ten security policemen standing in my bedroom, I wasn't scared. I was absolutely shocked at myself, at the fact that I wasn't frightened, that I had actually responded with anger and that I handled it. So I think that the whole experience has revealed things to us about ourselves, and made us a hell of a lot stronger people. We've experienced a kind of togetherness and unity and support which has made for a new strength of commitment. I think it all goes to show that the state's strategy of trying to instil fear into us is not working, that people are getting stronger, not weaker. People are equipping themselves to handle the increased repression.

Roger: Before those detentions, most people's attitudes would have been that if you're white and you're detained, you're going to have a fairly easy time. Now we know that's not true. Whites have been subjected to exactly the same kinds of pressures as everybody else – the blacks – have been dealing with, and we've coped.

Lisa: I feel I now have a broader sense of history, of where whites fit into the general political scene. I no longer feel that sense of alienation or apology that a lot of people have about being white in South Africa. It's now absolutely clear to me that there's a place for all of us in the struggle, that we all have skills and talents, that we are all useful and important, and we're actually very rooted in this country. I'm not saying that I'm glad we all had to go through the experience of the detentions, but I do think we've gained some valuable insights from the experience.

For months, the government refused to respond to calls for the detainees to be charged or released, maintaining that the security police were preparing a huge conspiracy trial that would demonstrate why they were all a threat to state security.

Sunday Times, **27 December 1981:** A massive security trial – or a series of separate trials – is expected early in the new year, according to informed sources. Sources closely involved in security affairs said it had become clear recently that the authorities were building up to a major trial in which a number of people now in detention will feature. The Minister of Police, Mr Louis le Grange, this week confirmed that 'within months' a number of detainees would be charged with 'serious offences'. And the head of the Security Branch, Lieutenant-General Johan Coetzee, said a member of the Attorney-General's office had been assigned to his branch to help formulate the charges. Charges facing trade unionists and labour leaders now in detention could include terrorism and furthering the aims of the banned African National Congress, he said. He said some of the people now in detention would be state witnesses and would testify against their colleagues.

One source said it appeared likely that the security authorities would try hard to link a number of activities – sabotage acts, boycotts of products, anti-Republic Day protests, and trade union activities – into a single conspiracy. Internationally, South Africa's penchant for detention without trial is a constant point of attack, and some form of show trial would be politically important for the government as a means of seeking to justify its security actions. According to the Detainees Parents' Support Committee, at least 5000 people have been detained since 1963, most of whom were released and never charged. Last year, it records, 127 minors were detained, of whom only 26 were charged. This year, 581 people were detained.

The mass trial did not materialize. In the end, one detainee stood alone in the dock: a woman named Barbara Hogan. A part-time graduate student and community worker, Hogan was the first woman to be charged with treason since the mass trial of ANC and Congress Alliance members in 1956-61, and the first South African to be prosecuted for treason in a case that involved no violence against the state. Hogan's work for the ANC had been confined to gathering information about trade unions and community organizations for her contact in Botswana; she was a tiny cog in the ANC's machinery, uninvolved in military operations. Yet her trial revealed the tremendous threat to the government posed by whites working for the ANC, no matter how low-key their role, as well as the value attached to white members by the ANC itself.

By the time her trial had ended, when Hogan returned to her cell for six weeks to await judgment, she had begun steeling herself for a guilty verdict and a harsh sentence. Her only consolation was that, unlike during the previous year of solitary confinement, when she saw no one but her security police interrogators whom she later sued for assault,[17] she was now permitted a few books, food parcels, and three half-hour visits a week. During the wait for judgment, she reflected on the historical significance of her case. ➤

Barbara Hogan was convicted of High Treason and sentenced to ten years in prison, with no leave to appeal – an unprecedented sentence that was condemned throughout the world. As South Africa's first white woman political prisoner since the 1960s, she served the first year of her sentence in virtual solitary confinement, until she was joined by another white woman convicted of treason, Jansie Lourens.

Police photo used as evidence in Niehaus-Lourens trial: Niehaus in police custody, points out gas works he planned to sabotage.

Barbara Hogan, September 1982, Johannesburg Women's Prison: I believe that the state felt under quite a bit of pressure to produce a big treason trial. Then, when the whole thing started to disintegrate, it kind of just came down to me. Now I think the judge is under a lot of pressure to come through with a conviction on treason. I think they really want to set a precedent with this one.

I have mixed feelings about all the press coverage of this case. I mean, there are so many people who've risked so much more than me and stand to lose so much more, and who actually achieved so much more. When you think of the hundreds of people who go totally unnoticed by the media, who never get any attention, who just get detained and tried and sentenced and no one ever knows, I sometimes think there's been entirely too much emphasis on my case.

This emphasis on me being white and female, that's also problematic. I know it's important, but it still bothers me, this whole focus on 'the young white woman'. It's part of the tremendous sensationalization of the case. I know that 'myths' are important. Myths were certainly a part of my motivation. I guess we all need that. It's just that when you're in the position of being part of the myth-making, it's easier to be critical. I don't want to only be recorded as the young white woman, but at the same time I know that it's really valuable to reinforce the growing importance of whites, and women, in the struggle. Just as long as it doesn't contribute to an individualistic view of my involvement. Because it's all part of a continuum, ultimately.

The trial of two Afrikaans-speaking students, Lourens and her fiancé, Carl Niehaus, a former deacon of the Dutch Reformed Church, was an even more wrenching experience for the government and its supporters. Niehaus was sentenced to fifteen years in prison and Lourens to four, for active work on behalf of the ANC: producing pamphlets, planting pamphlet bombs, learning a secret ANC code for transmitting information to the ANC outside the country, attempting to recruit ANC members, helping people flee the country for military training, and reconnoitering the Johannesburg gas works for possible sabotage. Yet, in full knowledge of the fact that any statement he made would be used against him, Niehaus spoke out boldly during his trial about what he saw as the unavoidable recourse to violence against the apartheid system.

Carl Niehaus, under cross-examination in the Rand Supreme Court, 22 November, 1983: Initially, I was very concerned about the use of violence. On one side, there is violence which is institutionalized in South African society; on the other side, there is the the kind of violence employed by the ANC. The ANC line also happens to agree with my Christian principles. I would like to draw a parallel with Nazi Germany, where the churches very lamely went along with the system. A small number of people in the church disagreed, and there were people, like Dietrich Bonhoeffer, who wanted to assassinate Hitler. I think we can favourably compare the position in South African churches to those in Germany at that time.

Prosecutor Jan Swanepoel: Would you go along with the assassination of the head of the South African government?
Carl Niehaus: I wouldn't have done it.
Prosecutor Jan Swanepoel: Is there a line? Can the ANC kill innocent people in the streets of Pretoria, but not the Prime Minister?
Carl Niehaus: I think the line is drawn by innocent people dying in the homelands. I would understand it (killing P.W. Botha) if – and I repeat if – it is going to bring an end to the horror of this system. It may be an option. It is important to distinguish between the (May 1983) Pretoria bomb and saying that the assassination of the Prime Minister would bring about political change.

Prosecutor Jan Swanepoel: Let's not beat about the bush. Why is it not necessary to kill the head of state?
Carl Niehaus: If the Prime Minister of this country wants to continue to the same position as Nazi Germany, then it will be necessary. As long as it is possible not to kill people, you shouldn't. When it becomes necessary, then it has to be done. It is necessary to continue with the armed struggle and that inevitably means that people will be killed. It is not that the ANC enjoys exploding bombs – it has been forced to it by the South African government, and as long as the situation goes on, bombs will continue to explode, I am convinced of it.

No amount of arguing can change one simple fact that is paramount in the law and order situation in our country today; pursue legitimate political goals within the framework of the law and you will not be touched. But get into the Niehaus situation, in which illegality at the behest of subversive movements and leadership abounds, and you are bound to get into conflict with the law. A further warning is that from the very start, his activities were laid bare by the authorities. He was a child in an adult world of political intrigue. Niehaus was foolish, but all will not be lost if others at least learn from his stupidity. Nobody should be fooled by nice-sounding and high-flown ideals such as those propagated by the African National Congress and its apologists. The ANC, the South African Communist Party and its followers are committed to the illegal and violent overthrow of South Africa's political, social and economic system. Killing and violence are their solutions.

But the most damning indictment of Niehaus's activities is that after all his actions, one can find absolutely nothing that he has contributed to real social change in South Africa. His course of action is a self-defeating one. This was the same course followed by people like Robert Adam, Renfrew Christie, and Guy Berger,[19] all people who were recruited through their connections to the universities and convicted in the last few years. How many more must follow before the ANC and its sympathizers realize the futility and destructiveness of their chosen course? All of these people have become involved in illegal activities via the National Union of South African Students, student Projects Committees and other so-called democratic organizations. Make sure that neither you nor any of those close to you fall into the ANC/SACP trap which is baited by NUSAS, the UDF and other noble-sounding organizations.

Security Police General Johan Coetzee, speaking on SABC, 15 March 1982: Statements that sabotage plots against the South African government were planned by so-called 'freedom fighters' of the African National Congress are wrong. These plots have been masterminded by white agents, and black ANC agents were sent in as cannon fodder to do the dirty work. I think the claim of the ANC that they have support among the black people at grassroots level is false, and this is very amply demonstrated by the recent incident where they had to import people from the United Kingdom and from Belgium and from Canada to come and launch this conspiracy, to attack what was obviously a status target: the headquarters of the military. I think it demonstrates that they haven't got the support of the black people which they claim they have.

It was hard enough for the government to accept that English-speaking whites could turn 'traitor', but the defiance of Afrikaners – from advocate Bram Fischer to poet Breyten Breytenbach[18] – was always a peculiarly cruel blow to the (mainly) Afrikaner government. Thus Niehaus and Lourens were castigated as naive, misled by activists and organizations inside the country, and used by ANC agents outside.

STUDENTS AND

STATE REPRESSION

The government's need to vilify white involvement in the ANC is tied in with the deep-rooted racist assumption that all blacks – even clever and conniving communist ones – need whites to tell them what to do. For example, when the ANC launched a spectacular rocket attack on the Voortrekkerhoogte military base in August 1981, the Chief of the South African security police, General Johan Coetzee, claimed that the sabotage had been plotted by whites who infiltrated South Africa from Europe and North America.

Few believe this caricature of the ANC as white brains manipulating black cannon fodder. Evidence at ANC trials and the little information that people manage to glean from non-government sources show the ANC to be a largely black but non-racial organization which embraces whites as members and even leaders. To an increasing number of blacks and whites, the ANC is the future, liberated South Africa in embryo.

The War

C. The Ungovernable

Sipho, a member of the Congress of South African Students: Students are seeing their problems in the schools as part of the entire system. From the time they leave school every day their problems aren't over. The trains and buses home are late and overcrowded or the fares have gone up again. When they get home they are hungry because the wages are too low and General Sales Tax and rents have gone up.[20] Police are teargassing them at school and hunting people for passes outside school.

Now the government has come up with this new constitution and the elections. This same government has closed down their schools, rather than give in to their demands. It is not surprising that students are not fooled by the talk of reform. That is why more and more students are throwing their weight behind their own organizations and bodies which will represent their interests – organizations like the Student Representative Councils, the Congress of South African Students, the Azanian Students' Organization and the United Democratic Front.

When tens of thousands of black students walked out of their classrooms and on to the streets in early 1984, and stayed there for the rest of the year, it looked as if the long predicted replay of 16 June 1976 had finally come to pass. But by the end of 1984, it was clear that a far more profound and far less controllable uprising was underway, involving not only students, but workers and the communities. The grievances that sparked the initial boycott in the high schools of Pretoria's black township of Atteridgeville were much the same as those that instigated the 1976 and 1980 schools unrest, except that the boycotters of 1984 had learned from the experience of their predecessors. Their demands were now more sophisticated and specific: the right to elect Student Representative Councils to negotiate directly with the government, the free distribution of textbooks to all students, an end to age restrictions preventing older students from attending school, a ban on excessive corporal punishment, and an end to sexual harassment of students by teachers.

The government's response echoed that of 1976 and 1980: the boycotted schools were closed, forcing thousands of politicized students into the role of full-time protestors. To the angry youth, no matter how much the government talked of reform, nothing had changed since 1976. Demands were still ignored and protesting students were still being killed by police. But the students realized that, in the years since Soweto, the government had not been able to stamp out the fire of resistance. With teargas and bullets, the police were conducting a fairly effective holding operation – isolating unrest, sometimes preventing it from spreading – but neither the government's reform nor its repression had succeeded in breaking a relentless militancy. As the boycotts raged from school to school, involving as many as 220,000 students by mid-1984, the protest against inferior and irrelevant education also widened.

At the time of the protests against the August elections for the new Coloured and Indian parliaments, the number of boycotting students tripled. The security police arrested nearly two hundred people in a vain bid to derail the boycott. The pitiful voter turn-out notwithstanding, the government proclaimed the poll a representative mandate and held elaborate ceremonies in Cape Town to open Parliament and install P.W. Botha as executive State President, with powers to handpick the Cabinet, control the even more powerful State Security Council, and dissolve the new Parliament at will.[21]

Although the government tried to switch the spotlight to the pomp in Cape Town, the main drama was unfolding in the black townships of the Vaal Triangle industrial area (covering only one per-cent of South Africa's land but accounting for half its service industries), which erupted in violent protests that left thirty-one dead, hundreds injured and thousands homeless.

A close examination of the casualties provides some important clues as to the root cause of what grew into the most sustained and widespread uprising since 1976. The six-year-old boy shot dead by police while playing on the verandah of his home recalled the martyrs of past unrest. The four township councillors stoned, hacked to death and set alight by residents represented an unprecedented level of black anger, focused with a vehemence never before witnessed in South Africa. In the past, blacks had non-violently demonstrated their rejection of the community councils offered them as an alternative to participation in central government – the urban African corollary of the Coloured and Indian houses of Parliament and homeland 'independence' – but Pretoria had ignored their boycott of the December 1983 council elections. So, in early 1984, a mysterious group calling itself the 'South African Suicide Squad' tried using a different language: the petrol-bombing of councillors' homes and businesses.

United Democratic Front pamphlet, issued in Cape Town, 14 September 1984: Botha's new apartheid parliaments get going this week. Today, Botha himself will be elected State President. Yesterday, Hendrickse (elected Coloured member of Parliament and appointed Cabinet Minister without Portfolio), Rajbansi (Indian delegate) and Botha's other junior partners took their seats in their kitchen parliaments. But who wants them? They don't represent us. More than 80 per cent of Coloureds and Indians who could have voted stayed away. Almost nobody voted! Millions of African people were not even allowed to vote. Yet Hendrickse and Rajbansi dare to speak for us!

In Cape Town, only four out of every 100 voted. Yet they open their parliaments here – what an insult to the people of Cape Town! While Hendrickse and Rajbansi enjoy their banquets and fancy houses, more than 35 of UDF's leaders are in detention. Thousands of Cape Town's people continue to have their shacks bulldozed. For Botha and his junior partners, it is the beginning of the 'new deal' road, a road that leads nowhere! Millions support the UDF call: We are one South Africa – we demand one Parliament! Release our leaders! Detentions will not stop our struggle for freedom!

Johannes Rantete, a resident of the Vaal township of Sebokeng: During the last few days of August, residents in the Vaal Triangle were informed that on Monday, the third day of September, no one should go to work, as it would be the day of protest against the rent hikes. Early on the morning of Friday, 31 August, pamphlets were distributed by the town council, warning residents that if they didn't go to work on Monday they would lose their jobs and lose their houses, and in turn, the future of their children would be doomed. Those pamphlets didn't have any influence on people. Saturday and Sunday came and passed. Then came the greatest day in the history of Sebokeng, the day of protest, the day of deaths, the day of arrests and the day of teargas and smoke. This day is historically named 'Bloody Monday'. The slogans that ruled on Bloody Monday were 'Amandla! Ngawethu'! and 'Asinamali'! (Power is ours! We have no money!) The increase in rents would have driven many families away from their houses. Black families are really experiencing some hardships. Things are becoming worse and worse for them. The General Sales Tax has increased. The majority are being paid less. Many people are being retrenched from their work, thus increasing already high unemployment.

The presence of the police in the townships often brought the strikes to the boiling point. Wherever they appeared with their vehicles, people began to gather and riots followed. If the police had not made continual appearances in the townships, and if they had stopped patrolling with their helicopters, there would have been no such warm riots as the Vaal area experienced.[22]

Leaflet distributed in Soweto on 17 February 1984 by the South African Suicide Squad: Why bombings on community councillors? Ninety per cent of Soweto rejected your councils and your leadership because Community Councils entrench apartheid. You crooked the people of Soweto by promising to reduce rents. We warn councillors to resign or the worst is ahead.

UDF National Publicity Secretary Terror Lekota, at a solidarity meeting with Tumahole residents in Johannesburg, 19 July 1984: The week of violence in Tumahole is a direct result of the new black local authorities system and action should be taken against those who serve on the new councils. People should stay out of the shops and premises of councillors because they have made common cause with apartheid. We predicted at the national launch of the UDF a year ago that black residents would find it impossible to afford the new municipalities. These areas simply do not have the business income of white areas and will have to rely on pushing up rents. There is no way that the masses of the people can meet these expenses. We call for the immediate resignation of councillors in these puppet bodies – the time is now. I believe a very disastrous situation is developing in this country, especially after what I have seen in Tumahole.

The bombings continued and by mid-1984, armed guards had been brought into the townships to protect the councillors from their supposed constituents. Candidates in the Coloured and Indian elections also became targets. The battle line between the people and the government – and its agents, black or white – was now sharper than ever before, but the line between civilians and South Africa's armed opponents was blurring. Whether or not the South African Suicide Squad had ANC links or allegiances, a grassroots military initiative against the government was clearly underway. This, coupled with evidence from the state's own security trials, showing a sophisticated knowledge of guns and bombs among guerillas who had never left the country, seemed to vindicate the ANC's updated strategy to rely more and more on local military training.[23]

Another early warning that blacks saw the councillors as Pretoria's impotent fall guys came in July, when a rent increase imposed by these black officials in the rural township of Tumahole led to a week of demonstrations, detentions and violent clashes with the police. In the past, there was no link between Tumahole, isolated in the heart of Afrikaner farmland, and other centres of resistance, but with the founding of the United Democratic Front, Tumahole and many other rural areas were hooked into a national network.[24] Tumahole's civic association, its chapter of the Congress of South African Students, and other local organizations all affiliated to the UDF.

UDF National Publicity Secretary Terror Lekota had been in the township when 1000 protesters clashed with police, and he was detained at a roadblock. Lekota was later able to report that while he was being held at the local police station, he saw the police repeatedly assault a detainee who looked like a man found dead in his cell the next day. The detainee, Johannes Ngalo, was buried under the banners of the UDF and its local affiliates. It was the UDF which arranged for a private post-mortem, led the call for a probe into Ngalo's death, organized memorial services around the country, and pointed to the government's new black local authorities system and its 'puppet' councillors as the root of the unrest.

The warning of what Tumahole's residents called 'the struggle of the poor' was not heeded. Two months later, after the same kind of unrest in response to the same

kind of rent increases led to physical attacks on councillors in the Vaal Triangle, the warning was taken seriously. Councillors went into hiding, emerging only to announce the scrapping of rent increases or their own resignations. The government went through the well-rehearsed response it had given to every protest since the 1950s – condemning 'agitators', detaining 'instigators', and banning meetings – yet this uniquely virulent uprising baffled South Africa's rulers. Unrest in the highly politicized townships of the big cities was predictable; the despair of blacks in the underdeveloped rural areas was understandable; but the Vaal Triangle had been peaceful since the Sharpeville massacre of 1960 – even during 1976 – and had been expected to remain so.

The Urban Foundation had poured vast sums of money into Sebokeng, Sharpeville's neighbouring township. Private industries, building societies and construction firms had invested heavily in home-ownership schemes. Yet this 'model township', was now smouldering, nearly every shop burned down, houses, schools and administrative offices reduced to rubble. Also in ruins was the very much-touted theory of a black middle class 'with something to lose' as a buffer against political unrest.

An even worse blow to the government than the crumbling of the would-be middle-class buffer was the failure of the authorities' concessions to cool the still-simmering townships and the still-boycotting students. The cancellation of rent increases was met with calls for further reductions, even after council officials and police went door-to-door, demanding rent from residents. The Department of Education and Training's constitution for Student Representative Councils was rejected as government-imposed, and when officials reopened schools and offered to let students write exams in mid-1985, the Congress of South African Students resolved to continue the boycott until they were permitted to write exams earlier, so as to avoid losing a full year of study. School and community issues were now inseparable: students linked their continued boycott to the rent issue, and the communities backed the students' campaign for an Education Charter to spell out the Freedom Charter's demand that 'the doors of learning and culture shall be opened to all'.

This uncompromising response to the government's concessions also spawned a sense of unity between communities fighting similar issues in different parts of South Africa. More than 40,000 people converged on Evaton and Sharpeville for the funerals of twenty-five of those killed in the Vaal Triangle. This outpouring of solidarity, grief and anger climaxed when a funeral procession marched straight at the armed police, shouting, 'We do not want any police here! We have come to bury our heroes and we want to do it with respect and dignity – go away!' The police retreated into their armoured personnel carriers, but later arrested 666 people for violating the government's ban on political gatherings.

The Citizen, **4 September 1984:** The riot situations in a number of Vereeniging and East Rand black townships were very serious and still fluid, the Minister of Law and Order, Mr Louis le Grange, said. The Minister said he had received a report on the situation which 'at this early stage' showed that 'certain adults have again used children and youngsters to do their dirty work for them'. He said it appeared that the instigators had used alleged house rental increases as an excuse to launch a well-timed and well-planned riot situation in a number of superbly controlled black urban townships, which were known for a long time as being model townships with regard to their administration in general.

'There was no sign before and in fact no reason for any unhappiness about house rentals in the affected townships,' Mr le Grange said. The Minister stressed that the affected areas were not slum areas. 'The affected areas are being occupied by a strong black middle class who did not complain about the administration of their black councillors before the riots'.

Soweto Civic Association member Isaac Mogase, speaking at the Evaton funeral, 16 September, 1984: Your struggle for rents in the Vaal area is our struggle for rents in Soweto. Your struggle against political domination by a minority regime is our struggle. Your struggle for freedom and justice is the struggle of our people throughout the country.

Cyril Ramaphosa, General-Secretary of the National Union of Mineworkers: It is clear that the Labour Relations Act neutralizes the workers' most effective weapon: the surprise element of strike. Our experience during the recent wage dispute proves that co-operating with the state by following procedures laid down in its labour laws does not serve our purpose. My members are asking themselves whether doing everything above board is worth it. The police acted just as if it had been an illegal strike.[25]

SABC, 10 October 1984: The Minister of Law and Order, Mr Louis le Grange, made the categorical statement at the National Party's Transvaal Congress that the United Democratic Front is pursuing the same revolutionary goals as the banned ANC, and is actively promoting a climate of revolution. Linking the UDF with the ANC through association is an easy exercise – and association it has to be, because the UDF purposefully and understandably avoids any overt formal ties with the terrorist organization.

Any cursory examination of the UDF reveals the following: that it goes along with the principles of the Freedom Charter, to which the ANC subscribes; that more than 90 per cent of its office-bearers were members of the ANC or the outlawed South African Communist Party; that ANC leader Nelson Mandela features among its patrons; that banned ANC publications increasingly feature the UDF as 'brothers in the struggle'; that the UDF, in common with the ANC, is openly committed to using extra-parliamentary methods to affect change, although it claims to be opposed to violence.

These are but the generally known indicators of what the UDF is up to, and the direction in which it is trying to push the country. Much is secret and remains unknown. Much more is known by the South African security authorities, but they find it expedient at this stage not to divulge the information. However, in the final analysis, it is incumbent upon the South African authorities to neutralize that which could lead to the implementation of what Mr le Grange called 'the UDF's revolutionary goals' with whatever actions it deems necessary.

The sustained political activity of 1984 was by no means confined to community and student organizations. Like community residents, students and unorganized workers, the trade unions learned that the lesson of the year was that extra-legal channels were more effective than legal ones. South Africa's first legal black strike, at the beginning of the year, taught workers at the Transvaal's African Explosives and Chemical Industries that the months of negotiations and the thirty days notice of intention to strike required by the reformed Labour Relations Act gave employers too great an advantage, for large numbers of workers were dismissed as a result. Similarly, the 90,000-strong National Union of Mineworkers lost faith in the legal path it followed in the run-up to its August strike, and its leadership hinted that the future might see a return to illegal strikes and community support action.

To the government, the key difference between the political activity of today and that of past years was the existence of a national political body that united communities, workers and students — African, Coloured, Indian and white. Many of the United Democratic Front's 645 affiliates were located in the flashpoints of the unrest today. Therefore, the state reasoned, the UDF was behind it all, and the ANC was behind the UDF.

The government has been branding the UDF and ANC front since the UDF's inception, detaining its leaders, harassing its members, raiding its offices, and banning its meetings, and the latest tirade by the Minister of Police seemed an ominous indication that the government was considering a ban on the organization. The UDF's national executive — minus three-quarters of its members who were being held under 'preventive detention' orders — counter-attacked.

The government's attacks on those who sought to change South Africa through open, legal means only served to prove an increasing number of the government's opponents that peaceful change was just not possible. More and more young blacks were deciding to fight the next round with arms, and more and more often their parents supported the move. Two mothers in Soweto spoke about their response to their children's decision to leave South Africa for military training.

First Soweto mother: At first I felt bitter, but now I think that I am with my son in every step he is taking.

What are those steps?

Soweto mother: Well, according to what he says, he is following the rest of the people of this country who are fighting for the struggle. In fact, those are his encouraging words whenever he writes. He always tells me to have courage because he is fighting for the struggle. That is why he left.

Do you feel that he will succeed?

Soweto mother: Well, I can't say, because some of them don't succeed; when they come back, they are shot or put in jail. But he is a freedom fighter, he is in the struggle. On that point I stand with him.

You call him a 'freedom fighter'; to the government, he's a 'terrorist'.

Soweto mother: I don't understand why they are called terrorists, because they are not terrorizing anybody – they are fighting for our rights. I think they have resorted to violence because so many times they sent people to try to talk, but nothing was done. We blacks, we are just kept like children, who are told what to do, where to go, how far to go. We cannot even talk freely. I think our children are on the right track because they see these things. We adults were satisfied until our children woke up and started to point out things that we didn't notice. So our children are on the right track.

Is this a matter that you can talk about freely?

Soweto mother: No I always keep it to myself. The police have come twice, asking for him. They come at night, knocking at doors and windows. They tell me if I get a letter from him, I must show it to the police – if I hear that he is around, I must bring him to the police. The other time they told me I was wanted at the police station and they picked me up for questioning.

What do you tell them?

Soweto mother: I will never help them. I don't wish them to get to him because I know he can be crippled for life, like the other young men who have been under the police. Many, many died under police hands. So I cannot help them.

Second Soweto mother: I think our children are more angry than us. My daughter left in 1977. She didn't even tell me she's going to escape the country. Last year when I was in Lesotho I met her, and it was then she told me she was going to be fighting.

How did you feel?

Soweto mother: Well, I feel it's for her own rights, and the good of the country. If I could do something, I should help too.

Do you think she'll succeed?

Soweto mother: Oh well, she's got every hope. Everybody believes in something. Like I, for instance, believe in church. I believe it'll help me. She believes in what she's doing, that it's going to help us all one day. I'm missing her terribly, but I've taken it. I'm depressed, but I'm looking forward to the day when I'll see Mandela again.

United Democratic Front statement, issued at a Johannesburg press conference, 10 October 1984: Mr le Grange's ill-advised statements represent the pinnacle of a sustained and vicious propaganda campaign against the UDF and its affiliates. He is using veiled threats, innuendo, false conclusions and misinformation to create a climate in which the government will be able to take repressive action against the UDF. His allegations of links between the UDF and the ANC are totally without foundation and cannot be substantiated. We make no apology for the fact that parts of our leadership have been members of the ANC. Even the Minister cannot deny that they have a proud history of struggle against this evil system and that they command the respect and support of the majority of our people.

The government is trying to divert attention from its own bankruptcy and inability to govern, by blaming the UDF for the conflict and turmoil which is currently tearing our land apart. The government's undemocratic constitution has been rejected, international isolation is unparalleled, and the economic crisis looms large in the face of the falling rand. The government has lost control. South Africa faces a bleak future in the hands of the present government.

Banning the UDF would contribute nothing toward alleviating the present crisis, but would exacerbate it. It would show the government's determination to stifle all legitimate and peaceful opposition. The UDF merely articulates the aspirations of the majority of the people, and these aspirations cannot be wished away by a ban. In a word, we have come here to say: Long live the UDF! Ban apartheid!

'My Mother', by Chris van Wyk:

*My mother could never carry me
while they used the warmth of her womb
to forge their hearts into hatred*

*My mother could never wean me
because they dried her out
until her tits were arid tufts of drought*

*My mother could never embrace me
while she kept house for them
held their children*

*My mother is
a boesman meid
a kaffir girl
a koelie aunty[26]
who wears beads of sweat around her neck
and chains round her ankles*

*But, defrocked of dignity
my mother has broken free of the heirlooms
of oppression*

*These days she dresses in the fatigues of those
grown tired of serving evil gods*

Now my mother is dressed to kill

The South African government had hoped that the Nkomati non-aggression accord it signed with neighbouring Mozambique in March of 1984 would so cripple the ANC that guerilla attacks would subside. Instead, the attacks continued unabated, with a new trend emerging: the first significant direct combat between guerillas and the police. The ANC had clashed with the police and the army on isolated occasions before (notably, the 1978 shoot-out in the middle of Johannesburg that led to the first execution of an ANC guerilla, Solomon Mahlangu) but after the Nkomati Accord, a spate of incidents saw guerillas confront government forces. In May, four men fought a gun battle with police after a rocket attack on a Durban oil refinery. The next month, a detainee overpowered police and escaped from custody while being transported from one police station to another on a Johannesburg highway. In July, and again in August, men armed with AK-47 rifles ambushed police on patrol in Soweto, and in November, guerillas clashed with the Bophuthatswana homeland army.

Another trend had emerged since the Nkomati Accord was signed: an increase in ANC sabotage attacks. The government chose to express the trend differently, emphasizing the rise in civilian casualties. When a bomb exploded in Durban, narrowly missing two truckloads of soldiers, but killing five pedestrians, the incident was portrayed by the police and the media not as a bungled attempt to hit a military target, but as a successful effort to kill civilians.

Rand Daily Mail, **14 July 1984:** No arrests have yet been made in connection with Thursday's killer bomb blast in Durban, in which five people were killed and 29 injured. Although the African National Congress has not claimed responsibility for the blast, the Minister of Law and Order, Mr Louis le Grange, blamed the organization for the attack during an inspection tour of the bomb scene yesterday.

Speaking at the scene, Mr le Grange said more and more civilians would be killed, maimed and injured in future, as the ANC opted for softer civilian targets in the wake of police successes against them. 'The ANC is desperate and has been hit for a six ever since the Nkomati Accord, and our successes in apprehending insurgents in the past few months. The ANC is not concerned with loss of life and Oliver Tambo himself has warned that more civilians would be victims of future ANC operations,' he said.[27]

The body of a man killed in yesterday's bomb blast in Durban lies amidst the wreckage of the explosion.

CAR-BOMB CARNAGE

Four die, 21 injured

Cold, but warm weekend ahead

Two drug arrests

In fact, the ANC had a strict policy of avoiding civilian casualties and was the first liberation movement to sign the Geneva Convention (which the South African government refused to do). Until the early 1980s, ANC incidents consisted mainly of attacks on symbolic government targets and vital infrastructure, with the few human targets being policemen and paid informers, usually blacks. However, as the frequency and intensity of ANC activity increased, civilians — black and white — were unintentionally but inevitably wounded and killed.

When the ANC's attacks were largely confined to the sabotage of township railway lines and raids on black police stations, most whites had been able to dismiss the guerillas as a few poorly-trained radicals 'hurting their own people'. But when nineteen whites and blacks were killed by a bomb in the streets of Pretoria in 1983, many white South Africans then readily accepted the government's argument that the ANC was committed to naked terrorism, aimed at innocent civilians. (The fact that the blast was aimed at the Defence Force Headquarters, and half those killed were military personnel was obscured by the media fixation on 'the car bomb outrage'.)

For blacks, however, the Pretoria blast marked a watershed of a different kind. Two young men, Themba, a social worker, and Vuyani, a field officer for a Christian organization, voiced the growing support in the black community for the ANC's guerilla war, and the acceptance of the inevitablity of civilian casualties.

Themba: Blacks generally took the Pretoria bombing as a signal that freedom is near. People said, even with those unfortunate people from Mamelodi (a black township outside Pretoria) who died in the incident, that of course it's bad, but it could not be helped. They were not the target as such, but they were caught in the crossfire. And others pointed to the large numbers of white army guys killed and said, 'You see, the movement is now hitting at real targets, not lifeless targets like electrical installations and so on.' They saw it as a good revenge.

Vuyani: Irrespective of the colour of who was killed, the reaction of so many blacks was that this is revolution, this is what armed struggle is all about. The regime tried to play up the racial thing, that the ANC is killing its own people, but it didn't work. People accept that there must be casualties. In fact, the regime itself has conditioned people to accept casualties with its deaths in detention and other brutalities. The Pretoria blast was successful in that it made people aware that there is a war in South Africa. Ordinary blacks aren't worried about violence – they experience violence every day. People are expecting change to be violent. They are ready for it.

How would you assess support for the ANC inside the country?

Themba: You find a vast difference between the thinking that existed five years ago and the present thinking, because people realize that all other means have been tried and failed. And they believe that the ANC can bring about a change in this country. I can predict with confidence that within a few years' time, the ANC will have liberated zones: areas within the country where people from outside can easily be accepted and protected, to do whatever tasks they're supposed to carry out in South Africa.

Vuyani: If the lack of co-operation of the people with the system is anything to go by, and instead what the people do is to hide the fighting cadres of the ANC – if that is the measurement for a liberated zone – then I can say that this is happening already, that there are liberated zones in the eastern Transvaal and northern Natal. The para-military police and the army have been surprised a number of times in these areas, by finding these people, who are supposed to be just simple peasants, knowing nothing, resisting with arms. Although we never get to hear about these skirmishes in the press.

What about the idea of people leaving the country to join the ANC? Is that ever talked about, or are people scared to discuss the issue?

Themba: I think that's an open secret. It is being discussed in trains and buses. If you ask somebody, 'It's quite some time that I haven't been seeing Mr A. Where's he gone to?', then he says, 'No, that guy has left, he has joined the forces.' So that one, it's not treated as a sacred cow.

Vuyani: But most of the time you find that you wouldn't hear of such information immediately, until it's been established that whoever has left is safe and out of the country. No matter how close you are to that person, he wouldn't inform you as to what his plans are.

Have you ever known of someone who left the country and then actually seen the person back inside?

Themba: Several times.

Vuyani: On seeing such a person you start feeling a bit excited, but you bring yourself under control. And then you normally find that people call you aside and say, 'Hey, we don't want people to know about so-and-so, so keep quiet about it.' But then people are often so happy to see that person, to know he's gone out and come back, that you'll hear people saying, 'The boys are around, the boys are here!'

There have been so many trials in which people have been convicted for possession of ANC literature. Has this made people scared to read ANC publications?

Themba: No, no. People are still very keen to get that stuff. They read it and they circulate it. How you get it, well, there's a network of circulation, and then it's a matter of bumping against it. But there are many people who bump against it regularly. You find sometimes that you wake up in the morning, you go to your postbox, and you find something from the ANC. How you got it, you don't know, but it's there.

There are organized underground groups, who have quite a wide variety of ANC publications which they read secretly and discuss, and then pass on to similar study groups. Especially among the youth, you find that they read all the publications with keen interest. People also listen quite keenly to (the ANC's) Radio Freedom, although in recent years it's been difficult to get the station. But people keep trying different frequencies: Lusaka, Angola, Addis

Ababa, Madagascar and the External Service of Radio Moscow all carry ANC programmes.

Themba: I should also point out, it's not that people take everything that's being received from outside without question. These underground study groups have a special task of constructively criticizing what has been presented, and in turn, of compiling something which they will feed the external mission of the ANC. It's a two-way process, where the latest information is fed out in the hope that once the external ANC get the latest information, they will put it into scientific terms and the ANC line, and feed it back inside the country.

The publications and pamphlets of the ANC are produced in Lusaka, London and East Berlin, then mailed and smuggled into South Africa. The frequency of prosecutions for possession of ANC literature is evidence that, despite the risk, many heed the call of the underground movement to pass on its message clandestinely. It is difficult to gauge the scope and success of the ANC's media campaign, but Jonas, a lawyer from the rural eastern Transvaal, felt it important to counter the assumption that awareness and support for the ANC is limited to the urban areas.

Jonas: People think that it is those in the urban areas who are so advanced, that they have the most access to ANC literature, but I'll tell you, it spreads first in these rural areas, before it ever reaches the cities. The cities are the last place to get the things we see regularly. I always try to explain to my friends from Joburg and Durban that they don't realize how much politically conscious in that direction the people are in the rural areas. It makes sense, anyway, because if there was to be an infiltration, who would be the first to give an ANC cadre water? It will be the people in the bush. Who will be the first to give him shelter? It will be the people in the bush. And that's why so many of them have been arrested in this area. There are many, many of these cadres who come into the country and then stay in the bush first, for a long, long time, to look at the situation.

Some people have spoken about areas of South Africa where the ANC can freely infiltrate and receive support. Do you believe such areas exist?

Jonas: It's not safe to start talking that a certain place is a liberated area, for obviously it will then be clamped down. That's not clever, you'd better just keep quiet about that. But, yes, I think there are liberated areas, definitely. In the rural areas, for that matter, much more than in the cities.

Do people listen to the ANC's radio at all around here?

Jonas: Oh yes, they do, they do. But it's an offence to listen. If they find you listening, they'll arrest you. So again, I can't say much about that.

There's a widely held assumption that most rural people are not politicized, that they support the homeland system. Are you saying that this is not true?

Jonas: Let me put it to you this way: my clientèle is 90 per cent from the rural areas, yet I do quite a few political cases. I'm satisfied that the rural people are very highly politically conscious, and they don't need anybody from outside to tell them what their problems are. Because they live through this whole thing, they are politicized by their living conditions, by removals. It's a lie to say that they need someone to instigate them – they don't. I think all they need, maybe, is political marshalling of their anger. If that is marshalled it can only take one direction, and that is of resistance.

As for the homelands, you'll find that there's a group that does support the homelands, purely out of ignorance, out of lack of understanding what this whole thing is about. But then you find a very good slice of educated people who are completely opposed to the homelands, who live within the homelands, but who don't support them at all. They regard the homeland leaders as sell-outs, finish and klaar (that's it). But then you find also that these chaps are shrewd, these homeland leaders. They mobilize support, they create a political base, which is a watchdog to people who want to attack the system. One must be wary of saying anything against a homeland leader,

for fear it would be reported back, and action would be taken against you. But I think the forces of change will soon put them under pressure. Nobody wants to be left out when the real thing starts to happen. If they move too late – well, we all know the position of Muzorewa in Zimbabwe.

So despite the influence of the homeland system, you still maintain there is great political consciousness in the rural areas?

Jonas: Let me give you an example. I've just been with a lady here, she's an aunt to a certain chap who is, in fact, one of those sentenced to be executed for ANC offences. I mean, how did that young man, who grew up here, come to be politically conscious to the extent that he felt he must take up arms? He is one who comes from right here, in the bush, supposed to be a citizen of a homeland. Now this must be a clear example of what people feel like in the homelands. I think the homelands are going to be the most sensitive areas for the government to handle in the future.

A problem is that the newspapers are lazy to come down here and collect information, and the government certainly doesn't try to publicize what's going on in the rural areas, so as a result, people really don't know what goes on here. But the black people here, they know about what's happening. They are excited. They cannot express that excitement, because they might be suspected of having contact with the ANC, and maybe promoting the aims of those people. But, in their hearts, when these attacks happen, it wouldn't for one minute make them sad. They could buy beer and celebrate after that.

Is there an awareness of people leaving the country to go for military training?

Jonas: Yes, definitely. People know that their children are leaving. My own brother is not here. My mother must be aware of that. I mean, we're not theorizing. We live this thing.

The ANC is alive within this whole structure of South African society. It's there, it's there. Some of the things one is scared to say, but it's there. I can't tell you who goes about telling them about it, but the people know about the ANC. Other groups have gone to the countryside to try and organize support, but they were told in no uncertain terms that they did not want to hear anything except from 'the movement'. You see, the ANC is an old organization and it started with the old people, so our parents know about it. We grew up knowing that there was a person named Mandela. People know the ANC songs, and they like to sing them. I was shocked when I went to a recent funeral here, a political funeral, by the type of songs the youth was singing. I was surprised; I never thought they would be so openly militant in such a bush area. I think they sang more militant songs than I ever heard in my student days or in the urban areas.

The South African government's opponents are not only increasingly militant, but increasingly confident. They speak routinely of life 'after liberation'. A group of young blacks in Natal envisaged the process of liberation as involving various stages, each of which would present its own challenges.

Mzwakhe: In the short term, we are involved in a national democratic struggle, and we see the basis for mobilizing quite a wide range of people to establish a democratic South Africa, led by the goals of the Freedom Charter for some kind of redistribution of wealth, some greater participation in education, health, housing.

Zodwa: There are those who criticize this idea of working in two stages: first the national democratic struggle, and then moving on to establish a socialist state. But the way we see it, the state has divided us into so many different ethnic categories and classes, that we're going to need to work hard in that first stage to rid ourselves of all these divisions.

Ahmed: It's not only us who see liberation coming in stages. I think people are aware that the government is planning for a transition period, and they are aware that someone like Gatsha Buthelezi is going to be used as a middle man, as a kind of Muzorewa. We are also aware that, even after liberation, there still may not be peace, because there will still be somebody coming to destabilize us. And we may be forced to take up arms to protect ourselves. We're seeing it right now, in the frontline states: if somebody supports South Africa, he's not involved in a 'terrorist' movement – it's a 'resistance' movement, and South Africa will fund him.

Moses: You know, it's because of our concern over what this society is going to be like after liberation, that we are very critical now, even of the forces of liberation. We worry sometimes that if there's a very heavy bias here on the military side of our struggle, what that will mean is that more and more people must go outside, and that means fewer people to remain here and organize people into trade unions and community groups. Already, we have the problem that people lack confidence to see that they have the ability to run their own lives. Now, increased militarization may mean that we have less emphasis on this kind of basic struggle, which may mean that people will not have enough political depth to carry through the whole reconstruction phase.

An over-emphasis on the military side not only obscures the struggle, but actually emasculates people of their power, because it tends to indicate to people that they are going to be liberated from the outside. But as people begin to understand more about the nature of the war that is being fought, they're being forced to realize that they themselves must become actively involved in the struggle-in their community, in their workplace, wherever.

Zodwa: I think that people must be prepared now for the sort of economic policies that are envisioned by the liberation movement. But people are being conditioned to be selfish and individualistic by the present system. We would hope that, through struggle, people can begin to learn what it means to live in a society where sharing resources is the basic principle that governs. When we say that the struggle must be democratic, it should go far beyond being just some cliché. It should mean that all people must have the concrete experience of participating in struggle and seeing their ability to take control of their lives.

Ahmed: There's also a very pragmatic aspect to all this talk about what will happen after liberation, and that has to do with the very powerful and sophisticated state that faces us, and the fact that the vast majority of people have been oppressed to an extent where skills among blacks are very far and few between. We need to also be developing the capabilities we'll need to maintain this very complex economy when we take over. So we're also very busy building the future South Africa, purely on a practical level, preparing ourselves to reconstruct a liberated society after the war.

Saulsville/Atteridgeville Youth Organization representative, at a United Democratic Front rally in Lenasia, 30 July 1984: We must be difficult to control. We must render the instruments of oppression difficult to work. We must escalate all forms of resistance. We must make ourselves ungovernable.

SABC, 23 October 1984: Regardless of the extent to which grievances – and there are many – have played a role, the impetus behind the sustained campaign of violence and lawlessness has sprung rather from a transparent attempt at establishing an 'ungovernable' citizenry. It therefore comes as no surprise that this very concept of ungovernability abounds in the contemporary literature of leftist radical organizations. The objective of the agitators, most of whom are apparently militant youths, is nothing less than the revolutionary overthrow of the present dispensation.

While the African National Congress is known for its anti-government guerilla attacks, its leaders also seem wary about any over-emphasis on military rather than political activity. The ANC President's first public statement of 1984 exhorted all South Africans to 'create conditions in which the country will become increasingly ungovernable'. Although the call went unreported in the censored South African media, it was nevertheless picked up and propagated inside the country.

In response to the cataclysmic events of August and September 1984, the government, too, latched on to this concept of 'ungovernability', and used it to justify its planned revenge on the ungovernable.

By the time SABC listeners heard that commentary, a military invasion of the ungovernable Vaal townships was well underway. At 2 a.m. on 23 October 1984, 7000 army troops and para-military police rolled into Sebokeng on armoured personnel carriers and began banging on doors and routing residents from bed, spending the next ten hours searching every single one of the township's 20,000 houses, before moving on to raid Sharpeville and Boipatong. Soldiers armed with R-1 rifles were stationed every ten metres throughout the townships and residents not permitted out of their homes until the troops had finished each search, dipped people's fingers in red dye, and stuck orange stickers on their houses and cars, reading 'Co-operation for peace and security – I am your friend – trust me'. Although the invasion was allegedly launched 'to rid the areas of criminal and revolutionary elements' the government conceded that there were no revolutionaries among the 354 people arrested. In a military tradition usually reserved for martial law zones, people were immediately tried and sentenced – for pass offences and minor common law crimes – by special courts set up in the townships.

Blacks called the brown-uniformed force, that invaded their homes in the dead of the night, 'the boys from the border'. Young white men who watched the government-approved version of the invasion on SABC-TV realized that their impending military conscription might not take them to a far-away border, but instead could force them to fight blacks living in the townships next door.

.(JOH)SEBOKENG, South Africa, Oct. 23 - SEALED OFF - Troops line a road as they seal off Sebokeng township Tuesday in one of the largest house to house searches ever carried out in South Africa. About 7,000 soldiers and police participated in the search of thousands of homes in the black township. Some 348 persons were reported arrested. (AP Laserphoto) (jtm30818mbr/argus)84 Slug: South Africa

October 1984 marked the first public admission that the South African Defence Force was fighting its own people.[28] The liberal press saw it as 'a confession that the unruly parts of the country are occupied enemy territory, an exercise not in law enforcement, but in reconquest'.[29] The Minister of Law and Order confirmed that 'as far as we're concerned, it is war, plain and simple'.[30] For the government's black and white opponents in the UDF, the military siege of the Vaal townships was a formal declaration that South Africa was in the midst of a civil war.

What form would this civil war take? How would the people of South Africa make themselves ungovernable? Some answers came on the 5th and 6th of November 1984, when the community organizations and the boycotting students joined with the independent trade unions in a general strike in South Africa's industrial heartland of the Transvaal. The country's largest and most effectively organized union, the Federation of South African Trade Unions, the powerful and once Black Consciousness-aligned Council of Unions of South Africa, and other independent trade unions had never before committed their membership to the political demands of the United Democratic Front, but when the army marched into workers' homes, the unions had to respond. The debate over the role of the working class in a popular front was suspended; together, the unions and the UDF organized a two-day work stay-away to demand that the army and police withdraw from the townships, rent and bus fare increases be stopped, community councillors resign, political detainees be released, dismissed workers be reinstated, and the government's 'unfair taxation' cease.

The Transvaal Regional Stay-Away Committee, representing the unions and the UDF's affiliates, popularized its call for a strike with the distribution of 400,000 pamphlets. The government countered with as many leaflets, air-dropped from military helicopters and handed out by police at roadblocks, urging residents to 'stand up once and for all and defy these organizations which give us orders' and

Letter written by a young white South African man to a friend in exile, October 1984: A lot has happened since I last wrote. The army moved into Sebokeng and various other townships on the East Rand last week and cordoned off the area and searched every house. The operation was initiated at 2 a.m. – can you imagine being woken up by the SADF in your bedroom? I don't known what it accomplished, because the flare-ups in the townships continue to happen daily. The consequences of going to call-ups and being sent on manoeuvres such as that of Sebokeng is the final straw for a number of guys like me. Most of the old gang from Durbs (Durban) are ignoring their call-ups and others are leaving the country. I'll see you at Christmas and you can tell me what life's like in exile, though I'd like to try and stay inside and dodge as long as possible.

Trevor Manuel, United Democratic Front Acting Publicity Secretary, 23 October 1984: The authorities are looking for something they could not find under the beds and in wardrobes. The anger of the people over rentals and the lack of participation in government does not hide in those places. The government's high-handedness and arrogance is a foretaste of things to come. The UDF warning of a impending civil war is now a reality.

ignore the stay-away lest they lost their jobs. Inkatha Chief Gatsha Buthelezi chorused the government's anti-stay-away call, condemning 'politically motivated criminal elements' and 'young hoodlums' for fomenting 'misdirected anger which will get us nowhere'.[31]

Yet as many as 800,000 people refused to go to work and 400,000 students boycotted classes. The strike was more than 80 per cent effective among workers from the besieged Vaal townships, and in the east Rand, where heavy industry and organized labour is concentrated.[32] The SASOL (oil-from-coal) and ISCOR (iron and steel) para-statals ground to a halt, despite threats to fire workers who joined the strike.[33] The transport system designed to carry workers to the Transvaal's industrial centre was abandoned. In the east Rand township of Tembisa, workers stoned buses and virtually ambushed trains by placing concrete sleepers on the railway line, setting carriages alight, and even preventing the fire brigade from reaching the burning trains. In Soweto, residents petrol-bombed bank branches, killing a policeman, and stoned to death a policeman guarding a town councillor's house.

By the second day of the strike, the army had again moved into the townships, although this time, a blanket ban on information on the use of troops was imposed. At least thirty people were dead, mainly as a result of battles that pitted residents, throwing stones from behind barricades of gutted cars and buses, against fully armed riot police and soldiers.

The trade unions' foray into the political arena, bolstered by the communities and students, was a stunning success: the stay-away strike had been the most successful in South African history.[34] The combined force of the muscle of organized labour and the back-up of the UDF's affiliated organizations had dealt the government a body blow that sent the politicians, the police and the army reeling, and by mid-1985, President Botha had been forced to declare a State of Emergency.

Thami Mali, chairman of the Traansvaal Regional Stay-Away Committee, 7 November 1984: The response to the stay-away proves beyond doubt that trade unions, students and community organizations, rather than Gatsha Buthelezi's Inkatha, enjoy the support of the people. It has actually shown that we have power in our hands; it showed that we can bring the machinery of this country to a standstill.[35] We cannot go back any more now. Our duty is to step up resistance and to create an ungovernable situation, and actually force the state to declare some of these areas as liberated zones.

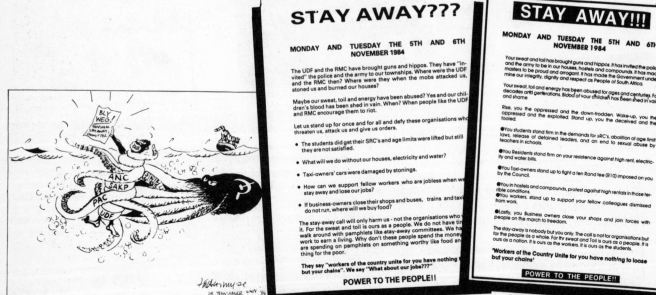

Government pamphlet   Stay-away committee pamphlet

If the government and its opponents agree on nothing else, it is that South Africa's future will be resolved through war — and more importantly, that it will be a very different kind of war. Neither a conventional military conflict nor a traditional peasant-based insurgency is envisaged. Likewise, the battle for majority rule in this advance industrial state is not expected to follow the pattern of past anti-colonial struggles in Africa or anywhere else in the world. Whether the battles are confined to sporadic incidents of sabotage and political unrest, as the government anticipates, or escalate to revolutionary proportions, as the government's opponents would hope, all sides agree that the military conflict may not be the most vital component of South Africa's war. The factories, communities and schools will also be battlefields. The weapons may often be guns and petrol bombs, but the South African people will also fight the government with strikes and meetings, songs and pamphlets. While there is wide agreement that South Africa is already in the early stages of a civil war, there is a great range of opinion as to the future course of this very different war.

Selection Park, Soweto residents, Ben Motsuenyane, Anglo-American Corporation personnel manager: We're not interested in having five-star hotels opening their doors to us; we are interested in power-sharing – nothing else. We want the right to participate in the economy of South Africa, to which we, as blacks, have made a supreme contribution. These skyscrapers that you see here in Johannesburg – black lives have been lost in building them. The very foundation on which Johannesburg is built – the mines – these are the graves of black people. Yet we are relegated to the most barren and economically unviable homelands, which are nothing else but reservoirs of workers for cheap labour.

Johannesburg schoolgirls, Roseanne: Ever since we became a nation, we've always been at war with ourselves in South Africa, and with the people outside.
Michelle: I know everybody in this country hasn't got the same rights and I would like to give them more rights – without doing my position any harm.

Do you think it's possible to change things for the majority of people in the country without changing your own position?

Michelle: Well, that's why I'm glad I'm not the government. I don't know how they're going to do that.

So how do you think that this situation might be changed?

Richard Molewa, Anglo-American Life Assurance administrator: I think that change is going to be brought about by the suffering masses. And if you're going to ask me, will it be peacefully or violently, I'll tell you: there already is violence in this country anyway, because the white minority government is ruling over us by violence and nothing else.
Ben Motsuenyane: And, I'd like to ask you, which minority in the world has ever given up its position of authority freely and without violence? Never. And the longer the minority resists, the more bloodshed there will be. Even the mildest blacks are toughening by the day, politically. Our children are far more angry and impatient than us – they are not prepared to wait any longer. And they are not prepared to accept all this cosmetic covering of repressive legislation, these so-called reforms. With this homeland system, our children are being declared aliens in the land of their birth – unlike us, who have had some few urban rights. My young daughter, for example, has been declared a citizen of Bophuthatswana – she doesn't even know where that place is! So it's no wonder our children now feel they have nothing to lose, but the country to win.

Tshediso Matona, national organizer for the Congress of South African Students: I think the events that are happening now are a very good indicator of what is going to happen in the future. We're seeing mass action by people challenging the system, workers involved in strikes and demanding higher wages, students challenging the education system. You have an element within the white group who are identifying with the cause of the oppressed people, and you also have an intensification of the armed struggle. I'm not underestimating the South African government's strength, and I know it's going to take a long time for change to come, because it is clear that the government is committed to defending the system. They'll fight until the bitter end to defend it. But still, I think of liberation every day. I believe that sometime in the future, the people's cause will triumph. I actually see freedom in sight.

SABC, 22 June 1981:

P.W. Botha: The vast majority of whites and brown people and black people don't want violence in our country. They want to go on with their work, they want to have their children properly educated, they want peaceful community and family life. I believe that when I say this, the vast number of South Africans are in favour of peaceful coexistence.

Announcer: You have, on a few occasions, warned people who preached revolution to be careful because they were playing with fire. Can you give us more details?

P.W. Botha: Yes, what I said was that the state will have to exercise its power to control matters in such a way that decent people will be able to live decent lives. They will be protected, we will apply force, and some people already burnt their fingers. I want to warn again today that the state is capable of applying much greater power, should it become necessary to maintain order. We have only used part of the state capacity to maintain order and peaceful life, and we are determined to keep South Africa in good order and in a peaceful situation.

Announcer: You have stated your viewpoint on this in the past, but can you explain your views on the release of Nelson Mandela?

P.W. Botha: The government is not in favour of the release of Mr Mandela. He has been found guilty, an independent judiciary decided that he shall serve a term in prison, and I have nothing to add to that.

Announcer: But there are people abroad who say he is one of the recognized leaders.

P.W. Botha: He might be one of the recognized leaders, but he is not a constitutionally chosen leader and we have enough elected leaders in South Africa with whom we can deliberate and consult, in spite of the irresponsible elements and their actions, and in spite of pressures from outside, and in spite of the intimidation.

Announcer: Finally, Mr Botha, in this current security situation which faces South Africa, have you a message to South Africans, and also to people outside?

P.W. Botha: Yes. We are living in a dangerous world, a world threatened by Russian expansionism and satellites supporting that expansionism. We are living in a world of terrorism, a dangerous world of chaotic conditions, of people trying to overthrow stable governments and a stable way of life. We also have our specific problems in southern Africa and we must be prepared to accept the challenges and to work harder, not only to leave it to the government to maintain order, but to make our own contributions as individual citizens, to motivate ourselves in such a way that we contribute our share behind the backs of our security forces to maintain stability and progress and development in southern Africa.

Annette and Leon Maré, eastern Transvaal farmers: We're supporting the National Party. You can't go too fast with this business of changing, because you've got to bridge a big gap. I think things are going at the right pace now. We shouldn't be in too much of a hurry. You can't do it overnight. It'll take time.

Jonas, rural Transvaal lawyer: You don't go and draw up a constitution as four million people and exclude twenty million people and hope to have peace. You can't do that. We won't allow ourselves to be excluded forever. We've got a right to live here, to work here and to help decide the affairs of this country. I think violence could be avoided if the government was prepared to meet the aspirations of the black people of this country. But they are not prepared, so there's only one way to describe the conflict that lies ahead: it's inevitable. Obviously the South African government is heavily armed, it's got a lot of sophisticated weaponry. But that didn't save the Shah of Iran. He had the best machinery in the world, but it didn't save him. So it's not just that. It goes beyond arms to win this struggle.

White student, Pietermaritzburg: There's going to be a lot of blood spilled, unfortunately, before things are settled in this country. There definitely will be a black government here, whether it's tomorrow, or in ten years time. The way I look at things, there's no way I'll have children in this country because, just to quote a few lines from a Dylan song, this government has thrown 'the worst fear that can ever be hurled: the fear to bring children into the world.'[36] I couldn't bring children into a society like this, not the way things are now.

Mama Luke, Crossroads squatter camp: There will be some war before things change in South Africa. I think so, because all these years we have been talking and talking and asking and we are only being put in jail. The radio always talks about the 'terrorists', but I think the terrorists are those people who could not stand it anymore. I am old, perhaps it is late for me to get my freedom. But I am fighting for my children's future.

Harald Pakendorf, editor of *Die Vaderland:* A one man, one vote situation is just not on the table, because that would mean we'd be swamped. There is one important difference between Rhodesia and South Africa: if you're unhappy in Rhodesia, or Zimbabwe – you must remember that only a third of all Rhodesian whites are actually Rhodesian-born – there are 350 million English-speakers in the world to whom you can go and you won't feel unhappy. You may not like the weather and the food may not be exactly to your liking, but they all speak English and go to the same church and the same school system.

Now, if you're an Afrikaner in South Africa, it's all you've got. We're not only about having a swimming pool and a Mercedes. It's our country, we have nothing else. So when I say there's going to no one man, one vote situation in a unitary state, that's what it's about — we are not about to give ourselves away.

On the other hand, we know what's coming. If you look at the statistics, people are realizing that in the year 2000, nine out of every ten people will be people of colour. And it is the realization that makes people uneasy. In any situation of change, people get uneasy, because they know they will lose something. And what they stand to gain, you can try and sell to them – as

security for their children and our future – but that isn't something you can take to the bank.

What we are looking to is a situation in which we can continue to be the white tribe of Africa without having to rule over other people or other people rule over us. That's basically what all Nationalist Party politics are about at this stage. And we know that if we bring about changes, they must be perceived to be real by the blacks – not by us. In the past, our politics had been to try and tell our whites, 'Look, what we've changed hasn't made a big difference.' Well, we know we're not supposed to do that; we're not supposed to tell the blacks, 'Look, you've got more pay in your pockets and the buses run on time, the schools have improved, there are better hospitals, and your child can grow up to be a doctor and you can get to be an MP – within the confederation.' Now, if we say that and it doesn't happen, we're in trouble. We must bring about real change soon. And in that way, we'll undercut the ANC.

Terror Lekota, National Publicity Secretary, United Democratic Front: Just as the Nats are clinging tenaciously and selfishly to life all by themselves, and denying our people full participation in South Africa, so, too, an increasing number of uncompromising freedom fighters is being born. From those shacks of Crossroads, Inanda (Durban township) and Orlando (Soweto township), we are seeing people who will sacrifice everything, including their own lives, to see to it that injustice is done away with and that freedom one day comes to this country.

Do you worry about the threat of the UDF being banned?

Robert, trade unionist: Being banned doesn't mean anything. So many organizations are banned, so many people are banned. It doesn't make any difference. They just ban the public existence of the thing. Look, they banned the ANC, but they didn't eradicate the ANC's stand with the people. I mean, it is with the people, it is with the majority of the people in South Africa. No matter how many guns the system has, they can't kill all the people who support the ANC. And they can't ban the ANC from our hearts.

SABC, 25 May 1983: Political reform is underway in South Africa, more rapid in its tempo, more wide-ranging in its scope, more comprehensive in its involvement of all communities, and more firmly fixed in its goals of justice and security for all than anything that has gone before. But it is an illusion to suppose that its further development, or any other form of peaceful political reform, would put an end to ANC terrorism. The ANC is a self-declared revolutionary movement, dedicated to the violent overthrow of the state and imposition of a communist order on the Soviet pattern. As an instrument of the Kremlin, its aims are to seize power for itself, and to achieve strategic dominance for the Soviets in southern Africa. Its means necessarily include terrorist intimidation. The Soviet potential for expansion in this region and the very future of the ANC depend on creating and exploiting mass confusion and alienation, on destroying the process of peaceful constitutional reform. The ANC is not amenable to debate on a just political dispensation, for that is not what it and its backers are after – they're out to seize power. The only answer is to stop them.

Rand Daily Mail, **6 September 1984:** The detailed secrets of the Russian limpet mine – now Public Menace Number One – were disclosed for the first time yesterday by police explosives experts. The public was urged to study the deadly explosive device which has been used to bomb five buildings on the Reef in three weeks, leaving 16 people injured. A massive manhunt for the terrorists placing the bombs is continuing on a round-the-clock basis, police said. Teams of bomb disposal specialists assisted by sniffer dogs have been placed on 24-hour-standby throughout the country to deal with any bomb or bomb scare. Do you know a limpet mine? Would you be able to recognize one? What would you do with it if you saw one? Major Paul Hattingh of the police explosives section had this advice for the public: 'Watch out for anything out of place – abandoned suitcases, parcels, strange metal parts where they should not be, and so on – and do not be scared to inform the police, even if it turns out to be a false alarm.' Today's terrorist, says Major Hattingh, works with professional equipment.

Reverend Frank Chikane, theologian and United Democratic Front Transvaal Vice-President: I am confident. I know things will change – the problem is the 'how' part of it. But I don't see any form of peaceful change. We can debate and debate about violence and non-violence, as Christians, but that kind of intellectualizing is not going to change the course of events here. The simple fact is that the war has started. And as long as South Africa refuses to talk to the ANC, then the ANC is going to continue fighting. And the more people rise up inside to say 'We want our rights' and then the government suppresses them, the more they will resort to arms and the ANC will become a home for them.

I've tried to talk to these guys when I was detained – the very ones who were interrogating me. They tried to threaten me, to say, 'You see how powerful South Africa is, you are wasting your time, your people will only die if they try to fight against the system.' But I always argue that it doesn't depend on how powerful a system is – the people will organize themselves to be equally powerful and destroy the system. Once a man has reached the stage where he doesn't care any more, even for his own life, then he becomes dangerous. So we are becoming dangerous. And this, the oppressor doesn't even know. I think the most tragic aspect of the oppressor vis-à-vis the oppressed is that the oppressor never knows the true feelings of the oppressed. So one day, he'll get a surprise.

Freedom song heard at protest meetings:

Those who are against us,
We shall reckon with them,
The day we take our land back –
Their names are written down.

When there's a roll call of our heroes,
I wonder if my name will be on that roll,
I wonder what it will be like
When we sit with Tambo
And tell him about the fall of the Boers.

Freedom Song:

There is Sasolburg/the Supreme
Court/Warmbaths/Koeberg/Pitoli[37]
Going up in flames,
We are going there,
The Umkhonto boys have arrived,
We are going there – Hayi, hayi,
We are going forward,
Don't be worried,
The boys know their job,
Let Afrika return!

Freedom songs:

We, the workers, demand the land back,
We demand our land back,
Even if it means blood and death.

We shall part with our parents
And go to other countries,
To fight for our country, South Africa,
Don't cry mama,
Even if I die,
I shall have died
For my country, South Africa.

Thandi, community organiser: People no longer aspire for the little the government is offering them. The government is saying, 'Half a loaf is better than no bread at all', but the people are aware that that half loaf is poisoned. So they say to hell with that half loaf – we fight for our freedom. And when the government answers back with teargas and bullets, people just say, 'The harsher the system becomes, the faster we go to our freedom.' I mean, how many jails are they going to build? They can't arrest all of us. At funerals these days, you hear people saying, 'For every martyr they kill, there'll be ten more to take his place.' That's the kind of momentum there is right now – it's like a time bomb has been set.

Freedom song:

Forward we shall march,
Forward we shall march,
Forward we shall march to a people's government.

One day we will march,
One day we will march,
One day we will march from Soweto to Pretoria!

Notes:

1 An Introduction to the System

1. Afrikaners are descendants of the original Dutch settlers, who speak Afrikaans and make up 60 per cent of the white population.

2. A compulsory subject in all white secondary schools in the Transvaal, Orange Free State and the Cape. The Department of Education lists its six components as 'spiritual preparedness, physical preparedness, first aid, fire fighting, and emergency plan for schools and general affairs'.

3. Cited in a South African Human Sciences Research Council report: 'Open Air Education in the RSA', 1979; veld schools have been an extension of the Youth Preparedness programme of the Transvaal Education Department since 1976.

4. From a Standard 8 English-speaking girls' camp lecture cited by Gavin Evans in 'The Role of the Military in Education in South Africa', Economic History dissertation, University of Cape Town, 1983.

5. The Johannesburg College of Education's 'Report to the Rector on an Investigation into Aspects of Veld School' concludes that its avowed aim of environmental education is eclipsed by 'intellectual coercion which is tantamount to indoctrination'.

6. Nineteenth-century Boer pioneers who fled British rule in the Cape and migrated north by oxwagon.

7. A common government reference to black Africans, from the Bantu languages of southern Africa.

8. In early 1980, the government dispatched Agricultural Secretary Sarel Hayward to the Transvaal farming areas on the borders with Botswana, Zimbabwe and Mozambique, where he told farmers, 'We need men of steel to stay and farm our strategic border areas', and unveiled a financial assistance scheme designed to stem the exodus of border farmers. The Promotion of the Density of Population in Designated Areas Act of 1980 included R14 million in soft loans to border farmers. N.B. The South African rand was worth about 20 per cent more than the US dollar in the late 1970s, but was worth about 20 per cent less than the dollar by the early 1980s, and only about half as much as the dollar in 1984.

9. Regional South African Defence Force units, established in 1982 for local 'area defence' and manned mainly by reservists of up to the age of 55 years.

10. A prejudice epitomized by the 'Hoggenheimer' cartoons in the Afrikaans press lampooning Sir Ernest Oppenheimer, founder of the Anglo-American Corporation.

11. The steady decrease in the real value of black earnings is documented by Jeremy Keenan in 'Trickle Up: African Income and Employment', South African Review: One, Ravan Press, Johannesburg, 1983.

12. Estimate of Anglo's assets from The Economist, 1 May 1982; quotes from Oppenheimer from Le Monde, 26 February 1984.

2 Resistance

1. ANC leader Nelson Mandela launched the organization's military wing, Umkhonto we Sizwe (Spear of the Nation) in 1961, and led an underground sabotage campaign until his arrest in 1962. In 1964, Mandela was sentenced to life imprisonment, along with other members of the ANC High Command. ANC President Oliver Tambo, who had left the country, has since co-ordinated underground activity in South Africa, and the ANC's diplomatic mission, from exile.

2. According to University of the Witwatersrand academic Tom Lodge ('The African National Congress in South Africa: 1976-1982: Guerilla War and Armed Propaganda', paper presented in Washington D.C., November 1982), Congress of South African Students' founding president Ephraim Mogale was an ANC member who was active in the northern Transvaal, organizing youth clubs, producing pamphlets, establishing a discussion group called the Communist Advance Movement, and recruiting people for military training. COSAS was banned in August 1985.

3. The biblical allusion, 'hewers of wood and drawers of water', was used by former Prime Minister Hendrik Verwoerd. The de Lange Report on Education was tabled in Parliament in 1981.

4. Academic critiques of the validity of the 'skills shortage' range from Charles Meth's dismissal of the crisis as a 'smokescreen' for the attempt to co-opt a black middle class ('Class Formation: Skills Shortage and Black Advancement', South African Review: One, Ravan Press, 1983) to Linda Chisholm's conclusion that its 'purpose appears to be as much to intensify ideological controls over workers and wed them more firmly to capitalist values as it is to provide for South Africa's manpower needs' ('Redefining Skills: Black Education in South Africa in the 1980s', Comparative Education, XIX, 3, 1983.

5. This slogan (English/Zulu/Afrikaans) became popular in the 1960s and by the 1970s it was commonplace at protest meetings. Note that the home language of most Coloureds is Afrikaans; also that some observers attribute support for socialist theories in Coloured schools to the influence of former members of the (Non-European) Unity Movement of South Africa, which had some impact on protest politics in the 1940s and 1950s. Unlike African schools, Coloured schools were often staffed by white teachers, many of whom supported non-racialism, and one of the initial demands of the boycotting Cape students was the unconditional reinstatement of three white teachers who were fired after showing sympathy with the students.

6. In 1980 and 1981, the Foreign Correspondents Association of Southern Africa was outraged by reports in pro-government newspapers blaming the media for the June 16th unrest. On 16 June 1982, police banned the media from 'trouble spots' and held more than forty journalists at gunpoint at the Protea police station for several hours. By 16 June 1984, journalists' access to Soweto and other black townships was restricted to police-chaperoned tours in army personnel carriers. With the government's declaration of a State of Emergency in July 1985, journalists were restricted from any 'demarcated area' and subsequently all filming, videoing and photographing of unrest was banned.

7. 'Brown' is a term used by the government to differentiate Coloureds from black Africans; many people of mixed race refer to themselves as black or 'so-called' Coloured.

8. Figures are from the Directory of South African Trade Unions, South African Labour and Development Research Unit, University of Cape Town, 1984. The African Mineworkers' Union led a week-long strike on the Rand in 1946 which was crushed by the state at a cost of twelve dead and 1200 wounded. The fledgling National Union of Mineworkers flexed its muscles for the first time in September 1984, winning a pay rise victory just hours ahead of a deadline for the first legal strike by black miners in the gold fields.

9. The Intimidation Act of 1982 allows police to detain workers suspected of 'intimidating' other workers.

10. Although the original back-pay claim was for R850,000, the out-of-court settlement in late 1983 paid out R800 apiece for 270 workers.

11. In 'The B & S Closure: Rationalization or Reprisal?' South African Labour Bulletin, X, 1, August–September 1984, Jeremy Keenan presents evidence showing that the company used the closure to rid itself of MAWU members. In Work In Progress, 34, 1984, Georgina Jaffee uses the Brits workers as a case study of the survival strategies of the unemployed.

12. The first, and most successful, consumer boycott in South African history was the ANC-led potato boycott, in protest at the treatment of farm labourers in the eastern Transvaal in 1959.

13. The South African government solidified its links with conservative Christian groups, such as the American Institute for Religion and Democracy, in the late 1970s, with 'Muldergate' funds (for illicit secret government projects).

14. Speaking in Parliament, 27 March 1984.

15. Reverend Chikane's suspension was condemned by the local church board and some six hundred Kagiso residents submitted a petition to the director of the church in September 1981, demanding Chikane's reinstatement. After negotiations with the Apostolic Faith Mission elders broke down, Chikane decided not to protest further against his suspension, and after his release from jail, he took a position with the Institute for Contextual Theology in Johannesburg.

16. The Publications Appeal Board lifted the ban on the Freedom Charter on 30 January 1984, saying it could not accept that the document belonged exclusively to the ANC, but warning that irresponsible use of it could contravene security laws. The ANC applauded the unbanning as heralding 'the mass acceptance of the Charter, despite the previous prohibitions, which has forced the regime to concede defeat'.

17. 'Azania' is a controversial name for South Africa, conceived by the Pan-Africanist Congress in the 1960s, and popularized by Black Consciousness supporters in the 1970s. It is rejected by the ANC, who claim it derives from an Arab word meaning a 'place of slaves' in East Africa. The Azanian Students' Organization retained the name for historical and tactical reasons, despite its move away from Black Consciousness and its sanctioning of co-operation with 'progressive whites'.

18. The only Black Consciousness trial since 1976 was that of former Soweto Students' Representative

Council member Khotso Seathlo and other members of the Nigeria-based South African Youth Revolutionary Council, comprised of exiled 1976-era student leaders who had shunned both the ANC and the PAC. The thesis that 'the impotence and bankruptcy of Black Consciousness as an ideology of liberation' is the 'lesson of the Soweto revolt' is argued by Stephen Davis in *Season of War: Insurgency in South Africa, 1977-1980,* forthcoming from Yale University Press. Another factor in the waning of support for Black Consciousness was the defection of many of its prominent exiled leaders to the ANC.

19. Fischer died while serving a sentence of life imprisonment for his support for the ANC and the South African Communist Party; Slovo is an ANC and SACP leader in exile; and Goldberg was sentenced to life in prison for ANC activities, together with Nelson Mandela. Goldberg was released in 1985, under a conditional amnesty that required him to forswear violence, but he reaffirmed his commitment to the ANC after leaving South Africa.

20. The Matanzima brothers rule the 'independent' homeland of Transkei, and Thebehali is the former 'mayor' of Soweto.

21. A lawyer with degrees from Columbia University and Oxford, Pixley Seme founded the ANC (first called the South African Native National Congress) in 1912.

22. There have been only two PAC trials since 1976, the 1979 trial of Zephania Mothopeng and seventeen others and the 1983 trial of Joe Thloloe, and little popular support has been evidenced inside South Africa.

23. Radio Freedom is the official voice of the ANC, broadcast via shortwave from Tanzania, Zambia, Angola, Ethiopia and Madagascar.

24. *Sowetan,* 2 July 1981.

25. Mandela's middle name.

26. Military riot control vehicles.

27. On 21 March 1960, police killed sixty-seven blacks involved in a peaceful protest against the pass laws in the Transvaal black township of Sharpeville; the government declared a national state of emergency, and a month later banned the ANC and the PAC.

28. 'Mayibuye i Africa', 'Let Africa return!' a slogan associated with the ANC.

29. Declassified and reported by Davis, op. cit. Davis gives a 'conservative estimate' of 12,500 South Africans involved outside the country with liberation movements, 9000 as members of the ANC. He also notes that before the Soweto uprisings, the

average age of ANC guerillas was 35 years, but that one year later, the country, the average age had dropped to 28 years.

30. An in-depth study of the government's prosecution of guerilla fighters post-1976 is Glenn Moss's 'Political Trials, South Africa: 1976–1979', Development Studies Group, Johannesburg, 1979, which cites the Pretoria Twelve trial. The South African government portrays the ANC as controlled by the South African Communist Party, which is, in turn, controlled by Moscow. The ANC maintains that the SACP (formed in 1921 and forced underground by the 1950 Suppression of Communism Act) is but one of the ANC's allies, and that the ANC receives military aid from the Soviet Union, but also humanitarian assistance from Europe, Africa, eastern bloc countries and the United Nations, among others.

31. Mandela, ANC Secretary-General Walter Sisulu and other top ANC leaders were held at the Robben Island maximum security prison off Cape Town until 1982, when they were moved to Pollsmoor Prison on the Cape mainland. White political prisoners are held in Pretoria Central Prison.

32. A rubber version of the sjambok (a rhino-hide whip) developed for police 'crowd control'.

33. Sentence commuted to life imprisonment in 1983, after an international clemency campaign.

34. The Terrorism Act of 1967 was incorporated into the 1982 International Security Act.

35. Quoted in Lodge, op cit.

36. Albert Luthuli was ANC president from 1953 until the 1960 banning, and won the 1961 Nobel Peace prize.

37. First published in *Staffrider,* November–December 1979, Johannesburg.

3 Reform

1. The first statement ended a hostile meeting with the now-defunct Coloured Representative Council on 9 November 1979. The second assertion was first made at the September 1979 Transvaal National Party Congress. The third quote is from a speech to Pretoria and Verwoerdburg National Party representatives at Pretoria City Hall in March 1982. The last statement is from a speech to a National Party meeting in November 1981.

2. From the *Financial Mail,* 22 June 1980, quoted in 'Riding the Tiger: Reform and Repression in South Africa', National Union of SA Students, 1982.

3. Dr Andries Treurnicht's

breakaway Conservative Party and Jaap Marais's fringe Herstigte Nasionale (Reconstituted National) Party criticized the constitutional proposals as a betrayal of apartheid principles that would 'sell-out' white voters to entrench the National Party–big business alliance. The liberal parliamentary opposition, the Progressive Federal Party, criticized the proposals for excluding blacks and creating a potential dictatorship through the powerful new executive State Presidency. According to the *Sunday Express* (4 September 1983), the National Party spent R4 million to R5 million on the referendum, with R2 million specifically budgeted for advertising.

4. Carstens stood for election as a candidate of the opposition Progressive Federal Party in the 1977 Johannesburg provincial elections, but said, 'My personal views have absolutely nothing to do with this contract'.

5. Claimed as the work of the ANC, as a protest against Koornhof's visit.

6. As of the end of 1985, this promise remains unfulfilled.

7. It took until the 1984 session of Parliament, after much revision, before all three bills became law.

8. The 10.7 per cent voter turn-out in the December 1983 elections to choose black local authorities in Soweto represented a slight improvement over the 6 per cent poll of 1978, with a countrywide poll of 21 per cent. However, government opponents claimed that the actual voting percentages were actually far smaller than indicated by the official figures, because more than half those eligible to vote were not on the voters' rolls. The Soweto poll brought the defeat of the unpopular incumbent leader of the Soweto Community Council, David Thebehali, by E.T. Tshabalala, who soon became just as unpopular as his predecessor.

9. Tour organized on 3 July 1980 by the Department of Foreign Affairs and Information for the Foreign Correspondents Association of South Africa.

10. While blacks are not allowed to own land in the black townships, as part of the 1979 reform initiative they were permitted to buy houses under terms of a 99-year-lease, whereby blacks could own the house, but not the land on which it was built. The government announced the mass sale of state-owned housing at 'bargain' prices in July 1983, but as of April 1984, only 8000 of the 500,000 houses had been sold.

11. Founder of the Anglo-American Corporation in 1917 and father of Harry

Oppenheimer.

12. *Financial Mail,* 11 March 1977.

13. *Sowetan,* 5 June 1981.

14. In February 1984, Minister of Co-operation and Development Piet Koornhof announced that blacks would be able to trade in defined central business districts, previously reserved for whites, 'but in terms of prescribed conditions'.

15. A 'laager' is a defensive formation of oxwagons drawn up by the Boers in the nineteenth century against attacking Zulus, now used to mean a gathering for protection.

16. In January 1982, SABC-TV ordered producers to devise ways of including Coloureds and Indians in programmes on the previously all-white channel.

17. Alexander, a former political prisoner (Unity Movement supporter) and current director of the South African Centre for Higher Education in Cape Town, was addressing the Career Opportunity Research and Information Centre in Cape Town, 22 September 1982.

18. The effective seizure of power by the military has been documented by scholars ranging in political outlook from Deon Geldenhuys and Hennie Kotze of the Rand Afrikaans University ('Aspects of Political Decision-Making in South Africa', *South African Journal of Political Science,* 1983) to the National Union of South African Students ('Total War in South Africa: Militarization and the Apartheid State, 1983'.)

19. The National Supplies and Procurement Act was first used in 1975, to compel companies to make tents for troops in Angola.

20. Statement by P.W. Botha in the *New York Times,* 24 March 1982.

21. A concern for the 'hearts and minds' of the local population was first expressed by British Military High Commissioner Sir Gerald Templar in 1952, during the Malayan counter-insurgency campaign.

22. Although Koevoet is effectively part of the SADF, the unit was constituted as a police unit so as to bypass United Nations Resolution 435, which calls for the withdrawal or disarmament of all military units, but allows for the continued operation of police units, according to Deputy Police Commissioner Lieutenant-General Victor Verster (*Cape Times,* 18 January 1984).

23. Paulus was sentenced to death in December 1983.

24. The western-backed National Front for the Liberation of Angola (FNLA), led by Holden Roberto and Jonas Savimbi with his South African-supported

National Union for the Total Independence of Angola (UNITA) fought unsuccessfully against the MPLA, led by the late Agostinho Neto, who became Angola's first president after independence.

25. The introduction of the San to the consumer society has taken its toll: alcoholism is rife, and apparently not discouraged by the SADF.

26. Interview by Gavin Evans, quoted in his dissertation for the University of Cape Town, 'The Role of the Military in Education in South Africa,' 1983. Note that 40 per cent of South Africa's soldiers are black, according to Kenneth Grundy, *Soldiers Without Politics: Blacks in the South African Armed Forces,* University of California Press, 1983.

27. The voluntary commando system had been a dismal failure, leaving regional commando units critically undermanned, hence the emphasis on the 'Dad's Army' to protect the National Key Points such as power stations, to aid in counter-insurgency operations in rural areas, and in manning police roadblocks and effecting crowd control in the urban areas.

28. Steele was the third of ten conscientious objectors between 1977 and 1983, when the Defence Force allowed COs from the recognized 'peace churches', such as Jehovah's Witnesses, to do non-combatant military service, while selective (political) COs were imprisoned for up to two years and/or fined.

29. A secular theory adopted by the Church as a morally responsible reflection on warfare, and developed further by theologians like St Thomas Aquinas, St Augustine and John Calvin.

30. The new law allows for six years of community service or non-combatant duty for objectors from recognized peace churches, but those who choose that option are subject to control measures which severely restrict their political activities.

31. There is no record of support for Buthelezi's role in KwaZulu from either Mandela or Sisulu. Mandela's essay that is quoted by Buthelezi, 'Our Struggle Needs Many Tactics', was written in 1958, to clarify the decision of the South African Coloured People's Organization (a member of the Congress Alliance) to participate in elections for Coloured parliamentary seats (before the Coloured were struck off the voter's roll). Mandela supported this tactic, citing a lack of sufficient unity and solidarity to sustain a boycott, and a need to exploit the parliamentary forum 'to put forth the case for a democratic and progressive

South Africa'.

32. In a speech by ANC Secretary-General Alfred Nzo, 26 June 1980, London. Nzo was misquoted by the press, which reported that he had called Buthelezi an 'interloper'.

33. In a speech to the KwaZulu Legislative Assembly, April 1983.

34. At a press conference in Pretoria, 3 November 1983. The secret Broederbond (Brotherhood) society was founded in 1918 to help Afrikaners wrench political and economic power from English-speaking capitalists.

35. A resolution passed by the Progressive Federal Party's ruling federal council in Johannesburg, November 1984, called for an end to conscription, and prompted the resignation of the PFP's former Defence spokesman, Harry Schwarz. In a similar motion in October 1984, the Natal PFP congress noted that the party's lack of direction on the military issue was 'leading to disillusionment from potential party supporters on university campuses'.

36. South African Associated Newspapers closed the *Rand Daily Mail* in April 1985, citing a R45-million loss in recent years, but the move was widely criticized as politically motivated. With the exception of the small, independent Johannesburg *Weekly Mail* the English-language, liberal, opposition press is controlled by the South African Association Newspapers morning group and the Argus chain of mainly afternoon papers. Anglo-American mining concerns own 40 per cent shares in Argus and Argus owns 40 per cent of SAAN. The government-supporting Afrikaans press is controlled by two Afrikaans concerns, Nasionale Pers and Perskor. These four media monopolies control nearly 90 per cent of South Africa's newspapers, the highest newspaper ownership concentration in the world. In April 1984, three of the country's five biggest black publications passed from white liberal control into the hands of Nasionale Pers, when publishing magnate Jim Bailey sold *City Press, Drum* and *True Love.* Nasionale Pers managing director Ton Vosloo's explanation made it clear that there was a political as well as an economic motive behind the black press venture: 'Our very future depends on building bridges of communication between Afrikaners and blacks, and to develop a peaceable way of life in our common part of the continent.'

37. Kensington is a white suburb of Johannesburg.

38. With at least 70,000 black miners on strike, the July 1982

labour action was the largest to hit the mining industry since 1946.

39. Hardline former Minister of Justice and Police.

40. The government's Steyn Commission on the Mass Media produced a report in early 1982 which recommended stricter press controls, such as a formal register of approved journalists, but the liberal press agreed instead to set up its own media council, which has led to further self-censorship.

41. The exposé of the Information Department's international propaganda campaign in 1978–9 curtailed the more blatant 'dirty tricks', but South Africa's international influence-buying efforts continued. The government spent more than R1.2 million placing advertisements in foreign newspapers in 1983–4, and devoted R16 million annually to the SABC's external network.

42. Figures from S. Clarke, 'Financial Aspects of Economic Sanctions on South Africa', International University Exchange Fund, 1980 and *South African Panorama,* May 1983.

43. The $45 million shipment was exposed in a documentary aired by Boston's WGBH-TV, 16 January 1980. In March 1982, a US Congressional committee concluded that the CIA had been 'seriously negligent' in the affair. Executives of the Space Research Corporation served six-month prison terms for violating federal export regulations.

44. A study by the American Friends Service Committee and the Washington Office on Africa, released in January 1984, showed that the US government had quietly licensed the commercial export of more than $28.3 million worth of military technology to South Africa since 1981. A comprehensive study by *Africa News* (22 October 1984) showed a steady rise in strategic exports to South Africa from the US since the Reagan administration lifted the ban on sales of commercial goods to the military and police, relaxed restrictions on sales of computers and aircraft in 1982 and 1983, and broadened the definition of acceptable commercial exports. The US has since allowed regular licensing of nuclear equipment and selected items from the government's index of sensitive military technology. South Africa's closest foreign military alliance was with Israel, which trained and exchanged military personnel and sold missiles, aircraft, weapons and electronics to the SADF.

45. Black members of a West Indian cricket team that toured South Africa in 1983 were declared 'honorary whites' and

paid handsomely by the South African government. After the boycott-breaking tour got the players banned for life from international sport, they told the *Sunday Times* (15 January 1984) that 'the heartache and the jeers' had forced many of the players to flee their Caribbean homes.

46. This quote is added from the *Rand Daily Mail,* 28 January 1982.

47. A survey of 551 black production workers in industrial areas of the Transvaal, Port Elizabeth and Natal, conducted by Professor Lawrence Schlemmer, head of the Centre for Applied Social Sciences at the University of Natal, and financed by the US State Department, showed that while black anger had risen dramatically in the 1980s, 75 per cent of blacks reject disinvestment as a means of 'frightening the South African government into getting rid of apartheid'. The *Sunday Times* (23 September 1984) splashed the headline 'Blacks Snub Anti-SA Lobby' across the front page, but buried in the inside pages of the paper Professor Schlemmer's concession that perhaps 'too great an incentive was given to reject the disinvestment position by mentioning the effect on job creation in the wording of the questions'. A 1978 Schlemmer survey showing massive support for Chief Gatsha Buthelezi has since been repudiated in subsequent surveys by Schlemmer and others. Although Schlemmer also headed the South African Institute of Race Relations, the body publicly disassociated itself from the study.

4 Repression

1. South Africa's Institute of Crime Prevention and Rehabilitation puts the country's prison population at 440 people per 100,000 population, as compared with 189 per 100,000 in the US. In 1984, pass law prosecutions were transferred from the Department of Co-operation and Development's Courts to the Magistrates' Courts of the Department of Justice. Less than 1 per cent of the nearly 284,000 people prosecuted for pass offences in 1983 had legal representation.

2. *Grassroots,* May 1981.

3. *Pace,* December 1983–January 1984.

4. At the September 1984 Cape Congress of the National Party, P. W. Botha announced that he had decided to abandon the government's policy of preferential treatment for Coloureds in the Cape and grant permanent residence to Africans who were legally in the region, but in

November 1984, the Chief Commissioner for the Western Cape said the 'Coloured labour preference policy' was still in force.

5. *Cape Times,* 6 December 1983.

6. All figures on population removals from *Forced Removals in South Africa,* Surplus People Project, Cape Town, 1983, the most comprehensive study to date on the effects of the government's removal policies. While Minister of Co-operation and Development Piet Koornhof branded the study 'propaganda', he admitted in Parliament in June 1984 that the number of blacks resettled in the homelands in 1983 was nearly double the number in previous years.

7. The Deputy Minister of Development and Land Affairs, Hennie van der Walt, ushered in the era of 'voluntary removals' in June 1983 with an admission that 'we made mistakes in the past', but that 'consultation' would guide the government's removals in the future.

8. *International Herald Tribune,* 8 May 1984. In September 1985 the Appeal Court found the Mogora removal illegal.

9. *Rand Daily Mail,* 10 June 1983.

10. In a speech opening a new shopping complex in Lebowa, 6 December 1980.

11. In an address to the Ciskei National Assembly, 3 August 1984.

12. According to the *Argus,* 7 July 1984, Ciskei's 'Israeli connection' was developing into an embarrassment for the Israeli and South African governments, and Israel was attempting to discourage further ties with the homeland. Yet in November 1984, the West Bank settlement of Ariel became the first municipal authority outside of southern Africa to confer a degree of recognition on Ciskei, when its mayor signed an agreement 'twinning' Ariel and Ciskei's capital of Bisho. Other major homeland investors include Taiwan, West Germany, the US, Italy and Hong Kong.

13. 'Ruling With the Whip', Nicholas Haysom, October 1983, was compiled from interviews and sworn statements taken in Ciskei by lawyers and medical doctors.

14. The balkanization of South Africa via the government's homeland policy; this statement is quoted in 'State of the Nation: Crisis in the Border Bantustan', South African Students' Press Union, December 1983.

15. *Rand Daily Mail,* 24 July 1984.

16. *Rand Daily Mail,* 18 January 1982.

17. Provisions of the 1984 Labour Relations Amendment Bill and the National Manpower Commission report tabled in Parliament in 1984.

18. This document was first published in the June 1981 issue of *Work in Progress.* Minister le Grange's defence of its author in reply to a question in Parliament in August 1981.

19. Tom Mashinini worked for a union affiliated to the Trade Union Council of South Africa, but subsequently resigned in protest against the refusal of the conservative labour grouping to speak out against detention without trial. Emma Mashinini is General Secretary of the Commercial and Catering Workers Union of South Africa.

20. Portuguese for 'the struggle continues', a slogan of the anti-colonial wars of Africa's Portuguese colonies. The preceding slogans are identified with the South African Congress of Trade Unions.

21. *The Star* calculates that fifty-four people died in detention between 1963 and 1984. Of these, half were said by police to have committed suicide, seven to have died accidentally, and ten to have died of natural causes, while the circumstances of at least eight were said to be unknown. These figures do not represent all deaths in detention in the homelands.

22. Dipale went missing after unsuccessfully trying to get police to investigate an attempt on his life by unknown gunmen in Soweto. When he was found dead in a police cell four days later, security police claimed he was to have been charged in court the next day for 'terrorist' activities.

23. References to union leaders Oscar Mpetha and Thozamile Gqwetha, student leader Wantu Zenzile, and Women's Federation leaders Florence Mkhize and Helen Joseph.

24. Reverend Allan Hendrickse, head of the Coloured Labour Party, whose support for the tri-racial Parliament is crucial to Pretoria.

25. From an interview in the *Sunday Times Magazine,* London, February 1981.

26. Leaders of anti-colonial wars in Kenya, Mozambique and Zimbabwe.

27. Ferrus's family publicly denied claims by Labour Party leader Hendrickse that the funeral was 'hijacked for cheap publicity' against the will of the family, saying it was Ferrus's 'wish to be buried under the banner of the ANC, the organization to which he belonged'.

28. Botha's statement and the anonymous pamphlet were quoted in the *Sunday Tribune,* 3 August 1980.

29. The defamation of Tutu continued even after he won the 1984 Nobel Peace Prize. Although the government officially maintained a stony silence, the Bishop was denounced in pro-government newspapers and on the SABC. In November 1984, Tutu was elected Anglican Bishop of Johannesburg.

30. According to *The Star* (26 November 1984), the National Student Federation, the umbrella body of conservative students groups in Johannesburg, Pietermaritzburg and Cape Town, spent R75,000 on publications, advertisements and office rental since its inception in mid-1984. NSF President Crystal refused to reveal the source of his funding, but said it came from the 'commercial world'.

31. The Progressive Federal Party member of Parliament for Port Elizabeth, John Malcomess, called for a police probe of the intimidation campaign in May 1983, with no results. The Johannesburg campaign received press publicity, but no official investigation. According to the Cape Town Detention Action Committee, there were more than 1600 incidents of right-wing violence in South Africa between 1964 and 1978, with hundreds more reported since then.

32. This poem appeared in *Dome,* 1, 1982, the official newspaper of the University of Natal (Durban) Students' Representative Council. The many names in the poem refer to people killed in detention, imprisoned, executed by the government, and victims of political assassinations after leaving South Africa (a list which includes Joe Gqabi in Zimbabwe in 1981, Ruth First in Mozambique in 1982, and Jeanette Schoon and her six-year-old daughter, Katryn, in Angola in 1984.)

33. The week that Langa was killed a close friend of his, artist and poet Dikobe Ben Martins, was jailed for ten years for ANC activities. In a rare display of government concern for a political assassination case, police claimed to have arrested Langa's killers, and announced that he had been murdered by the ANC for being a spy. The ANC denied the charge, maintaining that Langa, like so many others before him, was assassinated because of his ANC leanings.

34. The 1984 death in detention of Paris Malatji highlighted a new method of detention being used by security police: holding people under the Criminal Procedure Act, but treating them as security detainees.

35. Carl Niehaus was convicted of High Treason and sentenced to fifteen years imprisonment.

36. Two men who refused to testify in a Pietermaritzburg treason trial in 1984 received the stiffest prison sentences to date: three and four years.

37. From *Inside,* Jeremy Cronin, Ravan Press, 1983. John Matthews was sentenced in 1964 to fifteen years imprisonment, for activities on behalf of Umkhonto we Sizwe.

38. Mange's death sentence was the first imposed for treason since the 1942 trial of Nazi sympathizer Robey Leibbrandt, who was pardoned after the National Party came to power.

39. Although some of the defendants were homeland citizens, South African courts still consider that they owe allegiance to the South African state.

40. A special glass dock was built to confine James Mange and eleven black co-defendants in the 1979 treason trial, (see pages 128-9) and a special enlarged dock was built to hold the forty-three white mercenaries in the 1982 trial relating to the Seychelles coup attempt and ensuing plane hijacking.

41. Despite the stepped-up security, Pietermaritzburg's courts were hit by two blasts over the next three months.

42. A sign of support for the ANC.

43. Eastern bloc weapons supplied to the ANC's military wing, Umkhonto we Sizwe.

44. Portuguese acronym for the Front for the Liberation of Mozambique, the war-time guerilla movement and ruling party of the People's Republic of Mozambique.

45. The propaganda stunt was exposed by the Mozambican News Agency, which showed that, according to the synchronised clock attached to the recorder which tapes all conversations between Maputo's control tower and incoming and outgoing aircraft, the raid on Matola had finished a full ten minutes before 'Mike Zero One' radioed his message. The Green Leader fraud is chronicled in *None But Ourselves: Masses vs. Media in the Making of Zimbabwe,* Julie Frederikse, Ravan Press, Johannesburg, 1982; Zimbabwe Publishing House, Harare, 1983; Heinemann Educational Books, London, 1984; and Penguin, New York, 1984.

46. The US State Department went on record confirming South Africa's support for the MNR in *Africa Report,* January 1983.

47. South African Parliament, 3 February 1983.

48. By 1984, the South African government publicly admitted its support for Jonas Savimbi's UNITA. The Lesotho Liberation Army was originally formed in 1979 as the armed wing of the Basotholand Congress Party

opposition movement, but lost credibility in the 1980s when it appeared that its cadres were launching attacks on Lesotho from the Free State, with apparent South African support. In 1984, Lesotho opposition figures confirmed that the South African government had helped them form a new political alliance against the Lesotho government at a meeting in Pretoria. South African training and support for Zimbabwe dissidents has been revealed in numerous trials in Harare.

49. East London *Daily Dispatch,* 12 November 1983.

50. In Februry 1984, South Africa and Angola initialled an agreement in Lusaka creating a joint monitoring commission to oversee the withdrawal of South African troops from southern Angola and South Africa subsequently released Namibia's most prominent political prisoner, SWAPO leader Andimba Toivo ja Toivo.

51. *Citizen,* 16 April 1984.

52. Pretoria was so determined not to acknowledge its support publicly for the MNR and other surrogate guerilla movements in the region that it refused to release documentation vital to the September 1984 secret trial of national serviceman Roland Hunter and two others, thereby allowing them to escape prosecution for treason. Hunter had procured documents from the SADF's Directorate of Special Tasks proving South African support for the MNR, the Lesotho Liberation Army and Zimbabwe's 'dissidents'.

5 The war

1. An April 1984 SABC internal memorandum gave guidelines for promoting the constitution by expanding radio services for blacks, and a secret SABC working group formulated a 'plan of action' in May for SATV's role in persuading Coloureds and Indians to vote.

2. Njikelana's essay, in *Work in Progress,* 32, 1984, was a reply to General Workers' Union General-Secretary Dave Lewis's explanation of why his union would not affiliate to the UDF, in *WIP,* 29, 1983. In July, 1984, the alleged role of 'white bureaucratic intellectuals' in dissuading unions from political affiliation led to a breakaway from the Federation of South African Trade Unions and the formation of the United Mining, Metal and Allied Workers' Union, whose leader, Andrew Zulu, maintained, 'You can't limit politics in this country to the factory floor.'

3. The first Indians were brought to South Africa to work as indentured labourers on sugar plantations in 1860. Gandhi came to Natal in 1893 on legal business, then stayed to found the Natal Indian Congress, in response to the Indian Disenfranchisement Bill. In 1906, he led the first passive resistance campaign against a pass law for Indians in the Transvaal, which finally succumbed to the campaign in 1913.

4. The National Forum Committee was founded in Hammanskraal on 11-12 June 1983, with two hundred Black Consciousness organizations represented. It was not until late 1984 that the South African Council on Sport formally threw its support to the UDF, but SACOS had never taken the kind of anti-UDF stand reflected in that pamphlet.

5. In a speech to a 16 June 1983 commemoration meeting in Lenasia.

6. Bishop Abel Muzorewa was Prime Minister of the 1979 government of 'Zimbabwe-Rhodesia', but lost overwhelmingly to guerilla leader Robert Mugabe in the 1980 British-supervised independence elections.

7. Until the early 1980s, most political prisoners (mainly ANC supporters) had been banned upon their release. Fifty-five banning orders automatically expired on 1 July 1983, in terms of the new Internal Security Act, but ten people had their banning orders reimposed.

8. Despite the contempt Buthelezi expressed in late 1983, a year later he said he had written to ANC President Oliver Tambo, giving 'a clear and unambiguous statement that Inkatha wishes to co-operate with the ANC'. In that same speech, in Ulundi in October 1984, Buthelezi said it was 'silly' for the UDF to hide its working relationship with the ANC's external mission.

9. Holliday served seven years in prison for furthering the aims of the ANC.

10. The former head of the Christian Institute, Reverend Naudé was one of three whites banned in October 1977, when scores of Black Consciousness leaders and organizations were banned. He was unbanned seven years later, a seeming sop to international opinion at the height of the nationwide protests against the new constitution.

11. Leader of the Garment Workers Union for over two decades, until the 1950 Suppression of Communism Act forced his resignation.

12. Simon van der Stel was the second Dutch East India Company governor of the Cape (after Jan van Riebeeck), who imported French Huguenots to bolster the settler stock, and introduced wineries to the Stellenbosch region – hence the nickname, Simon 'of the vat'. Barney Barnato, a businessmen from London's East End and rival speculator of Cecil Rhodes, lost the struggle for control of the Kimberley diamond fields in the 1880s to Rhodes's De Beers Consolidated.

13. In late 1984, big business began openly critizing government — a reflection of growing private sector dissatisfaction with ideological policies seen as running counter to economic realities; in September 1985, a delegation of top business leaders held talks with the ANC in Zambia.

14. The Progressive Federal Party initially refused to serve on the President's Council until it included blacks, and campaigned against the constitution in the 1983 referendum, then did an about-face, claiming that 'politics is about compromise and sometimes a man has to get his hands a little dirty'.

15. About 46,000 immigrants became South African citizens under the October 1984 Citizenship Amendment Act, and the SADF issued a 'friendly' warning to new male citizens to register for military service.

16. Aggett was found hanged in his cell in February 1982. (see from pages 116-8.)

17. Despite the corroboration of Hogan's testimony by the district surgeon who had examined her bruises in prison, the Magistrate's Court ruled in favour of the police.

18. Breytenbach, a distinguished Afrikaans poet and painter in exile, was sentenced to nine years in prison for returning to South Africa to set up a clandestine anti-apartheid movement for whites. He was released after serving seven years.

19. Adam and Christie were both sentenced to ten years in prison for furthering the aims of the ANC; Berger served two years in prison for sending information to the ANC-aligned South African Congress of Trade Unions.

20. General Sales Tax was increased from 7 to 10 per cent in July 1984, a move the government's opponents claim was necessitated by the R2 billion a year cost of administering apartheid. The quote is from *SASPU National,* August 1984.

21. While a number of foreign envoys boycotted the Cape Town ceremonies, the guest of honour at Botha's inauguration was the rebel Angolan UNITA leader, Jonas Savimbi, whose presence reinforced speculation that South Africa was stalling on its promised withdrawal from southern Angola.

22. From *The Third Day of September: An Eye-Witness Account of the Sebokeng Rebellion of 1984,* Johannes Rantete, Ravan Press Storyteller Series, 1, 1984.

23. ANC President Oliver Tambo claimed that the ANC had deployed more guerilas in South Africa since the signing of the Nkomati Accord (*Zimbabwe Herald,* 5 April 1984), and indications that the ANC had stepped up supply and logistical support to guerilas in the country came in November 1984, when South African police unearthed large caches of arms and ammunition, apparently destined for the urban areas.

24. In June 1984, the Cape Town branch of the UDF organized a rural conference, which led to the founding of many more UDF branches in rural areas.

25. Quote from *Solidarity News Service,* 12 October 1984. The strike was led by 64,000 miners who had not been informed of a last-minute management concession to union demands. Seven miners were killed and hundreds injured when management called in the police.

26. Published in *Staffrider,* V, 1, 1982, Ravan Press. 'Boesman' (Bushman), 'Kaffir' and 'Koelie' are derogatory terms for Coloured, African and Asian.

27. At a Harare press conference on 10 August 1984, ANC President Tambo conceded that the Durban operation had been mishandled, and called the unintended civilian deaths 'unacceptable'.

28. Minister of Defence General Magnus Malan unabashedly maintained that the use of troops in the townships was 'nothing new', saying that 43,000 soldiers had been deployed in police work between January 1983 and June 1984. The police themselves are heavily militarized, equipped with armoured cars and automatic weapons, and trained in counter-insurgency.

29. *Sunday Express,* 28 October 1984.

30. *Leadership South Africa,* October 1984.

31. Even in the wake of the success of the stay-away, Buthelezi continued to accuse its organizers of dividing blacks and 'harming the cause of liberation'. The pro-government Afrikaans newspaper, *Beeld* (7 November 1984) lauded Buthelezi for his anti-stay-away stance, and urged the government to take 'action which will also strengthen the hand of the moderate Buthelezis of the country'. The liberal press felt similarly threatened by the strike: *The Star* (6 November 1984) asked in an editorial, 'Do these unions believe they can achieve anything by an

unstructured mass political gesture except polarization and violence?'

32. Figures from the Labour Monitoring Group, comprising six top Johannesburg academics (*Star,* 20 November 1984). An overall average 60 per cent stay-away in the Pretoria-Witwatersand-Vereeniging area was the consensus figure of employers and the media.

33. 6500 SASOL workers, 90 per cent of the workforce, were fired for their participation in the stay-away. The Chemical Workers' Industrial Union charged that SASOL had used the strike as an excuse to rid itself of the union. Few other employers took action against their workers for participation in the stay-away.

34. According to University of the Witwatersrand Professor Edward Webster, who made a detailed study of eighteen stay-away strikes since the launching of the first one in May 1950. The Associated Chambers of Commerce said industries had effectively lost two days' production as a result of the November 5–6 stay-away.

35. Mali was detained the next day, along with the entire Transvaal Regional Stay-Away Committee, including the President of the Federation of South African Trade Unions, Chris Dhlamini and General-Secretary of the Council of South African Unions, Piroshaw Camay. Columnist Allister Sparks (*Star,* 20 November 1984) described the detentions of these two leaders, whose powerful unions had until then remained aloof from protest politics, as 'the single most foolish actions in 36 years of Nationalist rule' because the government thereby 'politicized the black union movement at a stroke'. By the end of 1985, some 500,000 workers had launched a politically overt labour federation, the Congress of South African Trade Unions.

36. 'It's alright, ma, I'm only dying', by Bob Dylan.

37. Allusions to successful ANC bombings and sabotage operations. 'Pitoli' is an African name for Pretoria, where a deadly bomb exploded in 1983.

Illustration Captions and Credits

p.6 Soweto June 1976 *(The Cape Times* 19 Jun 1976); Pretoria bombing 21 May 1983 *(The Star* 21 May 1983)
p.7 Lessons of Christian National Education: test papers from a Pretoria primary school 1981.
p.8 Schoolgirl with her nanny *(Biddy Partridge).*
p.9 Schoolgirl cadets marching *(Paul Wienberg).*
p.11 Farmer and his son, Magaliesburg *(Paul Weinberg)*
p.12 *top* Child labour on a white farm, Springs, Transvaal *(Wendy Schweggman); bottom* 'Another border weapon for farmers' *(Farmer's Weekly* 18 Nov 1981)
p.13 Newspaper vendors sleeping rough in Cape Town *(Jimi Matthews).*
p.14 'Remember June 16' Congress of South African Students (COSAS) poster
p.15 'Each one teach one' COSAS graphic
p.16 *top right* Mobil advertisement *(Finance Week* 22-8 Sep 1983; *top left* Control Data advertisement; *bottom left* Escom advertisement *(South African Panorama* May 1980)
p.17 *top* Leaflet produced by university students during the schools boycott 1980; *bottom* 'Away with Kaferkaans' – Soweto 1976 *(Peter Magubane/IDAF)*
p.18 *top left* Spray-paint graffiti, Pretoria school *(Drum* Aug 1980); *top right* Coloured and Indian students demonstrating during the 1980 schools boycott *(Drum* Jun 1980); *bottom* 16 June 1982 Riot police in Soweto *(Drum)*
p.19 16 June 1984 police-supervised press tour of Soweto *(Wendy Schweggman)*
p.20 *top* 16 June 1981 Soweto students aid victim of police shooting *(Drum)*
pp.20/21 Leaflets produced by students featuring the photo of the first victim of the 16 June 1976 unrest, 13-year-old Hector Petersen
p.22 Meeting of striking meatworkers, Cape Town 1980 *(Richard Wicksteed); inset* Contact Group advertisement for 'strike-management' consultancy *(Financial Mail,* 11 Feb 1983).
p.23 Metal and Allied Workers Union meeting, Johannesburg, Sep 1983 *(Paul Weinberg).*
p.24 Cape Town bus terminus 1 May 1984 *(Jimi Matthews).*
p.25 Striking B & S workers meeting in Brits church hall 1983 *(Paul Weinberg).*
pp.24/25 Cartoons from workers' newspaper
p.26 'A trade union is . . .' *Izwilethu,* Official Newsletter of the Council of Unions of South Africa Mar/Apr 1984)
p.27 *top* Meat Boycott pamphlets; *bottom* residents attending a civic meeting in Cape Town *(Jimi Matthews)*
p.28 Youth meeting in Cape Town *(Jimi Matthews)*
pp.28/29 Community newspapers
p.30 *top* 'Workers and tenants . . . unite' (from a photograph by *Jimi Matthews); bottom left* Women's solidarity poster; *bottom right* Vaal Organisation of Women banner, South African Women's Day Afrapix
p.31 Bishop Desmond Tutu *(Paul Weinberg)*
p.32 Reverend Frank Chikane, Regina Mundi Church, Soweto 16 June 1984 *(Wendy Schweggman)*
p.33 *top* 'Muslims against oppression', poster in Cape Town *(Jimi Matthews); bottom* Trade unionist, Oscar Mpetha addresses rally protesting at detention of Father Smangaliso Mkatshwa 1984 *(Paul Weinberg)*
p.34 The text of the Freedom Charter reprinted on its twenty-fifth anniversary *(Sunday Post* 29 Jun 1980)
p.35 Black People's Convention poster paying tribute to Steve Biko.
p.36 Steve Biko's funeral (IDAF)
p.37 Anti-Republic Day poster (from a photograph by *Wendy Schweggman)*
p.39 *left* Release Mandela Committee advertisement, July 1984; *right Sunday Post* poster 16 Mar 1980
pp.40/41 Republic Day. *top left* Prime Minister P. W. Botha reviews troops, Durban 1981 *(Paul Weinberg); top centre* and *top right* Republic Day Festival Durban 1981 *(Biddy Partridge). bottom left* Republic Day 1981, Johannesburg *(Biddy Partridge); Rand Daily Mail* poster 28 May 1981. Definition of 'republic' and 'Whose Republic Day?', 'Reject Republic Day Celebrations', graphics from student newsletter, *Challenge.*
p.42 'Freedom fighter' by Mzwakhe (from *Staffrider* vol. 5, no. 1 1982)
p.44 *left* Sharp advertisement *(Sunday Times,* 29 Mar 1981); *right top to bottom Paratus* Mar 1982; *Sunday Post* 6 Jan 1980;. *Sowetan* 7 Jun 1982
p.45 *left The Citizen* 3 Nov 1981; *right* advertisement in *Sunday Times* 24 May 1981
p.46 *left* Leyland advertisement *(Sunday Tribune* 2 Aug 1981); *right Paratus* Mar 1982
p.47 *Scope* 20 Jun 1980
p.48 *top* Poster by MEDU Art Ensemble; *bottom top Rand Daily Mail,* 20 Aug 1981; *left* (picture) *Rand Daily Mail* 21 Dec 1982; *right Rand Daily Mail* 19 Oct 1983
p.50 'Zulu, Sotho . . .', Sasol advertisement; 'Black is bountiful', Makro advertising feature; 'Black Power', advertisement for advertising space in *Pace* magazine *(Clarion* 19 Sep 1978); 'What South Africa needs . . .', Escom advertisement; Taskelder advertisement *(New Dawn,* Jul 1980); 'Black Personnel Manager', Paul Tingley Selection advertisement
p.51 Campaign material for a 'Yes' vote in the 1983 Referendum.
p.52 *top* Worker at Johannesburg factory, 1983 Referendum day: Vote 'No'! ('Cha' in Sotho and Zulu); *bottom* Conservative Party rally in Johannesburg before1983 Referendum: Vote No! *(Wendy Schweggman)*
p.53 As p.51
pp.54/55 Crowds protesting Minister Koornof's visit to Soweto 15 October 1980 were kept at bay by police dogs *(Howard Barrell)*
p.56 *top* Anti-Community Council posters; *bottom* see p.54
p.57 *top* Slogans painted on the house of a Coloured member of the President's Council, Eldorado Park, Johannesburg, 1980; *bottom* see p.54
p.58 *top* Poster protest, Soweto highway: outdoor gatherings of more than one person are prohibited *(Wendy Schweggman); bottom* Anti-Community Council articles from *Ilizwi LaseRhini (Grahamstown Voice)*
p.59 *The Star* 26 Feb 1981
p.60 *top* Publicity for *Soweto Today* guide; Urban Foundation logo
pp.60/61 *bottom* Mobil 'Win a Television Set' Competition pamphlet, 1981
p.62 J. Walter Thompson (South Africa) advertisement
p.63 OK department store advertisement
p.64 Autumn Harvest wine advertisement (Biddy Partridge)
p.65 *left* SABC advertisement *(Financial Mail* 3 Apr 1981); *right* Radio Bantu advertisement *(Financial Mail* 20 Jun 1980).
p.67 *left Eastern Province Herald* 4 and 7 Apr 1984; *right Paratus,* Sep 1980
p.68 *left Daily News* 18 Apr 1984; *right* Johannesburg billboard *(Biddy Partridge)*
p.69 *top* Children's letters to 'boys on the border'; S.A. Border Patrol teeshirt; *bottom* SADF display captured 'terrorist' weapons during Namibia tour 1982 *(Julie Frederikse);* Anti-aircraft gun and dead SWAPO soldier *(Paratus* Jul 1980)
pp.70/71 National Defence Bonds advertisement *(To The Point,* 18 Aug 1978); Tabard insect repellent advertisement *(Armed Forces,* Nov 1981); *Grensvegter,* photocomic magazine cover; Canon advertisement *(Armed Forces,* Sep 1983); 'We are winners', sticker; Mobil advertisement from *National Service '80;* Paperback merchandising offer: 'Buy a paperback for your son or boyfriend on the border. We'll pay the postage . . .' *(Biddy Partridge);* 'To my Hero on the border': novelty ID card from the same shop; 'The SADF needs you!' *(Sunday Times,* 17 Oct 1982); Kit inspection, United Building Society advertisement *(Paratus,* May 1982); Wallet offer, Allied advertisement *(Paratus,* May 1982); Barclays advertisement
p.72 *top row,* Namibia press tour 1982 *(Julie Frederikse); Paratus* front cover Jun 1981; *bottom* Anti-aircraft ammunition captured from SWAPO *(Paratus,* Jul 1980)
p.74 Clipping from *Paratus,* Jan 1982; Vehicle mined by SWAPO *(The Warrior,* SADF newspaper)
p.75 One of the 'ethnic battalions' recruited by the security forces in Namibia poses for journalists during 1981 SADF press tour *(Julie Frederikse)*
p.76 *top* A volunteer trains with an R4 rifle (from 21 Battalion recruitment leaflet); *bottom* A sergeant of the 'Bushmen Battalion' *(Julie Frederikse)*
p.77 *top* Counter-insurgency poster (Northern Transvaal Command, SADF); *bottom* Masthead of *Kontak/Contact*
p.79 *top* Page from *Umanyano Lolutsha* (publication of Cape Youth Congress); *bottom* Cartoon strip *(The Eye* Sep 1983)
p.80 *top left* 21 Battalion parades in Johannesburg (21 Battalion recruitment leaflet); *bottom Paratus,* Jul 1980 Mar 1982
p.81 *top* and *bottom* Civil Defence (mock anti-'terrorist') exercise Johannesburg 1983 *(Wendy Schweggman); centre* Cape Town SADF military festival 1983 (Gideon Mendel).
p.82 Conscientious objectors' support group pamphlet
p.83 Cartoon from *Objector* (Western Cape anti-conscription newsletter) Nov 1983
pp.84/85 End Conscription Campaign sticker (p.84) and poster (p.85)
pp.86/87 *Objector* cover, Jul 1984; 'Cancel the Call-up' sticker; *bottom* Cartoon strip from *Marching Orders* (anti-conscription pamphlet)
pp.88/89 Chief Gatsha Buthelezi: on the speaking circuit (p.88) the stress is on moderation and free enterprise *(Drum);* with his Inkatha supporters (p.89) he emphasizes African tradition and his 'multi-strategy' approach to liberation *(top Paul Weinberg, bottom Drum).* Drawing of Buthelezi (p.88) from an Azanian Student Movement pamphlet
p.92 *Sunday Tribune* supplement, 14 Mar 1982
p.93 'Press is Gagged' poster Silkscreen Training Project poster
pp.94/95 Official Fact Sheets on the Republic of South Africa; *Reader's Digest* (SA edition) cover, Apr 1981
p.96 *top* Leyland Truck advertisement *(Financial Mail,* 30 Sep 1983); *bottom* GEC advertisement *(Financial Mail,* 6 May 1983)
p.97 *top left* Econostat advertisement *(The Economist,* 21 Jun 1980); *top right* Ford advertisement; *bottom* BP advertisement (Financial Mail, 23 Sep 1983)
p.98 *Salvo,* front page, Sep 1981
p.99 *top right* 'Pick 'n Pay' advertisement congratulating Zola Budd on her Olympic selection; *top left* and *bottom* Transvaal Anti-SAIC Committee and Transvaal Cricket Board pamphlet opposing AROSA Sri Lankan tour of South Africa
p.101 Poster by MEDU Art Ensemble
p.102 Detention Action Committee poster
p.103 *left* Police inspecting blacks' passes, Cape Town, 1983 *(Gideon Mendel); inset* Domestic worker shows her pass-book *(Wendy Schweggman); right* Letter from Department of Internal Affairs refusing passport to an African deemed to be a Ciskel citizen
pp.104 *top* A compound in the KwaZulu bantustar 1981 *(Nancy Durrell-McKenna/IDAF)*
pp.104/105 *left to right* Early morning: Cape Town squatter camp, dismantling shelter before police raid *(Afrapix);* Crossroads squatter camp 1983 *(Nigel Dickinson/IDAF);* Police in armoured personnel carrier oversee the destruction of a Cape Town squatter camp 1983 *(Gideon Mendel);* After police had flattened a Cape Town squatter camp *(Gideon Mendel);* The 'final solution': the only shop in the desolate new township of Khayelitsha *(Jimi Matthews)*
p.106 Mogopa residents meet to organize resistance to their forced removal *(Paul Weinberg); inset* One of the farmers who charged as much as R300 to transport the belongings of forcibly removed Mogopa residents to their 'homeland' *(Giedon Mendel)*
p.107 Saul Mhkize's funeral *(Wendy Schweggman).*

p.108 *top* Children play on the remains of vehicles belonging to a Reiger Park entrepreneur 1981 *(Biddy Partridge)*: *bottom* Demolition of flats in the old Coloured 'group area' of District Six, Cape Town *(Jimi Matthews)*

p.109 *top left* Bophuthatswana homeland leader Lucas Mangope with Sol Kerzner at the 1982 Sun City Golf Classic *(Paul Weinberg)*: *bottom left* Sun City Casino *(Sun City publicity photo)*; *bottom right* Workers' housing compound at Sun City, 1981 *(Biddy Partridge)*

p.110 *left* Lennox Sebe invites investment; *top right* advertisement for investment in Qwaqwa *(Growth May 1982)*; *bottom right* Transkei Development Corporation advertisement *(Financial Mail 16 Nov 1984)*

p.111 *top* A Johannesburg solidarity meeting in support of the Ciskei bus boycott; *centre* Anti-Ciskei independence sticker; *bottom* President Lennox Sebe and his wife greet South African Foreign Minister Pik Botha and his wife *(South African Information Service)*

p.112 'Resist Bantustan Violence' Silkscreen Training Project poster

p.113 Batlokwa, 1983 *(Paul Weinberg)*

p.114 *left* Huhudi Youth Organisation poster; *right* Anti-forced removals poster

p.115 'Solidarity with detained workers' Silkscreen Training Project poster

p.117 Neil Aggett's funeral: thousands marched through the streets of Johannesburg *(top Afrapix, bottom Paul Weinberg)*

p.118 *top* Neil Aggett's coffin is carried to the grave *(Afrapix)*; *bottom* Detainees' Parents' Support Committee conference in East London 1983 *(SASPU National)*

p.121 Graphic by Farah *(Staffrider vol. 5, no. 1 1982)*

pp.122/123 *left to right Campus News*, a fake pamphlet mimicking *NUSAS News*; NUSAS pamphlet refuting it; Anti-ANC pamphlet produced by the Student Moderate Alliance; A Pietermaritzburg right-wing students' group pamphlet attacking NUSAS students

pp.126/127 Anti-detention graphics, p.126 by Mzwakhe from *Staffrider* Apr/May 1979

p.129 *Natal Mercury* 16 Nov 1979

p.130 *top* South Africa Women's Day commemoration, Johannesburg, 1982 *(Biddy Partridge)*; *bottom* Lawyer Priscilla Jana at Women's Day commemoration Johannesberg 1984 *(Wendy Schweggman)*.

p.131 *top and bottom* Funeral of Lilian Ngoyi, a former ANC member Soweto *(Howard Barrell)*

p.133 Protests at Sobantu shooting (pictures from *Natal Witness*, Sep/Oct 1982)

p.134 *Natal Witness*, 4 Jun 1983

p.136 *top* South African troops return from raid on Angola, 1984 *(Wendy Schweggman)*; *bottom* SADF soldiers in Angola relax after a raid, with captured weapons, 1981 *(SADF publicity* photo)

p.137 *top* Tee shirts evoking SADF cross-border raids; *bottom Sunday Express* 8 March 1981 on SADF raid on Matola

p.138 The Pretoria bombing, 20 May 1983 *(Sunday Times* 22 May 1983)

p.139 Mozambican workers killed in South African raid on Matola jam factory 23 May 1983 *(Anders Nillson/AIM)*

p.140 *left* Matola raid *(Rand Daily Mail* 24 May 1983)*; map from *Newsweek* 6 Jun 1983

p.141 UNITA soldiers on parade *(Scope 29 Jun 1984)*

p.142 *top* Nkomati Accord *(Rand Daily Mail* 17 Mar 1984)*; Cartoon from *Die Vaderland*.

p.143 *top* 'Boomtime in Mozambique' *(Scope* cover 30 Mar 1984)*; *bottom* 'Blitzkrieg' *(Scope* 19 Oct 1984)

p.144 *Drum*. Sep 1980

p.145 London rally protesting P. W. Botha's 1984 visit *(Paul Weinberg)*

p.146 Student Union for Christian Action poster

p.147 *top* A student in possession of an anti-election sticker is harassed by police at a polling booth in Athlone: 22 August 1984 Coloured House of Representatives election *(Rashid Lombard)*; *bottom* Popular resentment towards a candidate for the Indian House of Parliament expressed in graffitti: Mr Osman lost his deposit *(Jimi Matthews)*.

pp.148/149 Community and trade union newspapers; anti-election posters; Photos, p.148, Scores of demonstrators were

injured when police broke up peaceful protests at the polling booth in Lenasia *(Wendy Schweggman; p.149, Johannesburg graffiti (Afrapix)*; Shaik Gabier, a Muslim leader, at the national launch of the UDF 20 August 1983 *(Jimi Matthews)*

p.150 *top* UDF launch, Cape Town 20 August 1983 *(Paul Weinberg)*; *bottom* Dancing and singing at a UDF women's rally in Cape Town *(Jimi Matthews)*

p.151 UDF posters for Million Signature Campaign and 20 August 1983 rally; *bottom* fake leaflet announcing postponement of the rally

p.152 *top* Joining the UDF's Million Signature Campaign, Cape Town 1984 *(Gideon Mendel)*; *bottom right* Allan Boesak launches the campaign *(Paul Weinberg)*; *bottom left* Anti-UDF, 'don't sign' smear pamphlets issued by right-wing students

p.153 *top* UDF newspaper and poster; *bottom* Workers' anti-election meeting, Athlone, Cape Aug 1984 *(Jimi Matthews)*; UDF pamphlet

p.154 Johannesburg graffiti 1984 *(Afrapix)*

p.156 Victims of the October 1983 Inkatha raid on the University of Zululand *(Omar Badsha/Afrapix)*

p.159 Veteran anti-apartheid campaigner, Helen Joseph receives a standing ovation at the UDF launch, Cape Town 20 August 1983 *(Wendy Schweggman)*

p.160 *top* University of the Witwatersrand demonstration in support of black protests against the new constitution, 1984 *(Wendy Schweggman)*; *bottom left to right* NUSAS poster; *Dome* University of Natal student newspaper) front cover; NUSAS poster

p.161 *left* Dome back cover; *right* NUSAS poster

p.162 Public meeting of Johannesburg Democratic Action Committee 1983 *(Wendy Schweggman)*

p.163 End Conscription Campaign poster

p.165 Picture of Carl Neihaus near the Johannesburg gas works taken by the police and used as evidence at his trial

p.166 NUSAS demonstrations and posters

p.167 Graphic by Simon Dunkley

p.168 Man kicks away teargas cannister. Duduza 18 May 1985

p.169 *top* Military parade on day of P. W. Botha's inauguration in Cape Town, 14 September 1984 *(Rashid Lombard)*; *inset* P. W. Botha as State President on 11c stamp; *bottom* The body of Sharpeville Deputy Mayor lies with a placard reading 'Away with the rent hike! Asinamali'. Sam Dhlamini was hacked to death by a crowd after he allegedly shot two youths *(ANP-Foto Amsterdam)*

p.170 *top* The funeral of Johannes Ngalo *(Wendy Schweggman)*; *bottom* People flee attack on black policeman's home in Duduza township 18 May 1985

p.171 Education Charter Campaign posters; *bottom* Zwide funeral of 14 people killed on Sharpeville Day at Port Elizabeth and Uitenhage

p.172 *top* National Union of Mineworkers logo; *bottom* UDF poster

p.174 *Rand Daily Mail*, 13 Jul 1984

p.175 Zwide funeral 1985 *(Gideon Mendel)*

p.176 Zwide: Bird shot at aftermath of funeral 1985 *(Gideon Mendel* APF)

p.177 Outside Soweto 14 trial *(Gideon Mendel)*

p.179 *top left* Sebokeng 23 October 1984; troops line a road as they seal off the township *(AP/Wide World Photos)*; *top right* SADF public relations leaflet; *bottom* End Conscription Campaign leaflet

p.180 *left* Cartoon linking Transvaal Stay-Away Committee with Soviet communism; *(Die Transvaler) centre* Government-issued pamphlet discouraging 'stay-away'; *right* Pro-'stay-away' pamphlet

p.181 *top* People stoning police vehicles Duduza 18 May 1985; *bottom* Ngalo Funeral 1984 *(Wendy Schweggman)*.

p.182 *top* 16 June 1984; police 'sneeze machine' teargassing the streets of Soweto *(Wendy Schweggman)*; *bottom* 'Power is ours! Let Afrika return!': one-man protest, Soweto highway 1983 *(Wendy Schweggman)*.

p.183 *top* James Ngalo, brother of the Tumahole man who died in police custody during the 1984 protest against rent increases demonstrates in the rural township *(Wendy Schweggman)*; *left* Randburg car dealer and his employee

(Wendy Schweggman); bottom Cape Town graffiti, 1983 *(Jimi Matthews)*.

p.184 *top* S.A. riot police fire tear smoke Duduza 18 May 1985 *(Gideon Mendal* AFP); *bottom* UDF Youth Rally in the Pretoria townships of Saulsville/Atteridgeville 1984 *(Paul Weinberg)*.

p.185 *top* Funeral of Atteridgeville schoolgirl killed in student unrest 1984 *(Wendy Schweggman)*; *bottom* Durban UDF rally 1983 *(Omar Badsha)*